500 BEST-EVER
CAKES & BAKES

500 BEST-EVER
CAKES
& BAKES

CONTRIBUTING EDITOR:
MARTHA DAY

LORENZ BOOKS

This edition published in 2001 by Lorenz Books

© Anness Publishing Limited 1996, 2001

Lorenz Books is an imprint of Anness Publishing Limited
Hermes House, 88–89 Blackfriars Road, London SE1 8HA
www.lorenzbooks.com

This edition distributed in Canada by Raincoast Books
9050 Shaughnessy Street, Vancouver, British Columbia V6P 6E5

A CIP catalogue record for this book is available from the British Library.

Publisher: Joanna Lorenz
Managing Editor: Linda Fraser
Designer: Siân Keogh
Photographers: Karl Adamson, Edward Allwright, David Armstrong, Steve Baxter, James Duncan, John Freeman, Michelle Garrett, Amanda Heywood, Tim Hill, Don Last, Michael Michaels
Recipes: Alex Barker, Carole Clements, Roz Denny, Christine France, Shirley Gill, Patricia Lousada, Norma MacMillan, Sue Maggs, Janice Murfitt, Annie Nichols, Louise Pickford, Katherine Richmond, Hilaire Walden, Steven Wheeler, Elizabeth Wolf-Cohen
Food for Photography: Carla Capalbo, Carole Handslip, Wendy Lee, Sarah Maxwell, Angela Nilsen, Jane Stevenson, Liz Trigg and Elizabeth Wolf-Cohen
Stylists: Madeleine Brehaut, Maria Kelly, Blake Minton, Kirsty Rawlings, Fiona Tillett

Previously published as *500 Fabulous Cakes & Bakes*

1 3 5 7 9 10 8 6 4 2

NOTES

For all recipes, quantities are given in both metric and imperial measures and, where appropriate, measures are also given in standard cups and spoons. Follow one set, but not a mixture, because they are not interchangeable.
Standard spoon and cup measures are level.
1 tsp = 5ml, 1 tbsp = 15ml, 1 cup = 250ml/8fl oz
Australian standard tablespoons are 20ml. Australian readers should use 3 tsp in place of 1 tbsp for measuring small quantities of gelatine, cornflour, salt, etc.
Medium eggs are used unless otherwise stated.

CONTENTS

Introduction

Baking is one of the most satisfying of all the culinary arts. It fills the house with the most wonderful aroma, gives ample reward for minimal effort and always meets with approval, especially from younger members of the family. Bake a batch of brownies, a fresh fruit pie, a crusty loaf of bread or a luxurious gâteau, and watch your rating rise!

This bonanza collection - five hundred of the finest recipes - is all you need to earn your champion baker's badge. It ranges from simple treats like drop scones and basic biscuits to elaborate cakes for special celebrations. Each recipe carries a full colour illustration of the finished bake, and the step-by-step instructions are so simple and straightforward that even a novice will find them easy to follow.

In fact, novice cooks often make the best bakers, preheating the oven in plenty of time, taking care to measure ingredients accurately and following recipe methods to the letter. All these elements are important in baking, which demands more precision than many other types of cooking. With a soup or stew you can happily sling in extra ingredients or cheat a little when it comes to exact quantities, but the balance of ingredients, the temperature and the timing are all very important when you are baking a cake or pastry. It is worth reading the chosen recipe carefully before you begin, doing any advance preparation such as browning almonds or softening butter, then setting out the ingredients in the style of the TV cook.

Advice on lining tins is given in individual recipes. Greaseproof paper is the traditional lining material, but non-stick baking paper is even easier to use and gives excellent results. To base-line a tin, place it on the paper and draw around the outside edge, then cut out the shape. Grease the base of the tin with a dab of oil or butter to hold the paper in place, then fit it in the tin. Grease the paper (if using greaseproof) and the sides of the tin.

Whether or not to grease tins used for pastry is a matter of choice. If the pastry is high in fat, such as shortcrust, flaky or puff, it is not usually necessary; however, spills from fillings may stick. When in doubt, grease the tins lightly.

If you are a novice baker, start with some of the simpler recipes, such as Chocolate-chip Cookies, Chive and Potato Scones or a Quick-mix Sponge. Try some of the delectable breads, from a traditional Plaited Loaf to the contemporary Saffron Focaccia.

You'll find every occasion amply catered for, from Valentine's Day through to a wedding. There are cakes for christenings, anniversaries and every possible birthday, from novelty teddies to telephones – including a mobile! For the family, the collection includes wonderful ways of keeping the cake tin and biscuit barrel brimming with healthy snacks, including a selection for those with dietary restrictions. With vegans in view, there's a special chocolate gâteau and a Dundee cake, and an entire chapter is devoted to low-fat cakes and bakes.

In *500 Best-Ever Cakes & Bakes* there's a sweet or savoury treat for every moment of the day, from breakfast Blueberry Muffins to a late-night slice of Pecan Tart. Tempted to embark on an immediate baking session? Go right ahead. Baking is a wonderfully therapeutic occupation – with sheer indulgence as the reward!

Farmhouse Biscuits

Delightfully wholesome, these farmhouse biscuits are ideal to serve with morning coffee.

Makes 18

115g/4oz/¹/₂ cup butter
   or margarine, at room
   temperature
90g/3¹/₂oz/7 tbsp light
   brown sugar
65g/2¹/₂oz/5 tbsp
   crunchy peanut butter
1 egg
50g/2oz/¹/₂ cup plain
   flour

2.5ml/¹/₂ tsp baking
   powder
2.5ml/¹/₂ tsp ground
   cinnamon
1.5ml/¹/₄ tsp salt
175g/6oz/1¹/₂ cups muesli
50g/2oz/¹/₂ cup raisins
50g/2oz/¹/₂ cup chopped
   walnuts

1 Preheat the oven to 180°C/350°F/Gas 4. Grease a baking sheet.

2 Cream the butter or margarine and sugar until light and fluffy. Beat in the peanut butter and then beat in the egg.

3 Sift the flour, baking powder, cinnamon and salt over the peanut butter mixture and stir to blend. Stir in the muesli, raisins and walnuts. Taste the mixture to see if it needs more sugar, as the sugar content of muesli varies.

4 Drop rounded tablespoonfuls of the mixture on to the prepared baking sheet about 2.5cm/1in apart. Press gently with the back of a spoon to spread each mound into a circle.

5 Bake until lightly coloured, about 15 minutes. With a palette knife, transfer to a wire rack to cool. Store in an airtight container.

Crunchy Oatmeal Biscuits

For nutty oatmeal biscuits, substitute an equal quantity of chopped walnuts or pecan nuts for the cereal.

Makes 14

175g/6oz/³/₄ cup butter or
   margarine, at room
   temperature
175g/6oz/³/₄ cup caster
   sugar
1 egg yolk
175g/6oz/1¹/₂ cups plain
   flour

5ml/1 tsp bicarbonate
   of soda
2.5ml/¹/₂ tsp salt
50g/2oz/²/₃ cup
   rolled oats
50g/2oz/²/₃ cup small
   crunchy nugget cereal

1 Cream the butter or margarine and sugar together until light and fluffy. Mix in the egg yolk.

2 Sift over the flour, bicarbonate of soda and salt, then stir into the butter mixture. Add the oats and cereal and stir to blend. Chill for at least 20 minutes.

3 Preheat the oven to 190°C/375°F/Gas 5. Grease a baking sheet.

4 Roll the mixture into balls. Place them on the baking sheet and flatten with the base of a floured glass.

5 Bake until golden, about 10–12 minutes. Then with a palette knife, transfer to a wire rack to cool. Store in an airtight container.

Apricot Yogurt Cookies

These cookies do not keep well, so it is best to eat them within two days, or to freeze them.

Makes 16

175g/6oz/1¹/₂ cups plain flour
5ml/1 tsp baking powder
5ml/1 tsp ground cinnamon
75g/3oz/scant 1 cup rolled oats
75g/3oz/¹/₂ cup light muscovado sugar
115g/4oz/¹/₂ cup chopped ready-to-eat dried apricots

15ml/1 tbsp flaked hazelnuts or almonds
150g/5oz/scant ²/₃ cup natural yogurt
45ml/3 tbsp sunflower oil
demerara sugar, to sprinkle

1 Preheat the oven to 190°C/375°F/Gas 5. Lightly oil a large baking sheet.

2 Sift together the flour, baking powder and cinnamon. Stir in the oats, sugar, apricots and nuts.

3 Beat together the yogurt and oil, then stir evenly into the mixture to make a firm dough. If necessary, add a little more yogurt.

4 Use your hands to roll the mixture into about 16 small balls, place on the baking sheet and flatten with a fork.

5 Sprinkle with demerara sugar. Bake for 15–20 minutes, or until firm and golden brown. Transfer to a wire rack to cool. Store in an airtight container.

Oat and Apricot Clusters

You can change the ingredients according to what's in your cupboard – try peanuts, pecan nuts, raisins or dates.

Makes 12

50g/2oz/4 tbsp butter or margarine
50g/2oz/4 tbsp clear honey
50g/2oz/¹/₂ cup medium oatmeal
50g/2oz/¹/₄ cup chopped ready-to-eat dried apricots

15ml/1 tbsp banana chips
15ml/1 tbsp dried coconut shreds
50–75g/2–3oz/ 2–3 cups cornflakes or crispy cereal

1 Place the butter or margarine and honey in a small pan and warm over a low heat, stirring until well blended.

2 Add the oatmeal, apricots, banana chips, coconut and cornflakes or crispy cereal and mix well.

3 Spoon the mixture into 12 paper cases, piling it up roughly. Transfer to a baking sheet and chill until set and firm.

Oaty Coconut Biscuits

The coconut gives these biscuits both a wonderful texture and a great taste.

Makes 48

*175g/6oz/2 cups
  quick-cooking oats
75g/3oz/1¹/₂ cups
  desiccated coconut
225g/8oz/1 cup butter
115g/4oz/¹/₂ cup caster
  sugar
50g/2oz/¹/₄ cup dark
  brown sugar
2 eggs*

*60ml/4 tbsp milk
7.5ml/1¹/₂ tsp vanilla
  essence
115g/4oz/1 cup
  plain flour, sifted
2.5ml/¹/₂ tsp bicarbonate
  of soda
2.5ml/¹/₂ tsp salt
5ml/1 tsp ground
  cinnamon*

1 Preheat the oven to 200°C/400°F/Gas 6. Spread the oats and coconut on a baking sheet. Bake for 8–10 minutes.

2 Cream the butter and sugars. Beat in the eggs, milk and vanilla. Fold in the dry ingredients. Add the oats and coconut. Drop spoonfuls of mixture on two greased baking sheets. Bake for 8–10 minutes. Cool on a wire rack.

Crunchy Jumbles

For even crunchier biscuits, add 50g/2oz/¹/₂ cup walnuts, coarsely chopped, with the cereal and chocolate chips.

Makes 36

*115g/4oz/¹/₂ cup butter
  or margarine, at room
  temperature
225g/8oz/1 cup caster
  sugar
1 egg
5ml/1 tsp vanilla essence
150g/5oz/1¹/₄ cups plain
  flour, sifted*

*2.5ml/¹/₂ tsp bicarbonate
  of soda
1.5ml/¹/₄ tsp salt
50g/2oz/2¹/₄ cups crisped
  rice cereal
175g/6oz/1 cup chocolate
  chips*

1 Preheat the oven to 180°C/350°F/Gas 4. Grease two baking sheets. Cream the butter or margarine and sugar until fluffy. Add the egg and vanilla essence. Add the flour and bicarbonate of soda and the salt and fold in.

2 Add the cereal and chocolate chips and mix thoroughly. Drop spoonfuls 5cm/2in apart onto baking sheets and bake for 10–12 minutes. Transfer to a wire rack to cool.

Cinnamon-coated Cookies

Walnut cookies are rolled in a cinnamon and sugar mixture to give a delicate spicy flavour.

Makes 30

Preheat the oven to 190°C/375°F/Gas 5. Grease two baking sheets. Cream 115g/4oz/¹/₂ cup butter, 225g/8oz/1 cup sugar and 5ml/1 tsp vanilla essence. Beat in 2 eggs and 50ml/2fl oz/¹/₄ cup milk. Sift over 350g/12oz/3 cups plain flour and 5ml/1 tsp bicarbonate of soda. Stir in 50g/2oz/¹/₂ cup chopped walnuts. Chill for 15 minutes then roll into balls. Roll the balls in a sugar and cinnamon mixture. Bake for 10 minutes, then cool on a wire rack.

Ginger Biscuits

So much tastier than shop-bought varieties, these ginger biscuits will disappear quickly, so make a large batch!

Makes 60

275g/10oz/2¹/₂ cups plain
    flour
5ml/1 tsp bicarbonate of
    soda
7.5ml/1¹/₂ tsp ground
    ginger
1.5ml/¹/₄ tsp ground
    cinnamon
1.5ml/¹/₄ tsp ground
    cloves

115g/4oz/¹/₂ cup butter
    or margarine, at room
    temperature
350g/12oz/1³/₄ cups
    caster sugar
1 egg, beaten
60ml/4 tbsp treacle
5ml/1 tsp fresh lemon
    juice

1 Preheat the oven to 160°C/325°F/Gas 3. Lightly grease three to four baking sheets.

2 Sift the flour, bicarbonate of soda and spices into a small bowl. Set aside.

3 Cream the butter or margarine and two-thirds of the sugar together. Stir in the egg, treacle and lemon juice. Add the flour mixture and mix in thoroughly with a wooden spoon to make a soft dough.

4 Shape the dough into 2cm/¾ in balls. Roll the balls in the remaining sugar and place about 5cm/2in apart on the baking sheets.

5 Bake until the biscuits are just firm to the touch, about 12 minutes. With a palette knife, transfer the biscuits to a wire rack and leave to cool.

Cream Cheese Spirals

These biscuits look so impressive and melt in the mouth, yet they are surprisingly easy to make.

Makes 32

225g/8oz/1 cup butter, at
    room temperature
225g/8oz/1 cup cream
    cheese
10ml/2 tsp caster sugar
225g/8oz/2 cups plain
    flour
1 egg white, beaten with
    15ml/1 tbsp water, for
    glazing

caster sugar, for
    sprinkling

For the filling
115g/4oz/1 cup finely
    chopped walnuts
115g/4oz/³/₄ cup light
    brown sugar
5ml/1 tsp ground
    cinnamon

1 Cream the butter, cream cheese and sugar until soft. Sift over the flour and mix until combined. Gather into a ball and divide in half. Flatten each half, wrap in greaseproof paper and chill for 30 minutes. Meanwhile, mix all the filling ingredients together and set aside.

2 Preheat the oven to 190°C/375°F/Gas 5. Grease two baking sheets. Working with one half of the dough at a time, roll out thinly into a 28cm/11in circle. Using a dinner plate as a guide, trim the edges with a knife.

3 Brush the surface with the egg white glaze, and then sprinkle evenly with half the filling.

4 Cut the circle into 16 segments. Starting from the base of the triangles, roll up to form spirals.

5 Place on the baking sheets and brush with the remaining glaze. Sprinkle with caster sugar. Bake until golden, about 15–20 minutes. Cool on a wire rack.

Italian Almond Biscotti

Serve biscotti after a meal, for dunking in sweet white wine, such as an Italian Vin Santo or a French Muscat.

Makes 48

200g/7oz/1¼ cups whole unblanched almonds
215g/7½ oz/scant 2 cups plain flour
90g/3½ oz/½ cup sugar
pinch of salt
pinch of saffron powder
2.5ml/½ tsp bicarbonate of soda
2 eggs
1 egg white, lightly beaten

1 Preheat the oven to 190°C/375°F/Gas 5. Grease and flour two baking sheets.

2 Spread the almonds on an ungreased baking sheet and bake until lightly browned, about 15 minutes. When cool, grind 50g/2oz/½ cup of the almonds in a food processor, blender, or coffee grinder until pulverized. Coarsely chop the remaining almonds in two or three pieces each. Set aside.

3 Combine the flour, sugar, salt, saffron powder, bicarbonate of soda and ground almonds in a bowl and mix to blend. Make a well in the centre and add the eggs. Stir to form a rough dough. Transfer to a floured surface and knead until well blended. Knead in the chopped almonds.

4 Divide the dough into three equal parts. Roll into logs about 2.5cm/1in diameter. Place on one of the prepared sheets, brush with the egg white and bake for 20 minutes. Remove from the oven. Lower the oven temperature to 140°C/275°F/Gas 1.

5 With a very sharp knife, cut into each log at an angle making 1cm/½ in slices. Return the slices on the baking sheets to the oven and bake for 25 minutes. Transfer to a wire rack to cool.

Orange Biscuits

These classic citrus-flavoured biscuits are ideal for a tasty treat at any time of the day.

Makes 30

115g/4oz/½ cup butter, at room temperature
200g/7oz/1 cup sugar
2 egg yolks
15ml/1 tbsp fresh orange juice
grated rind of 1 large orange
200g/7oz/1¾ cups plain flour
15ml/1 tbsp cornflour
2.5ml/½ tsp salt
5ml/1 tsp baking powder

1 Cream the butter and sugar until light and fluffy. Add the yolks, orange juice and rind, and continue beating to blend.

2 In another bowl, sift together the flour, cornflour, salt and baking powder. Add to the butter mixture and stir until it forms a dough. Wrap the dough in greaseproof paper and chill for 2 hours.

3 Preheat the oven to 190°C/375°F/Gas 5. Grease two baking sheets. Roll spoonfuls of the dough into balls and place 2.5–5cm/1–2in apart on the baking sheets.

4 Press down with a fork to flatten. Bake until golden brown, about 8–10 minutes. Using a palette knife, transfer to a wire rack to cool.

Raspberry Sandwich Biscuits

These biscuits may be stored in an airtight container with sheets of greaseproof paper between the layers.

Makes 32

175g/6oz/1 cup blanched almonds	5ml/1 tsp vanilla essence
175g/6oz/1½ cups plain flour	1 egg white
	1.5ml/¼ tsp salt
175g/6oz/¾ cup butter, at room temperature	25g/1oz/¼ cup flaked almonds
115g/4oz/½ cup caster sugar	250ml/8fl oz/1 cup raspberry jam
grated rind of 1 lemon	15ml/1 tbsp fresh lemon juice

1 Process the blanched almonds and 45ml/3 tbsp flour in a food processor or blender until finely ground. Cream the butter and sugar together until light and fluffy. Stir in the lemon rind and vanilla. Add the ground almonds and remaining flour and mix well. Gather into a ball, wrap in greaseproof paper, and chill for 1 hour.

2 Preheat the oven to 160°C/325°F/Gas 3. Line two baking sheets wih greaseproof paper. Divide the biscuit mixture into four equal parts. Working with one section at a time, roll out to a thickness of 3mm/⅛ in on a lightly floured surface. With a 6cm/2½in fluted pastry cutter, stamp out circles. Using a 2cm/¾in piping nozzle or pastry cutter, stamp out the centres from half the circles. Place the rings and circles 2.5cm/1in apart on the baking sheets.

3 Whisk the egg white with the salt until just frothy. Chop the flaked almonds. Brush the biscuit rings with the egg white, then sprinkle over the almonds. Bake until lightly browned, about 12–15 minutes. Cool for a few minutes on the baking sheets then transfer to a wire rack.

4 In a saucepan, melt the jam with the lemon juice until it comes to a simmer. Brush the jam over the biscuit circles and sandwich together with the rings.

Christmas Cookies

Decorate these delicious cookies with festive decorations or make them at any time of year.

Makes 30

175g/6oz/¾ cup unsalted butter, at room temperature	grated rind of 1 lemon
	1.5ml/¼ tsp salt
285g/10oz/1½ cups caster sugar	285g/10oz/2½ cups plain flour
1 egg	**For decorating (optional)**
1 egg yolk	coloured icing and small decorations
5ml/1 tsp vanilla essence	

1 Preheat the oven to 180°C/350°F/Gas 4. With an electric mixer, cream the butter until soft. Add the sugar gradually and continue beating until light and fluffy. Using a wooden spoon, slowly mix in the whole egg and the egg yolk. Add the vanilla essence, lemon rind and salt. Stir to mix well. Add the flour and stir until blended. Gather the mixture into a ball, wrap in greaseproof paper, and chill for 30 minutes.

2 On a floured surface, roll out the mixture about 3mm/⅛in thick. Stamp out shapes or rounds with biscuit cutters. Bake until lightly coloured, about 8 minutes. Transfer to a wire rack and leave to cool completely before icing and decorating, if wished.

Apricot Specials

Try other dried fruit, such as peaches or prunes, to vary the flavour of these special bars.

Makes 12

90g/3¹/₂oz/generous
    ¹/₂ cup light brown
    sugar
75g/3oz/³/₄ cup plain
    flour
75g/3oz/6 tbsp cold
    unsalted butter, cut
    in pieces

For the topping
150g/5oz/generous
    ¹/₂ cup dried apricots
250ml/8fl oz/1 cup water
grated rind of 1 lemon
65g/2¹/₂oz/generous ¹/₄
    cup caster sugar
10ml/2 tsp cornflour
50g/2oz/¹/₂ cup chopped
    walnuts

1 Preheat the oven to 180°C/350°F/Gas 4. In a mixing bowl, combine the brown sugar and flour. With a pastry blender, cut in the butter until the mixture resembles coarse breadcrumbs.

2 Transfer to a 20cm/8in square baking tin and press level. Bake for 15 minutes. Remove from the oven but leave the oven on.

3 Meanwhile, for the topping, combine the apricots and water in a saucepan and simmer until soft; about 10 minutes. Strain the liquid and reserve. Chop the apricots.

4 Return the apricots to the saucepan and add the lemon rind, caster sugar, cornflour and 60ml/4 tbsp of the soaking liquid. Cook for 1 minute.

5 Cool slightly before spreading the topping over the base. Sprinkle over the walnuts and bake for 20 minutes more. Cool in the tin before cutting into bars.

Brandy Snaps

You could serve these brandy snaps without the cream filling to eat with rich vanilla ice cream.

Makes 18

50g/2oz/4 tbsp butter, at
    room temperature
150g/5oz/generous
    ¹/₂ cup caster sugar
20ml/1 rounded tbsp
    golden syrup
40g/1¹/₂oz/¹/₃ cup plain
    flour

2.5ml/¹/₂ tsp ground
    ginger

For the filling
250ml/8fl oz/1 cup
    whipping cream
30ml/2 tbsp brandy

1 Cream together the butter and sugar until light and fluffy, then beat in the golden syrup. Sift over the flour and ginger and mix together. Transfer the mixture to a work surface and knead until smooth. Cover and chill for 30 minutes.

2 Preheat the oven to 190°C/375°F/Gas 5. Grease a baking sheet. Working in batches of four, shape the mixture into walnut-size balls. Place well apart on the baking sheet and flatten slightly. Bake until golden and bubbling, about 10 minutes.

3 Remove from the oven and leave to cool for a few moments. Working quickly, slide a palette knife under each one, turn over, and wrap around the handle of a wooden spoon (have four spoons ready). If they firm up too quickly, reheat for a few seconds to soften. When firm, slide the brandy snaps off and place on a wire rack to cool.

4 When all the brandy snaps are cool, prepare the filling. Whip the cream and brandy until soft peaks form. Pipe into each end of the brandy snaps just before serving.

Chocolate Pretzels

Pretzels come in many flavours – here is a chocolate version
to bake and enjoy.

Makes 28

*150g/5oz/1¼ cups plain
  flour*
1.5ml/¼ tsp salt
*20g/¾ oz/6 tbsp
  unsweetened cocoa
  powder*
*115g/4oz/½ cup butter,
  at room temperature*

*130g/4½oz/scant ⅔ cup
  sugar*
1 egg
*1 egg white, lightly
  beaten, for glazing*
*sugar crystals, for
  sprinkling*

1 Sift together the flour, salt and cocoa powder. Set aside.
Lightly grease two baking sheets. Cream the butter until light.
Add the sugar and continue beating until light and fluffy. Beat
in the egg. Add the dry ingredients and stir to blend. Gather
the dough into a ball, wrap in clear film and chill for 1 hour.

2 Roll the dough into 28 small balls. Chill the balls until
needed. Preheat the oven to 190°C/375°F/Gas 5. Roll each
ball into a rope about 25cm/10in long. With each rope, form a
loop with the two ends facing you. Twist the ends and fold
back on to the circle, pressing in to make a pretzel shape.
Place on the baking sheets.

3 Brush the pretzels with the egg white. Sprinkle sugar
crystals over the tops and bake in the oven until firm, about
10–12 minutes. Transfer to a wire rack to cool.

Ginger Cookies

If your children enjoy cooking with you, mixing and
rolling the dough, or cutting out different shapes, this is the
ideal recipe to let them practise on.

Makes 16

*115g/4oz/8 tbsp soft
  brown sugar*
*115g/4oz/½ cup soft
  margarine*
pinch of salt
few drops vanilla essence
*175g/6oz/1½ cup
  wholemeal flour*

*15g/½oz/1 tbsp cocoa,
  sifted*
10ml/2 tsp ground ginger
a little milk
*glacé icing and glacé
  cherries, to decorate*

1 Preheat the oven to 190°C/375°F/Gas 5. Cream the sugar,
margarine, salt and vanilla essence together until very soft
and light.

2 Work in the flour, cocoa and ginger, adding a little milk, if
necessary, to bind the mixture. Knead lightly on a floured
surface until smooth.

3 Roll out the dough on a lightly floured surface to about
5mm/1¼in thick. Stamp out shapes using biscuit cutters and
place on baking sheets.

4 Bake the cookies for 10–15 minutes, leave to cool on the
baking sheets until firm, then transfer to a wire rack to cool
completely. Decorate with the glacé icing and glacé cherries.

Chocolate Macaroons

Roll one side of the macaroons in chopped nuts and bake nut-side up for a crunchier variation.

Makes 24

50g/2oz plain chocolate, melted
175g/6oz/1¹/₂ cups blanched almonds
225g/8oz/1 cup caster sugar
3 egg whites
2.5ml/¹/₂ tsp vanilla essence
1.5ml/¹/₄ tsp almond essence
icing sugar, for dusting

1 Preheat the oven to 160°C/325°F/Gas 3. Line two baking sheets with greaseproof paper then grease. Grind the almonds in a food processor or blender. Transfer to a bowl, then blend in the sugar, egg whites, vanilla and almond essence. Stir in the chocolate. The mixture should just hold its shape; if too soft, chill for 15 minutes.

2 Shape the mixture into walnut-size balls. Place on the baking sheets and flatten slightly. Brush with a little water; dust with icing sugar. Bake until just firm, 10–12 minutes. With a palette knife, transfer to a wire rack to cool.

Chocolate-orange Sponge Drops

Light and crispy, with a marmalade filling, these sponge drops are truly decadent.

Makes 14–15

2 eggs
50g/2oz/¹/₄ cup caster sugar
2.5ml/¹/₂ tsp grated orange rind
50g/2oz/¹/₂ cup plain flour
60ml/4 tbsp fine shred orange marmalade
40g/1¹/₂oz plain chocolate, cut into small pieces

1 Preheat the oven to 200°C/400°F/Gas 6. Line three baking sheets with baking paper. Put the eggs and sugar in a bowl over a pan of simmering water. Whisk until thick and pale. Remove from the pan and whisk until cool. Whisk in the orange rind. Sift the flour over and fold it in gently.

2 Put 28–30 dessertspoonfuls of the mixture on the baking sheets. Bake for 8 minutes, until golden. Cool slightly, then transfer to a wire rack. Sandwich pairs together with marmalade. Melt the chocolate and drizzle over the drops.

Coconut Macaroons

Have a change from after-dinner mints, and serve these delicious coconut macaroons with coffee instead.

Makes 24

Preheat the oven to 180°C/350°F/Gas 4. Grease two baking sheets. Sift 40g/1¹/₂ oz/¹/₃ cup plain flour and 1.5ml/1¹/₄ tsp salt into a bowl, then stir in 225g/8oz/4 cups desiccated coconut. Pour in 170ml/5¹/₂fl oz/scant ¾ cup sweetened condensed milk. Add 5ml/1 tsp vanilla essence; stir from the centre to a thick mixture. Drop tablespoonfuls of the mixture 2.5cm/1in apart on the baking sheets. Bake until golden brown, about 20 minutes. Cool on a wire rack.

Peanut Butter Biscuits

For added crunchiness, stir in 75g/3oz/½ cup peanuts, coarsely chopped, with the peanut butter.

Makes 24

150g/5oz/1¼ cups plain flour
2.5ml/½ tsp bicarbonate of soda
2.5ml/½ tsp salt
115g/4oz/½ cup butter, at room temperature
170g/5¾ oz/scant 1 cup light brown sugar
1 egg
5ml/1 tsp vanilla essence
260g/9½oz/scant 1¼ cups crunchy peanut butter

1 Sift together the flour, bicarbonate of soda and salt and set aside. In another bowl, cream the butter and sugar together until light and fluffy.

2 In a third bowl, mix the egg and vanilla, then gradually beat into the butter mixture. Stir in the peanut butter and the chopped peanuts, if using, and blend thoroughly. Stir in the dry ingredients. Chill for 30 minutes, or until firm.

3 Preheat the oven to 180°C/350°F/Gas 4. Grease two baking sheets. Spoon out rounded teaspoonfuls of the dough and roll into balls.

4 Place the balls on the baking sheets and press flat with a fork into circles about 6cm/2½in in diameter, making a criss-cross pattern. Bake in the oven until lightly coloured, about 12–15 minutes. Transfer to a wire rack to cool.

Chocolate-chip Cookies

A perennial favourite with all the family, these cookies contain walnuts as well as chocolate chips.

Makes 24

115g/4oz/½ cup butter or margarine, at room temperature
45g/1¾ oz/scant ¼ cup caster sugar
100g/3¾ oz/generous ½ cup dark brown sugar
1 egg
2.5ml/½ tsp vanilla essence
175g/6oz/1½ cups plain flour
2.5ml/½ tsp bicarbonate of soda
1.5ml/¼ tsp salt
175g/6oz/1 cup chocolate chips
50g/2oz/½ cup walnuts, chopped

1 Preheat the oven to 180°C/350°F/Gas 4. Lightly grease two large baking sheets. With an electric mixer, cream the butter or margarine and both the sugars together until light and fluffy.

2 In another bowl, mix the egg and the vanilla essence, then gradually beat into the butter mixture. Sift over the flour, bicarbonate of soda and salt and stir. Add the chocolate chips and walnuts, and mix to combine well.

3 Place heaped teaspoonfuls of the dough 5cm/2in apart on the baking sheets. Bake in the oven until lightly coloured, about 10–15 minutes. Transfer to a wire rack to cool.

Almond Tile Biscuits

These biscuits are named after the French roof tiles they so closely resemble.

Makes about 24

65g/2¹/₂oz/scant ¹/₂ cup whole blanched almonds, lightly toasted
65g/2¹/₂oz/¹/₃ cup caster sugar
40g/1¹/₂oz/3 tbsp unsalted butter, softened
2 egg whites
2.5ml/¹/₂ tsp almond essence
40g/1¹/₂oz/¹/₃ cup plain flour, sifted
50g/2oz/¹/₂ cup flaked almonds

1 Preheat the oven to 200°C/400°F/Gas 6. Grease well two baking sheets. Place the almonds and 30ml/2 tbsp of the sugar in a blender or food processor and process until finely ground, but not pasty.

2 Beat the butter until creamy, add the remaining sugar and beat until light and fluffy. Gradually beat in the egg whites until the mixture is well blended, then beat in the almond essence. Sift the flour over the butter mixture and fold in, then fold in the almond mixture.

3 Drop tablespoonfuls of the mixture on to the baking sheets 15cm/6in apart. With the back of a wet spoon, spread each mound into a paper-thin 7.5cm/3in circle. Sprinkle with the flaked almonds.

4 Bake the biscuits, one sheet at a time, for 5–6 minutes until the edges are golden and the centres still pale. Remove the baking sheet to a wire rack and, working quickly, use a palette knife to loosen the edges of a biscuit. Lift the biscuit on the palette knife and place over a rolling pin, then press down the sides of the biscuit to curve it. Repeat with the remaining biscuits, and leave to cool.

Brittany Butter Biscuits

These little biscuits are similar to shortbread, but richer in taste and texture.

Makes 18–20

6 egg yolks, lightly beaten
15ml/1 tbsp milk
250g/9oz/2 cups plain flour
175g/6oz/generous ³/₄ cup caster sugar
200g/7oz/scant 1 cup lightly salted butter at room temperature, cut into small pieces

1 Preheat the oven to 180°C/350°F/Gas 4. Lightly butter a large baking sheet. Mix 15ml/1 tbsp of the egg yolks with the milk for a glaze. Set aside.

2 Sift the flour into a large bowl and make a central well. Add the egg yolks, sugar and butter and, using your fingertips, work them together until smooth and creamy. Gradually blend in the flour to form a smooth but slightly sticky dough.

3 Using floured hands, pat out the dough to 8mm/⅛in thick and cut out circles using a 7.5cm/3in biscuit cutter. Transfer the circles to the baking sheet, brush with egg glaze, then score to create a lattice pattern.

4 Bake for 12–15 minutes until golden. Cool in the tin on a wire rack for 15 minutes, then transfer to the wire rack to cool completely.

Ginger Florentines

These colourful, chewy biscuits are delicious served with vanilla or other flavoured ice cream.

Makes 30

50g/2oz/4 tbsp butter
115g/4oz/¹/₂ cup
caster sugar
50g/2oz/¹/₄ cup mixed
glacé cherries, chopped
25g/1oz/generous 1 tbsp
candied orange peel,
chopped
50g/2oz/¹/₂ cup flaked
almonds
50g/2oz/¹/₂ cup chopped
walnuts

25g/1oz/1 tbsp glacé
ginger, chopped
30ml/2 tbsp plain flour
2.5ml/¹/₂ tsp ground
ginger

To finish
50g/2oz plain chocolate,
melted
50g/2oz white chocolate,
melted

1 Preheat the oven to 180°C/350°F/Gas 4. Beat the butter and sugar together until light and fluffy. Thoroughly mix in all the remaining ingredients, except the melted plain and white chocolate.

2 Line some baking sheets with non-stick baking paper. Put four small spoonfuls of the mixture on to each sheet, spacing them well apart to allow for spreading. Flatten the biscuits and bake for 5 minutes.

3 Remove the biscuits from the oven and flatten with a wet fork, shaping them into neat rounds. Return to the oven for about 3–4 minutes, until they are golden brown. Work in batches if necessary.

4 Let them cool on the baking sheets for 2 minutes to firm up, and then transfer them to a wire rack. When they are cold and firm, spread plain chocolate on the undersides of half the biscuits and white chocolate on the undersides of the rest.

Christmas Biscuits

These are great fun for children to make as presents, and any shape of biscuit cutter can be used.

Makes about 12

75g/3oz/6 tbsp butter
50g/2oz/generous ¹/₂ cup
icing sugar
finely grated rind of
1 small lemon
1 egg yolk
175g/6oz/1¹/₂ cups plain
flour

pinch of salt

To decorate
2 egg yolks
red and green edible food
colouring

1 Beat the butter, sugar and lemon rind together until pale and fluffy. Beat in the egg yolk, and then sift in the flour and the salt. Knead together to form a smooth dough. Wrap and chill for 30 minutes.

2 Preheat the oven to 190°C/375°F/Gas 5. On a lightly floured surface, roll out the dough to 3mm/¹/₈in thick. Using a 6cm/2¹/₂in fluted cutter, stamp out as many biscuits as you can, with the cutter dipped in flour to prevent it from sticking to the dough.

3 Transfer the biscuits on to lightly greased baking sheets. Mark the tops lightly with a 2.5cm/1in holly leaf cutter and use a 5mm/¹/₄in plain piping nozzle for the berries. Chill for 10 minutes, until firm.

4 Meanwhile, put each egg yolk into a small cup. Mix red food colouring into one and green food colouring into the other. Using a small, clean paintbrush, carefully paint the colours on to the biscuits. Bake for 10–12 minutes, or until they begin to colour around the edges. Let them cool slightly on the baking sheets, then transfer to a wire rack.

Traditional Sugar Biscuits

These lovely old-fashioned biscuits would be ideal to serve at an elegant tea party.

Makes 36

350g/12oz/3 cups plain
  flour
5ml/1 tsp bicarbonate
  of soda
10ml/2 tsp baking
  powder
1.5ml/¹/₄ tsp grated
  nutmeg
115g/4oz/¹/₂ cup butter
  or margarine, at room
  temperature

225g/8oz/generous 1 cup
  caster sugar
2.5ml/¹/₂ tsp vanilla
  essence
1 egg
120ml/4fl oz/¹/₂ cup milk
coloured or demerara
  sugar, for sprinkling

1 Sift the flour, bicarbonate of soda, baking powder and nutmeg into a small bowl. Set aside. Cream the butter or margarine, caster sugar and vanilla essence together until the mixture is light and fluffy. Add the egg and beat to mix well.

2 Add the flour mixture alternately with the milk, stirring with a wooden spoon to make a soft dough. Wrap the dough in clear film and chill for 30 minutes.

3 Preheat the oven to 180℃/350℉/Gas 4. Roll out the dough on a lightly floured surface to a 3mm/¹/₈in thickness. Cut into circles with a biscuit cutter.

4 Transfer the biscuits to ungreased baking sheets. Sprinkle each one with sugar. Bake until golden, 10–12 minutes. With a palette knife, transfer the biscuits to a wire rack to cool.

Spicy Pepper Biscuits

Despite the warm, complex flavour added by the spices, these light biscuits are simple to make.

Makes 48

200g/7oz/¹/₄ cup plain
  flour
50g/2oz/¹/₄ cup cornflour
10ml/2 tsp baking
  powder
2.5ml/¹/₂ tsp ground
  cardamom
2.5ml/¹/₂ tsp ground
  cinnamon
2.5ml/¹/₂ tsp grated
  nutmeg
2.5ml/¹/₂ tsp ground
  ginger
2.5ml/¹/₂ tsp ground
  allspice
2.5ml/¹/₂ tsp salt

2.5ml/¹/₂ tsp freshly
  ground black pepper
225g/8oz butter or
  margarine, at room
  temperature
90g/3¹/₂ oz/¹/₂ cup light
  brown sugar
2.5ml/¹/₂ tsp vanilla
  essence
5ml/1 tsp finely grated
  lemon rind
50ml/2fl oz/¹/₄ cups
  whipping cream
75g/3oz/³/₄ cup finely
  ground almonds
50ml/2 tbsp icing sugar

1 Preheat the oven to 180℃/350℉/Gas 4 . Sift the flour, cornflour, baking powder, spices, salt and pepper into a bowl.

2 Cream the butter or margarine and brown sugar until light and fluffy. Beat in the vanilla essence and lemon rind.

3 With the mixer on low speed, add the flour mixture alternately with the cream, beginning and ending with flour. Stir in the ground almonds.

4 Shape the dough into 2cm/³/₄in balls. Place them on ungreased baking sheets about 2.5cm/1in apart. Bake until golden brown underneath, about 15–20 minutes.

5 Leave to cool on the baking sheets for about 1 minute before transferring to a wire rack to cool completely. Before serving, sprinkle lightly with icing sugar.

Sultana Cornmeal Biscuits

These little yellow biscuits come from the Veneto region of Italy, and Marsala wine enhances their regional appeal.

Makes about 48

65g/2½oz/⅓ cup sultanas
50g/2oz/½ cup finely ground yellow cornmeal
175g/6oz/1½ cups plain flour
7.5ml/1½ tsp baking powder

pinch of salt
225g/8oz/1 cup butter
200g/7oz/1 cup granulated sugar
2 eggs
15ml/1 tbsp Marsala or 5ml/1 tsp vanilla essence

1 Soak the sultanas in a small bowl of warm water for 15 minutes. Drain. Preheat the oven to 180°C/350°F/Gas 4. Sift the cornmeal and flour, the baking powder and the salt together into a bowl.

2 Cream the butter and sugar together until light and fluffy. Beat in the eggs, one at a time. Beat in the Marsala or vanilla essence. Add the dry ingredients to the batter, beating until well blended. Stir in the sultanas.

3 Drop heaped teaspoonfuls of batter on to a greased baking sheet in rows about 2in apart. Bake for 7–8 minutes, or until the biscuits are golden brown at the edges. Remove to a wire rack to cool.

Mexican Cinnamon Biscuits

Pastelitos **are traditional sweet shortbreads at weddings in Mexico, dusted in icing sugar to match the bride's dress.**

Makes 20

115g/4oz/½ cup butter
25g/1oz/2 tbsp caster sugar
115g/4oz/1 cup plain flour
50g/2oz/¼ cup cornflour

1.5ml/¼ tsp ground cinnamon
30ml/2 tbsp chopped mixed nuts
25g/1oz/¼ cup icing sugar, sifted

1 Preheat the oven to 160°C/325°F/Gas 3. Lightly grease a baking sheet. Place the butter and sugar in a bowl and beat until pale and creamy.

2 Sift in the plain flour, cornflour and cinnamon and gradually work in with a wooden spoon until the mixture comes together. Knead lightly until completely smooth.

3 Take tablespoonfuls of the mixture, roll into 20 small balls and arrange on the baking sheet. Press a few chopped nuts into the top of each one and then flatten slightly.

4 Bake the biscuits for about 30–35 minutes, until pale golden. Remove from the oven and, while they are still warm, toss them in the sifted icing sugar. Leave the biscuits to cool on a wire rack before serving.

Toasted Oat Meringues

Meringues needn't be plain. Try these oaty ones for a lovely crunchy change.

Makes 12

50g/2oz/generous ¹/₂ cup rolled oats	7.5ml/1¹/₂ tsp cornflour
2 egg whites	175g/6oz/³/₄ cup caster sugar
1.5ml/¹/₄ tsp salt	

1 Preheat the oven to 140℃/275℉/Gas 1. Spread the oats on a baking sheet and toast in the oven until golden, for about 10 minutes. Lower the heat to 120℃/250℉/Gas ¹/₂. Grease and flour a baking sheet.

2 Beat the egg whites and salt until they start to form soft peaks. Sift over the cornflour and continue beating until the whites hold stiff peaks. Add half the sugar; whisk until glossy. Add the remaining sugar and fold in, then fold in the oats.

3 Place tablespoonfuls of the mixture on to the baking sheet and bake for 2 hours, then turn off the oven. Turn over the meringues, and leave in the oven until cool.

Meringues

Make these classic meringues as large or small as you like. Serve as a tea-time treat or as an elegant dessert.

Makes about 24

4 egg whites	2.5ml/¹/₂ tsp vanilla or almond essence (optional)
1.5ml/¹/₄ tsp salt	
275g/10oz/1¹/₄ cups caster sugar	250ml/8fl oz/1 cup whipping cream

1 Preheat the oven to 110℃/225℉/Gas ¹/₄. Grease and flour two large baking sheets. Beat the egg whites and salt in a metal bowl. When they start to form soft peaks, add half the sugar and continue beating until the mixture holds stiff peaks.

2 With a large metal spoon, fold in the remaining sugar and vanilla or almond essence, if using. Pipe or spoon the meringue mixture on to the baking sheets. Bake for 2 hours, turn off the oven. Loosen the meringues, invert, and set in another place on the sheets to prevent sticking. Leave in the oven until cool. Whip the cream and use to fill the meringues.

Chewy Chocolate Biscuits

If you have a weakness for chocolate, add 75g/3oz/¹/₂ cup chocolate chips to the mixture with the nuts.

Makes 18

Preheat the oven to 180℃/350℉/Gas 4. Line two baking sheets with greaseproof paper and grease. Using an electric mixer, beat 4 egg whites until frothy. Sift over 275g/10oz/2 cups icing sugar and 5ml/1 tsp coffee. Add 15ml/1 tbsp water, beat on low speed to blend, then on high until thick. Fold in 115g/4oz/1 cup chopped walnuts. Place generous spoonfuls of the mixture 2.5cm/1in apart on the sheets. Bake for 12–15 minutes. Transfer to a wire rack to cool.

Lavender Cookies

Instead of lavender you can use other flavourings, such as cinnamon, lemon, orange or mint.

Makes about 30

150g/5oz/⅔ cup butter
115g/4oz/½ cup
   granulated sugar
1 egg, beaten
15ml/1 tbsp dried
   lavender flowers

175g/6oz/1½ cups
   self-raising flour
leaves and flowers,
   to decorate

1 Preheat the oven to 180°C/350°F/Gas 4. Grease two baking sheets. Cream the butter and sugar together, then stir in the egg. Mix in the lavender flowers and the flour.

2 Drop spoonfuls of the mixture on to the baking sheets. Bake for about 15–20 minutes, until the biscuits are golden. Serve with some fresh leaves and flowers to decorate.

Chocolate Amaretti

As an alternative decoration, lightly press a few coffee sugar crystals on top of each cookie before baking.

Makes 24

150g/5oz/scant 1 cup
   blanched, toasted
   whole almonds
115g/4oz/½ cup caster
   sugar
15ml/1 tbsp unsweetened
   cocoa powder

30ml/2 tbsp icing sugar
2 egg whites
pinch of cream of tartar
5ml/1 tsp almond essence
flaked almonds,
   to decorate

1 Preheat the oven to 160°C/325°F/Gas 3. Line a large baking sheet with non-stick baking paper or foil. In a food processor fitted with a metal blade, process the toasted almonds with half the sugar until they are finely ground but not oily. Transfer to a bowl and sift in the cocoa and icing sugar; stir to blend. Set aside.

2 Beat the egg whites and cream of tartar until stiff peaks form. Sprinkle in the remaining sugar 15ml/1 tbsp at a time, beating well after each addition, and continue beating until the whites are glossy and stiff. Beat in the almond essence.

3 Sprinkle over the almond mixture and gently fold into the egg whites until just blended. Spoon the mixture into a large piping bag fitted with a plain 1cm/½in nozzle. Pipe 4cm/1½in rounds, 2.5cm/1in apart, on the baking sheet. Press a flaked almond into the centre of each.

4 Bake the cookies for 12–15 minutes or until they appear crisp. Remove the baking sheet to a wire rack to cool for 10 minutes. With a metal palette knife, remove the cookies to the wire rack to cool completely.

Melting Moments

These biscuits are very crisp and light – and they really do melt in your mouth.

Makes 16–20

40g/1¹/₂oz/3 tbsp butter
  or margarine
65g/2¹/₂oz/5 tbsp lard
75g/3oz/scant ¹/₂ cup
  caster sugar
¹/₂ egg, beaten
a few drops of vanilla or
  almond essence

150g/5oz/1¹/₄ cups
  self-raising flour
rolled oats, for coating
4–5 glacé cherries,
  quartered, to decorate

1 Preheat the oven to 180℃/350℉/Gas 4. Beat together the butter or margarine, lard and sugar, then gradually beat in the egg and vanilla or almond essence.

2 Stir the flour into the beaten mixture, with floured hands, then roll into 16–20 small balls. Spread the rolled oats on a sheet of greaseproof paper and toss the balls in them to coat evenly.

3 Place the balls, spaced slightly apart, on two baking sheets, place a piece of cherry on top of each and bake for about 15–20 minutes, until lightly browned. Allow the biscuits to cool on the sheets for 5 minutes before transferring to a wire rack to cool completely.

Easter Biscuits

This is a seasonal recipe, but these biscuits can be enjoyed at any time of the year.

Makes 16–18

115g/4oz/¹/₂ cup butter
  or margarine
75g/3oz/scant ¹/₂ cup
  caster sugar, plus
  extra for sprinkling
1 egg, separated
200g/7oz/1¾ cups plain
  flour

2.5ml/¹/₂ tsp mixed spice
2.5ml/¹/₂ tsp ground
  cinnamon
50g/2oz/4 tbsp currants
15ml/1 tbsp chopped
  mixed peel
15–30ml/1–2 tbsp milk

1 Preheat the oven to 200℃/400℉/Gas 6. Lightly grease two baking sheets. Cream together the butter or margarine and sugar until light and fluffy, then beat in the egg yolk.

2 Sift the flour and spices over the egg mixture, then fold in with the currants and peel, adding sufficient milk to make a fairly soft dough.

3 Turn the dough on to a floured surface, knead lightly until just smooth, then roll out using a floured rolling pin, to about a 5mm/¹/₄in thickness. Cut the dough into circles using a 5cm/2in fluted biscuit cutter. Transfer the circles to the baking sheets and bake for 10 minutes.

4 Beat the egg white, then brush over the biscuits. Sprinkle with caster sugar and return to the oven for a further 10 minutes, until golden. Transfer to a wire rack to cool.

Shortbread

Once you have tasted this shortbread, you'll never buy a packet from a shop again.

Makes 8

150g/5oz/generous ¹/₂ cup unsalted butter, at room temperature

115g/4oz/¹/₂ cup caster sugar

150g/5oz/1¹/₄ cups plain flour

65g/2¹/₂oz/¹/₂ cup rice flour

1.5ml/¹/₄ tsp baking powder

1.5ml/¹/₄ tsp salt

1 Preheat the oven to 160°C/325°F/Gas 3. Lightly grease a 20cm/8in shallow round cake tin. Cream the butter and sugar together until light and fluffy. Sift over the flours, baking powder and salt, and mix well.

2 Press the mixture neatly into the prepared tin, smoothing the surface with the back of a spoon. Prick all over with a fork, then score into eight equal wedges.

3 Bake until golden, about 40–45 minutes. Leave in the tin until cool enough to handle, then unmould and recut the wedges while still hot. Store in an airtight container.

Flapjacks

For a spicier version, add 5ml/1 tsp ground ginger to the melted butter.

Makes 8

50g/2oz/¹/₄ cup butter

20ml/1 rounded tbsp golden syrup

65g/2¹/₂oz/scant ¹/₂ cup dark brown sugar

115g/4oz/generous 1 cup quick-cooking oats

1.5ml/¹/₄ tsp salt

1 Preheat the oven to 180°C/350°F/Gas 4. Line and grease a 20cm/8in shallow round cake tin. Place the butter, golden syrup and sugar in a pan over a low heat. Cook, stirring, until melted and combined.

2 Remove from the heat and add the oats and salt. Stir the mixture to blend. Spoon the mixture into the prepared tin and smooth the surface. Place in the centre of the oven and bake until golden brown, 20–25 minutes. Leave in the tin until cool enough to handle, then unmould and cut into wedges while still hot. Store in an airtight container.

Chocolate Delights

This method of making biscuits ensures they are all of a uniform size.

Makes 50

25g/1oz plain chocolate
25g/1oz bitter cooking
    chocolate
225g/8oz/2 cups plain
    flour
2.5ml/½ tsp salt
225g/8oz/1 cup unsalted
    butter, at room
    temperature

225g/8oz/generous 1 cup
    caster sugar
2 eggs
5ml/1 tsp vanilla essence
115g/4oz/1 cup finely
    chopped walnuts

1 Melt the chocolate in the top of a double boiler, or in a heatproof bowl set over a pan of gently simmering water. Set aside. In a bowl, sift together the flour and salt. Set aside.

2 Cream the butter until soft. Add the sugar and continue beating until the mixture is light and fluffy. Mix the eggs and vanilla essence, then gradually stir into the butter mixture. Stir in the chocolate, then the flour. Finally, stir in the nuts.

3 Divide the mixture into four equal parts, and roll each into a 5cm/2in diameter log. Wrap tightly in foil and chill or freeze until firm.

4 Preheat the oven to 190°C/375°F/Gas 5. Grease two baking sheets. With a sharp knife, cut the logs into 5mm/¼in slices. Place the circles on the baking sheets and bake until lightly coloured, about 10 minutes. Using a palette knife, transfer to a wire rack to cool.

Cinnamon Treats

Place these biscuits in a heart-shaped basket, as here, and serve them up with love.

Makes 50

250g/9oz/generous
    2 cups plain flour
2.5ml/½ tsp salt
10ml/2 tsp ground
    cinnamon

225g/8oz/1 cup unsalted
    butter, at room
    temperature
225g/8oz/generous 1 cup
    caster sugar
2 eggs
5ml/1 tsp vanilla essence

1 Sift together the flour, salt and cinnamon together into a bowl. Set aside.

2 Cream the butter until soft. Add the sugar and continue beating until the mixture is light and fluffy. Beat the eggs and vanilla essence together, then gradually stir into the butter mixture. Stir in the dry ingredients.

3 Divide the mixture into four equal parts, then roll each into a 5cm/2in diameter log. Wrap tightly in foil and chill or freeze until firm.

4 Preheat the oven to 190°C/375°F/Gas 5. Grease two baking sheets. With a sharp knife, cut the logs into 5mm/¼in slices. Place the rounds on the baking sheets and bake until lightly coloured, about 10 minutes. Using a palette knife, transfer to a wire rack to cool.

Chunky Chocolate Drops

Do not allow these cookies to cool completely on the baking sheet or they will break when you try to lift them.

Makes 18

175g/6oz plain chocolate
115g/4oz/1/2 cup unsalted
   butter
2 eggs
90g/31/2oz/1/2 cup
   granulated sugar
50g/2oz/1/4 cup (packed)
   light brown sugar
40g/11/2oz/1/3 cup plain
   flour
25g/1oz/1/4 cup
unsweetened cocoa
powder
5ml/1 tsp baking powder
10ml/2 tsp vanilla
   essence

pinch of salt
115g/4oz/1 cup pecan
   nuts, toasted and
   coarsely chopped
175g/6oz/1 cup plain
   chocolate chips
115g/4oz fine quality
   white chocolate,
   chopped into 5mm/
   1/4in pieces
115g/4oz fine quality
   milk chocolate,
   chopped into 5mm/
   1/4in pieces

1 Preheat the oven to 160°C/325°F/Gas 3. Grease two large baking sheets. In a medium saucepan over a low heat, melt the plain chocolate and butter until smooth, stirring frequently. Remove from the heat to cool slightly.

2 Beat the eggs and sugars for 2–3 minutes until pale and creamy. Gradually beat in the melted chocolate mixture. Beat in the flour, cocoa, baking powder, vanilla and salt, just to blend. Add the nuts, chocolate chips and chocolate pieces.

3 Drop 4–6 heaped tablespoonfuls of the mixture on to each baking sheet 10cm/4in apart and flatten each to a round about 7.5cm/3in. Bake for 8–10 minutes until the tops are shiny and cracked and the edges look crisp.

4 Remove the baking sheets to a wire rack to cool for about 2 minutes, until the cookies are just set, then remove them to the wire rack to cool completely. Continue to bake in batches.

Chocolate Crackle-tops

These cookies are best eaten on the day they are baked, as they dry slightly on storage.

Makes 38

200g/7oz plain chocolate,
   chopped
90g/31/2oz/7 tbsp
   unsalted butter
115g/4oz/1/2 cup caster
   sugar
3 eggs
5ml/1 tsp vanilla essence
215g/71/2oz/scant 2 cups
   plain flour

25g/1oz/1/4 cup
   unsweetened cocoa
   powder
2.5ml/1/2 tsp baking
   powder
pinch of salt
175g/6oz/11/2 cups icing
   sugar, for coating

1 Heat the chocolate and butter over a low heat until smooth, stirring frequently. Remove from the heat. Stir in the sugar, and continue stirring until dissolved. Add the eggs, one at a time, beating well after each addition; stir in the vanilla. In a separate bowl, sift together the flour, cocoa, baking powder and salt. Gradually stir into the chocolate mixture until just blended. Cover and chill for at least 1 hour.

2 Preheat the oven to 160°C/325°F/Gas 3. Grease two or three large baking sheets. Place the icing sugar in a small, deep bowl. Using a teaspoon, scoop the dough into small balls and roll in your hands into 4cm/11/2in balls.

3 Drop the balls, one at a time, into the icing sugar and roll until heavily coated. Remove each ball with a slotted spoon and tap against the bowl to remove any excess sugar. Place on the baking sheets 4cm/11/2in apart.

4 Bake the cookies for 10–15 minutes or until the tops feel slightly firm when touched with your fingertip. Remove the baking sheets to a wire rack for 2–3 minutes, then with a palette knife remove the cookies to the wire rack to cool.

Chocolate-chip Oat Biscuits

Oat biscuits are given a delicious lift by the inclusion of chocolate chips. Try caramel chips for a change, if you like.

Makes 60

115g/4oz/1 cup plain flour
2.5ml/¹/₂ tsp bicarbonate of soda
1.5ml/¹/₄ tsp baking powder
1.5ml/¹/₄ tsp salt
115g/4oz/¹/₂ cup butter or margarine, at room temperature
115g/4oz/generous ¹/₂ cup caster sugar
90g/3¹/₂oz/generous ¹/₂ cup light brown sugar
1 egg
2.5ml/¹/₂ tsp vanilla essence
75g/3oz/scant ¹/₂ cup rolled oats
175g/6oz/1 cup plain chocolate chips

1 Preheat the oven to 180°C/350°F/Gas 4. Grease three or four baking sheets. Sift the flour, bicarbonate of soda, baking powder and salt into a mixing bowl. Set aside.

2 With an electric mixer, cream the butter or margarine and the sugars together. Add the egg and vanilla, and beat until light and fluffy. Add the flour mixture and beat on low speed until thoroughly blended. Stir in the rolled oats and plain chocolate chips, mixing well with a wooden spoon. The dough should be crumbly.

3 Drop heaped teaspoonfuls on to the baking sheets, about 2.5cm/1in apart. Bake until just firm around the edges but still soft in the centres, about 15 minutes. With a palette knife, transfer the biscuits to a wire rack to cool.

Chocolate and Coconut Slices

These tasty family favourites are easier to slice if they are allowed to cool overnight.

Makes 24

175g/6oz/2 cups crushed digestive biscuits
50g/2oz/¹/₄ cup caster sugar
pinch of salt
115g/4oz/¹/₂ cup butter or margarine, melted
75g/3oz/1¹/₂ cups desiccated coconut
250g/9oz plain chocolate chips
250ml/8fl oz/1 cup sweetened condensed milk
115g/4oz/1 cup chopped walnuts

1 Preheat the oven to 180°C/350°F/Gas 4. In a bowl, combine the crushed biscuits, sugar, salt and butter or margarine. Press the mixture evenly over the base of an ungreased 33 x 23cm/13 x 9in baking dish.

2 Sprinkle the coconut over the biscuit base, then scatter over the chocolate chips. Pour the condensed milk evenly over the chocolate. Sprinkle the walnuts on top. Bake in the oven for 30 minutes. Unmould on to a wire rack and leave to cool.

Nut Lace Wafers

To create a different taste, add some finely grated orange peel to these delicate biscuits.

Makes 18

65g/2¹/₂oz/scant ¹/₂ cup
   blanched almonds
50g/2oz/¹/₄ cup butter
40g/1¹/₂oz/¹/₃ cup plain
   flour

90g/3¹/₂oz/¹/₂ cup caster
   sugar
30ml/2 tbsp double cream
2.5ml/¹/₂ tsp vanilla
   essence

1 Preheat the oven to 190°C/375°F/Gas 5. Lightly grease two baking sheets.

2 With a sharp knife, chop the almonds as finely as possible. Alternatively, use a food processor or blender to chop the nuts very finely.

3 Melt the butter in a saucepan over a low heat. Remove from the heat and stir in the remaining ingredients and the finely chopped almonds.

4 Drop teaspoonfuls 6cm/2¹/₂in apart on the prepared sheets. Bake until golden, about 5 minutes. Cool on the baking sheets briefly, just until the wafers are stiff enough to remove. With a palette knife, transfer to a wire rack to cool.

Oatmeal Lace Rounds

These rich, nutty biscuits are very quick and simple to make and will be enjoyed by everyone.

Makes 36

165g/5¹/₂oz/²/₃ cup butter
   or margarine
130g/4¹/₂oz/1¹/₄ cups
   quick-cooking
   porridge oats
170g/5³/₄ oz/³/₄ cup dark
   brown sugar
155g/5¹/₄oz/²/₃ cup caster
   sugar

40g/1¹/₂oz/¹/₃ cup plain
   flour
1.5ml/¹/₄ tsp salt
1 egg, lightly beaten
5ml/1 tsp vanilla essence
65g/2¹/₂oz/ generous
   ¹/₂ cup pecan nuts or
   walnuts, finely
   chopped

1 Preheat the oven to 180°C/350°F/Gas 4. Lightly grease two baking sheets.

2 Melt the butter or margarine in a saucepan over a low heat. Set aside. In a mixing bowl, combine the oats, brown sugar, caster sugar, flour and salt. Make a well in the centre and add the butter or margarine, egg and vanilla. Mix until blended, then stir in the chopped nuts.

3 Drop rounded teaspoonfuls of the mixture about 5cm/2in apart on the prepared baking sheets. Bake in the oven until lightly browned on the edges and bubbling all over, about 5–8 minutes. Cool on the baking sheets for 2 minutes, then transfer to a wire rack to cool completely.

Nutty Chocolate Squares

These delicious squares are incredibly rich, so cut them smaller if you wish.

Makes 16

2 eggs
10ml/2 tsp vanilla essence
1.5ml/¹/₄ tsp salt
175g/6oz/1¹/₂ cups pecan nuts, coarsely chopped
50g/2oz/¹/₂ cup plain flour
50g/2oz/¹/₄ cup caster sugar

120ml/4fl oz/¹/₂ cup golden syrup
75g/3oz plain chocolate, finely chopped
40g/1¹/₂oz/3 tbsp butter
16 pecan nut halves, to decorate

1 Preheat the oven to 160°C/325°F/Gas 3. Line the base and sides of a 20cm/8in square baking tin with greaseproof paper and lightly grease the paper.

2 Whisk together the eggs, vanilla and salt. In another bowl, mix together the chopped pecan nuts and flour. Set both aside until needed.

3 In a saucepan, bring the sugar and golden syrup to the boil. Remove from the heat, stir in the chocolate and butter, and blend thoroughly with a wooden spoon. Mix in the beaten egg mixture, then fold in the pecan nut mixture.

4 Pour the mixture into the baking tin and bake until set, about 35 minutes. Cool in the tin for 10 minutes before unmoulding. Cut into 5cm/2in squares and press pecan nut halves into the tops while warm. Cool on a wire rack.

Raisin Brownies

Cover these brownies with a light chocolate frosting for a truly decadent treat, if you wish.

Makes 16

115g/4oz/¹/₂ cup butter or margarine
50g/2oz/¹/₂ cup cocoa powder
2 eggs
225g/8oz/generous 1 cup caster sugar

5ml/1 tsp vanilla essence
40g/1¹/₂oz/¹/₃ cup plain flour
75g/3oz/³/₄ cup chopped walnuts
75g/3oz/generous ¹/₂ cup raisins

1 Preheat the oven to 180°C/350°F/Gas 4. Line the base and sides of a 20cm/8in square baking tin with greaseproof paper and grease the paper.

2 Gently melt the butter or margarine in a small saucepan. Remove from the heat and stir in the cocoa powder. With an electric mixer, beat the eggs, sugar and vanilla together until light. Add the cocoa mixture and stir to blend.

3 Sift the flour over the cocoa mixture and gently fold in. Add the walnuts and raisins and scrape the mixture into the prepared baking tin.

4 Bake in the centre of the oven for 30 minutes. Leave in the tin to cool before cutting into 5cm/2in squares and removing. The brownies should be soft and moist.

Chocolate-chip Brownies

A double dose of chocolate is incorporated into these melt-in-the-mouth brownies.

Makes 24

115g/4oz plain chocolate	pinch of salt
115g/4oz/½ cup butter	150g/5oz/1¼ cups plain
3 eggs	flour
200g/7oz/1 cup sugar	175g/6oz/1 cup chocolate
2.5ml/½ tsp vanilla	chips
essence	

1 Preheat the oven to 180°C/350°F/Gas 4. Then line a 33 x 23cm/13 x 9in baking tin with greaseproof paper and grease the paper.

2 Melt the chocolate and butter together in the top of a double boiler, or in a heatproof bowl set over a pan of gently simmering water.

3 Beat together the eggs, sugar, vanilla and salt. Stir in the chocolate mixture. Sift over the flour and fold in. Add the chocolate chips.

4 Pour the mixture into the baking tin and spread evenly. Bake until just set, about 30 minutes. The brownies should be slightly moist inside. Leave to cool in the tin.

5 To turn out, run a knife all around the edge and invert on to a baking sheet. Remove the paper. Place another sheet on top and invert again. Cut into bars for serving.

Marbled Brownies

Flavoursome and impressive in appearance, these fancy brownies are also great fun to make.

Makes 24

	For the plain mixture
225g/8oz plain chocolate	50g/2oz/4 tbsp butter, at
75g/3oz/⅓ cup butter	room temperature
4 eggs	175g/6oz/¾ cup cream
300g/11oz/1½ cups sugar	cheese
150g/5oz/1¼ cups plain	90g/3½ oz/1½ cups
flour	sugar
2.5ml/½ tsp salt	2 eggs
5ml/1 tsp baking powder	25g/1oz/4 tbsp plain
10ml/2 tsp vanilla	flour
essence	5ml/1 tsp vanilla essence
115g/4oz/1 cup walnuts,	
chopped	

1 Preheat the oven to 180°C/350°F/Gas 4 . Then line a 33 x 23cm/13 x 9in baking tin with greaseproof paper and grease.

2 Melt the chocolate and butter over a very low heat, stirring. Set aside to cool. Meanwhile, beat the eggs until light and fluffy. Gradually beat in the sugar. Sift over the flour, salt and baking powder and fold to combine.

3 Stir in the cooled chocolate mixture. Add the vanilla and walnuts. Measure and set aside 475ml/16fl oz/2 cups of the chocolate mixture. For the plain mixture, cream the butter and cream with an electric mixer. Add the sugar and continue beating until blended. Beat in the eggs, flour and vanilla.

4 Spread the unmeasured chocolate mixture in the tin. Pour over the plain mixture. Drop spoonfuls of the reserved chocolate mixture on top.

5 With a palette knife, swirl the mixtures to marble. Do not blend completely. Bake until just set, 35–40 minutes. Turn out when cool and cut into squares for serving.

Oatmeal and Date Brownies

These brownies are marvellous as a break-time treat. The secret of chewy, moist brownies is not to overcook them.

Makes 16
150g/5oz plain chocolate
50g/2oz/4 tbsp butter
75g/3oz/scant 1 cup
    quick-cooking
    porridge oats
25g/1oz/3 tbsp
    wheatgerm
25g/1oz/⅓ cup milk
    powder
2.5ml/½ tsp baking
    powder

2.5ml/½ tsp salt
50g/2oz/½ cup chopped
    walnuts
50g/2oz/⅓ cup dates,
    chopped
50g/2oz/¼ cup molasses
    sugar
5ml/1 tsp vanilla essence
2 eggs, beaten

1 Break the chocolate into a heatproof bowl and add the butter. Place over a pan of simmering water and stir until completely melted.

2 Cool the chocolate, stirring occasionally. Preheat the oven to 180°C/350°F/Gas 4. Grease and line a 20cm/8in square cake tin.

3 Combine all the dry ingredients together in a bowl, then beat in the melted chocolate, vanilla and eggs. Pour the mixture into the cake tin, level the surface and bake in the oven for 20–25 minutes until firm around the edges yet still soft in the centre.

4 Cool the brownies in the tin, then chill in the fridge. When they are more solid, turn them out of the tin and cut into 16 squares.

Banana Chocolate Brownies

Nuts traditionally give brownies their chewy texture. Here oat bran is used instead, creating a wonderful alternative.

Makes 9
75ml/5 tbsp cocoa
    powder
15ml/1 tbsp caster sugar
75ml/5 tbsp milk
3 large bananas, mashed
215g/7½oz/1 cup soft
    light brown sugar

5ml/1 tsp vanilla essence
5 egg whites
75g/3oz/¾ cup self-
    raising flour
75g/3oz/⅔ cup oat bran
icing sugar, for dusting

1 Preheat the oven to 180°C/350°F/Gas 4. Line a 20cm/8in square cake tin with non-stick baking paper.

2 Blend the cocoa and caster sugar with the milk. Add the bananas, soft brown sugar and vanilla essence. Lightly beat the egg whites with a fork. Add the chocolate mixture and continue to beat well. Sift the flour over the mixture and fold in with the oat bran. Pour into the prepared tin.

3 Cook in the oven for 40 minutes, or until firm. Cool in the tin for 10 minutes, then turn out on to a wire rack. Cut into squares and lightly dust with icing sugar before serving.

White Chocolate Brownies

If you wish, hazelnuts can be substituted for the macadamia nuts in the topping.

Serves 12

150g/5oz/1 cup plain
  flour
2.5ml/½ tsp baking
  powder
pinch of salt
175g/6oz fine quality
  white chocolate,
  chopped
90g/3½ oz/½ cup caster
  sugar
115g/4oz/½ cup unsalted
  butter, cut into pieces

2 eggs, lightly beaten
5ml/1 tsp vanilla essence
175g/6oz semi-sweet
  chocolate chips

For the topping

200g/7oz milk chocolate,
  chopped
215g/7½ oz/1 cup
  unsalted macadamia
  nuts, chopped

1 Preheat the oven to 180°C/350°F/Gas 4. Grease a 23cm/9in springform tin. Sift together the flour, baking powder and salt, and set aside.

2 In a medium saucepan over a moderate heat, melt the white chocolate, sugar and butter until smooth, stirring frequently. Cool slightly, then beat in the eggs and vanilla. Stir in the chocolate chips. Spread evenly in the prepared tin, smoothing the top.

3 Bake for 20–25 minutes until a toothpick inserted 5cm/2in from the side of the tin comes out clean. Remove from the oven to a heatproof surface, sprinkle chopped milk chocolate over the surface (avoid touching the side of tin) and return to oven for 1 minute.

4 Remove from the oven and, using the back of a spoon, gently spread out the softened chocolate. Sprinkle with the macadamia nuts and gently press into the chocolate. Cool on a wire rack for 30 minutes; chill for 1 hour. Run a sharp knife around the side of the tin to loosen; then unclip and remove. Cut into thin wedges to serve.

Maple-Pecan Nut Brownies

This recipe provides a delicious adaptation of the classic American chocolate brownie.

Makes 12

115g/4oz/½ cup butter,
  melted
75g/3oz/½ cup light soft
  brown sugar
90ml/6 tbsp maple syrup
2 eggs
115g/4oz/1 cup
  self-raising flour

75g/3oz/¼ cup pecan
  nuts, chopped
115g/4oz/⅔ cup plain
  chocolate chips
50g/2oz/¼ cup unsalted
  butter
12 pecan nut halves, to
  decorate

1 Preheat the oven to 180°C/350°F/Gas 4. Line and grease a 25 x 18cm/10 x 7in cake tin.

2 Beat together the melted butter, sugar, 60ml/4 tbsp of the maple syrup, eggs and flour for 1 minute, or until smooth. Stir in the nuts and transfer to the cake tin. Smooth the surface and bake for 30 minutes, until risen and firm to the touch. Cool in the tin for 10 minutes, then transfer to a wire rack to cool completely.

3 Melt the chocolate chips, butter and remaining syrup over a low heat. Cool slightly, then spread over the cake. Press in the pecan nut halves, leave to set for about 5 minutes, then cut into bars.

American Chocolate Fudge Brownies

This is the classic American recipe, but omit the frosting if you find it too rich.

Makes 12

175g/6oz/³/₄ cup butter
40g/1¹/₂oz/6 tbsp cocoa powder
2 eggs, lightly beaten
175g/6oz/1 cup soft light brown sugar
2.5ml/¹/₂ tsp vanilla essence
115g/4oz/1 cup chopped pecan nuts

50g/2oz/¹/₂ cup self-raising flour

For the frosting
115g/4oz plain chocolate
25g/1oz/2 tbsp butter
15ml/1 tbsp soured cream

1 Preheat the oven to 180°C/350°F/Gas 4. Grease then line a 20cm/8in square shallow cake tin with greaseproof paper. Melt the butter in a pan and stir in the cocoa powder. Set aside to cool.

2 Beat together the eggs, sugar and vanilla essence in a bowl, then stir in the cooled cocoa mixture with the nuts. Sift over the flour and fold into the mixture with a metal spoon.

3 Pour the mixture into the cake tin and bake in the oven for 30–35 minutes, until risen. Remove from the oven (the mixture will still be quite soft and wet, but it cooks further while cooling) and leave to cool in the tin.

4 To make the frosting, melt the chocolate and butter together in a pan and remove from the heat. Beat in the soured cream until smooth and glossy. Leave to cool slightly, and then spread over the top of the brownies. When set, cut into 12 pieces.

Fudge-glazed Chocolate Brownies

These brownies are just about irresistible, so hide them from friends – or make lots!

Makes 16

250g/9oz bittersweet chocolate, chopped
25g/1oz unsweetened chocolate, chopped
115g/4oz/¹/₂ cup unsalted butter, cut into pieces
90g/3¹/₂ oz/¹/₂ cup light brown sugar
50g/2oz/¹/₄ cup granulated sugar
2 eggs
15ml/1 tbsp vanilla essence
65g/2¹/₂ oz/¹/₂ cup plain flour
115g/4oz/1 cup pecans or walnuts, toasted and chopped

150g/5oz white chocolate, chopped
pecan halves, to decorate (optional)

Fudgy Chocolate Glaze
175g/6oz bittersweet chocolate, chopped
50g/2oz/4 tbsp unsalted butter, cut into pieces
30ml/2 tbsp corn or golden syrup
10ml/2 tsp vanilla essence
5ml/1 tsp instant coffee

1 Preheat oven to 180°C/350°F/Gas 4. Line a 20cm/8in square baking tin with foil then grease the foil.

2 In a saucepan over a low heat, melt the dark chocolates and butter. Off the heat, add the sugars and stir for 2 minutes. Beat in the eggs and vanilla; blend in the flour. Stir in the nuts and white chocolate. Pour into the tin. Bake for 20–25 minutes. Cool in the tin for 30 minutes then lift, using the foil, on to a wire rack to cool for 2 hours.

3 For the glaze, melt all the ingredients in a pan until smooth, stirring. Chill for 1 hour then spread over the brownies. Chill until set then cut into squares.

Chocolate Raspberry Macaroon Bars

Any seedless preserve, such as strawberry or apricot, can be substituted for the raspberry in this recipe.

Makes 16 – 18

115g/4oz/¹/₂ cup unsalted
  butter, softened
50g/2oz/¹/₂ cup icing
  sugar
25g/1oz/¹/₄ cup
  unsweetened cocoa
  powder
pinch of salt
5ml/1 tsp almond essence
120g/4oz/1¹/₄ cups plain
  flour

15ml/1 tbsp raspberry
  flavour liqueur
175g/6oz/1 cup milk
  chocolate chips
175g/6oz/1¹/₂ cups finely
  ground almonds
4 egg whites
pinch of salt
200g/7oz/1 cup caster
  sugar
2.5ml/¹/₂ tsp almond
  essence
50g/2oz/¹/₂ cup flaked
  almonds

For the topping
150g/5oz/¹/₂ cup seedless
  raspberry preserve

1 Preheat the oven to 160°C/325°F/Gas 3. Then line a 23 x 33cm/9 x 13in baking tin with foil and grease. Beat together the butter, sugar, cocoa and salt until blended. Beat in the almond essence and flour to make a crumbly dough.

2 Turn the dough into the tin and smooth the surface. Prick with a fork. Bake for 20 minutes until just set. Remove from the oven and increase the temperature to 190°C/375°F/Gas 5. Combine the raspberry preserve and liqueur. Spread over the cooked crust, then sprinkle with the chocolate chips.

3 In a food processor fitted with a metal blade, process the almonds, egg whites, salt, sugar and almond essence. Pour over the jam layer, spreading evenly. Sprinkle with almonds.

4 Bake for 20 – 25 minutes until the top is golden and puffed. Cool in the tin for 20 minutes. Carefully remove from the tin and cool completely. Peel off the foil and cut into bars.

Chewy Fruit Muesli Slice

The apricots give these slices a wonderful chewy texture and the apple keeps them moist.

Makes 8

75g/3oz/scant ¹/₂ cup
  ready-to-eat dried
  apricots, chopped
1 eating apple, cored and
  grated
150g/5oz/1¹/₄ cups Swiss-
  style muesli

150ml/¹/₄ pint/²/₃ cup
  apple juice
15g/¹/₂oz/1 tbsp
  sunflower margarine

1 Preheat the oven to 190°C/375°F/Gas 5. Place all the ingredients in a large bowl and mix well.

2 Press the mixture into a 20cm/8in round non-stick sandwich tin and bake for 35 – 40 minutes, or until lightly browned and firm. Mark the muesli slice into wedges and leave to cool in the tin.

Blueberry Streusel Slice

If you are short of time, use ready-made pastry for this delightful streusel.

Makes 30

225g/8oz shortcrust
   pastry
50g/2oz/¹/₂ cup plain
   flour
1.5ml/¹/₄ tsp baking
   powder
40g/1¹/₂oz/3 tbsp butter
   or margarine
25g/1oz/2 tbsp fresh
   white breadcrumbs

50g/2oz/¹/₃ cup soft light
   brown sugar
1.5ml/¹/₄ tsp salt
50g/2oz/4 tbsp flaked or
   chopped almonds
30ml/4 tbsp blackberry or
   bramble jelly
115g/4oz/1 cup
   blueberries, fresh
   or frozen

1 Preheat the oven to 180°C/350°F/Gas 4. Roll out the pastry on a lightly floured surface and line an 18 x 28cm/7 x 11in Swiss roll tin. Prick the base evenly with a fork.

2 Rub together the plain flour, baking powder, butter or margarine, breadcrumbs, sugar and salt until really crumbly, then mix in the almonds.

3 Spread the pastry with the jelly, sprinkle with the blueberries, then cover evenly with the streusel topping, pressing down lightly. Bake for 30–40 minutes, reducing the temperature after 20 minutes to 160°C/325°F/Gas 3.

4 Remove from the oven when golden on the top and the pastry is cooked through. Cut into slices while still hot, then allow to cool.

Sticky Date and Apple Bars

If possible allow this mixture to mature for 1–2 days before cutting – it will get stickier and even more delicious!

Makes 16

115g/4oz/¹/₂ cup
   margarine
50g/2oz/¹/₃ cup soft dark
   brown sugar
50g/2oz/4 tbsp golden
   syrup
115g/4oz/³/₄ cup chopped
   dates
115g/4oz/generous 1 cup
   rolled oats

115g/4oz/1 cup
   wholemeal self-raising
   flour
225g/8oz/2 eating apples,
   peeled, cored and
   grated
5–10ml/1–2 tsp lemon
   juice
20–25 walnut halves

1 Preheat the oven to 190°C/375°F/Gas 5. Then line an 18–20cm/7–8in square or rectangular loose-based cake tin. In a large pan, heat the margarine, sugar, syrup and dates, stirring until the dates soften completely.

2 Gradually work in the oats, flour, apples and lemon juice until well mixed. Spoon into the tin and spread out evenly. Top with the walnut halves.

3 Bake for 30 minutes, then reduce the temperature to 160°C/325°F/Gas 3 and bake for 10–20 minutes more, until firm to the touch and golden. Cut into squares or bars while still warm, or wrap in foil when nearly cold and keep for 1–2 days before eating.

Figgy Bars

Make sure you have napkins handy when you serve these deliciously sticky bars.

Makes 48

350g/12oz/1¹/₂ cups dried figs
3 eggs
175g/6oz/³/₄ cup caster sugar
75g/3oz/³/₄ cup plain flour
5ml/1 tsp baking powder
2.5ml/¹/₂ tsp ground cinnamon
1.5ml/¹/₄ tsp ground cloves
1.5ml/¹/₄ tsp grated nutmeg
1.5ml/¹/₄ tsp salt
75g/3oz/³/₄ cup finely chopped walnuts
30ml/2 tbsp brandy or cognac
icing sugar, for dusting

1 Preheat the oven to 160°C/325°F/Gas 3. Then line a 30 x 20 x 3cm/12 x 8 x 1½in baking tin with greaseproof paper and grease the paper.

2 With a sharp knife, chop the figs roughly. Set aside. In a bowl, whisk the eggs and sugar until well blended. In another bowl, sift together the dry ingredients, then fold into the egg mixture in several batches.

3 Scrape the mixture into the baking tin and bake until the top is firm and brown, about 35–40 minutes. It should still be soft underneath.

4 Leave to cool in the tin for 5 minutes, then unmould and transfer to a sheet of greaseproof paper lightly sprinkled with icing sugar. Cut into bars.

Lemon Bars

A surprising amount of lemon juice goes into these bars, but you will appreciate why when you taste them.

Makes 36

50g/2oz/¹/₂ cup icing sugar
175g/6oz/1¹/₂ cups plain flour
2.5ml/¹/₂ tsp salt
175g/6oz/³/₄ cup butter, cut in small pieces

For the topping

4 eggs
350g/12oz/1¹/₂ cups caster sugar
grated rind of 1 lemon
120ml/4fl oz/¹/₂ cup fresh lemon juice
175ml/6fl oz/³/₄ cup whipping cream
icing sugar, for dusting

1 Preheat the oven to 160°C/325°F/Gas 3. Grease a 33 x 23cm/13 x 9in baking tin.

2 Sift the sugar, flour and salt into a bowl. With a pastry blender, cut in the butter until the mixture resembles coarse breadcrumbs. Press the mixture into the base of the tin. Bake until golden brown, about 20 minutes.

3 Meanwhile, for the topping, whisk the eggs and sugar together until blended. Add the lemon rind and juice, and mix well.

4 Lightly whip the cream and fold into the egg mixture. Pour over the still warm base, return to the oven, and bake until set, about 40 minutes. Cool completely before cutting into bars. Dust with icing sugar.

Spiced Raisin Bars

If you like raisins, these gloriously spicy bars are for you. Omit the walnuts if you prefer.

Makes 30

100g/3³/₄ oz/scant 1 cup
   plain flour
7.5ml/1¹/₂ tsp baking
   powder
5ml/1 tsp ground
   cinnamon
2.5ml/¹/₂ tsp grated
   nutmeg
1.5ml/¹/₄ tsp ground
   cloves
1.5ml/¹/₄ tsp mixed spice

215g/7¹/₂oz/1¹/₂ cups
   raisins
115g/4oz/¹/₂ cup butter
   or margarine, at room
   temperature
90g/3¹/₂oz/¹/₂ cup sugar
2 eggs
170g/5³/₄ oz/scant ¹/₂ cup
   black treacle
50g/2oz/¹/₂ cup walnuts,
   chopped

1 Preheat the oven to 180°C/350°F/Gas 4. Then line a 33 x 23cm/13 x 9in baking tin with greaseproof paper and grease the paper.

2 Sift together the flour, baking powder and spices. Place the raisins in another bowl and toss with a few tablespoons of the flour mixture.

3 With an electric mixer, cream the butter or margarine and sugar together until light and fluffy. Beat in the eggs, one at a time, then the black treacle. Stir in the flour mixture, raisins and walnuts.

4 Spread evenly in the baking tin. Bake until just set, about 15–18 minutes. Cool in the tin before cutting into bars.

Toffee Meringue Bars

Two delicious layers complement each other beautifully in these easy-to-make bars.

Makes 12

50g/2oz/4 tbsp butter
215g/7¹/₂oz/scant
   1¹/₄ cups dark brown
   sugar
1 egg
2.5ml/¹/₂ tsp vanilla
   essence
65g/2¹/₂oz/9 tbsp plain
   flour
2.5ml/¹/₂ tsp salt
1.5ml/¹/₄ tsp grated
   nutmeg

For the topping
1 egg white
1.5ml/¹/₄ tsp salt
15ml/1 tbsp golden syrup
90g/3¹/₂oz/¹/₂ cup caster
   sugar
50g/2oz/¹/₂ cup walnuts,
   finely chopped

1 Combine the butter and brown sugar in a saucepan and heat until bubbling. Set aside to cool.

2 Preheat the oven to 180°C/350°F/Gas 4. Line the base and sides of a 20cm/8in square cake tin with greaseproof paper and grease the paper.

3 Beat the egg and vanilla into the cooled sugar mixture. Sift over the flour, salt and nutmeg and fold in. Spread in the base of the cake tin.

4 For the topping, beat the egg white with the salt until it holds soft peaks. Beat in the golden syrup, then the sugar, and continue beating until the mixture holds stiff peaks. Fold in the nuts and spread on top. Bake for 30 minutes. Cut into bars when completely cool.

Chocolate Walnut Bars

These double-decker bars should be stored in the fridge in an airtight container.

Makes 24

50g/2oz/²/₃ cup walnuts
55g/2¼oz/generous
  ¼ cup caster sugar
100g/3¾ oz/scant 1 cup
  plain flour, sifted
90g/3½ oz/6 tbsp cold
  unsalted butter, cut
  into pieces

90ml/6 tbsp water
25g/1oz/¼ cup
  unsweetened cocoa
  powder
90g/3½oz/½ cup caster
  sugar
5ml/1 tsp vanilla essence
1.5ml/¼ tsp salt
2 eggs
icing sugar, for dusting

For the topping
25g/1oz/2 tbsp unsalted
  butter

1 Preheat the oven to 180°C/350°F/Gas 4. Grease the base and sides of a 20cm/8in square baking tin.

2 Grind the walnuts with a few tablespoons of the sugar in a food processor or blender. In a bowl, combine the ground walnuts, remaining sugar and flour. Rub in the butter until the mixture resembles coarse breadcrumbs. Alternatively, use a food processor. Pat the walnut mixture evenly into the base of the baking tin. Bake for 25 minutes.

3 Meanwhile, for the topping, melt the butter with the water. Whisk in the cocoa powder and sugar. Remove from the heat, stir in the vanilla essence and salt, then cool for 5 minutes. Whisk in the eggs until blended. Pour the topping over the baked crust.

4 Return to the oven and bake until set, about 20 minutes. Set the tin on a wire rack to cool, then cut into bars and dust with icing sugar.

Hazelnut Squares

These crunchy, nutty squares are made in a single bowl. What could be simpler?

Makes 9

50g/2oz plain chocolate
65g/2½oz/5 tbsp butter
  or margarine
225g/8oz/generous 1 cup
  caster sugar
50g/2oz/½ cup plain
  flour
2.5ml/½ tsp baking
  powder

2 eggs, beaten
2.5ml/½ tsp vanilla
  essence
115g/4oz/1 cup skinned
  hazelnuts, roughly
  chopped

1 Preheat the oven to 180°C/350°F/Gas 4. Grease a 20cm/8in square baking tin.

2 In a heatproof bowl set over a pan of barely simmering water, melt the chocolate and butter or margarine. Remove the bowl from the heat.

3 Add the sugar, flour, baking powder, eggs, vanilla and half of the hazelnuts to the melted mixture and stir well with a wooden spoon.

4 Pour the mixture into the prepared tin. Bake in the oven for 10 minutes, then sprinkle the reserved hazelnuts over the top. Return to the oven and continue baking until firm to the touch, about 25 minutes.

5 Cool in the tin, set on a wire rack for 10 minutes, then unmould on to the rack and cool completely. Cut into squares before serving.

Fruity Tea bread

Serve this bread thinly sliced, toasted or plain, with butter or cream cheese and jam.

Makes one 23 x 13cm/9 x 5in loaf

225g/8oz/2 cups plain
  flour
115g/4oz/generous ¹/₂ cup
  caster sugar
15ml/1 tbsp baking
  powder
2.5ml/¹/₂ tsp salt
grated rind of 1 large
  orange
160ml/5¹/₂fl oz/generous
  ²/₃ cup fresh orange
  juice

2 eggs, lightly beaten
75g/3oz/6 tbsp butter or
  margarine, melted
115g/4oz/1 cup fresh
  cranberries or
  bilberries
50g/2oz/¹/₂ cup chopped
  walnuts

1 Preheat the oven to 180°C/350°F/Gas 4. Then line a
23 x 13cm/9 x 5in loaf tin with greaseproof paper and
grease the paper.

2 Sift the flour, sugar, baking powder and salt into a mixing
bowl. Then stir in the orange rind. Make a well in the centre
and add the fresh orange juice, eggs and melted butter or
margarine. Stir from the centre until the ingredients are
blended; do not overmix. Add the berries and walnuts and
stir until blended.

3 Transfer the mixture to the prepared tin and bake until a
skewer inserted in the centre of the loaf comes out clean,
about 45–50 minutes. Leave to cool in the tin for 10 minutes
before transferring to a wire rack to cool completely.

Date and Pecan Loaf

Walnuts may be used instead of pecan nuts to make this
luxurious tea bread.

Makes one 23 x 13cm/9 x 5in loaf

175g/6oz/1 cup chopped
  stoned dates
175ml/6fl oz/³/₄ cup
  boiling water
50g/2oz/4 tbsp unsalted
  butter, at room
  temperature
50g/2oz/¹/₃ cup dark
  brown sugar
50g/2oz/¹/₄ cup caster
  sugar
1 egg, at room
  temperature

30ml/2 tbsp brandy
165g/5¹/₂oz/generous
  ¹/₄ cup plain flour
10ml/2 tsp baking
  powder
2.5ml/¹/₂ tsp salt
4ml/³/₄ tsp freshly grated
  nutmeg
75g/3oz/³/₄ cup coarsely
  chopped pecan nuts

1 Place the dates in a bowl and pour over the boiling water.
Set aside to cool. Preheat the oven to 180°C/350°F/Gas 4. Line
a 23 x 13cm/9 x 5in loaf tin with greaseproof paper and then
grease the paper.

2 With an electric mixer, cream the butter and sugars until
light and fluffy. Beat in the egg and brandy, then set aside.

3 Sift the flour, baking powder, salt and nutmeg together,
at least three times. Fold the dry ingredients into the sugar
mixture in three batches, alternating with the dates and water.
Fold in the nuts.

4 Pour the mixture into the prepared tin and bake until a
skewer inserted in the centre comes out clean, about 45–
50 minutes. Leave the loaf to cool in the tin for 10 minutes
before transferring to a wire rack to cool completely.

Wholemeal Banana Nut Loaf

A hearty and filling loaf, this would be ideal as a winter tea-time treat.

Makes one 23 x 13cm/9 x 5in loaf

115g/4oz/¹/₂ cup butter,
    at room temperature
115g/4oz/generous ¹/₂ cup
    caster sugar
2 eggs, at room
    temperature
115g/4oz/1 cup plain
    flour
5ml/1 tsp bicarbonate of
    soda

1.5ml/¹/₄ tsp salt
5ml/1 tsp ground
    cinnamon
50g/2oz/¹/₂ cup
    wholemeal flour
3 large ripe bananas
5ml/1 tsp vanilla essence
50g/2oz/¹/₂ cup chopped
    walnuts

1 Preheat the oven to 180°C/350°F/Gas 4. Line the base and sides of a 23 x 13cm/9 x 5in loaf tin with greaseproof paper and grease the paper.

2 With an electric mixer, cream the butter and sugar together until light and fluffy. Add the eggs, one at a time, beating well after each addition.

3 Sift the plain flour, bicarbonate of soda, salt and cinnamon over the butter mixture and stir to blend. Then stir in the wholemeal flour.

4 With a fork, mash the bananas to a purée, then stir into the mixture. Stir in the vanilla and nuts.

5 Pour the mixture into the prepared tin and spread level. Bake until a skewer inserted in the centre comes out clean, about 50–60 minutes. Leave to stand for 10 minutes before transferring to a wire rack to cool completely.

Apricot Nut Loaf

Apricots, raisins and walnuts combine to make a lovely light tea bread.

Makes one 23 x 13cm/9 x 5in loaf

115g/4oz/¹/₂ cup dried
    apricots
1 large orange
75g/3oz/generous ¹/₂ cup
    raisins
150g/5oz/²/₃ cup caster
    sugar
85ml/5¹/₂ tbsp/¹/₃ cup oil
2 eggs, lightly beaten

250g/9oz/generous
    2 cups plain flour
10ml/2 tsp baking
    powder
2.5ml/¹/₂ tsp salt
5ml/1 tsp bicarbonate of
    soda
50g/2oz/¹/₂ cup chopped
    walnuts

1 Place the apricots in a bowl, cover with lukewarm water and leave to stand for 30 minutes. Preheat the oven to 180°C/350°F/Gas 4. Line a 23 x 13cm/9 x 5in loaf tin with greaseproof paper and grease the paper.

2 With a vegetable peeler, remove the orange rind, leaving the pith. Chop the strips finely.

3 Drain the apricots and chop coarsely. Place in a bowl with the orange rind and raisins. Squeeze the peeled orange. Measure the juice and add enough hot water to obtain 175ml/6fl oz/¾ cup liquid. Add the orange juice mixture to the apricot mixture. Stir in the sugar, oil and eggs. Set aside.

4 In another bowl, sift together the flour, baking powder, salt and bicarbonate of soda. Fold the flour mixture into the apricot mixture in three batches, then stir in the walnuts.

5 Spoon the mixture into the prepared tin and bake until a skewer inserted in the centre of the loaf comes out clean, about 55–60 minutes. If the loaf browns too quickly, protect the top with a sheet of foil. Cool in the tin for 10 minutes, then transfer to a wire rack to cool completely.

Bilberry Tea bread

A lovely crumbly topping makes this tea bread extra special.

Makes 8 pieces

50g/2oz/4tbsp butter or margarine, at room temperature
175g/6oz/¾ cup caster sugar
1 egg, at room temperature
120ml/4fl oz/½ cup milk
225g/8oz/2 cups plain flour
10ml/2 tsp baking powder
2.5ml/½ tsp salt

275g/10oz/¾ cup fresh bilberries, or blueberries

For the topping

115g/4oz/½ cup sugar
40g/1½oz/⅓ cup plain flour
2.5ml/½ tsp ground cinnamon
50g/2oz/4 tbsp butter, cut into pieces

1 Preheat the oven to 190°C/375°F/Gas 5. Grease a 23cm/9in baking dish.

2 With an electric mixer, cream the butter or margarine with the sugar until light and fluffy. Add the egg, beat to combine, then mix in the milk until well blended.

3 Sift over the flour, baking powder and salt and stir just enough to blend the ingredients. Add the berries and stir. Transfer to the baking dish.

4 For the topping, place the sugar, flour, cinnamon and butter in a mixing bowl. Cut in with a pastry blender until the mixture resembles coarse breadcrumbs. Sprinkle the topping over the mixture in the baking dish. Bake until a skewer inserted in the centre comes out clean, about 45 minutes. Serve warm or cold.

Dried Fruit Loaf

Use any combination of dried fruit you like in this delicious tea bread.

Makes one 23 x 13cm/9 x 5in loaf

450g/1lb/2¾ cups mixed dried fruit, such as currants, raisins, chopped dried apricots and dried cherries
300ml/½ pint/1¼ cups cold strong tea
200g/7oz/generous 1 cup dark brown sugar
grated rind and juice of 1 small orange

grated rind and juice of 1 lemon
1 egg, lightly beaten
200g/7oz/1³/₄ cups plain flour
15ml/1 tbsp baking powder
1.5ml/¼ tsp salt

1 In a bowl, mix the dried fruit with the cold tea and leave to soak overnight.

2 Preheat the oven to 180°C/350°F/Gas 4. Line the base and sides of a 23 x 13cm/9 x 5in loaf tin with greaseproof paper and grease the paper.

3 Strain the fruit, reserving the liquid. In a bowl, combine the sugar, orange and lemon rind, and fruit. Pour the orange and lemon juice into a measuring jug; if the quantity is less than 250ml/8fl oz/1 cup, then top up with the soaking liquid. Stir the citrus juices and egg into the dried fruit mixture.

4 Sift the flour, baking powder and salt together into another bowl. Stir into the fruit mixture until blended.

5 Transfer to the tin and bake until a skewer inserted in the centre comes out clean; about 1¼ hours. Leave in the tin for 10 minutes before unmoulding.

Corn Bread

Serve this bread as an accompaniment to a meal, with soup, or take it on a picnic.

Makes one 23 x 13cm/9 x 5in loaf

115g/4oz/1 cup plain
  flour
65g/2¹/₂oz/generous
  ¹/₄ cup caster sugar
5ml/1 tsp salt
15ml/1 tbsp baking
  powder
175g/6oz/scant 1¹/₂ cups
  cornmeal or polenta

350ml/12fl oz/1¹/₂ cups
  milk
2 eggs
75g/3oz/6 tbsp butter,
  melted
115g/4oz/¹/₂ cup
  margarine, melted

1 Preheat the oven to 200°C/400°F/Gas 6. Then line a 23 x 13cm/9 x 5in loaf tin with greaseproof paper and grease the paper.

2 Sift the flour, sugar, salt and baking powder into a mixing bowl. Add the cornmeal or polenta and stir to blend. Make a well in the centre. Whisk together the milk, eggs, melted butter and margarine. Pour the mixture into the well. Stir until just blended; do not overmix.

3 Pour into the tin and bake until a skewer inserted in the centre comes out clean, about 45 minutes. Serve hot or at room temperature.

Spicy Sweetcorn Bread

An interesting variation on basic corn bread; adjust the number of chillies used according to taste.

Makes 9 squares

3–4 whole canned
  chillies, drained
2 eggs
475ml/16fl oz/2 cups
  buttermilk
50g/2oz/4 tbsp butter,
  melted
50g/2oz/¹/₂ cup plain
  flour

5ml/1 tsp bicarbonate
  of soda
10ml/2 tsp salt
175g/6oz/scant 1¹/₂ cups
  cornmeal or polenta
350g/12oz/2 cups canned
  sweetcorn or frozen
  sweetcorn, thawed

1 Preheat the oven to 200°C/400°F/Gas 6. Line the base and sides of a 23cm/9in square cake tin with greaseproof paper and lightly grease the paper.

2 With a sharp knife, finely chop the canned chillies and set aside until needed.

3 In a large bowl, whisk the eggs until frothy, then whisk in the buttermilk. Add the melted butter.

4 Sift the flour, bicarbonate of soda and salt together into another large bowl. Fold into the buttermilk mixture in three batches, then fold in the cornmeal or polenta in three batches. Finally, fold in the chillies and sweetcorn.

5 Pour the mixture into the tin and bake until a skewer inserted in the centre comes out clean; about 25–30 minutes. Leave in the tin for 2–3 minutes before unmoulding. Cut into squares and serve warm.

Sweet Sesame Loaf

Lemon and sesame seeds make a great partnership in this light tea bread.

Makes one 23 x 13cm/9 x 5in loaf

75g/3oz/6 tbsp sesame
  seeds
275g/10oz/2¹/₂ cups plain
  flour
12.5ml/2¹/₂ tsp baking
  powder
5ml/1 tsp salt
50g/2oz/4 tbsp butter or
  margarine, at room
  temperature

130g/4¹/₂oz/scant ²/₃ cup
  sugar
2 eggs, at room
  temperature
grated rind of 1 lemon
350ml/12fl oz/1¹/₂ cups
  milk

1 Preheat the oven to 180°C/350°F/Gas 4. Carefully line a 23 x 13cm/9 x 5in loaf tin with greaseproof paper and then grease the paper.

2 Reserve 25g/1oz/2 tbsp of the sesame seeds. Spread the rest on a baking sheet and bake in the oven until lightly toasted, about 10 minutes.

3 Sift the flour, baking powder and salt into a bowl. Stir in the toasted sesame seeds and set aside.

4 Cream the butter or margarine and sugar together until light and fluffy. Beat in the eggs, then stir in the lemon rind and milk. Pour the milk mixture over the dry ingredients and fold in with a large metal spoon until just blended.

5 Pour into the tin and sprinkle over the reserved sesame seeds. Bake until a skewer inserted in the centre comes out clean, about 1 hour. Cool in the tin for 10 minutes. Turn out on to a wire rack to cool completely.

Cardamom and Saffron Tea Loaf

An aromatic sweet bread ideal for afternoon tea, or lightly toasted for breakfast.

Makes one 900g/2lb loaf

generous pinch of saffron
  strands
750ml/1¹/₄ pints/3 cups
  lukewarm milk
25g/1oz/2 tbsp butter
1kg/2¹/₄ lb/8 cups strong
  plain flour
2 sachets easy-blend
  dried yeast

40g/1¹/₂ oz/3 tbsp caster
  sugar
6 cardamom pods, split
  open and seeds
  extracted
115g/4oz/scant ³/₄ cup
  raisins
30ml/2 tbsp clear honey
1 egg, beaten

1 Crush the saffron straight into a cup containing a little of the warm milk and leave to infuse for 5 minutes. Rub the butter into the flour, then mix in the yeast, sugar, cardamom seeds and raisins.

2 Beat the remaining milk with the honey and egg, then mix this into the flour, along with the saffron milk and strands, to form a firm dough. Turn out the dough and knead it on a lightly floured surface for 5 minutes.

3 Return the dough to the mixing bowl, cover with oiled clear film and leave in a warm place until doubled in size.

4 Preheat the oven to 200°C/400°F/Gas 6. Grease a 900g/2lb loaf tin. Turn the dough out on to a floured surface, punch down, knead for 3 minutes, then shape into a fat roll and fit into the tin. Cover with a sheet of lightly oiled clear film and stand in a warm place until the dough begins to rise again.

5 Bake the loaf for 25 minutes until golden brown and firm on top. Turn out on to a wire rack and as it cools brush the top with clear honey.

Courgette Tea bread

Like carrots, courgettes are a vegetable that work well in baking, adding moistness and lightness to the bread.

Makes one 23 x 13cm/9 x 5in loaf

50g/2oz/4 tbsp butter	5ml/1 tsp baking powder
3 eggs	5ml/1 tsp salt
250ml/8fl oz/1 cup vegetable oil	5ml/1 tsp ground cinnamon
285g/10^1/$_2$oz/1^1/$_2$ cups sugar	5ml/1 tsp grated nutmeg
2 unpeeled courgettes, grated	1.5ml/^{1}/$_4$ tsp ground cloves
275g/10oz/2^1/$_2$ cups plain flour	115g/4oz/1 cup chopped walnuts
10ml/2 tsp bicarbonate of soda	

1 Preheat the oven to 180°C/350°F/Gas 4. Line the base and sides of a 23 x 13cm/9 x 5in loaf tin with greaseproof paper and grease the paper.

2 In a saucepan, melt the butter over a low heat. Set aside until needed.

3 With an electric mixer, beat the eggs and oil together until thick. Beat in the sugar, then stir in the melted butter and the courgettes. Set aside.

4 In another bowl, sift all the dry ingredients together three times. Carefully fold into the courgette mixture. Fold in the chopped walnuts.

5 Pour into the tin and bake until a skewer inserted in the centre comes out clean, about 60–70 minutes. Leave to stand for 10 minutes before turning out on to a wire rack to cool.

Mango Tea bread

A delicious tea bread with an exotic slant – baked with juicy ripe mango.

Makes two 23 x 13cm/9 x 5in loaves

275g/10oz/2^1/$_2$ cups plain flour	285g/10^1/$_2$oz/1^1/$_2$ cups sugar
10ml/2 tsp bicarbonate of soda	120ml/4fl oz/^{1}/$_2$ cup vegetable oil
10ml/2 tsp ground cinnamon	1 large ripe mango, peeled and chopped
2.5ml/^{1}/$_2$ tsp salt	85g/3^1/$_4$oz/generous 1^1/$_2$ cups desiccated coconut
115g/4oz/1^1/$_2$ cup margarine, at room temperature	65g/2^1/$_2$oz/^{1}/$_2$ cup raisins
3 eggs, at room temperature	

1 Preheat the oven to 180°C/350°F/Gas 4. Line the base and sides of two 23 x 13cm/9 x 5in loaf tins with greaseproof paper and grease the paper.

2 Sift together the flour, bicarbonate of soda, cinnamon and salt. Set aside until needed.

3 Cream the margarine until soft. Beat in the eggs and sugar until light and fluffy. Beat in the oil.

4 Fold the dry ingredients into the creamed ingredients in three batches, then fold in the mango, two-thirds of the coconut and the raisins.

5 Spoon the batter into the tins. Sprinkle over the remaining coconut. Bake until a skewer inserted in the centre comes out clean, about 50–60 minutes. Leave to stand for 10 minutes before turning out on to a wire rack to cool completely.

American-style Corn Sticks

If you don't have a corn-stick mould, use éclair tins or a bun tray and reduce the cooking time by 10 minutes.

Makes 6

1 egg
120ml/4fl oz/¹/₂ cup milk
15ml/1 tbsp vegetable oil
115g/4oz/scant 1 cup
  cornmeal or polenta

50g/2oz/¹/₂ cup plain
  flour
10ml/2 tsp baking
  powder
45ml/3 tbsp caster sugar

1 Preheat the oven to 190°C/375°F/Gas 5. Grease a cast-iron corn-stick mould.

2 Beat the egg in a small bowl. Stir in the milk and vegetable oil, and set aside.

3 In a mixing bowl, stir together the cornmeal or polenta, flour, baking powder and sugar. Pour in the egg mixture and stir with a wooden spoon to combine.

4 Spoon the mixture into the prepared mould. Bake until a skewer inserted in the centre of a corn stick comes out clean, about 25 minutes. Cool in the mould on a wire rack for 10 minutes before unmoulding.

Savoury Sweetcorn Bread

For a spicy bread, stir 30ml/2 tbsp chopped fresh chillies into the mixture with the cheese and sweetcorn.

Makes 9

2 eggs, lightly beaten
250ml/8fl oz/1 cup
  buttermilk
115g/4oz/1 cup plain
  flour
115g/4oz/scant 1 cup
  cornmeal or polenta
10ml/2 tsp baking
  powder

2.5ml/¹/₂ tsp salt
15ml/1 tbsp caster sugar
115g/4oz/1 cup Cheddar
  cheese, grated
225g/8oz/1¹/₃ cups
  sweetcorn, fresh or
  frozen and thawed

1 Preheat the oven to 200°C/400°F/Gas 6. Then grease a 23cm/9in square baking tin.

2 Combine the eggs and buttermilk in a small bowl and whisk until well mixed. Set aside.

3 In another bowl, stir together the flour, cornmeal or polenta, baking powder, salt and sugar. Add the egg mixture and stir with a wooden spoon to combine. Stir in the cheese and sweetcorn.

4 Pour the mixture into the baking tin. Bake until a skewer inserted in the centre comes out clean, about 25 minutes. Unmould the bread on to a wire rack and leave to cool. Cut into squares before serving.

Herb Popovers

Popovers are delicious flavoured with herbs, and served as a snack or starter.

Makes 12

3 eggs
250ml/8fl oz/1 cup milk
25g/1oz/2 tbsp butter, melted
75g/3oz/³/₄ cup plain flour

1.5ml/¹/₄ tsp salt
1 small sprig each mixed fresh herbs, such as chives, tarragon, dill and parsley

1 Preheat the oven to 220°C/425°F/Gas 7. Grease 12 small ramekins or individual baking cups.

2 With an electric mixer, beat the eggs until blended. Beat in the milk and melted butter. Sift together the flour and salt, then beat into the egg mixture to combine thoroughly.

3 Strip the herb leaves from the stems and chop finely. Mix together and measure out 30ml/2 tbsp. Stir the measured herbs into the batter.

4 Half-fill the prepared ramekins or baking cups. Bake until golden; 25–30 minutes. Do not open the oven door during baking time or the popovers may collapse. For drier popovers, pierce each one with a knife after 30 minutes baking time and then bake for a further 5 minutes. Serve the herb popovers hot.

Cheese Popovers

Serve these popovers simply as an accompaniment to a meal, or make a filling and serve them as a starter.

Makes 12

3 eggs
250ml/8fl oz/1 cup milk
25g/1oz/2 tbsp butter, melted
75g/3oz/³/₄ cup plain flour

1.5ml/¹/₄ tsp salt
1.5ml/¹/₄ tsp paprika
25g/1oz/¹/₃ cup freshly grated Parmesan cheese

1 Preheat the oven to 220°C/425°F/Gas 7. Grease 12 small ramekins or individual baking cups.

2 With an electric mixer, beat the eggs until blended. Beat in the milk and melted butter. Sift together the flour, salt and paprika, then beat into the egg mixture. Add the Parmesan cheese and stir in.

3 Half-fill the prepared cups and bake until golden, about 25–30 minutes. Do not open the oven door or the popovers may collapse. For drier popovers, pierce each one with a knife after about 30 minutes baking time and then bake for another 5 minutes. Serve hot.

Sweet Potato and Raisin Bread

Serve buttered slices of this subtly-spiced loaf at coffee or tea time.

Makes one 900g/2lb loaf

350g/12oz/3 cups flour
10ml/2tsp baking powder
2.5ml/½ tsp salt
5ml/1 tsp ground cinnamon
2.5ml/½ tsp grated nutmeg
450g/1lb mashed cooked sweet potatoes

90g/3½ oz light brown sugar
115g/4oz/½ cup butter or margarine, melted and cooled
3 eggs, beaten
75g/3oz/generous ½ cup raisins

1 Preheat the oven to 180°C/350°F/Gas 4. Grease a 900g/2lb loaf dish or tin.

2 Sift the flour, baking powder, salt, cinnamon, and nutmeg into a small bowl. Set aside.

3 With an electric mixer, beat the mashed sweet potatoes with the brown sugar, butter or margarine, and eggs until well mixed.

4 Add the flour mixture and the raisins. Stir with a wooden spoon until the flour is just mixed in.

5 Transfer the batter to the prepared dish or tin. Bake until a skewer inserted in the centre of the loaf comes out clean, about 1–1¼ hours.

6 Let the bread cool in the pan on a wire rack for 15 minutes, then unmould from the dish or tin on to the wire rack and leave to cool completely.

Lemon and Walnut Tea bread

Beaten egg whites give this citrus-flavour loaf a lovely light and crumbly texture.

Makes one 23 x 13cm/9 x 5in loaf

115g/4oz/½ cup butter or margarine, at room temperature
90g/3½oz/½ cup sugar
2 eggs, at room temperature, separated
grated rind of 2 lemons
30ml/2 tbsp lemon juice

215g/7½oz/scant 2 cups plain flour
10ml/2 tsp baking powder
120ml/4fl oz/½ cup milk
50g/2oz/½ cup chopped walnuts
1.5ml/¼ teaspoon salt

1 Preheat the oven to 180°C/350°F/Gas 4. Then line a 23 x 13cm/9 x 5in loaf tin with greaseproof paper and grease the paper.

2 Cream the butter or margarine with the sugar until light and fluffy. Beat in the egg yolks. Add the lemon rind and juice and stir until blended. Set aside.

3 In another bowl, sift together the flour and baking powder three times. Fold into the butter mixture in three batches, alternating with the milk. Fold in the walnuts. Set aside.

4 Beat the egg whites and salt until stiff peaks form. Fold a large spoonful of the egg whites into the walnut mixture to lighten it. Fold in the remaining egg whites carefully until the mixture is just blended.

5 Pour the batter into the prepared tin and bake until a skewer inserted in the centre of the loaf comes out clean, about 45–50 minutes. Cool in the tin for 5 minutes before turning out on to a wire rack to cool completely.

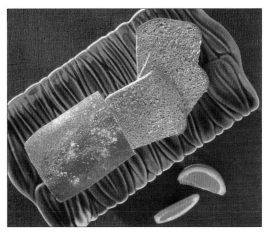

Date and Nut Maltloaf

Choose any type of nut you like to include in this very rich and fruit-packed tea bread.

Makes two 450g/1lb loaves

300g/11oz/2 cups strong plain flour

275g/10oz/2 cups strong plain wholemeal flour

5ml/1 tsp salt

75g/3oz/6 tbsp soft brown sugar

1 sachet easy-blend dried yeast

50g/2oz/4 tbsp butter or margarine

15ml/1 tbsp black treacle

60ml/4 tbsp malt extract

scant 250ml/8fl oz/1 cup lukewarm milk

115g/4oz/¹⁄₂ cup chopped dates

50g/2oz/¹⁄₂ cup chopped nuts

75g/3oz/generous ¹⁄₂ cup sultanas

75g/3oz/generous ¹⁄₂ cup raisins

30ml/2 tbsp clear honey, to glaze

1 Sift the flours and salt into a large bowl, then tip in the wheat flakes from the sieve. Stir in the sugar and yeast.

2 Put the butter or margarine in a small pan with the treacle and malt extract. Stir over a low heat until melted. Leave to cool, then combine with the milk.

3 Stir the milk mixture into the dry ingredients and knead thoroughly for 15 minutes until the dough is elastic.

4 Knead in the fruits and nuts. Transfer the dough to an oiled bowl, cover with clear film and leave in a warm place for about 1¹⁄₂ hours, until the dough has doubled in size.

5 Grease two 450g/1lb loaf tins. Knock back the dough and knead lightly. Divide in half, form into loaves and place in the tins. Cover and leave in a warm place for 30 minutes, until risen. Meanwhile, preheat the oven to 190°C/375°F/Gas 5.

6 Bake for 35–40 minutes, until well risen. Cool on a wire rack. Brush with honey while warm.

Orange Wheatloaf

Perfect just with butter as a breakfast tea bread and lovely for banana sandwiches.

Makes one 450g/1lb loaf

275g/10oz/2¹⁄₄ cups wholemeal plain flour

2.5ml/¹⁄₂ tsp salt

25g/1oz/2 tbsp butter

25g/1oz/2 tbsp soft light brown sugar

¹⁄₂ sachet easy-blend dried yeast

grated rind and juice of ¹⁄₂ orange

1 Sift the flour into a large bowl and return any wheat flakes from the sieve. Add the salt and rub in the butter lightly with your fingertips.

2 Stir in the sugar, yeast and orange rind. Pour the orange juice into a measuring jug and use hot water to make up to 200ml/7fl oz/scant 1 cup (the liquid should not be more than hand hot).

3 Stir the liquid into the flour and mix to a soft ball of dough. Knead gently on a lightly floured surface until quite smooth and elastic.

4 Place the dough in a greased 450g/1lb loaf tin and leave in a warm place until nearly doubled in size. Preheat the oven to 220°C/425°F/Gas 7.

5 Bake the bread for 30–35 minutes, or until it sounds hollow when tapped underneath. Tip out of the tin and cool on a wire rack.

Orange and Honey Tea bread

Honey gives a special flavour to this tea bread. Serve just with a scraping of butter.

Makes one 23 x 13cm/9 x 5in loaf

385g/13¹/₂oz/scant
3¹/₂cups plain flour
12.5ml/2¹/₂ tsp baking
powder
2.5ml/¹/₂ tsp bicarbonate
of soda
2.5ml/¹/₂ tsp salt
25g/1oz/2 tbsp margarine
250ml/8fl oz/1 cup clear
honey
1 egg, at room
temperature, lightly
beaten
25ml/1¹/₂ tbsp grated
orange rind
175ml/6fl oz/³/₄ cup
freshly squeezed
orange juice
115g/4oz/1 cup chopped
walnuts

1 Preheat the oven to 160°C/325°F/Gas 3. Line the base and sides of a 23 x 13cm/9 x 5in loaf tin with greaseproof paper and grease the paper.

2 Sift the flour, baking powder, bicarbonate of soda and salt together in a bowl.

3 Cream the margarine until soft. Stir in the honey until blended, then stir in the egg. Add the orange rind and stir to combine thoroughly.

4 Fold the flour mixture into the honey and egg mixture in three batches, alternating with the orange juice. Stir in the chopped walnuts.

5 Pour into the prepared tin and bake in the oven until a skewer inserted in the centre comes out clean, about 60 – 70 minutes. Leave for 10 minutes before turning out on to a wire rack to cool completely.

Apple Loaf

Ring the changes with this loaf by using different nuts and dried fruit.

Makes one 23 x 13cm/9 x 5in loaf

1 egg
250ml/8fl oz/1 cup
bottled or home-made
apple sauce
50g/2oz/4 tbsp butter or
margarine, melted
100g/3³/₄oz/scant ³/₄ cup
dark brown sugar
45g/1³/₄oz/scant ¹/₄ cup
caster sugar
275g/10oz/2¹/₂ cups plain
flour
10ml/2 tsp baking
powder
2.5ml/¹/₂ tsp bicarbonate
of soda
2.5ml/¹/₂ tsp salt
5ml/1 tsp ground
cinnamon
2.5ml/¹/₂ tsp grated
nutmeg
65g/2¹/₂oz/¹/₂ cup
currants or raisins
50g/2oz/¹/₂ cup pecan
nuts or walnuts,
chopped

1 Preheat the oven to 180°C/350°F/Gas 4. Line the base and sides of a 23 x 13cm/9 x 5in loaf tin with greaseproof paper and grease the paper.

2 Break the egg into a bowl and beat lightly. Stir in the apple sauce, butter or margarine and both sugars. Set aside.

3 In another bowl, sift together the flour, baking powder, bicarbonate of soda, salt, cinnamon and nutmeg. Fold the dry ingredients, including the currants or raisins and the nuts, into the apple sauce mixture in three batches.

4 Pour into the prepared tin and bake in the oven until a skewer inserted in the centre of the loaf comes out clean, about 1 hour. Leave to stand in the tin for 10 minutes, then turn out on to a wire rack to cool completely.

Fruit and Brazil Nut Tea bread

Mashed bananas are a classic ingredient in tea breads, and help to create a moist texture.

Makes one 23 x 13cm/9 x 5in loaf

225g/8oz/2 cups plain flour
10ml/2 tsp baking powder
5ml/1 tsp mixed spice
115g/4oz/½ cup butter, diced
115g/4oz/¾ cup light soft brown sugar
2 eggs, lightly beaten
30ml/2 tbsp milk
30ml/2 tbsp dark rum

2 bananas, peeled and mashed
115g/4oz/½ cup dried figs, chopped
50g/2oz/½ cup brazil nuts, chopped

To decorate
8 whole brazil nuts
4 whole dried figs, halved
30ml/2 tbsp apricot jam
5ml/1 tsp dark rum

1 Preheat the oven to 180°C/350°F/Gas 4. Grease and base-line a 23 x 13cm/9 x 5in loaf tin. Sift the flour, baking powder and mixed spice into a bowl. Rub in the butter until the mixture resembles fine breadcrumbs. Stir in the sugar.

2 Make a well in the centre and work in the eggs, milk and rum until combined. Stir in the remaining ingredients and transfer to the loaf tin.

3 Press the whole brazil nuts and halved figs gently into the mixture, to form an attractive pattern. Bake for 1¼ hours, or until a skewer inserted in the centre comes out clean. Cool in the tin for 10 minutes, then transfer to a wire rack.

4 Heat the jam and rum together in a small saucepan. Increase the heat and boil for 1 minute. Remove from the heat and pass through a fine sieve. Cool the glaze slightly, brush over the warm cake, and leave to cool completely.

Glazed Banana Spiced Loaf

The lemony glaze perfectly sets off the flavours in this banana tea bread.

Makes one 23 x 13cm/9 x 5in loaf

115g/4oz/½ cup butter, at room temperature
165g/5½oz/generous ⅔ cup caster sugar
2 eggs, at room temperature
215g/7½oz/scant 2 cups plain flour
5ml/1 tsp salt
5ml/1 tsp bicarbonate of soda
2.5ml/½ tsp grated nutmeg
1.5ml/¼ tsp mixed spice

1.5ml/¼ tsp ground cloves
175ml/6fl oz/¾ cup soured cream
1 large ripe banana, mashed
5ml/1 tsp vanilla essence

For the glaze
115g/4oz/1 cup icing sugar
15–30ml/1–2 tbsp lemon juice

1 Preheat the oven to 180°C/350°F/Gas 4. Line a 23 x 13cm/9 x 5in loaf tin with greaseproof paper and grease the paper.

2 Cream the butter and sugar until light and fluffy. Add the eggs, one at a time, beating well after each addition.

3 Sift together the flour, salt, bicarbonate of soda, nutmeg, mixed spice and cloves. Add to the butter mixture and stir to combine well. Add the soured cream, banana and vanilla and mix to just blend. Pour into the prepared tin.

4 Bake until the top springs back when touched lightly, about 45–50 minutes. Cool in the tin for 10 minutes. Turn out on to a wire rack.

5 For the glaze, combine the icing sugar and lemon juice, then stir until smooth. Place the cooled loaf on a rack set over a baking sheet. Pour the glaze over the loaf and allow to set.

Banana Bread

For a change, add 50 – 75g/2 – 3oz/½ – ¾ cup chopped walnuts with the dry ingredients or pecan nuts.

Makes one 21 x 11cm/8½ x 4½in loaf

200g/7oz/1¾ cups plain
  flour
11.5ml/2¼ tsp baking
  powder
2.5ml/½ tsp salt
4ml/¾ tsp ground
  cinnamon (optional)
60ml/4 tbsp wheatgerm

65g/2½oz/5 tbsp butter,
  at room temperature
115g/4oz/generous ½ cup
  caster sugar
4ml/¾ tsp grated lemon
  rind
3 ripe bananas, mashed
2 eggs, beaten

1 Preheat the oven to 180°C/350°F/Gas 4. Grease and flour a 21 x 11cm/8½ x 4½in loaf tin.

2 Sift the flour, baking powder, salt and cinnamon, if using, into a bowl. Stir in the wheatgerm.

3 In another bowl, combine the butter with the caster sugar and grated lemon rind. Beat thoroughly until the mixture is light and fluffy.

4 Add the mashed bananas and eggs, and mix well. Add the dry ingredients and blend quickly and evenly.

5 Spoon into the loaf tin. Bake for 50 – 60 minutes or until a wooden skewer inserted in the centre comes out clean. Cool in the tin for 5 minutes, then turn out on to a wire rack to cool completely.

Banana Orange Loaf

For the best banana flavour and a really good, moist texture, make sure the bananas are ripe for this cake.

Makes one 23 x 13cm/9 x 5in loaf

90g/3½oz/generous
  ⅔ cup wholemeal
  plain flour
90g/3½oz/generous
  ¾ cup plain flour
5ml/1 tsp baking powder
5ml/1 tsp ground mixed
  spice
45ml/3 tbsp flaked
  hazelnuts, toasted

2 large ripe bananas
1 egg
30ml/2 tbsp sunflower oil
30ml/2 tbsp clear honey
finely grated rind and
  juice of 1 small orange
4 orange slices, halved
10ml/2 tsp icing sugar

1 Preheat the oven to 180°C/350°F/Gas 4. Brush a 23 x 13cm/9 x 5in loaf tin with sunflower oil and line the base with non-stick baking paper.

2 Sift the flours with the baking powder and spice into a large bowl, adding any bran that is caught in the sieve. Stir the hazelnuts into the dry ingredients.

3 Peel and mash the bananas. Beat in the egg, oil, honey and the orange rind and juice. Stir evenly into the dry ingredients.

4 Spoon into the prepared tin and smooth the top. Bake for 40 – 45 minutes, or until firm and golden brown. Turn out on to a wire rack to cool.

5 Sprinkle the orange slices with the icing sugar and grill until golden. Use to decorate the cake.

Marmalade Tea bread

If you prefer, leave the top of the loaf plain and serve sliced and lightly buttered instead.

Makes one 22 x 11cm/8½ x 4½in loaf

200g/7oz/1¾ cups
  plain flour
5ml/1 tsp baking powder
6.5ml/1¼ tsp ground
  cinnamon
90g/3½oz/7 tbsp butter
  or margarine
50g/2oz/⅓ cup soft light
  brown sugar

60ml/4 tbsp chunky
  orange marmalade
1 egg, beaten
about 45ml/3 tbsp milk
60ml/4 tbsp glacé icing
  and shreds of orange
  and lemon rind,
  to decorate

1 Preheat the oven to 160°C/325°F/Gas 3. Lightly butter a 22 x 11cm/8½ x 4½in loaf tin, then line the base with greaseproof paper and grease the paper.

2 Sift the flour, baking powder and cinnamon together, toss in the butter, then rub in until the mixture resembles coarse breadcrumbs. Stir in the sugar.

3 In a separate bowl, mix together the marmalade, egg and most of the milk, then stir into the flour mixture to make a soft dropping consistency, adding more milk if necessary.

4 Transfer the mixture to the tin and bake for 1¼ hours, or until firm to the touch. Leave the cake to cool for 5 minutes, then turn on to a wire rack, peel off the lining paper, and leave to cool completely.

5 Drizzle the glacé icing over the top of the cake and decorate with the orange and lemon rind.

Cherry Marmalade Muffins

Purists say you should never serve a muffin cold, so enjoy these fresh from the oven.

Makes 12

225g/8oz/2 cups self-
  raising flour
5ml/1 tsp ground mixed
  spice
75g/3oz/scant ½ cup
  caster sugar
115g/4oz/½ cup glacé
  cherries, quartered

30ml/2 tbsp orange
  marmalade
150ml/¼ pint/⅔ cup
  milk
50g/2oz/4 tbsp sunflower
  margarine
marmalade, to glaze

1 Preheat the oven to 200°C/400°F/Gas 6. Lightly grease 12 deep muffin cups with oil.

2 Sift together the flour and spice, then stir in the sugar and glacé cherries.

3 Mix the marmalade with the milk and beat into the dry ingredients with the margarine. Spoon into the greased cups. Bake for 20–25 minutes, until golden brown and firm. Turn out on to a wire rack and brush the tops of the muffins, with warmed marmalade.

Spiced Date and Walnut Cake

Nuts and dates are a classic flavour combination. Use pecan nuts instead of walnuts, if you wish.

Makes one 900g/2lb cake

300g/11 oz/2³/₄ cups wholemeal self-raising flour
10ml/2 tsp mixed spice
150g/5oz/generous ³/₄ cup chopped dates
50g/2oz/¹/₂ cup chopped walnuts
60ml/4 tbsp sunflower oil
115g/4oz/³/₄ cup dark muscovado sugar
300ml/¹/₂ pint/1¹/₄ cups milk
walnut halves, to decorate

1 Preheat the oven to 180°C/350°F/Gas 4. Line a 900g/2lb loaf tin with greaseproof paper and grease the paper.

2 Sift together the flour and spice, adding back any bran from the sieve. Stir in the dates and walnuts.

3 Mix the oil, sugar and milk, then stir evenly into the dry ingredients. Spoon into the loaf tin and arrange the walnut halves on top.

4 Bake the cake in the oven for about 45–50 minutes, or until golden brown and firm. Turn out the cake, remove the lining paper, and leave to cool on a wire rack.

Prune and Peel Rock Buns

The fruit content of these scones gives them plenty of flavour – and they're a low-fat option too!

Makes 12

225g/8oz/2 cups plain flour
10ml/2 tsp baking powder
75g/3oz/¹/₂ cup demerara sugar
50g/2oz/¹/₂ cup chopped ready-to-eat dried prunes
50g/2oz/¹/₃ cup chopped mixed peel
finely grated rind of 1 lemon
50ml/2fl oz/¹/₄ cup sunflower oil
75ml/5 tbsp skimmed milk

1 Preheat the oven to 200°C/400°F/Gas 6. Lightly oil a large baking sheet. Sift together the flour and baking powder, then stir in the sugar, prunes, peel and lemon rind.

2 Mix the oil and milk, then stir into the mixture, to make a dough which just binds together.

3 Spoon into rocky heaps on the baking sheet and bake for 20 minutes, until golden. Leave to cool on a wire rack.

Raisin Bran Buns

Serve these buns warm or at room temperature, on their own, with butter, or with cream cheese.

Makes 15

50g/2oz/4 tbsp butter or margarine	75g/3oz/generous ¹/₂ cup raisins
40g/1¹/₂oz/¹/₃ cup plain flour	65g/2¹/₂oz/scant ¹/₂ cup dark brown sugar
50g/2oz/¹/₂ cup wholemeal flour	50g/2oz/¹/₄ cup caster sugar
7.5ml/1¹/₂ tsp bicarbonate of soda	1 egg
1.5ml/¹/₄ tsp salt	250ml/8fl oz/1 cup buttermilk
5ml/1 tsp ground cinnamon	juice of ¹/₂ lemon
25g/1oz/generous 1 cup bran	

1 Preheat the oven to 200°C/400°F/Gas 6. Lightly grease 15 bun-tray cups. Put the butter or margarine in a saucepan and melt over a gentle heat. Set aside.

2 In a mixing bowl, sift together the flours, bicarbonate of soda, salt and cinnamon. Add the bran, raisins and sugars and stir until blended.

3 In another bowl, mix together the egg, buttermilk, lemon juice and melted butter. Add the buttermilk mixture to the dry ingredients and stir in lightly and quickly until just moistened. Do not mix until smooth.

4 Spoon the mixture into the prepared bun-tray cups, filling them almost to the top. Half-fill any empty cups with water. Bake until golden, about 15–20 minutes. Remove to a wire rack to cool slightly or serve immediately.

Raspberry Crumble Buns

The crumble topping adds an unusual twist to these lovely fruit buns.

Makes 12

175g/6oz/1¹/₂ cups plain flour	grated rind of 1 lemon
50g/2oz/¹/₄ cup caster sugar	**For the crumble topping**
45g/1³/₄ oz/scant ¹/₃ cup light brown sugar	25g/1oz/¹/₄ cup finely chopped pecan nuts or walnuts
10ml/2 tsp baking powder	50g/2oz/¹/₃ cup dark brown sugar
1.5ml/¹/₄ tsp salt	45ml/3 tbsp plain flour
5ml/1 tsp ground cinnamon	5ml/1 tsp ground cinnamon
115g/4oz/¹/₂ cup butter, melted	45ml/3 tbsp butter, melted
1 egg	
120ml/4fl oz/¹/₂ cup milk	
150g/5oz/³/₄ cup fresh raspberries	

1 Preheat the oven to 180°C/350°F/Gas 4. Lightly grease 12 bun-tray cups or use 12 paper cases. Sift the flour into a bowl. Add the sugars, baking powder, salt and cinnamon, and stir to blend.

2 Make a well in the centre. Place the butter, egg and milk in the well and mix until just combined. Stir in the raspberries and lemon rind. Spoon the mixture into the prepared bun tray, filling the cups almost to the top.

3 For the crumble topping, mix the nuts, dark brown sugar, flour and cinnamon in a bowl. Add the melted butter and stir to blend.

4 Spoon some of the crumble over each bun. Bake until browned, about 25 minutes. Transfer to a wire rack to cool slightly. Serve warm.

Banana and Pecan Muffins

As a variation on this recipe, substitute an equal quantity
of walnuts for the pecan nuts.

Makes 8

150g/5oz/1¼ cups plain
   flour
7.5ml/1½ tsp baking
   powder
50g/2oz/4 tbsp butter or
   margarine, at room
   temperature
150g/5oz caster sugar

1 egg
5ml/1tsp teaspoon
   vanilla essence
3 bananas, mashed
50g/2oz/½ cup pecan
   nuts, chopped
75ml/5tbsp milk

1 Preheat the oven to 190℃/375℉/Gas 5. Lightly grease
8 deep muffin cups. Sift the flour and baking powder into a
small bowl. Set aside.

2 With an electric mixer, cream the butter or margarine and
sugar together. Add the egg and vanilla and beat until fluffy.
Mix in the banana.

3 Add the pecan nuts. With the mixer on low speed, beat in
the flour mixture alternately with the milk.

4 Spoon the mixture into the prepared muffin cups, filling
them two-thirds full. Bake until golden brown and a skewer
inserted into the centre of a muffin comes out clean, about
20–25 minutes.

5 Let the muffins cool in the cups on a wire rack for about
10 minutes. To loosen, run a knife gently around each muffin
and unmould on to the wire rack. Leave to cool 10 minutes
longer before serving.

Blueberry and Cinnamon Muffins

These moist and "moreish" muffins appeal equally to
adults and children.

Makes 8

115g/4oz/1 cup plain
   flour
15ml/1tbsp baking
   powder
pinch of salt
65g/2½ oz/¼ cup light
   brown sugar
1 egg

175ml/6fl oz/¾ cup milk
45ml/3tbsp vegetable oil
10ml/2tsp ground
   cinnamon
115g/4oz/⅔ cup fresh or
   thawed frozen
   blueberries

1 Preheat the oven to 190℃/375℉/Gas 5. Lightly grease
8 deep muffin cups.

2 With an electric mixer, beat the first eight ingredients
together until smooth. Fold in the blueberries.

3 Spoon the mixture into the muffin cups, filling them
two-thirds full. Bake until a skewer inserted in the centre of a
muffin comes out clean, about 25 minutes.

4 Let the muffins cool in the cups on a wire rack for about
10 minutes, then unmould them on to the wire rack and allow
to cool completely, to serve slightly warm.

Carrot Buns

Carrots give these buns a lovely moist consistency, and a delightful taste too.

Makes 12

175g/6oz/³/₄ cup margarine, at room temperature
90g/3¹/₂oz/generous ¹/₂ cup dark brown sugar
1 egg, at room temperature
15ml/1 tbsp water
225g/8oz/1¹/₂ cups grated carrots

150g/5oz/1¹/₄ cups plain flour
5ml/1 tsp baking powder
2.5ml/¹/₂ tsp bicarbonate of soda
5ml/1 tsp ground cinnamon
1.5ml/¹/₄ tsp grated nutmeg
2.5ml/¹/₂ tsp salt

1 Preheat the oven to 180°C/350°F/Gas 4. Grease a 12-cup bun tray or use paper cases.

2 With an electric mixer, cream the margarine and sugar until light and fluffy. Beat in the egg and water, then stir in the carrots.

3 Sift over the flour, baking powder, bicarbonate of soda, cinnamon, nutmeg and salt. Stir to blend.

4 Spoon the mixture into the prepared bun tray, filling the cups almost to the top. Bake until the tops spring back when touched lightly, about 35 minutes. Leave to stand for about 10 minutes in the bun tray before transferring to a wire rack to cool completely.

Dried Cherry Buns

Dried cherries have a wonderful tart flavour, quite unlike glacé cherries.

Makes 16

250ml/8fl oz/1 cup plain yogurt
175g/6oz/³/₄ cup dried cherries
115g/4oz/¹/₂ cup butter, at room temperature
175g/6oz/generous ³/₄ cup caster sugar
2 eggs, at room temperature

5ml/1 tsp vanilla essence
200g/7oz/generous 1³/₄ cups plain flour
10ml/2 tsp baking powder
5ml/1 tsp bicarbonate of soda
1.5ml/¹/₄ tsp salt

1 In a mixing bowl, combine the yogurt and cherries. Cover and leave to stand for 30 minutes. Preheat the oven to 180°C/350°F/Gas 4. Grease 16 bun-tray cups or use paper cases.

2 With an electric mixer, cream the butter and sugar together until light and fluffy. Add the eggs, one at a time, beating well after each addition. Add the vanilla and the cherry mixture and stir to blend. Set aside.

3 In another bowl, sift together the flour, baking powder, bicarbonate of soda and salt. Fold into the cherry mixture in three batches.

4 Fill the prepared cups two-thirds full. For even baking, half-fill any empty cups with water. Bake until the tops spring back when touched lightly, about 20 minutes. Transfer to a wire rack to cool completely.

Chelsea Buns

A traditional English recipe, Chelsea buns enjoy wide popularity elsewhere in the world.

Makes 12

225g/8oz/2 cups strong
  white flour
2.5ml/¹/₂ tsp salt
40g/1¹/₂oz/3 tbsp
  unsalted butter
7.5ml/1¹/₂ tsp easy-blend
  dried yeast
120ml/4fl oz/¹/₂ cup milk

1 egg, beaten
75g/3oz/¹/₂ cup mixed
  dried fruit
25g/1oz/2¹/₂ tbsp chopped
  mixed peel
50g/2oz/¹/₃ cup soft light
  brown sugar
clear honey, to glaze

1 Preheat the oven to 190°C/375°F/Gas 5. Grease a 18cm/7in square tin. Sift together the flour and salt; rub in 25g/1oz/2 tbsp of the butter.

2 Stir in the yeast and make a central well. Slowly add the milk and egg, stirring, then beat until the dough leaves the sides of the bowl clean.

3 Knead the dough until smooth. Place in an oiled bowl, cover and set aside until doubled in size. Transfer to a floured surface and roll it out to a rectangle 30 x 23cm/12 x 9in.

4 Mix the dried fruits, peel and sugar. Melt the remaining butter and brush over the dough. Scatter over the fruit mixture, leaving a 2.5cm/1in border. Roll up the dough from a long side. Seal the edges, then cut into 12 slices.

5 Place the slices, cut-sides up, in the greased tin. Cover and set aside until doubled in size. Bake for 30 minutes, until a rich golden brown. Brush with honey and leave to cool slightly in the tin before turning out.

Sticky Nut Buns

These buns will be popular, so save time by making double the recipe and freezing half for another occasion.

Makes 12

160ml/5¹/₂ fl oz/generous
  ²/₃ cup lukewarm milk
15ml/1 tbsp easy-blend
  dried yeast
30ml/2 tbsp caster sugar
450g/1lb/4 cups strong
  white flour
5ml/1 tsp salt
115g/4oz/¹/₂ cup cold
  butter, cut into small
  pieces
2 eggs, lightly beaten
finely grated rind of 1
  lemon

**For the topping and
filling**
275g/10oz/1³/₄ cups dark
  brown sugar
65g/2¹/₂oz/5 tbsp butter
120ml/4fl oz/¹/₂ cup
  water
75g/3oz/³/₄ cup chopped
  pecan nuts or walnuts
45ml/3 tbsp caster sugar
10ml/2 tsp ground
  cinnamon
165g/5¹/₂oz/generous
  1 cup raisins

1 Preheat the oven to 180°C/350°F/Gas 4. Mix the milk, yeast and sugar and leave until frothy. Combine the flour and salt, and rub in the butter. Add the yeast mixture, eggs and lemon rind. Stir to a rough dough. Knead until smooth, then return to the bowl, cover and leave until doubled in size.

2 Cook the brown sugar, butter and water in a heavy saucepan until syrupy, about 10 minutes. Place 15ml/1 tbsp syrup in the base of twelve 4cm/¹/₂in muffin cups. Sprinkle a thin layer of nuts in each, reserving the remainder.

3 Punch down the dough; roll out to a 45 x 30cm/18 x 12in rectangle. Combine the caster sugar, cinnamon, raisins and reserved nuts. Sprinkle over the dough. Roll up tightly from a long edge and cut into 2.5cm/1in rounds. Place in the muffin cups, cut-sides up. Leave to rise for 30 minutes.

4 Bake until golden, about 25 minutes. Invert the tins on to a baking sheet, leave for 5 minutes, then remove the tins. Cool on a wire rack, sticky-sides up.

Oatmeal Buttermilk Muffins

These easy-to-make muffins make a healthy treat for breakfast, or a snack at any time.

Makes 12

75g/3oz/1 cup rolled oats
250ml/3fl oz/1 cup buttermilk
115g/4oz/¹⁄₂ cup butter, at room temperature
75g/3oz/¹⁄₂ cup dark brown sugar, firmly packed

1 egg, at room temperature
115g/4oz/1 cup flour
5ml/1 tsp baking powder
1.5ml/¹⁄₄ tsp baking soda
25g/1oz/¹⁄₄ cup rains

1 In a bowl, combine the oats and buttermilk and leave to soak for 1 hour.

2 Grease a 12-cup muffin pan or use paper cases.

3 Preheat the oven to 200°C/400°F/Gas 6. With an electric mixer, cream the butter and sugar until light and fluffy. Beat in the egg.

4 In another bowl, sift together the flour, baking powder, bicarbonate of soda, and salt. Stir into the butter mixture, alternating with the oat mixture. Fold in the raisins. Do not overmix. .

5 Fill the prepared cups two-thirds full. Bake until a cake tester inserted in the centre comes out clean, 20–25 minutes. Transfer to a rack to cool.

Pumpkin Muffins

Molasses adds a delicious flavour to these spicy muffins. For a change, add dried apricots instead of currants.

Makes 14

150g/5oz/²⁄₃ cup butter or margarine, at room temperature
175g/6oz/¹⁄₄ cup dark brown sugar, firmly packed
115g/4oz/¹⁄₃ cup molasses
1 egg, at room temperature, beaten
225g/8oz/1 cup cooked or canned pumpkin

200g/7oz/1³⁄₄ cups flour
1.5ml/¹⁄₄ tsp salt
5ml/1 tsp bicarbonate of soda
10ml/1 tsp ground cinnamon
5ml/1 tsp grated nutmeg
50g/2oz/¹⁄₄ cup currants or raisins

1 Preheat the oven to 200°C/400°F/Gas 6. Grease 14 muffin cups or use paper cases.

2 With an electric mixer, cream the butter or margarine. Add the sugar and molasses and beat until light and fluffy.

3 Add the egg and pumpkin and stir until well blended.

4 Sift over the flour, salt, bicarbonate of soda, cinnamon, and nutmeg. Fold just enough to·blend; do not overmix.

5 Fold in the currants or raisins.

6 Spoon the batter into the prepared muffin cups, filling them three-quarters full.

7 Bake for 12–15 minutes until the tops spring back when touched lightly. Serve warm or cold.

Blueberry Muffins

Hot blueberry muffins with a hint of vanilla are an American favourite for breakfast, brunch or tea.

Makes 12

350g/12oz/3 cups plain flour
10ml/2 tsp baking powder
1.5ml/¼ tsp salt
115g/4oz/½ cup caster sugar
2 eggs, beaten

300ml/½ pint/1¼ cups milk
115g/4oz/½ cup butter, melted
5ml/1 tsp vanilla essence
175g/6oz/1½ cups blueberries

1 Preheat the oven to 200°C/400°F/Gas 6. Grease a 12-cup muffin tin.

2 Sift the flour, baking powder and salt into a large mixing bowl and stir in the sugar.

3 Place the eggs, milk, butter and vanilla essence in a separate bowl and whisk together well.

4 Fold the egg mixture into the dry ingredients with a metal spoon, then gently stir in the blueberries.

5 Spoon the mixture into the muffin cups, filling them to just below the top. Place the muffin tin on the top shelf of the oven and bake for 20–25 minutes, until the muffins are well risen and lightly browned. Leave the muffins in the tin for about 5 minutes, and then turn them out on to a wire rack to cool. Serve warm or cold.

Apple and Cranberry Muffins

Not too sweet but good and spicy, these muffins will be a favourite with family and friends.

Makes 12

50g/2oz/4 tbsp butter
1 egg
90g/3½oz/½ cup caster sugar
grated rind of 1 orange
120ml/4fl oz/½ cup fresh orange juice
150g/5oz/1¼ cups plain flour
5ml/1 tsp baking powder
2.5ml/½ tsp bicarbonate of soda
5ml/1 tsp ground cinnamon

2.5ml/½ tsp grated nutmeg
2.5ml/½ tsp mixed spice
1.5ml/¼ tsp ground ginger
1.5ml/¼ tsp salt
1–2 eating apples
175g/6oz/1½ cups cranberries
50g/2oz/½ cup chopped walnuts
icing sugar, for dusting (optional)

1 Preheat the oven to 180°C/350°F/Gas 4. Grease a 12-cup muffin tin or use paper cases. Melt the butter over a gentle heat. Set aside to cool.

2 Place the egg in a mixing bowl and whisk lightly. Add the melted butter and whisk to combine, then add the sugar, orange rind and juice. Whisk to blend.

3 In a large bowl, sift together the flour, baking powder, bicarbonate of soda, spices and salt. Quarter, core and peel the apples. With a sharp knife, chop coarsely.

4 Make a well in the dry ingredients and pour in the egg mixture. With a spoon, stir until just blended. Add the apples, cranberries and walnuts and stir to blend.

5 Fill the cups three-quarters full and bake until the the tops spring back when touched lightly, about 25–30 minutes. Transfer to a wire rack to cool. Dust with icing sugar before serving, if desired.

Yogurt and Honey Muffins

For a more substantial texture, fold in 50g/2oz/½ cup chopped walnuts with the flour.

Makes 12

50g/2oz/4 tbsp butter
75ml/5 tbsp clear honey
250ml/8fl oz/1 cup plain yogurt
1 large egg, at room temperature
grated rind of 1 lemon
50ml/2fl oz/¼ cup lemon juice

150g/5oz/¼ cup plain flour
175g/6oz/½ cup wholemeal flour
7.5ml/1½ tsp bicarbonate of soda
1.5ml/¼ tsp grated nutmeg

1 Preheat the oven to 190°C/375°F/Gas 5. Grease a 12-cup muffin tin or use paper cases.

2 In a saucepan, melt the butter and honey. Remove from the heat and set aside to cool slightly.

3 In a bowl, whisk together the yogurt, egg, lemon rind and juice. Add the butter and honey mixture. Set aside.

4 In another bowl, sift together the dry ingredients. Fold them into the yogurt mixture to blend.

5 Fill the prepared cup two-thirds full. Bake until the tops spring back when touched lightly, about 20–25 minutes. Cool in the tin for 5 minutes before turning out. Serve warm or at room temperature.

Prune Muffins

Prunes bring a delightful moisture to these tasty and wholesome muffins.

Makes 12

1 egg
250ml/8fl oz/1 cup milk
120ml/4fl oz/½ cup vegetable oil
45g/1¾ oz/scant ¼ cup caster sugar
25g/1oz/2 tbsp dark brown sugar
275g/10oz/2½ cups plain flour

10ml/2 tsp baking powder
2.5ml/½ tsp salt
1.5ml/¼ tsp grated nutmeg
115g/4oz/½ cup cooked stoned prunes, chopped

1 Preheat the oven to 200°C/400°F/Gas 6. Grease a 12-cup muffin tin or use paper cases.

2 Break the egg into a mixing bowl and beat with a fork. Beat in the milk and oil. Stir in the sugars and set aside.

3 Sift the flour, baking powder, salt and nutmeg into a mixing bowl. Make a well in the centre, pour in the egg mixture and stir until moistened. Do not overmix; the batter should be slightly lumpy. Finally, fold in the prunes.

4 Fill the prepared cups two-thirds full. Bake until golden brown, about 20 minutes. Leave to stand for 10 minutes before turning out. Serve warm or at room temperature.

Crunchy Muesli Muffins

The muesli in these muffins gives them an unusual texture and makes them ideal to serve for breakfast.

Makes 10

150g/5oz/1¼ cups plain
  flour
12.5ml/2½ tsp baking
  powder
30ml/2 tbsp caster sugar
200g/7oz/1½ cups
  toasted oat cereal with
  raisins

250ml/8fl oz/1 cup milk
50g/2oz/4tbsp butter,
  melted, or corn oil
1 egg, beaten

1 Preheat the oven to 200°C/400°F/Gas 6. Grease 10 cups of a muffin tin or use paper cases.

2 Sift the flour, baking powder and sugar together into a large bowl. Add the oat cereal and stir to blend.

3 In a separate bowl, combine the milk, melted butter or corn oil and the beaten egg. Add to the dry ingredients. Stir until moistened, but do not overmix.

4 Spoon the mixture into the cups, leaving room for the muffins to rise. Half-fill any empty cups with water. Bake in the oven for 20 minutes, or until golden brown. Transfer to a wire rack to cool.

Raspberry Muffins

If you are using frozen raspberries, work quickly as the cold berries make the mixture solidify.

Makes 12

115g/4oz/1 cup
  self-raising flour
115g/4oz/1 cup
  wholemeal self-raising
  flour
45ml/3 tbsp caster sugar
2.5ml/½ tsp salt
2 eggs, beaten

200ml/7fl oz/scant 1 cup
  milk
50g/2oz/4 tbsp butter,
  melted
175g/6oz/1 cup
  raspberries, fresh or
  frozen (defrosted for
  less than 30 minutes)

1 Preheat the oven to 190°C/375°F/Gas 5. Lightly grease a 12-cup muffin tin, or use paper cases. Sift the dry ingredients together, then tip in any wheat flakes left in the sieve.

2 Beat the eggs, milk and melted butter together and stir into the dry ingredients to make a thick batter.

3 Stir the raspberries in gently. If you mix too much the raspberries begin to disintegrate and colour the dough. Spoon into the cups or paper cases.

4 Bake for 30 minutes, until well risen and just firm. Leave to cool in the tin placed on a wire rack. Serve warm or cool.

Scones

Traditionally, scones should be served with butter, clotted or whipped cream and jam.

Makes 10–12

225g/8oz/2 cups plain flour	1 egg, beaten
15ml/1 tbsp baking powder	75ml/5 tbsp milk
50g/2oz/4 tbsp butter, diced	1 beaten egg, to glaze

1 Preheat the oven to 220°C/425°F/Gas 7. Lightly butter a baking sheet. Sift the flour and baking powder together, then rub in the butter.

2 Make a well in the centre of the flour mixture, add the egg and milk and mix to a soft dough using a round-bladed knife.

3 Turn out the scone dough on to a floured surface, and knead very lightly until smooth.

4 Roll out the dough to about a 2cm/¾ in thickness and cut into 10 or 12 circles using a 5cm/2in plain or fluted cutter dipped in flour.

5 Transfer to the baking sheet, brush with egg, then bake for about 8 minutes, until risen and golden. Cool slightly on a wire rack before serving.

Drop Scones

If you place the cooked scones in a folded dish towel they will stay soft and moist.

Makes 8–10

115g/4oz/1 cup plain flour	25g/1oz/2 tbsp butter, diced
5ml/1 tsp bicarbonate of soda	1 egg, beaten
5ml/1 tsp cream of tartar	150ml/¼ pint/ ⅔ cup milk

1 Lightly grease a griddle or heavy-based frying pan, then preheat it.

2 Sift the flour, bicarbonate of soda and cream of tartar together, then rub in the butter until the mixture resembles breadcrumbs. Make a well in the centre, then stir in the egg and sufficient milk to give the consistency of double cream.

3 Drop spoonfuls of the mixture, spaced slightly apart, on to the griddle or frying pan. Cook over a steady heat for 2–3 minutes, until bubbles rise to the surface and burst.

4 Turn the scones over and cook for a further 2–3 minutes, until golden underneath. Serve warm with butter and honey.

Wholemeal Scones

Split these wholesome scones in two with a fork while still warm and spread with butter and jam, if you wish.

Makes 16

175g/6oz/¾ cup cold
butter
350g/12oz/3 cups
wholemeal flour
150g/5oz/1¼ cups plain
flour
30ml/2 tbsp sugar

2.5ml/½ tsp salt
12.5ml/2½ tsp
bicarbonate of soda
2 eggs
175g/6fl oz/3¼ cup
buttermilk
35g/1¼oz/¼ cup raisins

1 Preheat the oven to 200°C/400°F/Gas 6. Grease and flour a large baking sheet.

2 Cut the butter into small pieces. Combine all the dry ingredients in a bowl. Add the butter and rub in until the mixture resembles coarse breadcrumbs. Set aside.

3 In another bowl, whisk together the eggs and buttermilk. Set aside 30ml/2 tbsp for glazing, then stir the remaining egg mixture into the dry ingredients until it just holds together. Stir in the raisins.

4 Roll out the dough to about 2cm/¾in thickness. Stamp out circles with a biscuit cutter. Place on the baking sheet and brush with the glaze.

5 Bake until golden, about 12–15 minutes. Allow to cool slightly before serving.

Orange and Raisin Scones

Split these scones when cool and toast them under a preheated grill. Butter them while still hot.

Makes 16

275g/10oz/2½ cups plain
flour
25ml/1½ tsp baking
powder
60g/2¼oz/generous/
¼ cup sugar
2.5ml/½ tsp salt
65g/2½oz/5 tbsp butter,
diced

65g/2½oz/5 tbsp
margarine, diced
grated rind of 1 large
orange
50g/2oz/scant ½ cup
raisins
120ml/4fl oz/½ cup
buttermilk
milk, to glaze

1 Preheat the oven to 220°C/425°F/Gas 7. Grease and flour a large baking sheet.

2 Combine the dry ingredients in a large bowl. Add the butter and margarine and rub in until the mixture resembles coarse breadcrumbs.

3 Add the orange rind and raisins. Gradually stir in the buttermilk to form a soft dough. Roll out the dough to about a 2cm/¾in thickness. Stamp out circles with a biscuit cutter. Place on the baking sheet and brush the tops with milk.

4 Bake until golden, about 12–15 minutes. Serve hot or warm, with butter, or whipped or clotted cream and jam.

Cheese and Chive Scones

Feta cheese makes an excellent substitute for butter in these tangy savoury scones.

Makes 9

115g/4oz/1 cup
  self-raising flour
150g/5oz/1 cup
  wholemeal self-raising
  flour
2.5ml/½ tsp salt
75g/3oz feta cheese

15ml/1 tbsp chopped
  fresh chives
150ml/¼ pint/⅔ cup
  milk, plus extra to
  glaze
1.5ml/¼ tsp cayenne
  pepper

1 Preheat the oven to 200°C/400°F/Gas 6. Sift the flours and salt into a mixing bowl. Add any bran left in the sieve.

2 Crumble the feta cheese and rub into the dry ingredients. Stir in the chives, then add the milk and mix to a soft dough.

3 Turn out on to a floured surface and lightly knead until smooth. Roll out to a 2cm/¾in thickness and stamp out scones with a 6cm/2½in biscuit cutter.

4 Transfer the scones to a non-stick baking sheet. Brush with milk, then sprinkle over the cayenne pepper. Bake in the oven for 15 minutes, or until golden brown. Serve warm or cold.

Sunflower Sultana Scones

Sunflower seeds give these wholesome fruit scones an interesting flavour and appealing texture.

Makes 10–12

225g/8oz/2 cups
  self-raising flour
5ml/1 tsp baking powder
25g/1oz/2 tbsp soft
  sunflower margarine
30ml/2 tbsp golden caster
  sugar
50g/2oz/scant ½ cup
  sultanas

30ml/2 tbsp sunflower
  seeds
150g/5oz/⅔ cup natural
  yogurt
about 30–45ml/
  2–3 tbsp skimmed
  milk

1 Preheat the oven to 230°C/450°F/Gas 8. Lightly oil a baking sheet. Sift the flour and baking powder into a bowl and rub in the margarine evenly.

2 Stir in the sugar, sultanas and half the sunflower seeds, then mix in the yogurt, with just enough milk to make a fairly soft, but not sticky, dough.

3 Roll out on a lightly floured surface to about a 2cm/¾ in thickness. Cut into 6cm/2½ in flower shapes or rounds with a biscuit cutter and lift on to the baking sheet.

4 Brush with milk and sprinkle with the reserved sunflower seeds, then bake for 10–12 minutes, until well risen and golden brown. Cool the scones on a wire rack. Serve split and spread with jam or low-fat spread.

Buttermilk Scones

If time is short, drop heaped tablespoonfuls of the mixture on to the baking sheet.

Makes 10

225g/8oz/2 cups plain
  flour
5ml/1 tsp baking powder
2.5ml/½ tsp bicarbonate
  of soda
5ml/1 tsp salt
50g/2oz/4 tbsp butter or
  margarine, chilled
175ml/6fl oz/¾ cup
  buttermilk

1 Preheat the oven to 220°C/425°F/Gas 7. Sift the flour, baking powder, bicarbonate of soda and salt into a mixing bowl. Cut in the butter or margarine with a fork until the mixture resembles coarse breadcrumbs.

2 Add the buttermilk and mix until well combined to form a soft dough. Turn the dough on to a lightly floured surface and knead for about 30 seconds.

3 Roll out the dough to a 1cm/½in thickness. Use a floured 6cm/2½in pastry cutter to cut out rounds. Transfer the rounds to a baking sheet and bake until golden brown, about 10–12 minutes. Serve hot with butter and honey.

Date Oven Scones

To ensure light, well-risen scones, don't handle the dough too much or roll it out too thinly.

Makes 12

225g/8oz/2 cups
  self-raising flour
pinch of salt
50g/2oz/4 tbsp butter
50g/2oz/¼ cup caster
  sugar
50g/2oz/⅓ cup chopped
  dates
150ml/¼ pint/⅔ cup milk
1 beaten egg, to glaze

1 Preheat the oven to 230°C/450°F/Gas 8. Sift the flour and salt into a bowl and, using a pastry blender or your fingers, rub in the butter until the mixture resembles fine breadcrumbs. Add the sugar and chopped dates, and stir to blend.

2 Make a well in the centre of the dry ingredients and add the milk. Stir with a fork until the mixture comes together in a fairly soft dough.

3 Turn the dough out on to a lightly floured surface and knead gently for 30 seconds. Roll it out to a 2cm/¾in thickness. Cut out circles with a biscuit cutter. Arrange them, not touching, on an ungreased baking sheet, then glaze with the beaten egg.

4 Bake in the oven for 8–10 minutes, or until well risen and golden brown. Using a palette knife, transfer the scones to a wire rack to cool completely.

Cheese and Marjoram Scones

A great success for a hearty tea. With savoury toppings, these scones can make a good basis for a light lunch.

Makes 18

115g/4oz/1 cup
  wholemeal flour
115g/4oz/1 cup
  self-raising flour
pinch of salt
45ml/1½oz/3 tbsp butter
1.5ml/¼ tsp dry mustard
10ml/2 tsp dried
  marjoram

50–75g/2–3oz/
  ½–¾ cup finely grated
  Cheddar cheese
120ml/4fl oz/½ cup milk,
  or as required
50g/2oz/½ cup pecan
  nuts or walnuts,
  chopped

1 Gently sift the two flours into a bowl and add the salt. Cut the butter into small pieces, and rub into the flour until the mixture resembles fine breadcrumbs.

2 Add the mustard, marjoram and grated cheese, and mix in sufficient milk to make a soft dough. Knead the dough lightly.

3 Preheat the oven to 220°C/425°F/Gas 7. Lightly grease two or three baking sheets. Roll out the dough on a floured surface to about a 2cm/¾in thickness and cut it out with a 5cm/2in square biscuit cutter. Place the scones, slightly apart, on the baking sheets.

4 Brush the scones with a little milk and then sprinkle the chopped pecan nuts or walnuts over the top. Bake for about 12 minutes. Serve warm, spread with butter.

Dill and Potato Cakes

The inclusion of dill in these potato cakes makes them quite irresistible.

Makes 10

225g/8oz/2 cups
  self-raising flour
40g/½oz/3 tbsp butter,
  softened
pinch of salt
15ml/1 tbsp finely
  chopped fresh dill

175g/6oz/scant 1 cup
  mashed potato,
  freshly made
30–45ml/2–3 tbsp milk

1 Preheat the oven to 230°C/450°F/Gas 8. Grease a baking sheet. Sift the flour into a bowl and add the butter, salt and dill. Mix in the mashed potato and enough milk to make a soft, pliable dough.

2 Roll out the dough on a well-floured surface until fairly thin. Cut into circles with a 7.5cm/3in biscuit cutter.

3 Place the potato cakes on the baking sheet, and bake for 20–25 minutes until risen and golden.

White Bread

There is nothing quite like the smell and taste of home-baked bread, eaten while still warm.

Makes two 23 x 13cm/9 x 5in loaves

50ml/2fl oz/¼ cup
lukewarm water
15ml/1 tbsp active dried
yeast
30ml/2 tbsp sugar
475ml/16fl oz/2 cups
lukewarm milk

25g/1oz/2 tbsp butter or
margarine, at room
temperature
10ml/2 tsp salt
about 900g/2lb/8 cups
strong flour

1 Combine the water, yeast and 15ml/1 tbsp of the sugar in a measuring jug and leave for 15 minutes until frothy.

2 Pour the milk into a large bowl. Add the remaining sugar, the butter or margarine, and salt. Stir in the yeast mixture, then stir in the flour, 150g/5oz/1¼ cups at a time, until a stiff dough is obtained.

3 Transfer the dough to a floured surface. Knead the dough until it is smooth and elastic, then place it in a large greased bowl, cover with a plastic bag, and leave to rise in a warm place until doubled in volume, about 2–3 hours.

4 Grease two 23 x 13cm/9 x 5in loaf tins. Punch down the dough and divide in half. Form into loaf shapes and place in the tins, seam-sides down. Cover and leave to rise again until almost doubled in volume, about 45 minutes. Meanwhile, preheat the oven to 190°C/375°F/Gas 5.

5 Bake until firm and brown, about 45–50 minutes. Turn out and tap the base of a loaf: if it sounds hollow the loaf is done. If necessary, return to the oven and bake for a few minutes longer. Turn out and cool on a wire rack.

Multigrain Bread

Try different flours, such as rye, cornmeal, buckwheat or barley to replace the wheatgerm and the soya flour.

Makes two 22 x 11cm/8½ x 4½in loaves

15ml/1 tbsp active dried
yeast
50ml/2fl oz/¼ cup
lukewarm water
65g/2½oz/¾ cup rolled
oats
475ml/16fl oz/2 cups
milk
10ml/2 tsp salt
50ml/2fl oz/¼ cup oil
50g/2oz/⅓ cup light
brown sugar

30ml/2 tbsp honey
2 eggs, lightly beaten
25g/1oz wheatgerm
175g/6oz/1½ cups soya
flour
350g/12oz/scant 2½ cups
wholemeal flour
about 450g/1lb/4 cups
strong flour

1 Combine the yeast and water, stir, and leave for about 15 minutes to dissolve. Place the oats in a large bowl. Scald the milk, then pour over the rolled oats. Stir in the salt, oil, sugar and honey. Leave until lukewarm.

2 Stir in the yeast mixture, eggs, wheatgerm, soya and wholemeal flours. Gradually stir in enough strong flour to obtain a rough dough. Transfer the dough to a floured surface and knead, adding flour if necessary, until smooth and elastic. Return to a clean bowl, cover and leave to rise in a warm place until doubled in volume, about 2½ hours.

3 Grease two 22 x 11cm/8½ x 4½in loaf tins. Punch down the risen dough and knead briefly. Then divide the dough into quarters. Roll each quarter into a cylinder 4cm/1½in thick. Twist together two cylinders and place in a tin; repeat for the remaining cylinders. Cover and leave to rise until doubled in volume again, about 1 hour. Meanwhile, preheat the oven to 190°C/375°F/Gas 5.

4 Bake until the bases sound hollow when tapped lightly, about 45–50 minutes. Turn out and cool on a wire rack.

Plaited Loaf

It doesn't take much effort to turn an ordinary dough mix into this work of art.

Makes one loaf

15ml/1 tbsp active dried yeast
5ml/1 tsp honey
250ml/8fl oz/1 cup lukewarm milk
50g/2oz/4 tbsp butter, melted

425g/15oz/3¾ cups strong flour
5ml/1 tsp salt
1 egg, lightly beaten
1 egg yolk, beaten with 5ml/1 tsp milk, to glaze

1 Combine the yeast, honey, milk and butter. Stir and leave for 15 minutes to dissolve.

2 In a large bowl, mix together the flour and salt. Make a central well; add the yeast mixture and egg. With a wooden spoon, stir from the centre, gradually incorporating the flour, to obtain a rough dough.

3 Transfer to a floured surface and knead until smooth and elastic. Place in a clean bowl, cover and leave to rise in a warm place until doubled in volume, about 1½ hours.

4 Grease a baking sheet. Punch down the dough and divide into three equal pieces. Roll each piece into a long thin strip. Begin plaiting with the centre strip, tucking in the ends. Cover loosely and leave to rise in a warm place for 30 minutes. Meanwhile, preheat the oven to 190°C/375°F/Gas 5. Brush the bread with the egg and milk glaze and bake until golden, about 40–45 minutes. Turn out on to a wire rack to cool.

Oatmeal Bread

A healthy, rustic-looking bread made with rolled oats as well as flour.

Makes two loaves

475ml/16fl oz/2 cups milk
25g/1oz/2 tbsp butter
50g/2oz/4 tbsp cup dark brown sugar
10ml/2 tsp salt
15ml/1 tbsp active dried yeast

50ml/2fl oz/¼ cup lukewarm water
400g/14oz/4 cups rolled oats
675–900g/1½–2lb/ 6–8 cups strong white flour

1 Scald the milk. Remove from the heat and stir in the butter, brown sugar and salt. Leave until lukewarm.

2 Combine the yeast and warm water in a large bowl and leave until frothy. Stir in the milk mixture. Add 275g/10oz/ 3 cups of the oats and enough flour to obtain a soft dough.

3 Transfer to a floured surface and knead until smooth and elastic. Place in a greased bowl, cover with a plastic bag, and leave until doubled in volume, about 2–3 hours.

4 Grease a large baking sheet. Transfer the dough to a lightly floured surface and divide in half. Shape into rounds. Place on the baking sheet, cover with a dish towel and leave to rise until doubled in volume, about 1 hour.

5 Preheat the oven to 200°C/400°F/Gas 6. Score the tops and sprinkle with the remaining oats. Bake until the bases sound hollow when tapped, about 45–50 minutes. Turn out on to wire racks to cool.

Country Bread

A filling bread made with a mixture of wholemeal and white flour.

Makes two loaves

350g/12oz/scant 2½ cups
  wholemeal flour
350g/12oz/3 cups plain
  flour
150g/5oz/1¼ cups strong
  plain flour
20ml/4 tsp salt
50g/2oz/4 tbsp butter, at
  room temperature
475ml/16fl oz/2 cups
  lukewarm milk

For the starter
15ml/1 tbsp active dried
  yeast
250ml/8fl oz/1 cup
  lukewarm water
150g/5oz/1¼ cups plain
  flour
1.5ml/¼ tsp caster sugar

1 Combine all the starter ingredients in a bowl. Cover and leave in a warm place for 2–3 hours.

2 Place the flours, salt and butter in a food processor and process just until blended, about 1–2 minutes. Stir together the milk and starter, then slowly pour into the processor, with the motor running, until the mixture forms a dough. Knead until smooth.

3 Place in an ungreased bowl, cover with a plastic bag, and leave to rise in a warm place until doubled in size, about 1½ hours. Knead again then return to the bowl and leave until tripled in size, about 1½ hours.

4 Grease a baking sheet. Divide the dough in half. Cut off one-third of the dough from each half and shape into four balls. Top each large ball with a small ball and press the centre with the handle of a wooden spoon to secure. Cover with a plastic bag, slash the top, and leave to rise.

5 Preheat the oven to 200°C/400°F/Gas 6. Dust the loaves with flour and bake until browned and the bases sound hollow when tapped, 45–50 minutes. Cool on a wire rack.

Wholemeal Rolls

To add interest when serving, make these individual rolls into different shapes if you wish.

Makes 12

15ml/2 tbsp active dried
  yeast
50ml/2fl oz/¼ cup
  lukewarm water
5ml/1 tsp caster sugar
175ml/6fl oz/¼ cup
  lukewarm buttermilk
1.5ml/¼ tsp bicarbonate
  of soda

5ml/1 tsp salt
40g/1½oz/3 tbsp butter,
  at room temperature
200g/7oz/scant 1½ cups
  wholemeal flour
150g/5oz/1¼ cups plain
  flour
1 beaten egg, to glaze

1 In a large bowl, combine the yeast, water and sugar. Stir, and leave for 15 minutes to dissolve.

2 Add the buttermilk, bicarbonate of soda, salt and butter and stir to blend. Stir in the wholemeal flour. Add just enough of the plain flour to obtain a rough dough.

3 Knead on a floured surface until smooth. Divide into three equal parts. Roll each into a cylinder, then cut in four.

4 Grease a baking sheet. Form the pieces into torpedo shapes, place on the baking sheet, cover and leave in a warm place until doubled in size.

5 Preheat the oven to 200°C/400°F/Gas 6. Brush the rolls with the egg. Bake until firm, about 15–20 minutes. Leave to cool on a wire rack.

Wholemeal Bread

A simple wholesome bread to be enjoyed by the whole family at any time.

Makes one 23 x 13cm/9 x 5in loaf

525g/1lb 5oz/generous 4 cups wholemeal flour	450ml/¾ pint/1¾ cups lukewarm water
10ml/2 tsp salt	30ml/2 tbsp honey
20ml/4 tsp active dried yeast	30ml/2 tbsp oil
	40g/1½oz wheatgerm
	milk, to glaze

1 Warm the flour and salt in a bowl in the oven at its lowest setting for 10 minutes. Meanwhile, combine the yeast with half of the water and leave to dissolve.

2 Make a central well in the flour. Pour in the yeast mixture, the remaining water, honey, oil and wheatgerm. Stir from the centre until smooth.

3 Grease a 23 x 13cm/9 x 5in loaf tin. Knead the dough just enough to shape into a loaf. Put it in the tin and cover with a plastic bag. Leave in a warm place until the dough is about 2.5cm/1in higher than the tin rim, about 1 hour.

4 Preheat the oven to 200°C/400°F/Gas 6. Brush the loaf with milk, and bake until the base sounds hollow when tapped, about 35–40 minutes. Cool on a wire rack.

Two-tone Bread

A tasty, malty bread that, when cut, reveals an attractive swirled interior.

Makes two 350g/12oz loaves

25ml/1½ tbsp active dried yeast	600ml/1 pint/2½ cups warm milk
120ml/4fl oz/½ cup warm water	65g/2½oz/5 tbsp butter or margarine, melted and cooled
55g/2¼oz/generous ¼ cup caster sugar	45ml/3 tbsp black treacle
675g/1½lb/6 cups strong plain flour	275g/10oz/2 cups strong wholemeal plain flour
7.5ml/½ tbsp salt	

1 Dissolve the yeast in the water with 5ml/1 tsp of the sugar. Sift 350g/12oz/3 cups of the white flour, the salt and remaining sugar. Make a well and add the yeast, milk and butter. Mix in gradually to form a smooth soft batter.

2 Divide the batter into two bowls. To one bowl, add 275g/10oz/2½ cups of the strong white flour and mix together to a soft dough. Knead until smooth. Shape into a ball, put into a greased bowl and rotate to grease all over. Cover with clear film.

3 Mix the treacle and wholemeal flour into the second bowl. Add enough of the remaining white flour to make a soft dough. Knead until smooth. Shape into a ball, put in a greased bowl and cover. Leave the doughs to rise in a warm place for about 1 hour until doubled in size. Grease two 22 x 11cm/8½ x 4½in loaf tins.

4 Preheat the oven to 220°C/425°F/Gas 7. Punch down the dough and divide each ball in half. Roll out half of the light dough to a 30 x 20cm/12 x 8in rectangle. Roll out half of the dark dough to the same size. Set the dark dough rectangle on the light one. Roll up tightly from a short side. Set in a loaf tin. Repeat. Cover the tins and leave the dough to rise until doubled in size. Bake for 30–35 minutes.

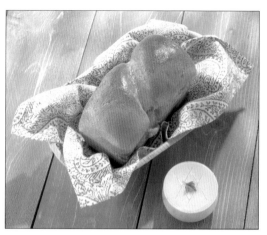

Pleated Rolls

Fancy home-made rolls show that every care has been taken to ensure a welcoming dinner party.

Makes 48 rolls

15ml/1tbsp active dried yeast	10ml/2tsp salt
475ml/16fl oz/2 cups lukewarm milk	2 eggs
115g/4oz/½ cup margarine	985g–1.2kg/2lb 3oz–2½lb/ scant 7–8 cups strong flour
50g/2oz/4tbsp sugar	50g/2oz/4tbsp butter

1 Combine the yeast and 120ml/4fl oz/½ cup milk in a large bowl. Stir and leave for 15 minutes to dissolve. Scald the remaining milk, leave to cool for 5 minutes, then beat in the margarine, sugar, salt and eggs. Leave until lukewarm.

2 Pour the milk mixture into the yeast mixture. Stir in half the flour with a wooden spoon. Add the remaining flour, 190g/5oz/1¼ cups at a time, to obtain a rough dough.

3 Transfer the dough to a floured surface, knead until elastic. Place in a clean bowl, cover with a plastic bag and leave to rise in a warm place until doubled in volume.

4 In a saucepan, melt the butter and set aside. Lightly grease two baking sheets. Punch down the dough and divide into four equal pieces. Roll each piece into a 30 x 20cm/12 x 8in rectangle, about 5mm/¼ in thick. Cut each of the rectangles into four long strips, then cut each strip into three 10 x 5cm/ 4 x 2in rectangles. Brush each rectangle with melted butter, then fold the rectangles in half, so that the top extends about 1cm/½ in over the bottom. Place the rectangles slightly overlapping on the baking sheet, with the longer sides facing up.

5 Cover and chill for 30 minutes. Preheat the oven to 180°C/350°F/Gas 4. Bake until golden, 18–20 minutes. Cool slightly before serving.

Cheese Bread

This flavoured bread is ideal to serve with hot soup for a hearty snack lunch.

Makes one 23 x 13cm/9 x 5in loaf

15ml/1 tbsp active dried yeast	10ml/2 tsp salt
250ml/8fl oz/1 cup lukewarm milk	90g/3½ oz/scant 1 cup grated mature Cheddar cheese
25g/1oz/2 tbsp butter	
425g/15oz/3¾ cups strong white flour	

1 Combine the yeast and milk. Stir and leave for 15 minutes to dissolve. Meanwhile, melt the butter, leave to cool, then add to the yeast mixture.

2 Mix the flour and salt together in a large bowl. Make a central well and pour in the yeast mixture. With a wooden spoon, stir from the centre to obtain a rough dough. If the dough seems too dry, add 30–45ml/2–3 tbsp water.

3 Transfer to a floured surface and knead until smooth and elastic. Return to the bowl, cover and leave to rise in a warm place until doubled in volume, about 2–3 hours.

4 Grease a 23 x 13cm/9 x 5in loaf tin. Punch down the dough and knead in the cheese to distribute it evenly. Twist the dough, form into a loaf shape and place in the tin, tucking the ends under. Leave in a warm place until the dough rises above the rim of the tin.

5 Preheat the oven to 200°C/400°F/Gas 6. Bake for 15 minutes, then lower the heat to 190°C/375°F/Gas 5 and bake until the base sounds hollow when tapped, about a further 30 minutes.

Poppyseed Knots

The poppyseeds look attractive and add a slightly nutty flavour to these rolls.

Makes 12
300ml/½ pint/1¼ cups
   lukewarm milk
50g/2oz/4tbsp butter, at
   room temperature
5ml/1 tsp caster sugar
10ml/2 tsp active dry
   yeast
1 egg yolk

10ml/2 tsp salt
500–575g/1lb 2oz/
   4–4½ cup 4oz plain
   flour
1 egg beaten with 10ml/2
   tsp of water, to glaze
poppyseeds, for
   sprinkling

1 In a large bowl, stir together the milk, butter, sugar and yeast. Leave for 15 minutes to dissolve. Stir in the egg yolk, salt and 275g/10oz/2½ cups of the flour. Add half the remaining flour and stir to obtain a soft dough.

2 Transfer to a floured surface and knead, adding flour if necessary, until smooth and elastic. Place in a bowl, cover and leave in a warm place until the dough doubles in volume, about 1½–2 hours.

3 Grease a baking sheet. Punch down the dough with your fist and cut into 12 pieces the size of golf balls. Roll each piece into a rope, twist to form a knot and place 2.5cm/1in apart on the sheet. Cover loosely and leave to rise in a warm place until doubled in volume, about 1–1½ hours.

4 Preheat the oven to 180°C/350°F/Gas 4. Brush the knots with the egg glaze and sprinkle over the poppyseeds. Bake until the tops are lightly browned, about 30 minutes. Cool slightly on a wire rack before serving.

Clover Leaf Rolls

For a witty touch, make one "lucky four-leaf clover" in the batch.

Makes 24
300ml/½ pint/1¼ cups
   milk
30ml/2 tbsp caster sugar
50g/2oz/4 tbsp butter, at
   room temperature
10ml/2 tsp active dried
   yeast

1 egg
10ml/2 tsp salt
450–500g/1 – 1¼lb/
   4 – 5 cups plain flour
melted butter, to glaze

1 Heat the milk to lukewarm, pour into a large bowl and stir in the sugar, butter and yeast. Leave for 15 minutes. Stir in the egg and salt. Gradually stir in 475g/1lb 2oz/4½ cups of the flour. Add just enough extra to obtain a rough dough. Knead until smooth. Place in a greased bowl, cover and leave in a warm place until doubled in size, about 1½ hours.

2 Grease two 12-cup bun trays. Punch down the dough, and make 72 equal-size balls.

3 Place three balls, in one layer, in each bun cup. Cover loosely and leave to rise in a warm place until doubled in size, about 1½ hours.

4 Preheat the oven to 200°C/400°F/Gas 6. Brush the rolls with glaze. Bake until lightly browned, about 20 minutes. Cool slightly on a wire rack before serving.

French Bread

For truly authentic bread you should use flour grown and milled in France.

Makes 2 loaves

15ml/1 tbsp active dried
   yeast
475ml/16fl oz/2 cups
   lukewarm water
15ml/1 tbsp salt

850 – 900g/1lb 14oz – 2lb/
   3½–4 cups plain flour
semolina or flour, for
   sprinkling

1 In a large bowl, combine the yeast and water, stir, and leave for 15 minutes. Stir in the salt.

2 Add the flour, 150g/5oz/1¼ cups at a time, to obtain a smooth dough. Knead for 5 minutes.

3 Shape into a ball, place in a greased bowl and cover with a plastic bag. Leave to rise in a warm place until doubled in size, about 2–4 hours.

4 On a lightly floured surface shape into two long loaves. Place on a baking sheet sprinkled with semolina or flour and leave to rise for 5 minutes.

5 Score the tops diagonally with a sharp knife. Brush with water and place in a cold oven. Place a pan of boiling water on the base of the oven and set the oven to 200°C/400°F/Gas 6. Bake until crusty and golden, about 40 minutes. Cool on a wire rack.

Croissants

Enjoy breakfast Continental-style with these melt-in-your-mouth croissants.

Makes 18

15ml/1 tbsp active dried
   yeast
325ml/11fl oz/1⅓ cups
   lukewarm milk
10ml/2 tsp caster sugar
12.5ml/1½ tsp salt
450g/1lb/4 cups plain
   flour

225g/8oz/1 cup cold
   unsalted butter
1 egg, beaten with
   10ml/2 tsp water, to
   glaze

1 In an electric mixer bowl, stir together the yeast and milk. Leave for about 15 minutes. Stir in the sugar, salt and about 150g/5oz/1¼ cups of the flour.

2 Using a dough hook, slowly add the remaining flour. Beat on a high speed until the dough pulls away from the sides of the bowl. Cover and leave to rise in a warm place until doubled in size, about 1½ hours. Knead until smooth, wrap in greaseproof paper and chill for 15 minutes.

3 Roll out the butter between two sheets of greaseproof paper to make two 15 x 10cm/6 x 4in rectangles. Roll out the dough to 30 x 20cm/12 x 8in. Interleave the butter with the dough. With a short side facing you, roll it out again to 30 x 20cm/12 x 8in. Fold in thirds again, wrap and chill for 30 minutes. Repeat procedure twice, then chill for 2 hours.

4 Roll out the dough to a rectangle about 3mm/⅛ in thick. Trim the sides. Cut into 18 equal-size triangles. Roll up from base to point. Place point-down on baking sheets and form crescents. Cover and leave to rise in a warm place until more than doubled in size, about 1–1½ hours.

5 Preheat the oven to 240°C/475°F/Gas 9. Brush with egg. Bake for 2 minutes. Lower the heat to 190°C/375°F/Gas 5 and bake until golden, about 10–12 minutes. Serve warm.

Individual Brioches

These buttery rolls with their distinctive topknots are delicious served with jam at coffee time.

Makes 8

15ml/1 tbsp active dried
    yeast
15ml/1 tbsp caster sugar
30ml/2 tbsp warm milk
2 eggs
about 200g/7oz/1¼ cups
    plain flour

2.5ml/½ tsp salt
75g/3oz/6 tbsp butter,
    cut into six pieces, at
    room temperature
1 egg yolk, beaten with
    10ml/2 tsp water, to
    glaze

1 Butter eight individual brioche or muffin tins. Put the yeast and sugar in a small bowl, add the milk and stir until dissolved. Leave to stand for 5 minutes, then beat in the eggs.

2 Put the flour and salt into a food processor, then, with the machine running, slowly pour in the yeast mixture. Scrape down the sides and process until the dough forms a ball. Add the butter and pulse to blend.

3 Transfer the dough to a buttered bowl and cover with a dish towel. Leave to rise in a warm place for 1 hour, then punch down.

4 Shape three-quarters of the dough into eight balls and put into the tins. Shape the last quarter into eight small balls, make a depression in the top of each large ball and set a small ball into it.

5 Leave to rise in a warm place for 30 minutes. Preheat the oven to 200°C/400°F/Gas 6.

6 Brush the brioches with the egg glaze. Bake for about 15–18 minutes, until golden brown. Transfer to a wire rack and leave to cool completely.

Dinner Milk Rolls

Making bread especially for your dinner guests is not only a wonderful gesture, it is also quite easy to do.

Makes 12–16

750g/1½lb/6 cups strong
    plain flour
10ml/2 tsp salt
25g/1oz/2 tbsp butter
1 sachet easy-blend dried
    yeast
450ml/¾ pint/1¾ cups
    lukewarm milk

cold milk, to glaze
poppy, sesame and
    sunflower seeds, or sea
    salt flakes, for
    sprinkling

1 Sift together the flour and salt into a large bowl. Rub in the butter, then stir in the yeast. Mix to a firm dough with the milk (you may not need it all).

2 Knead the dough for 5 minutes, then return to the bowl, cover with oiled clear film and leave to rise until doubled in volume.

3 Grease a baking sheet. Punch down the dough and knead again, then divide into 12–16 pieces and make into shapes of your choice. Place on the baking sheet, glaze the tops with milk, and sprinkle over your chosen seeds or sea salt flakes.

4 Leave to start rising again. Meanwhile, preheat the oven to 230°C/450°F/Gas 8. Bake the rolls for 12 minutes or until golden brown and cooked. Cool on a wire rack. Eat the same day as they will not keep.

Dill Bread

Tasty herb breads such as this are expensive to buy ready-made – if they can be found at all.

Makes two loaves

20ml/4 tsp active dried yeast	60ml/4 tbsp oil
475ml/16fl oz/2 cups lukewarm water	1 large bunch of dill, finely chopped
30ml/2 tbsp sugar	2 eggs, lightly beaten
1.05kg/2lb 5½ oz/scant 9½ cups strong flour	150g/5½ oz/⅔ cup cottage cheese
½ onion, chopped	20ml/4 tsp salt
	milk, to glaze

1 Mix together the yeast, water and sugar in a large bowl and leave for 15 minutes to dissolve. Stir in about half of the flour. Cover and leave to rise in a warm place for 45 minutes.

2 In a frying pan, cook the onion in 15ml/1 tbsp of the oil until soft. Set aside to cool, then stir into the yeast mixture. Stir the dill, eggs, cottage cheese, salt and the remaining oil into the yeast. Gradually add the remaining flour until the dough is too stiff to stir.

3 Transfer to a floured surface and knead until smooth and elastic. Place in a bowl, cover and leave to rise until doubled in volume, about 1–1½ hours.

4 Grease a large baking sheet. Cut the dough in half and shape into two rounds. Place on the sheet and leave to rise in a warm place for 30 minutes.

5 Preheat the oven to 190℃/375°F/Gas 5. Score the tops, brush with the milk to glaze and bake until browned, about 50 minutes. Transfer to a wire rack to cool.

Spiral Herb Bread

When you slice this unusual loaf, its herbal secret is revealed inside.

Makes two 23 x 13cm/9 x 5in loaves

30ml/2 tbsp active dried yeast	1 large bunch of parsley, finely chopped
600ml/1 pint/2½ cups lukewarm water	1 bunch of spring onions, chopped
425g/15oz/3¾ cups strong white flour	1 garlic clove, finely chopped
500g/1lb 2oz/generous 3½ cups wholemeal flour	salt and ground black pepper
15ml/1 tbsp salt	1 egg, lightly beaten
25g/1oz/2 tbsp butter	milk, for glazing

1 Combine the yeast and 50ml/2fl oz/¼ cup of the water, stir and leave for 15 minutes to dissolve.

2 Combine the flours and salt in a large bowl. Make a central well and pour in the yeast mixture and the remaining water. With a wooden spoon, stir to a rough dough. Transfer to a floured surface; knead until smooth. Return to the bowl, cover with a plastic bag, and leave until doubled in size.

3 Meanwhile, combine the butter, parsley, spring onions and garlic in a large frying pan. Cook over a low heat, stirring, until softened. Season and set aside.

4 Grease two 23 x 13cm/9 x 5in loaf tins. When the dough has risen, cut in half and roll each half into a rectangle 35 x 23cm/14 x 9in. Brush with the beaten egg; spread with the herb mixture. Roll up to enclose the filling, pinch the short ends to seal. Place in the tins, seam-sides down. Cover, leave in a warm place until the dough rises above the tin rims.

5 Preheat the oven to 190℃/375°F/Gas 5. Brush the loaves with milk and bake until the bases sound hollow when tapped, about 55 minutes. Cool on a wire rack.

Sesame Seed Bread

This delicious bread breaks into individual rolls. It is ideal for entertaining.

Makes one 23cm/9in loaf

10ml/2 tsp active dried
   yeast
300ml/½ pint/1¼ cups
   lukewarm water
200g/7oz/1¼ cups plain
   flour
200g/7oz/scant 1½ cups
   wholemeal flour

10ml/2 tsp salt
65g/2½oz/5 tbsp toasted
   sesame seeds
milk, to glaze
30ml/2 tbsp sesame
   seeds, for sprinkling

1 Combine the yeast and 75ml/5 tbsp of the water and leave to dissolve. Mix the flours and salt in a large bowl. Make a central well and pour in the yeast and water. Stir from the centre to obtain a rough dough.

2 Transfer to a floured surface and knead until smooth and elastic. Return to the bowl and cover with a plastic bag. Leave in a warm place until the dough has doubled in size, about 1½–2 hours.

3 Grease a 23cm/9in round cake tin. Punch down the dough and knead in the sesame seeds. Divide the dough into 16 balls and place in the tin. Cover with a plastic bag and leave in a warm place until risen above the rim.

4 Preheat the oven to 220°C/425°F/Gas 7. Brush the loaf with milk and sprinkle with the sesame seeds. Bake for 15 minutes. Lower the heat to 190°C/375°F/Gas 5 and bake until the base sounds hollow when tapped, about 30 minutes. Cool on a wire rack.

Rye Bread

To bring out the flavour of the caraway seeds, toast them lightly in the oven first.

Makes one loaf

200g/7oz/scant 1½ cups
   rye flour
475ml/16fl oz/2 cups
   boiling water
120ml/4fl oz/ ½ cup black
   treacle
65g/2½oz/5 tbsp butter,
   cut into pieces
15ml/1 tbsp salt
30ml/2 tbsp caraway
   seeds

15ml/1 tbsp active dried
   yeast
120ml/4fl oz/ ½ cup
   lukewarm water
about 850g/1lb 14oz/
   7½ cups plain flour
semolina or flour, for
   dusting

1 Mix the rye flour, boiling water, treacle, butter, salt and caraway seeds in a large bowl. Leave to cool.

2 In another bowl, mix the yeast and lukewarm water and leave to dissolve. Stir into the rye flour mixture. Stir in just enough plain flour to obtain a stiff dough. If it becomes too stiff, stir with your hands. Transfer to a floured surface and knead thoroughly until the dough is no longer sticky and is smooth and shiny.

3 Place in a greased bowl, cover with a plastic bag, and leave in a warm place until doubled in volume. Punch down the dough, cover, and leave to rise again for 30 minutes.

4 Preheat the oven to 180°C/350°F/Gas 4. Dust a baking sheet with semolina or flour.

5 Shape the dough into a ball. Place on the sheet and score several times across the top. Bake until the base sounds hollow when tapped, about 40 minutes. Cool on a wire rack.

Rosemary Focaccia

Italian flat bread is easy to make using a packet mix. Additions include olives and sun-dried tomatoes.

Makes two loaves

450g/1lb packet white
  bread mix
60ml/4 tbsp extra virgin
  olive oil
10ml/2 tsp dried
  rosemary, crushed
8 sun-dried tomatoes,
  chopped

12 black olives, stoned
  and chopped
200ml/7fl oz/scant 1 cup
  lukewarm water
sea salt flakes, for
  sprinkling

1 Combine the bread mix with half the oil, the rosemary, tomatoes, olives and water to form a firm dough.

2 Knead the dough on a lightly floured surface for about 5 minutes. Return to the mixing bowl and cover with a piece of oiled clear film. Leave the dough to rise in a warm place until doubled in size. Meanwhile, lightly grease two baking sheets and preheat the oven to 220°C/425°F/Gas 7.

3 Punch down the dough and knead again. Divide into two and shape into flat rounds. Place on the baking sheet, and make indentations with your fingertips. Trickle over the remaining olive oil and sprinkle with sea salt flakes.

4 Bake the focaccia for 12–15 minutes until golden brown and cooked. Turn out on to wire racks to cool. This bread is best eaten slightly warm.

Saffron Focaccia

A dazzling yellow bread that is both light in texture and distinctive in flavour.

Makes one loaf

pinch of saffron strands
150ml/¼ pint/⅔ cup
  boiling water
225g/8oz/2 cups plain
  flour
2.5ml/½ tsp salt
5ml/1 tsp easy-blend
  dried yeast
15ml/1 tbsp olive oil

For the topping

2 garlic cloves, sliced
1 red onion, cut into thin
  wedges
rosemary sprigs
12 black olives, stoned
  and coarsely chopped
15ml/1 tbsp olive oil

1 Place the saffron in a heatproof jug and pour in the boiling water. Leave to infuse until lukewarm.

2 Place the flour, salt, yeast and olive oil in a food processor. Turn on and gradually add the saffron and its liquid. Process until the dough forms a ball.

3 Turn on to a floured surface; knead for 10–15 minutes. Place in a bowl, cover and leave to rise until doubled in size, about 30–40 minutes.

4 Punch down the dough and roll into an oval shape about 1cm/½in thick. Place on a lightly greased baking sheet and leave to rise for 30 minutes.

5 Preheat the oven to 200°C/400°F/Gas 6. With your fingers, press indentations over the surface of the bread.

6 Cover with the topping ingredients, brush lightly with olive oil, and bake for 25 minutes or until the loaf sounds hollow when tapped on the base. Leave to cool on a wire rack.

Rosemary Bread

Sliced thinly, this herb bread is delicious with cheese or soup for a light meal.

Makes one 23 x 13cm/9 x 5in loaf

*1 sachet easy-blend dried
    yeast
175g/6oz/1¼ cups
    wholemeal flour
175g/6oz/1½ cups self-
    raising flour
25g/1oz/2 tbsp butter
50ml/2fl oz/¼ cup warm
    water
250ml/8fl oz/1 cup milk,
    at room temperature*

*15ml/1 tbsp sugar
5ml/1 tsp salt
15ml/1 tbsp sesame seeds
15ml/1 tbsp dried
    chopped onion
15ml/1 tbsp fresh
    rosemary leaves
115g/4oz/1 cup cubed
    Cheddar cheese
rosemary leaves and
    coarse salt, to decorate*

1 Mix the yeast with the flours in a large mixing bowl. Melt the butter. Then stir the warm water, milk, sugar, butter, salt, sesame seeds, onion and rosemary into the flour. Knead thoroughly until quite smooth.

2 Flatten the dough, then add the cheese cubes. Knead them in until they are well combined.

3 Place the dough into a clean bowl greased with a little melted butter. Cover with a dish towel and put in a warm place for 1½ hours, or until the dough has doubled in size.

4 Grease a 23 x 13cm/9 x 5in loaf tin with butter. Punch down the dough and shape into a loaf. Place in the tin, cover with the dish towel and leave for about 1 hour until doubled in size. Preheat the oven to 190°C/375°F/Gas 5.

5 Bake for 30 minutes. Cover the loaf with foil for the last 5–10 minutes of baking. Turn the bread out on to a wire rack to cool. Garnish with some rosemary leaves and coarse salt scattered on top.

Potato Bread

Don't add butter or milk to the potatoes when you mash them, or the dough will be too sticky.

Makes two 23 x 13cm/9 x 5in loaves

*20ml/4 tsp active dried
    yeast
250ml/8fl oz/1 cup
    lukewarm milk
225g/8oz potatoes, boiled
    (reserve 250ml/
    8fl oz/1 cup of the
    cooking liquid)*

*30ml/2 tbsp oil
20ml/4 tsp salt
850–900g/1lb
    4oz–2lb/3½–4 cups
    plain flour*

1 Combine the yeast and milk in a large bowl and leave to dissolve, about 15 minutes. Meanwhile, mash the potatoes.

2 Add the potatoes, oil and salt to the yeast mixture and mix well. Stir in the reserved cooking water, then stir in the flour, in six separate batches, to form a stiff dough. Knead until smooth, return to the bowl, cover, and leave in a warm place until doubled in size, about 1–1½ hours. Punch down, then leave to rise again for 40 minutes.

3 Grease two 23 x 13cm/9 x 5in loaf tins. Roll the dough into 20 small balls. Place two rows of balls in each tin. Leave until the dough has risen above the rims of the tins.

4 Preheat the oven to 200°C/400°F/Gas 6. Bake the dough for 10 minutes, then lower the heat to 190°C/375°F/Gas 5. Bake until the bases of the loaves sound hollow when tapped, about 40 minutes. Cool on a wire rack.

Irish Soda Bread

Easy to make, this distinctive bread goes well with soup, cheese and traditional, rustic-style dishes.

Makes one loaf

275g/10oz/2½ cups plain flour
150g/5oz/1 cup wholemeal flour
5ml/1 tsp bicarbonate of soda
5ml/1 tsp salt

25g/1oz/2 tbsp butter or margarine, at room temperature
300ml/½ pint/1¼ cups buttermilk
15ml/1 tbsp plain flour, for dusting

1 Preheat the oven to 200°C/400°F/Gas 6. Grease a baking sheet. Sift together the flours, bicarbonate of soda and salt. Make a central well and add the butter or margarine and buttermilk. Working from the centre, stir to combine the ingredients until a soft dough is formed.

2 With floured hands, gather the dough into a ball. Knead for 3 minutes. Shape the dough into a large round.

3 Place on the baking sheet. Cut a cross in the top with a sharp knife and dust with the flour. Bake until brown, about 40–50 minutes. Transfer to a wire rack to cool.

Sage Soda Bread

This wonderful loaf, quite unlike bread made with yeast, has a velvety texture and a powerful sage aroma.

Makes one loaf

225g/8oz/⅔ cups wholemeal flour
115g/4oz/1 cup strong white flour
2.5ml/½ tsp salt
5ml/1 tsp bicarbonate of soda

30ml/2 tbsp shredded fresh sage
300–450ml/½– ¾ pint/1¼–1¾ cups buttermilk

1 Preheat the oven to 220°C/425°F/Gas 7. Sift the dry ingredients into a bowl. Stir in the sage and add enough buttermilk to make a soft dough.

2 Shape the dough into a round loaf and place on a lightly greased baking sheet.

3 Cut a deep cross in the top. Bake in the oven for about 40 minutes, or until the loaf is well risen and sounds hollow when tapped on the base. Leave to cool on a wire rack.

Breadsticks

If preferred, use other seeds, such as poppy or caraway, in these sticks.

Makes 18–20

15ml/1 tbsp active dried yeast	5ml/1 tsp caster sugar
300ml/½ pint/1¼ cups lukewarm water	30ml/2 tbsp olive oil
425g/15oz/scant 4 cups plain flour	1 egg, beaten, to glaze
10ml/2 tsp salt	150g/5oz/10 tbsp sesame seeds, toasted
	coarse salt, for sprinkling

1 Combine the yeast and water, stir and leave for about 15 minutes. Place the flour, salt, sugar and olive oil in a food processor. With the motor running, slowly pour in the yeast mixture and process until the dough forms a ball.

2 Knead until smooth. Place in a bowl, cover and leave to rise in a warm place for 45 minutes. Grease two baking sheets.

3 Roll the dough into 18–20 30cm/12in sticks. Place on the baking sheets, brush with egg then sprinkle with sesame seeds and coarse salt. Leave to rise, uncovered, for 20 minutes.

4 Preheat the oven to 200°C/400°F/Gas 6. Bake until golden, about 15 minutes. Turn off the heat but leave in the oven for a further 5 minutes. Serve warm or cool.

Tomato Breadsticks

Once you've tried this simple recipe you'll never buy manufactured breadsticks again.

Makes 16

225g/8oz/2 cups plain flour	150ml/¼ pint/⅔ cup warm water
2.5ml/½ tsp salt	6 halves sun-dried tomatoes in olive oil, drained and chopped
7.5ml/½ tbsp easy-blend dried yeast	15ml/1 tbsp milk
5ml/1 tsp honey	10ml/2 tsp poppyseeds
5ml/1 tsp olive oil	

1 Place the flour, salt and yeast in a food processor. Add the honey and olive oil and, with the machine running, gradually pour in the water until the dough starts to cling together (you may not need all the water). Process for a further 1 minute.

2 Turn out the dough on to a floured surface and knead for 3–4 minutes, until springy and smooth. Knead in the sun-dried tomatoes. Form into a ball and place in a lightly oiled bowl. Leave to rise for 5 minutes.

3 Preheat the oven to 150°C/300°F/Gas 2. Divide the dough into 16 pieces and roll each piece into a 28 x 1cm/11 x ½in stick. Place on a lightly greased baking sheet and leave to rise in a warm place for 15 minutes.

4 Brush the sticks with milk and sprinkle with poppy seeds. Bake for 30 minutes. Leave to cool on a wire rack.

Walnut Bread

This rich bread could be served at a dinner party with the cheese course, or with a rustic ploughman's lunch.

Makes one loaf

420g/15oz/3 cups
    wholemeal flour
140g/5oz/1¼ cups strong
    flour
12.5ml/2½ tsp salt
500ml/18fl oz/2¼ cups
    lukewarm water

15ml/1tbsp clear honey
15ml/1tbsp active dried
    yeast
140g/5oz/1 cup walnut
    pieces, plus more to
    decorate
1 beaten egg, to glaze

1 Combine the flours and salt in a large bowl. Make a well in the centre and add 250ml/8fl oz/1 cup of the water, the honey and the yeast. Set aside until the mixture is frothy.

2 Add the remaining water. With a wooden spoon, stir from the centre, incorporating flour with each turn, to obtain a smooth dough. Add more flour if the dough is too sticky and use your hands if the dough becomes too stiff to stir.

3 Transfer to a floured board and knead, adding flour if necessary, until the dough is smooth and elastic. Place in a greased bowl and roll the dough around in the bowl to coat thoroughly on all sides. Cover with a plastic bag and leave in a warm place until doubled in volume. Punch down the dough and knead in the walnuts evenly.

4 Grease a baking sheet. Shape the dough into a round loaf and place on the baking sheet. Press in walnut pieces to decorate the top. Cover loosely with a damp cloth and leave to rise in a warm place until doubled in size, 25–30 minutes.

5 Preheat the oven to 220°C/425°F/Gas 7. With a sharp knife, score the top. Brush with the beaten egg. Bake for 15 minutes. Lower the heat to 190°C/375°F/Gas 5 and bake until the base sounds hollow when tapped, about 40 minutes. Cool on a rack.

Pecan Nut Rye Bread

A tasty homespun loaf that recalls the old folk cooking of the United States.

Makes two 21.5 x 11.5cm/8½ x 4½in loaves

25ml/1½ tbsp active
    dried yeast
700ml/22fl oz/2¾ cups
    lukewarm water
675g/1½lb/6 cups strong
    flour
500g/1¼lb/5 cups rye
    flour

30ml/2tbsp salt
15ml/1tbsp clear honey
10ml/2tsp caraway seeds,
    (optional)
115g/4oz/8tbsp butter, at
    room temperature
225g/8oz pecan nuts,
    chopped

1 Combine the yeast and 120ml/4fl oz/½ cup of the water. Stir and leave for 15 minutes to dissolve. In the bowl of an electric mixer, combine the flours, salt, honey, caraway seeds and butter. With the dough hook, mix on low speed until well blended.

2 Add the yeast mixture and the remaining water and mix on medium speed until the dough forms a ball. Transfer to a floured surface and knead in the pecan nuts.

3 Return the dough to a bowl, cover with a plastic bag and leave in a warm place until doubled, about 2 hours. Grease two 21.5 x 11.5cm/8½ x 4½ in loaf tins. Punch down the risen dough.

4 Divide the dough in half and form into loaves. Place in the tins, seam-sides down. Dust the tops with flour. Cover with plastic bags and leave to rise in a warm place until doubled in volume, about 1 hour.

5 Preheat the oven to 190°C/375°F/Gas 5. Bake until the bases sound hollow when tapped, 45–50 minutes. Transfer to wire racks to cool completely.

Prune Bread

Makes 1 loaf

225g/8oz/1 cup
  dried prunes
15ml/1 tbsp easy-blend
  dried yeast
75g/3oz/⅔ cup
  wholemeal flour
385 – 420g/13½
  – 15oz/3–4cups
  strong flour
2.5ml/½ tsp bicarbonate

of soda
5ml/1 tsp salt
5ml/1 tsp pepper
30g/1oz butter, at room
  temperature
175ml/6fl oz/¾ cup
  buttermilk
55g/2oz/½ cup
  walnuts, chopped
milk, for glazing

1 Simmer the prunes in water to cover until soft, or soak overnight. Drain, reserving 60ml/4 tbsp of the soaking liquid. Stone and chop the prunes.

2 Combine the yeast and the reserved prune liquid, stir and leave for 15 minutes to dissolve.

3 In a large bowl, stir together the flours, bicarbonate of soda, salt and pepper. Make a well in the centre.

4 Add the prunes, butter, and buttermilk. Pour in the yeast mixture. With a wooden spoon, stir from the centre, folding in more flour with each turn, to obtain a rough dough.

5 Transfer to a floured surface and knead until smooth and elastic. Return to the bowl, cover with a plastic bag and leave to rise in a warm place until doubled in volume, for about 1½ hours. Grease a baking sheet.

6 Punch down the dough with your fist, then knead in the walnuts. Shape the dough into a long, cylindrical loaf. Place on the baking sheet, cover loosely, and leave to rise in a warm place for 45 minutes. Preheat the oven to 220°C/425°F/Gas 7.

7 With a sharp knife, score the top. Brush with milk and bake for 15 minutes. Lower to 190°C/375°F/Gas 5 and bake for 35 minutes more, until the bottom sounds hollow. Cool.

Courgette Crown Bread

Adding grated courgettes and cheese to a loaf mixture will keep it tasting fresher for longer.

Serves 8

450g/1lb/3 cups coarsely
  grated courgettes
salt
500g/1¼ lb/5 cups plain
  flour
2 sachets easy-blend
  dried yeast

60ml/4 tbsp freshly
  grated Parmesan
  cheese
ground black pepper
30ml/2 tbsp olive oil
lukewarm water, to mix
milk, to glaze
sesame seeds, to garnish

1 Spoon the courgettes into a colander, sprinkling them lightly with salt. Leave to drain for 30 minutes, then pat dry with kitchen paper.

2 Mix the flour, yeast and Parmesan together and season with black pepper. Stir in the oil and courgettes, and add enough lukewarm water to make a firm dough.

3 Knead the dough on a lightly floured surface until smooth, then return to the mixing bowl, cover it with oiled clear film and leave it to rise in a warm place, until doubled in size. Meanwhile, grease and line a 23cm/9in round sandwich tin. Preheat the oven to 200°C/400°F/Gas 6.

4 Punch down the dough, and knead it lightly. Break into 8 balls, roll each one and arrange them, touching, in the tin. Brush the tops with milk and sprinkle over the sesame seeds.

5 Allow to rise again, then bake for 25 minutes or until golden brown. Cool slightly in the tin, then turn out on to a wire rack.

Raisin Bread

Makes 2 loaves

15ml/1 tbsp easy-blend
   dried yeast
450ml/¾ pint/1¾ cups
   lukewarm milk
150g/5oz raisins
65g/2½ oz4 tbsp currants
15ml/1 tbsp sherry or
   brandy
2.5/½ tsp grated nutmeg

grated rind of 1 large
   orange
60g/2¼ oz/7 tbsp sugar
15ml/1 tbsp salt
115g/4oz/8 tbsp
   butter, melted
700 – 850g/1lb 8oz – 1lb
   14oz strong flour
1 egg beaten with 15ml/
   1 tbsp cream

1 Stir the yeast with 120ml/4fl oz/½ cup of the milk and leave to stand for 15 minutes to dissolve. Mix the raisins, currants, sherry or brandy, nutmeg and orange rind together.

2 In another bowl, mix the remaining milk, sugar, salt and half the butter. Add the yeast mixture. With a wooden spoon, stir in half the flour, 150g/5oz at a time, until blended. Add the remaining flour as needed for a stiff dough.

3 Transfer to a floured surface and knead until smooth and elastic. Place in a greased bowl, cover and leave to rise in a warm place until doubled in volume, about 2½ hours.

4 Punch down the dough, return to the bowl, cover and leave to rise in a warm place for 30 minutes. Grease two 21.5 x 11.5cm/8½ x 4½ in bread tins. Divide the dough in half and roll each half into a 50 x 18cm/20 x 7in rectangle.

5 Brush the rectangles with the remaining melted butter. Sprinkle over the raisin mixture, then roll up tightly, tucking in the ends slightly as you roll. Place in the prepared tins, cover, and leave to rise until almost doubled in volume.

6 Preheat the oven to 200°C/400°F/Gas 6. Brush the loaves with the egg and milk. Bake for 20 minutes. Lower to 180°C/350°F/Gas 4 and bake until golden, 25 – 30 minutes more. Cool on racks.

Coconut Bread

This bread is delicious served with a cup of hot chocolate or a glass of fruit punch.

Makes 1 loaf

175g/6oz/¾ cup butter
115g/4oz/⅔ cup
   demerara sugar
225g/8oz/2 cups self-
   raising flour
200g/7oz/scant 2 cups
   plain flour
115g/4oz desiccated
   coconut
5ml/1 tsp mixed spice

10ml/2 tsp vanilla
   essence
15ml/1 tbsp rum
2 eggs
about 150ml/¼ pint/
   ⅔ cup milk
15ml/1 tbsp caster sugar,
   blended with 30ml/
   2 tbsp water, to glaze

1 Preheat the oven to 180°C/350°F/Gas 4. Grease two 450g/1lb loaf tins.

2 Place the butter and sugar in a large bowl and sift in the flour. Rub in the ingredients together with your fingertips until the mixture resembles fine breadcrumbs.

3 Add the coconut, mixed spice, vanilla essence, rum, eggs and milk and mix together well with your hands. If the mixture is too dry, moisten with milk. Knead on a floured board until firm and pliable.

4 Halve the mixture and place in the prepared loaf tins. Glaze with sugared water and bake for 1 hour until the loaves are cooked. Test with a skewer, the loaves are ready when the skewer comes out clean.

Danish Wreath

Serves 10–12

5ml/1 tsp easy-blend
    dried yeast
175ml/6fl oz/¾ cup milk
50g/2oz/4 tbsp sugar
450g/1lb/4 cups strong
    white flour
2.5ml/½ tsp salt
2.5ml/½ tsp vanilla
    essence
1 egg, beaten
2 x 115g/4oz/½ cup
    blocks unsalted butter

1 egg yolk beaten with
    10ml/2 tsp water
115g/4oz/1 cup icing
    sugar

For the filling
200g/7oz/generous 1 cup
    dark brown sugar
5ml/1 tsp ground
    cinnamon
50g/2oz/½ cup walnuts
    or pecans, plus extra

1 Mix the yeast, milk and 2.5ml/½ tsp of the sugar. Leave for 15 minutes to dissolve. Mix the flour, sugar and salt. Make a well; add the yeast, vanilla and egg to make a rough dough. Knead until smooth, wrap and chill.

2 Roll the butter to form two 15 x 10cm/6 x 4in rectangles. Roll the dough to a 30 x 20cm/12 x 8in rectangle. Place one butter rectangle in the centre. Fold the bottom third of dough over and seal the edge. Place the other butter rectangle on top and cover with the top third of the dough.

3 Roll the dough into a 30 x 20cm/12 x 8in rectangle. Fold into thirds. Wrap and chill for 30 minutes. Repeat twice more. After the third fold, chill for 1–2 hours. Grease a baking sheet.

4 Roll out the dough to a 63 x 15cm/25 x 6in strip. Mix the filling ingredients and spread over, leaving a 1cm/½in edge. Roll the dough into a cylinder, place on the sheet in a circle and seal the edges. Cover and leave to rise for 45 minutes.

5 Preheat the oven to 200°C/400°F/Gas 6. Slash the top every 5cm/2in, cutting 1cm/½in deep. Brush with the egg and milk. Bake for 35–40 minutes until golden. Cool. To serve, mix the icing sugar with some water, then drizzle over the wreath. Sprinkle with some nuts.

Kugelhopf

A traditional round moulded bread from Germany, flavoured with Kirsch or brandy.

Makes one ring loaf

100g/3¾ oz/¾ cup raisins
15ml/1 tbsp Kirsch or
    brandy
15ml/1 tbsp easy-blend
    dried yeast
120ml/4fl oz/½ cup
    lukewarm water
115g/4oz/½ cup unsalted
    butter, at room
    temperature
90g/3½oz/½ cup sugar
3 eggs, at room
    temperature

grated rind of 1 lemon
5ml/1 tsp salt
2.5ml/½ tsp vanilla
    essence
425g/15oz/3¾ cups
    strong white flour
120ml/4fl oz/½ cup milk
25g/1oz/¼ cup flaked
    almonds
80g/3¼oz/generous
    ½ cup whole blanched
    almonds, chopped
icing sugar, for dusting

1 In a bowl, combine the raisins and Kirsch or brandy. Combine the yeast and water, stir and leave for 15 minutes.

2 Cream the butter and sugar until thick and fluffy. Beat in the eggs, one at a time. Add the lemon rind, salt and vanilla. Stir in the yeast mixture. Add the flour, alternating with the milk, until well blended. Cover and leave to rise in a warm place until doubled in volume, about 2 hours.

3 Grease a 2.75 litre/4½ pint/11¼ cup kugelhopf mould, then sprinkle the flaked almonds evenly over the base. Work the raisins and chopped almonds into the dough, then spoon into the mould. Cover with a polythene bag, and leave to rise in a warm place until the dough almost reaches the top of the tin, about 1 hour.

4 Preheat the oven to 180°C/350°F/Gas 4. Bake until golden brown, about 45 minutes. If the top browns too quickly, cover with foil. Cool in the tin for 15 minutes, then turn out on to a wire rack. Dust the top lightly with icing sugar.

Open Apple Pie

If using eating apples for this pie, make sure they are firm-fleshed rather than soft.

Serves 8

1.5kg/3 – 3½lb tart eating
or cooking apples
45g/1¾oz/scant ¼ cup
sugar
10ml/2 tsp ground
cinnamon
grated rind and juice of
1 lemon
25g/1oz/2 tbsp butter,
diced
30 – 45ml/2 – 3 tbsp
honey, to glaze

For the pastry

275g/10oz/2½ cups plain
flour
2.5ml/½ tsp salt
115g/4oz/½ cup butter,
cut into pieces
60g/2¼oz/4½ tbsp
vegetable fat or lard,
cut into pieces
75 – 90ml/5 – 6 tbsp iced
water

1 For the pastry, sift the flour and salt into a bowl. Add the butter and fat and rub in until the mixture resembles coarse breadcrumbs. Stir in just enough water to bind the dough. Gather into a ball, wrap and chill for at least 20 minutes.

2 Preheat the oven to 200°C/400°F/Gas 6. Place a baking sheet in the oven.

3 Peel, core and slice the apples. Combine with the sugar, cinnamon, lemon rind and juice.

4 Roll out the pastry to a 30cm/12in circle. Use to line a 23cm/9in pie dish, leaving an overhanging edge. Fill with the apples. Fold in the edges and crimp loosely. Dot the apples with diced butter.

5 Bake on the hot baking sheet until the pastry is golden and the apples are tender, about 45 minutes.

6 Melt the honey in a saucepan and brush over the apples to glaze. Serve warm or at room temperature.

Apple and Cranberry Lattice Pie

Serves 8

grated rind of 1 orange
45ml/3 tbsp orange juice
2 large cooking apples
170g/6oz/1⅓ cups
cranberries
70g/2½oz/½ cup raisins
25g/1oz/4 tbsp walnuts,
chopped
215g/7½oz/generous 1
cup caster sugar
115g/4oz/½ cup dark
brown sugar
15g/½oz/2 tbsp plain
flour

For the crust

285g/10oz/2½ cups plain
flour
2.5ml/½ tsp salt
85g/3oz/6 tbsp cold
butter, cut into pieces
85g/3oz/½ cup cold
vegetable fat or lard,
cut into pieces
65 – 125ml/2 – 4fl oz iced
water

1 For the crust, sift the flour and salt, add the butter and fat and rub in well. Stir in enough water to bind the dough. Form into two equal balls, wrap and chill for at least 20 minutes.

2 Put the orange rind and juice into a bowl. Peel and core the apples and grate into the bowl. Stir in the cranberries, raisins, walnuts, all except 1 tbsp of the caster sugar, the brown sugar and flour. Place a baking sheet in the oven and preheat to 200°C/400°F/Gas 6.

3 Roll out one ball of dough about 3mm/⅛in thick. Transfer to a 23cm/9in pie plate and trim. Spoon the cranberry and apple mixture into the shell.

4 Roll out the remaining dough to a circle about 28cm/11in in diameter. With a serrated pastry wheel, cut the dough into 10 strips, 2cm/¾in wide. Place five strips horizontally across the top of the tart at 2.5cm/1in intervals. Weave in five vertical strips and trim. Sprinkle the top with sugar.

5 Bake for 20 minutes. Reduce heat to 180°C/350°F/Gas 4 and bake until the crust is golden and the filling is bubbling, about 15 minutes more.

Peach Leaf Pie

Serves 8

1.1kg/2¼lb ripe peaches
juice of 1 lemon
90g/3½oz/½ cup sugar
45ml/3 tbsp cornflour
1.5ml/¼ tsp grated
 nutmeg
2.5ml/½ tsp ground
 cinnamon
25g/1oz/2 tbsp butter,
 diced

For the pastry
275g/10oz/2½ cups plain
 flour
4ml/¾ tsp salt
115g/4oz/½ cup cold
 butter, cut into pieces
60g/2¼oz/4½ tbsp cold
 vegetable fat or lard,
 cut into pieces
75–90ml/5–6 tbsp iced
 water
1 egg beaten with 15ml/
 1 tbsp water

1 Make the pastry as described for Open Apple Pie on page 86. Gather into two balls, one slightly larger than the other. Wrap and chill for at least 20 minutes. Place a baking sheet in the oven and preheat to 220℃/425℉/Gas 7.

2 Drop the peaches into boiling water for 20 seconds, then transfer to a bowl of cold water. When cool, peel off the skins. Slice the flesh and combine with the lemon juice, sugar, cornflour and spices. Set aside.

3 Roll out the larger dough ball to 3mm/⅛in thick. Use to line a 23cm/9in pie tin. Chill. Roll out the remaining dough to 5mm/¼in thick. Cut out leaves 8cm/3in long. Mark veins. With the scraps, roll a few balls.

4 Brush the pastry base with egg glaze. Add the peaches and dot with the butter. To assemble, start from the outside edge and cover the peaches with a ring of leaves. Place a second, staggered ring above. Continue until covered. Place the balls in the centre. Brush with glaze. Bake on the hot baking sheet for 10 minutes. Lower the heat to 180℃/350℉/Gas 4 and bake for 35–40 minutes more.

Walnut and Pear Lattice Pie

For the lattice top, either weave strips of pastry or use a special pastry cutter to create a lattice effect.

Serves 6–8

450g/1lb shortcrust
 pastry
450g/2lb pears, peeled,
 cored and thinly sliced
50g/2oz/4 tbsp caster
 sugar
25g/1oz/2 tbsp plain
 flour
2.5ml/½ tsp grated
 lemon rind
25g/1oz/scant ¼ cup
 raisins or sultanas

25g/1oz/4 tbsp chopped
 walnuts
2.5ml/½ tsp ground
 cinnamon
50g/2oz/½ cup icing
 sugar
15ml/1 tbsp lemon juice
about 10ml/2 tsp cold
 water

1 Preheat the oven to 190℃/375℉/Gas 5. Roll out half of the pastry and use it to line a 23cm/9in tin that is about 5cm/2in deep.

2 Combine the pears, caster sugar, flour and lemon rind. Toss to coat the fruit. Mix in the raisins, nuts and cinnamon. Put the filling into the pastry case and spread it evenly.

3 Roll out the remaining pastry and use to make a lattice top. Bake the pie for 55 minutes or until the pastry is golden brown on top.

4 Combine the icing sugar, lemon juice and water in a bowl and stir until smooth. Remove the pie from the oven. Drizzle the glaze evenly over the top, on the pastry and filling. Leave the pie to cool in its tin on a wire rack.

Lemon Meringue Pie

A classic dish whose popularity never seems to wane.

Serves 8

225g/8oz shortcrust pastry	*25g/1oz/2 tbsp butter*
grated rind and juice of 1 large lemon	*45ml/3 tbsp cornflour*
	3 eggs, separated
250ml/8fl oz/1 cup plus 15ml/1 tbsp cold water	*pinch of salt*
	pinch of cream of tartar
115g/4oz/generous ½ cup caster sugar plus 90ml/6 tbsp extra	

1 Line a 23cm/9in pie dish with the pastry, folding under a 1cm/½in overhang. Crimp the edge and chill for 20 minutes.

2 Preheat the oven to 200°C/400°F/Gas 6. Prick the pastry case base, line with greaseproof paper and fill with baking beans. Bake for 12 minutes. Remove the paper and beans and bake until golden, 6–8 minutes more.

3 In a saucepan, combine the lemon rind and juice with 250ml/8fl oz/1 cup of the water, 115g/4oz/generous ½ cup of the sugar, and the butter. Bring to the boil.

4 Meanwhile, dissolve the cornflour in the remaining water. Add the egg yolks. Beat into the lemon mixture, return to the boil and whisk until thick, about 5 minutes. Cover the surface with greaseproof paper and leave to cool.

5 For the meringue, beat the egg whites with the salt and cream of tartar until stiffly peaking. Add the remaining sugar and beat until glossy.

6 Spoon the lemon mixture into the pastry case. Spoon the meringue on top, sealing it with the pastry rim. Bake until golden, 12–15 minutes.

Blueberry Pie

Serve this tangy blueberry pie with crème fraîche or double cream.

Serves 6–8

450g/1lb shortcrust pastry	*5ml/1 tsp grated orange rind*
500g/1¼lb/5 cups blueberries	*1.5ml/¼ tsp grated nutmeg*
165g/5½oz/generous ⅔ cup caster sugar	*30ml/2 tbsp orange juice*
45ml/3 tbsp plain flour	*5ml/1 tsp lemon juice*

1 Preheat the oven to 190°C/375°F/Gas 5. On a lightly floured surface, roll out half of the pastry and use it to line a 23cm/9in pie tin that is 5cm/2in deep.

2 Combine the blueberries, 150g/5oz/¾cup of the sugar, the flour, orange rind and nutmeg. Toss the mixture gently to coat all the fruit.

3 Pour the blueberry mixture into the pastry case and spread evenly. Sprinkle over the citrus juices.

4 Roll out the remaining pastry and cover the pie. Cut out small decorative shapes from the top. Use to decorate the pastry, and finish the edge.

5 Brush the top with water and sprinkle with the remaining caster sugar. Bake for 45 minutes, or until the pastry is golden brown. Serve warm or at room temperature.

Creamy Banana Pie

Do not prepare the topping for this pie too soon before serving or the banana slices will discolour.

Serves 6

200g/7oz/2¼ cups ginger
  biscuits, finely
  crushed
65g/2½oz/5 tbsp butter
  or margarine, melted
2.5ml/½ tsp grated
  nutmeg or ground
  cinnamon
175g/6oz/1 ripe banana,
  mashed
350g/12oz/1½ cups
  cream cheese, at room
  temperature

50ml/generous 3 tbsp
  thick natural yogurt
  or soured cream
45ml/3 tbsp dark rum or
  5ml/1 tsp vanilla
  essence

For the topping
250ml/8fl oz/1 cup
  whipping cream
3 – 4 bananas

1 Preheat the oven to 190°C/375°F/Gas 5. For the crust, combine the crushed biscuits, butter or margarine and spice. Mix thoroughly with a wooden spoon.

2 Press the biscuit mixture into a 23cm/9in pie dish, building up thick sides with a neat edge. Bake for 5 minutes, then leave to cool.

3 Beat the mashed bananas with the cream cheese. Fold in the yogurt or soured cream and rum or vanilla. Spread the filling in the biscuit case. Chill for at least 4 hours or preferably overnight.

4 For the topping, whip the cream until soft peaks form. Spread on the pie filling. Slice the bananas and arrange on top in a decorative pattern.

Red Berry Sponge Tart

When soft berry fruits are in season, serve this delicious tart warm with scoops of vanilla ice cream.

Serves 4

450g/1lb/4 cups soft
  berry fruits, such as
  raspberries, black-
  berries, blackcurrants,
  redcurrants,
  strawberries and
  blueberries
2 eggs

50g/2oz/¼ cup caster
  sugar, plus extra to
  taste (optional)
15ml/1 tbsp flour
75g/3oz/¾ cup ground
  almonds
vanilla ice cream, to
  serve

1 Preheat the oven to 190°C/375°F/Gas 5. Grease and line a 23cm/9in pie tin with greaseproof paper. Scatter the fruit in the base of the tin with a little sugar if the fruits are tart.

2 Beat the eggs and sugar together for about 3 – 4 minutes, or until they leave a thick trail across the surface. Combine the flour and almonds, then fold into the egg mixture with a palette knife, retaining as much air as possible.

3 Spread the mixture on top of the fruit base, bake in the preheated oven for 15 minutes, then turn out on to a serving plate .

De Luxe Mincemeat Tart

Serves 8

225g/8oz/2 cups plain
  flour
10ml/2 tsp ground
  cinnamon
50g/2oz/½ cup walnuts,
  finely ground
115g/4oz/½ cup butter
50g/2oz/4 tbsp caster
  sugar, plus extra for
  dusting
1 egg
2 drops vanilla essence
15ml/1 tbsp cold water

For the mincemeat

2 eating apples, peeled,
  cored and grated
225g/8oz/generous
  1½ cups raisins

115g/4oz/½ cup dried
  apricots, chopped
115g/4oz/½ cup ready-
  to-eat dried figs or
  prunes, chopped
225g/8oz green grapes,
  halved and seeded
50g/2oz/½ cup chopped
  almonds
finely grated rind of
  1 lemon
30ml/2 tbsp lemon juice
30ml/2 tbsp brandy or
  port
1.5ml/¼ tsp mixed spice
115g/4oz/generous ½ cup
  soft light brown sugar
25g/1oz/2 tbsp butter,
  melted

1 Process the flour, cinnamon, nuts and butter in a food processor or blender to make fine crumbs. Turn into a bowl and stir in the sugar. Beat the egg with the vanilla and water and stir into the dry ingredients. Form a soft dough, knead until smooth, wrap and chill for 30 minutes.

2 Mix the mincemeat ingredients together. Use two-thirds of the pastry to line a 23cm/9in, loose-based flan tin. Push the pastry well into the edges, then trim. Fill with the mincemeat.

3 Roll out the remaining pastry and cut into 1cm/½in strips. Arrange the strips in a lattice over the top of the pastry, wet the joins and press them together. Chill for 30 minutes.

4 Preheat a baking sheet in the oven at 190°C/375°F/Gas 5. Brush the pastry with water and dust with caster sugar. Bake the tart on the baking sheet for 30–40 minutes. Cool in the tin on a wire rack for 15 minutes. Then remove the tin.

Crunchy Apple and Almond Flan

Don't put sugar with the apples as this produces too much liquid. The sweetness is in the pastry and topping.

Serves 8

75g/3oz/6 tbsp butter
175g/6oz/1½ cups plain
  flour
25g/1oz/4 tbsp ground
  almonds
25g/1oz/2 tbsp caster
  sugar
1 egg yolk
15ml/1 tbsp cold water
1.5ml/¼ tsp almond
  essence
675g/1½lb cooking apples
25g/1oz/2 tbsp raisins

For the topping

115g/4oz/1 cup plain
  flour
1.5ml/¼ tsp ground
  mixed spice
50g/2oz/4 tbsp butter,
  cut in small cubes
50g/2oz/4 tbsp demerara
  sugar
50g/2oz/½ cup flaked
  almonds

1 To make the pastry, rub the butter into the flour until it resembles breadcrumbs. Stir in the almonds and sugar. Whisk the egg yolk, water and almond essence together and mix into the dry ingredients to form a soft dough. Knead until smooth, wrap, and leave to rest for 20 minutes.

2 For the topping, sift the flour and spice into a bowl and rub in the butter. Stir in the sugar and almonds. Roll out the pastry and use to line a 23cm/9in loose-based flan tin. Trim the top and chill for 15 minutes.

3 Preheat a baking sheet in the oven at 190°C/375°F/Gas 5. Peel, core and slice the apples thinly. Arrange in the flan in overlapping, concentric circles, doming the centre. Sprinkle with raisins.

4 Cover with the topping mixture, pressing it on lightly. Bake on the hot baking sheet for 25–30 minutes, or until the top is golden brown and the apples are tender (test them with a fine skewer). Leave the flan to cool in the tin for 10 minutes before serving.

Rhubarb and Cherry Pie

The unusual partnership of rhubarb and cherries works well in this pie.

Serves 8

450g/1lb rhubarb, cut
  into 2.5cm/1in pieces
450g/1lb canned stoned
  tart red or black
  cherries, drained
275g/10oz/scant 1½ cups
  caster sugar
45ml/3 tbsp quick-
  cooking tapioca

For the pastry
275g/10oz/2½ cups plain
  flour
5ml/1 tsp salt
75g/3oz/6 tbsp cold
  butter, cut in pieces
50g/2oz/4 tbsp cold
  vegetable fat or lard,
  cut in pieces
50–120ml/2–4fl oz/
  ¼–½ cup iced water
milk, for glazing

1 For the pastry, sift the flour and salt into a bowl. Add the butter and fat and rub in until the mixture resembles coarse breadcrumbs. Stir in enough water to bind. Form into two balls, wrap and chill for 20 minutes.

2 Preheat a baking sheet in the oven at 200°C/400°F/Gas 6. Roll out one pastry ball and use to line a 23cm/9in pie dish, leaving a 1cm/½in overhang.

3 Mix together the filling ingredients and spoon into the pastry case.

4 Roll out the remaining pastry, cut out four leaf shapes, and use to cover the pie leaving a 2cm/¾in overhang. Fold this under the pastry base and flute. Roll small balls from the scraps, mark veins in the leaves and use to decorate the pie.

5 Glaze the top and bake on the baking sheet until golden, 40–50 minutes.

Festive Apple Pie

Serves 8

900g/2lb cooking apples
15g/½oz/2 tbsp plain
  flour
115g/4oz/generous ½ cup
  caster sugar
25ml/1½ tbsp fresh
  lemon juice
2.5ml/½ tsp ground
  cinnamon
2.5ml/½ tsp mixed spice
1.5ml/¼ tsp ground
  ginger
1.5ml/¼ tsp grated
  nutmeg
1.5ml/¼ tsp salt

50g/2oz/4 tbsp butter,
  diced

For the pastry
275g/10oz/2½ cups plain
  flour
5ml/1 tsp salt
75g/3oz/6 tbsp cold
  butter, cut in pieces
50g/2oz/4 tbsp cold
  vegetable fat or lard,
  cut in pieces
50–120ml/2–
  4fl oz/¼–½ cup iced
  water

1 For the pastry, sift the flour and salt into a bowl. Add the butter and fat, and rub in until the mixture resembles coarse breadcrumbs. Stir in just enough water to bind. Form two balls, wrap and chill for 20 minutes.

2 Roll out one ball and use to line a 23cm/9in pie dish. Preheat a baking sheet in the oven at 220°C/425°F/Gas 7.

3 Peel, core and slice the apples. Toss with the flour, sugar, lemon juice, spices and salt. Spoon into the pastry case and dot with butter.

4 Roll out the remaining pastry. Place on top of the pie and trim to leave a 2cm/¾in overhang. Fold this under the pastry base and press to seal. Crimp the edge. Form the scraps into leaf shapes and balls. Arrange on the pie and cut steam vents.

5 Bake on the baking sheet for 10 minutes. Reduce the heat to 180°C/350°F/Gas 4 and bake for 40 minutes, until golden.

Black Bottom Pie

Serves 8

10ml/2 tsp gelatine
45ml/3 tbsp cold water
2 eggs, separated
150g/5oz/¾ cup caster
  sugar
15g/½oz/2 tbsp cornflour
2.5ml/½ tsp salt
475ml/16fl oz/2 cups
  milk
50g/2oz plain chocolate,
  finely chopped

30ml/2 tbsp rum
1.5ml/¼ tsp cream of
  tartar
chocolate curls, to
  decorate

For the crust
175g/6oz/2 cups
  gingernuts, crushed
65g/2½oz/5 tbsp butter,
  melted

1 Preheat the oven to 180°C/350°F/Gas 4. Mix the crushed gingernuts and melted butter. Press evenly over the base and side of a 23cm/9in pie plate. Bake for 6 minutes. Sprinkle the gelatine over the water and leave to soften.

2 Beat the egg yolks in a large mixing bowl and set aside. In a saucepan, combine half the sugar, the cornflour and salt. Gradually stir in the milk. Boil for 1 minute, stirring constantly. Whisk the hot milk mixture into the yolks, pour back into the saucepan and return to the boil, whisking. Cook for 1 minute, still whisking. Remove from the heat.

3 Pour 225g/8oz of the custard mixture into a bowl. Add the chopped chocolate and stir until melted. Stir in half the rum and pour into the pie crust. Whisk the softened gelatine into the plain custard until dissolved, then stir in the remaining rum. Set the pan in cold water to reach room temperature.

4 Beat the egg whites and cream of tartar until they peak stiffly. Add the remaining sugar gradually, beating thoroughly after each addition. Fold the custard into the egg whites, then spoon over the chocolate mixture in the pie crust. Chill until set, about 2 hours. Decorate with chocolate curls.

Pumpkin Pie

A North American classic, this pie is traditionally served at Thanksgiving.

Serves 8

40g/1½oz/scant ½ cup
  pecan nuts, chopped
250g/9oz puréed
  pumpkin
475ml/16fl oz/2 cups
  single cream
130g/4½oz/¾ cup light
  brown sugar
1.5ml/¼ tsp salt
5ml/1 tsp ground
  cinnamon
2.5ml/½ tsp ground
  ginger

1.5ml/¼ tsp ground
  cloves
1.5ml/¼ tsp grated
  nutmeg
2 eggs

For the pastry
165g/5½oz/1⅓ cups plain
  flour
2.5ml/½ tsp salt
115g/4oz/½ cup lard or
  vegetable fat
30–45ml/2–3 tbsp iced
  water

1 Preheat the oven to 220°C/425°F/Gas 7. For the pastry, sift the flour and salt into a mixing bowl. Rub in the fat until the mixture resembles coarse breadcrumbs. Sprinkle in enough water to form the mixture into a ball.

2 Roll out the pastry to a 5mm/¼in thickness. Use to line a 23cm/9in pie tin. Trim and flute the edge. Sprinkle the chopped pecan nuts over the base of the case.

3 Beat together the pumpkin, cream, sugar, salt, spices and eggs. Pour the pumpkin mixture into the pastry case. Bake for 10 minutes, then reduce the heat to 180°C/350°F/Gas 4 and continue baking until the filling is set, about 45 minutes. Leave the pie to cool in the tin, set on a wire rack.

Chocolate Nut Tart

This is a sophisticated tart – strictly for grown-ups!

Serves 6–8

*225g/8oz sweet
    shortcrust pastry
200g/7oz/1¼ cups dry
    amaretti biscuits
90g/3½oz/⅔ cup blanched
    almonds
50g/2oz/½ cup blanched
    hazelnuts*

*45ml/3 tbsp sugar
200g/7oz plain cooking
    chocolate
45ml/3 tbsp milk
50g/2oz/4 tbsp butter
45ml/3 tbsp amaretto
    liqueur or brandy
30ml/2 tbsp single cream*

1 Grease a shallow loose-based 25cm/10in tart tin. Roll out the pastry and use to line the tin. Trim the edge, prick the base with a fork and chill for 30 minutes.

2 Grind the amaretti biscuits in a blender or food processor. Tip into a mixing bowl. Set eight whole almonds aside and place the rest in the food processor or blender with the hazelnuts and sugar. Grind to a medium texture. Add the nuts to the amaretti, and mix well.

3 Preheat the oven to 190°C/375°F/Gas 5. In the top of a double boiler, melt the chocolate with the milk and butter. Stir until smooth.

4 Pour the chocolate mixture into the dry ingredients, and mix well. Add the liqueur or brandy and cream.

5 Spread the filling evenly in the pastry case. Bake for 35 minutes, or until the crust is golden brown and the filling has puffed up and is beginning to darken. Allow to cool to room temperature. Split the reserved almonds in half and use to decorate the tart.

Pecan Nut Tartlets

These delightful individual tartlets make an elegant dinner-party dessert.

Makes 6 10cm/4in tartlets

*450g/1lb shortcrust
    pastry
175g/6oz/1 cup pecan
    nut halves
3 eggs, beaten
25g/1oz/2 tbsp butter,
    melted*

*275g/10oz/1¼ cups
    golden syrup
2.5ml/½ tsp vanilla
    essence
115g/4oz/generous ½ cup
    caster sugar
15ml/1 tbsp plain flour*

1 Preheat the oven to 180°C/350°F/Gas 4. Roll out the pastry and use to line 6 10cm/4in tartlet tins. Divide the pecan nut halves between the pastry cases.

2 Combine the eggs with the butter, and add the golden syrup and vanilla essence. Sift over the caster sugar and flour, and blend. Fill the pastry cases with the mixture and leave until the nuts rise to the surface.

3 Bake for 35–40 minutes, until a skewer inserted in the centre comes out clean. Cool in the tins for 15 minutes, then turn out on to a wire rack.

Pear and Hazelnut Flan

A delicious flan for Sunday lunch. Grind the hazelnuts yourself if you prefer, or use ground almonds instead.

Serves 6–8

115g/4oz/1 cup plain
  flour
115g/4oz/¾ cup
  wholemeal flour
115g/4oz/½ cup
  sunflower margarine
45ml/3 tbsp cold water

5ml/1 tsp vanilla essence
50g/2oz/4 tbsp caster
  sugar
50g/2oz/4 tbsp butter,
  softened
2 eggs, beaten
45ml/3 tbsp raspberry
  jam
400g/14oz can pears in
  natural juice
few chopped hazelnuts, to
  decorate

For the filling

50g/2oz/½ cup self-
  raising flour
115g/4oz/1 cup ground
  · hazelnuts

1 For the pastry, stir the flours together, then rub in the margarine until the mixture resembles fine breadcrumbs. Mix to a firm dough with the water.

2 Roll out the dough and use to line a 23–25cm/9–10in flan tin, pressing it up the sides after trimming, so the pastry sits a little above the tin. Prick the base, line with greaseproof paper and fill with baking beans. Chill for 30 minutes.

3 Preheat the oven to 200°C/400°F/Gas 6. Place the flan tin on a baking sheet and bake blind for 20 minutes. Remove the paper and beans after 15 minutes.

4 Beat all the filling ingredients together except for the jam and pears. If too thick, stir in some of the pear juice. Reduce the oven temperature to 180°C/350°F/Gas 4. Spread the jam on the pastry case and spoon over the filling.

5 Drain the pears and arrange them, cut-side down, in the filling. Scatter over the nuts. Bake for 30 minutes until risen, firm and golden brown.

Latticed Peaches

This elegant dessert may be prepared using canned peach halves when fresh peaches are out of season.

Serves 6
For the pastry

115g/4oz/1 cup plain
  flour
45ml/3 tbsp butter or
  sunflower margarine
45ml/3 tbsp natural
  yogurt
30ml/2 tbsp orange juice
milk, to glaze

45ml/3 tbsp ground
  almonds
30ml/2 tbsp natural
  yogurt
finely grated rind of
  1 small orange
1.5ml/¼ tsp almond
  essence

For the sauce

1 ripe peach
45ml/3 tbsp orange juice

For the filling

3 ripe peaches

1 Lightly grease a baking sheet. Sift the flour into a bowl and rub in the butter or margarine. Stir in the yogurt and orange juice to make a firm dough. Roll out half the pastry thinly and stamp out six rounds with a 7.5cm/3in biscuit cutter.

2 Skin the peaches, halve and remove the stones. Mix together the almonds, yogurt, orange rind and almond essence. Spoon into the hollows of each peach half and place, cut-side down, on the pastry rounds.

3 Roll out the remaining pastry thinly and cut into thin strips. Arrange the strips over the peaches to form a lattice, brushing with milk to secure firmly. Trim the ends. Chill for 30 minutes. Preheat the oven to 200°C/400°F/ Gas 6. Brush with milk and bake for 15–18 minutes, until golden brown.

4 For the sauce, skin the peach and halve it to remove the stone. Place the flesh in a food processor or blender, with the orange juice, and purée until smooth. Serve the peaches hot, with the peach sauce spooned around.

Surprise Fruit Tarts

These delicious and simple little tarts are the perfect summer treat.

Serves 6

4 large or 8 small sheets
    frozen filo pastry,
    thawed
65g/2½oz/5 tbsp butter
    or margarine, melted
250ml/8fl oz/1 cup
    whipping cream
45ml/3 tbsp strawberry
    jam
15ml/1 tbsp Cointreau or
    other orange-flavour
    liqueur
115g/4oz/1 cup seedless
    black grapes, halved

115g/4oz/1 cup seedless
    white grapes, halved
150g/5oz fresh pineapple,
    cubed, or drained
    canned pineapple
    chunks
115g/4oz/¾ cup
    raspberries
30ml/2 tbsp icing sugar
6 sprigs fresh mint, to
    decorate

1   Preheat the oven to 180°C/350°F/Gas 4. Grease six cups of a bun tray. Stack the filo sheets and cut with a sharp knife or scissors into 24 squares 11cm/4½in.

2   Lay four squares of pastry in each of the six greased cups. Press the pastry firmly into the cups, rotating slightly to make star-shaped baskets. Brush the pastry baskets lightly with butter or margarine. Bake until the pastry is crisp and golden, 5–7 minutes. Cool on a wire rack.

3   In a bowl, lightly whip the cream until soft peaks form. Gently fold the strawberry jam and Cointreau into the cream.

4   Just before serving, spoon a little of the cream mixture into each pastry basket. Top with the fruit. Sprinkle with icing sugar and decorate each basket with a small sprig of mint.

Truffle Filo Tarts

The cups can be prepared a day ahead and stored in an air-tight container.

Makes 24 cups

3–6 sheets fresh or
    frozen (thawed) filo
    pastry, depending on
    size
45g/1½oz/3 tbsp unsalted
    butter, melted
sugar, for sprinkling
lemon rind, to decorate

Truffle mixture
250ml/8fl oz/1 cup
    double cream
225g/8oz bittersweet or
    semi-sweet chocolate,
    chopped
50g/2oz/4 tbsp unsalted
    butter, cut into pieces
30ml/2 tbsp brandy

1   Prepare the truffle mixture. In a saucepan over medium heat, bring the cream to the boil. Remove from the heat and add the chocolate, stirring until melted. Beat in the butter and add the brandy. Sieve into a bowl and chill for 1 hour.

2   Preheat the oven to 200°C/400°F/Gas 6. Grease a bun tray with 24 cups, each 4cm/1½in. Cut each filo sheet into 6cm/2½in squares. Cover with a damp dish towel. Keeping the filo sheets covered, place one square on a work surface. Brush lightly with melted butter, turn over and brush the other side. Sprinkle with a pinch of sugar. Butter another square and place it over the first at an angle. Sprinkle with sugar. Butter a third square and place over the first two, unevenly, so the corners form an uneven edge. Press the layered square into the tray. Continue to fill the tray.

3   Bake the filo cups for 4–6 minutes, until golden. Cool for 10 minutes on a wire rack in the tray. Remove from the tray and cool completely.

4   Stir the chocolate mixture, which should be just thick enough to pipe. Spoon the mixture into a piping bag fitted with a medium star nozzle and pipe a swirl into each cup. Decorate with lemon rind.

Apple Strudel

Ready-made filo pastry makes a good substitute for paper-thin strudel pastry in this classic Austrian dish.

Serves 10–12

75g/3oz/generous ½ cup raisins
30ml/2 tbsp brandy
5 eating apples
3 large cooking apples
90g/3½oz/generous ½ cup dark brown sugar
5ml/1 tsp ground cinnamon
grated rind and juice of 1 lemon

25g/1oz/½ cup dry breadcrumbs
50g/2oz/½ cup chopped pecan nuts or walnuts
12 sheets frozen filo pastry, thawed
175g/6oz/¾ cup butter, melted
icing sugar, for dusting

1 Soak the raisins in the brandy for 15 minutes.

2 Peel, core and thinly slice the apples. Combine with the rest of the filling ingredients, reserving half the breadcrumbs.

3 Preheat the oven to 190°C/375°F/Gas 5. Grease two baking sheets. Unfold the filo pastry and cover with a dish towel. One by one, butter and stack the sheets to make a six-sheet pile.

4 Sprinkle half the reserved breadcrumbs over the last sheet and spoon half the apple mixture at the bottom edge. Roll up from this edge, Swiss roll style. Place on a baking sheet, seam-side down and fold under the ends to seal. Repeat to make a second strudel. Brush both with butter.

5 Bake in the oven for 45 minutes, cool slightly, then dust with icing sugar.

Cherry Strudel

A refreshing variation on traditional apple strudel. Serve with whipped cream, if you like.

Serves 8

65g/2½oz/1¼ cups fresh breadcrumbs
175g/6oz/¾ cup butter, melted
200g/7oz/1 cup sugar
15ml/1 tbsp ground cinnamon

5ml/1 tsp grated lemon rind
450g/1lb/2 cups sour cherries, stoned
8 sheets filo pastry
icing sugar, for dusting

1 In a frying pan, fry the breadcrumbs in 65g/2½oz/5 tbsp of the butter until golden. Set aside.

2 In a large mixing bowl, toss together the sugar, cinnamon and lemon rind. Stir in the cherries.

3 Preheat the oven to 190°C/375°F/Gas 5. Grease a baking sheet. Unfold the filo sheets. Keep the unused sheets covered with damp kitchen paper. Lift off one sheet and place on a piece of greaseproof paper. Brush the pastry with butter. Sprinkle an eighth of the breadcrumbs over the surface.

4 Lay a second sheet of filo pastry on top, brush with butter and sprinkle with breadcrumbs. Continue until you have used up all the pastry.

5 Spoon the cherry mixture at the bottom edge of the strip. Starting at the cherry-filled end, roll up the dough Swiss roll style. Use the paper to flip the strudel on to the baking sheet, seam-side down. Carefully fold under the ends to seal. Brush the top with melted butter.

6 Bake the strudel for 45 minutes. Cool slightly, then dust with a fine layer of icing sugar.

Strawberry Tart

This tart is best assembled just before serving, but you can bake the pastry case and make the filling ahead.

Serves 6

350g/12oz rough-puff or puff pastry
225g/8oz/1 cup cream cheese
grated rind of ½ orange
30ml/2 tbsp orange liqueur or juice

45–60ml/3–4 tbsp icing sugar, plus extra for dusting (optional)
450g/1lb/4 cups ripe strawberries, hulled

1 Preheat the oven to 200°C/400°F/Gas 6. Roll out the pastry to about a 3mm/⅛in thickness and use to line a 28 x 10cm/11 x 4in rectangular flan tin. Trim the edges, then chill for 30 minutes.

2 Prick the base of the pastry all over. Line with foil, fill with baking beans and bake for 15 minutes. Remove the foil and beans and bake for 10 minutes, until the pastry is browned. Gently press down on the pastry base to deflate, then leave to cool on a wire rack.

3 Beat together the cheese, orange rind, liqueur or orange juice and icing sugar to taste. Spread the cheese filling in the pastry case. Halve the strawberries and arrange them on top of the filling. Dust with icing sugar, if you like.

Alsatian Plum Tart

Fruit and custard tarts, similar to a fruit quiche, are typical in Alsace. Sometimes they have a yeast dough base instead of pastry. You can use other seasonal fruits in this tart, or a mixture of fruit.

Serves 6–8

450g/1lb ripe plums, halved and stoned
30ml/2 tbsp kirsch or plum brandy
350g/12oz shortcrust or sweet shortcrust pastry
30ml/2 tbsp seedless raspberry jam

For the custard filling
2 eggs
25g/1oz/4 tbsp icing sugar
175ml/6 fl oz/¾ cup double cream
grated rind of ½ lemon
1.5ml/¼ tsp vanilla essence

1 Preheat the oven to 200°C/400°F/Gas 6. Mix the plums with the kirsch or brandy and set aside for about 30 minutes.

2 Roll out the pastry thinly and use to line a 23cm/9in pie tin. Prick the base of the pastry case all over and line with foil. Add a layer of baking beans and bake for 15 minutes until slightly dry and set. Remove the foil and the baking beans.

3 Brush the base of the pastry case with a thin layer of jam, then bake for a further 5 minutes. Remove the pastry case from the oven and transfer to a wire rack. Reduce the oven temperature to 180°C/350°F/Gas 4.

4 To make the custard filling, beat the eggs and sugar until well combined, then beat in the cream, lemon rind, vanilla and any juice from the plums.

5 Arrange the plums, cut-side down, in the pastry case and pour over the custard mixture. Bake for about 30–35 minutes until a knife inserted in the centre comes out clean. Serve the tart warm or at room temperature.

Almond Mincemeat Tartlets

Mince Pies with Orange Pastry

Makes 36

275g/10oz/2½ cups plain
  flour
75g/3oz/¾ cup icing
  sugar
5ml/1 tsp ground
  cinnamon
175g/6oz/¾ cup butter
50g/2oz/½ cup ground
  almonds
1 egg yolk
45ml/3 tbsp milk
450g/1lb jar mincemeat
15ml/1 tbsp brandy or
  rum

For the lemon filling

115g/4oz/½ cup butter or
  margarine
115g/4oz/½ cup caster
  sugar
175g/6oz/1½ cups self-
  raising flour
2 large eggs
finely grated rind of
  1 large lemon

For the lemon icing

115g/4oz/1 cup icing
  sugar
15ml/1 tbsp lemon juice

1 Sift the flour, sugar and cinnamon into a bowl and rub in the butter until it resembles breadcrumbs. Add the ground almonds and bind with the egg yolk and milk to a soft, pliable dough. Knead until smooth, wrap and chill for 30 minutes.

2 Preheat the oven to 375°F/190°C/Gas 5. On a lightly floured surface, roll out the pastry and cut out 36 fluted rounds with a pastry cutter. Mix the mincemeat with the brandy or rum and put a small teaspoonful in the bottom of each pastry case. Chill.

3 For the lemon sponge filling, whisk the butter or margarine, sugar, flour, eggs and lemon rind together until smooth. Spoon on top of the mincemeat, dividing it evenly, and level the tops. Bake for 20–30 minutes, or until golden brown and springy to the touch. Remove and leave to cool on a wire rack.

4 For the lemon icing, sift the icing sugar and mix with the lemon juice to a smooth coating consistency. Spoon into a piping bag and drizzle a zig-zag pattern over each tart. If you're short of time, simply dust the tartlets with icing sugar.

Homemade mince pies are so much nicer than shop-bought, especially with this flavoursome pastry.

Makes 18

225g/8oz/2 cups plain
  flour
30g/1½oz/scant ⅓ cup
  icing sugar
10ml/2 tsp ground
  cinnamon
150g/5oz/generous 1 cup
  butter

grated rind of 1 orange
about 60ml/4 tbsp iced
  water
225g/8oz/1½ cups
  mincemeat
1 egg, beaten, to glaze
icing sugar, for dusting

1 Sift together the flour, icing sugar and cinnamon. Rub in the butter until it resembles fine breadcrumbs. Stir in the grated orange rind.

2 Mix to a firm dough with the water. Knead lightly, then roll out to a 5mm/¼in thickness. Using a 7cm/2½in round biscuit cutter, stamp out 18 circles, then stamp out 18 smaller 5cm/2in circles.

3 Line two bun tins with the larger circles. Place a small spoonful of mincemeat into each pastry case and top with the smaller pastry circles, pressing the edges to seal.

4 Glaze the tops with egg and leave to rest in the fridge for 30 minutes. Preheat the oven to 200°C/400°F/Gas 6.

5 Bake for 15–20 minutes, or until golden brown. Remove to wire racks. Serve just warm, dusted with icing sugar.

Glacé Fruit Pie

Use half digestive and half gingernut biscuits for the crust, if you prefer.

Serves 10

15ml/1 tbsp rum
50g/2oz/4 tbsp mixed
  glacé fruit, chopped
475ml/16fl oz/2 cups
  milk
20ml/4 tsp gelatine
90g/3½oz/½ cup sugar
2.5ml/½ tsp salt
3 eggs, separated
250ml/8fl oz/1 cup
  whipping cream,
  whipped

chocolate curls, to
  decorate

For the crust
175g/6oz/2 cups
  digestive biscuits,
  crushed
75g/2½oz/5 tbsp butter,
  melted
15ml/1 tbsp sugar

1 Mix the digestive biscuits, butter and sugar. Press evenly over the base and sides of a 23cm/9in pie plate. Chill.

2 Stir together the rum and glacé fruit. Set aside. Pour 120ml/4fl oz/½ cup of the milk into a small bowl. Sprinkle over the gelatine and leave for 5 minutes to soften.

3 In the top of a double boiler, combine 50g/2oz/4 tbsp of the sugar, the remaining milk and salt. Stir in the gelatine mixture. Cook, stirring, until the gelatine dissolves. Whisk in the egg yolks and cook, stirring, until thick enough to coat the spoon. Pour the custard over the glacé fruit mixture, set in a bowl of iced water.

4 Beat the egg whites until they peak softly. Add the remaining sugar and beat just to blend. Fold a large dollop of the egg whites into the cooled gelatine mixture. Pour into the remaining egg whites and fold together. Fold in the cream.

5 Pour into the pie crust and chill until firm. Decorate with chocolate curls.

Chocolate Chiffon Pie

As the name suggests, this is a wonderfully smooth and light-textured pie.

Serves 8

200g/7oz plain chocolate,
  chopped
250ml/8fl oz/1 cup milk
15ml/1 tbsp gelatine
90g/3½oz/1 cup sugar
2 extra-large eggs,
  separated
5ml/1 tsp vanilla essence
1.5ml/¼ tsp salt
350ml/12fl oz/1½ cups
  whipping cream,
  whipped

whipped cream and
  chocolate curls, to
  decorate

For the crust
200g/7oz/2⅓ cups
  digestive biscuits,
  crushed
75g/3oz/6 tbsp butter,
  melted

1 Place a baking sheet in the oven and preheat to 180°C/350°F/Gas 4. Mix the biscuits and butter together and press over the base and sides of a 23cm/9in pie plate. Bake for 8 minutes.

2 Grate the chocolate in a blender or food processor. Place the milk in the top of a double boiler. Sprinkle over the gelatine and leave for 5 minutes to soften.

3 In the top of a double boiler, put 40g/1½oz/6 tbsp sugar, the chocolate and egg yolks. Stir until dissolved. Add the vanilla. Place the top in a bowl of ice and stir until the mixture reaches room temperature. Remove from the ice.

4 Beat the egg whites and salt until they peak softly. Add the remaining sugar and beat just to blend. Fold a dollop of egg whites into the chocolate mixture, then pour back into the whites and fold in.

5 Fold in the cream and pour into the pie crust. Freeze until just set, about 5 minutes, then chill for 3–4 hours. Decorate with whipped cream and chocolate curls.

Chocolate Pear Tart

Chocolate and pears have a natural affinity, well used in this luxurious pudding.

Serves 8

115g/4oz plain chocolate, grated
3 large firm, ripe pears
1 egg
1 egg yolk
120ml/4fl oz/½ cup single cream
2.5ml/½ tsp vanilla essence
45ml/3 tbsp caster sugar

For the pastry
150g/5oz/1¼ cups plain flour
1.5ml/¼ tsp salt
30ml/2 tbsp sugar
115g/4oz/½ cup cold unsalted butter, cut into pieces
1 egg yolk
15ml/1 tbsp lemon juice

1   For the pastry, sift the flour and salt into a bowl. Add the sugar and butter. Rub in until the mixture resembles coarse breadcrumbs. Stir in the egg yolk and lemon juice. Form a ball, wrap, and chill for 20 minutes.

2   Preheat the oven to 200°C/400°F/Gas 6. Roll out the pastry and use to line a 25cm/10in tart dish.

3   Sprinkle the pastry case with the grated chocolate.

4   Peel, halve and core the pears. Cut in thin slices crossways, then fan out slightly. Transfer the pears to the tart using a palette knife and arrange like wheel spokes.

5   Whisk together the egg and egg yolk, cream and vanilla. Ladle over the pears and sprinkle with sugar.

6   Bake on a baking sheet for 10 minutes. Reduce the heat to 180°C/350°F/Gas 4 and cook until the custard is set and the pears begin to caramelize, about 20 minutes more. Serve while still warm.

Pear and Apple Crumble Pie

You could use just one fruit in this pie if you prefer.

Serves 8

3 firm pears
4 cooking apples
175g/6oz/scant 1 cup caster sugar
30ml/2 tbsp cornflour
1.5ml/¼ tsp salt
grated rind of 1 lemon
30ml/2 tbsp fresh lemon juice
75g/3oz/generous ½ cup raisins
75g/3oz/¾ cup plain flour

5ml/1 tsp ground cinnamon
75g/3oz/6 tbsp cold butter, cut in pieces

For the pastry
150g/5oz/1¼ cups plain flour
2.5ml/½ tsp salt
65g/2½oz/5 tbsp cold vegetable fat or lard, cut in pieces
30ml/2 tbsp iced water

1   For the pastry, sift the flour and salt into a bowl. Add the fat and rub in until the mixture resembles breadcrumbs. Stir in enough water to bind. Form into a ball, roll out, and use to line a 23cm/9in pie dish, leaving a 1cm/½in overhang. Fold this under for double thickness. Flute the edge, then chill.

2   Preheat a baking sheet at 230°C/450°F/Gas 8. Peel, core and slice the fruit. Combine in a bowl with one-third of the sugar, the cornflour, salt, lemon rind and juice, and raisins.

3   For the crumble topping, combine the remaining sugar, flour, cinnamon and butter in a bowl. Rub in until the mixture resembles coarse breadcrumbs.

4   Spoon the filling into the pastry case. Sprinkle the crumbs over the top.

5   Bake on the baking sheet for 10 minutes, then reduce the heat to 180°C/350°F/Gas 4. Cover the pie loosely with foil and bake until browned, 35–40 minutes more.

Chocolate Lemon Tart

The unusual chocolate pastry complements the lemon filling superbly in this rich tart.

Serves 8–10

245g/8¼oz/1¼ cups
   caster sugar
6 eggs
grated rind of 2 lemons
160ml/5½fl oz/generous
   ⅔ cup fresh lemon
   juice
160ml/5½fl oz/generous
   ⅔ cup whipping cream
chocolate curls, to
   decorate

For the pastry
180g/6¼oz/generous
   1½ cups plain flour
30ml/2 tbsp cocoa
   powder
25g/1oz/4 tbsp icing
   sugar
2.5ml/½ tsp salt
115g/4oz/½ cup butter or
   margarine
15ml/1 tbsp water

1 Grease a 25cm/10in tart tin. For the pastry, sift the flour, cocoa powder, icing sugar and salt into a bowl. Set aside.

2 Melt the butter and water over a low heat. Pour over the flour mixture and stir until the dough is smooth.

3 Press the dough evenly over the base and sides of the tart tin. Chill while preparing the filling.

4 Preheat a baking sheet in the oven at 190°C/375°F/Gas 5. Whisk the sugar and eggs until the sugar is dissolved. Add the lemon rind and juice and mix well. Add the cream.

5 Pour the filling into the pastry case and bake on the hot baking sheet until the filling is set, 20–25 minutes. Cool on a wire rack, then decorate with chocolate curls.

Kiwi Ricotta Cheese Tart

A delicious filling in a rich pastry case creates an elegant dinner-party dessert.

Serves 8

75g/3oz/½ cup blanched
   almonds, ground
130g/3½ oz/½ cup sugar
900g/2lb/4 cups
   ricotta cheese
250ml/8fl oz/1 cup
   whipping cream
1 egg and 3 egg yolks
15ml/1 tbsp plain flour
pinch of salt
30ml/2 tbsp rum
grated rind of 1 lemon
30ml/2 tbsp lemon juice

30ml/2 tbsp honey
5 kiwi fruit

For the pastry
150g/5oz/1¼ cups
   plain flour
15ml/1 tbsp sugar
2.5ml/½ tsp each salt and
   baking powder
75g/3oz/6 tbsp butter
1 egg yolk
45–60ml/3–4 tbsp
   whipping cream

1 For the pastry, mix the flour, sugar, salt and baking powder. Add the butter and rub in. Mix in the egg yolk and cream to bind the pastry. Wrap and chill for 30 minutes.

2 Preheat the oven to 220°C/425°F/Gas 7. On a lightly floured surface, roll out the dough to a 3mm/⅛in thickness. Use to line a 23cm/9in springform tin. Prick the pastry all over with a fork. Line with crumpled greaseproof paper and fill with dried beans. Bake for 10 minutes. Remove the paper and beans and bake for another 6–8 minutes until golden. Reduce the oven temperature to 180°C/350°F/Gas 4.

3 Mix the almonds with 15ml/1 tbsp of the sugar. Beat the ricotta until creamy then add the cream, egg, yolks, remaining sugar, flour, salt, rum, lemon rind and 30ml/2 tbsp lemon juice. Beat, add the almonds and mix. Pour into pastry case and bake for 1 hour, until golden. Cool and chill. Mix the honey and remaining lemon juice. Halve the kiwis lengthways then slice. Arrange over tart and brush with the honey glaze.

Lime Tart

Use lemons instead of limes, with yellow food colouring, if
you prefer.

Serves 8
3 large egg yolks
400g/14oz can sweetened
    condensed milk
15ml/1 tbsp grated lime
    rind
120ml/4fl oz/½ cup fresh
    lime juice
green food colouring
    (optional)

120ml/4fl oz/½ cup
    whipping cream

For the base
115g/4oz/1⅓ cups
    crushed digestive
    biscuits
65g/2½oz/5 tbsp butter
    or margarine, melted

1 Preheat the oven to 180°C/350°F/Gas 4. For the base, place
the crushed biscuits in a bowl and add the butter or
margarine. Mix to combine.

2 Press the mixture evenly over the base and sides of a
23cm/9in pie dish. Bake for 8 minutes, then cool.

3 Beat the yolks until thick. Beat in the milk, lime rind and
juice and colouring, if using. Pour into the pastry case and
chill until set, about 4 hours. To serve, whip the cream. Pipe a
lattice pattern on top, or spoon dollops around the edge.

Fruit Tartlets

You could make one large fruit tart for an elegant dessert, if
you like.

Makes 8
175ml/6fl oz/¾ cup
    redcurrant jelly
15ml/1 tbsp fresh lemon
    juice
175ml/6fl oz/¾ cup
    whipping cream
675g/1½lb fresh fruit,
    such as strawberries,
    raspberries, kiwi fruit,
    peaches, grapes or
    currants, peeled and
    sliced as necessary

For the pastry
150g/5oz/generous ½ cup
    cold butter, cut in
    pieces
65g/2½oz/scant ½ cup
    dark brown sugar
45ml/3 tbsp cocoa
    powder
200g/7oz/1¾ cups plain
    flour
1 egg white

1 For the pastry, melt the butter, brown sugar and cocoa
over a low heat. Remove from the heat and sift over the flour.
Stir, then add enough egg white to bind. Form into a ball,
wrap, and chill for 30 minutes.

2 Grease eight 8cm/3in tartlet tins. Roll out the pastry
between two sheets of greaseproof paper. Stamp out eight
10cm/4in rounds with a fluted biscuit cutter.

3 Line the tartlet tins and prick the bases with a fork. Chill
for 15 minutes. Preheat the oven to 180°C/350°F/Gas 4.

4 Bake the pastry cases until firm, 20–25 minutes. Cool, then
turn out.

5 Melt the jelly with the lemon juice. Brush over the tartlet
bases. Whip the cream and spread thinly in the tartlet cases.
Arrange the fruit on top. Brush with the jelly glaze and serve.

Chocolate Cheesecake Tart

You can use just digestive biscuits for the base of this tart, if you prefer.

Serves 8

350g/12oz/1½ cups
  cream cheese
60ml/4 tbsp whipping
  cream
225g/8oz/generous 1 cup
  caster sugar
50g/2oz/½ cup cocoa
  powder
2.5ml/½ tsp ground
  cinnamon
3 eggs

whipped cream and
  chocolate curls, to
  decorate

For the base
75g/3oz/1 cup crushed
  digestive biscuits
40g/1½oz/scant 1 cup
  crushed amaretti
  biscuits
75g/3oz/6 tbsp butter,
  melted

1 Preheat a baking sheet in the oven at 180°C/350°F/Gas 4. For the base, mix the crushed biscuits and butter in a bowl. Press the mixture over the base and sides of a 23cm/9in pie dish. Bake for 8 minutes. Leave to cool. Keep the oven on.

2 Beat the cream cheese and cream together until smooth. Beat in the sugar, cocoa and cinnamon until blended.

3 Add the eggs, one at a time, beating just enough to blend.

4 Pour into the biscuit base and bake on the baking sheet for 25–30 minutes. The filling will sink down as it cools. Decorate with whipped cream and chocolate curls.

Frozen Strawberry Tart

For a frozen raspberry tart, use raspberries in place of the strawberries.

Serves 8

225g/8oz/1 cup cream
  cheese
250ml/8fl oz/1 cup
  soured cream
500g/1¼lb/5 cups frozen
  strawberries, thawed
  and sliced

For the base
115g/4oz/1⅓ cups
  crushed digestive
  biscuits
15ml/1 tbsp caster sugar
65g/2½oz/5 tbsp butter,
  melted

1 For the base, mix together the biscuits, sugar and butter. Press the mixture over the base and sides of a 23cm/9in pie dish. Freeze until firm.

2 Blend together the cream cheese and soured cream. Reserve 90ml/6 tbsp of the strawberries. Add the rest to the cream cheese mixture.

3 Pour the filling into the biscuit base and freeze until firm, about 6–8 hours. To serve, spoon some of the reserved strawberries on top.

Treacle Tart

A very rich dessert, popular with all the family.

Serves 4–6

175ml/6fl oz/¾ cup
  golden syrup
75g/3oz/1½ cups fresh
  white breadcrumbs
grated rind of 1 lemon
30ml/2 tbsp fresh lemon
  juice

For the pastry

175g/6oz/1½ cups plain
  flour
2.5ml/½ tsp salt
75g/3oz/6 tbsp cold
  butter, cut in pieces
40g/1½oz/3 tbsp cold
  margarine, cut in
  pieces
45–60ml/3–4 tbsp iced
  water

1 For the pastry, sift together the flour and salt, add the fats and rub in until the mixture resembles coarse breadcrumbs. Stir in enough water to bind. Form into a ball, wrap and chill for 20 minutes.

2 Roll out the pastry and use to line a 20cm/8in pie dish. Chill for 20 minutes. Reserve the pastry trimmings.

3 Preheat a baking sheet in the oven at 200°C/400°F/Gas 6. In a saucepan, warm the syrup until thin and runny. Stir in the breadcrumbs and lemon rind. Leave for 10 minutes, then stir in the lemon juice. Spread in the pastry case.

4 Roll out the pastry trimmings and cut into 12 thin strips. Lay six strips on the filling, then lay the other six at an angle over them to form a lattice.

5 Bake on the baking sheet for 10 minutes. Lower the heat to 190°C/375°F/Gas 5. Bake until golden, about 15 minutes more. Serve warm or cold.

Almond Syrup Tart

Serves 6

75g/3oz/1½ cups fresh
  white breadcrumbs
225g/8oz/1 cup golden
  syrup
finely grated rind of
  ½ lemon
10ml/2 tsp lemon juice
23cm/9in pastry case,
  made with basic, nut
  or rich shortcrust
  pastry

25g/1oz/4 tbsp flaked
  almonds
milk, to glaze (optional)
cream, custard, ice
  cream, to serve

1 Preheat the oven to 200°C/400°F/Gas 6. Combine the breadcrumbs with the syrup and the lemon rind and juice.

2 Spoon into the pastry case and spread out evenly. Sprinkle the flaked almonds evenly over the top.

3 Brush the pastry with milk to glaze, if you like. Bake for 25–30 minutes, until the pastry and filling are golden brown.

4 Transfer to a wire rack to cool. Serve warm or cold, with cream, custard or ice cream.

Tarte Tatin

A special *tarte tatin* tin is ideal, but an ovenproof frying pan can be used quite successfully.

Serves 8–10

225g/½lb puff or shortcrust pastry
10–12 large Golden Delicious apples
115g/4oz/½ cup butter, cut into pieces
115g/4oz/½ cup caster sugar
2.5ml/½ tsp ground cinnamon
crème fraîche or whipped cream, to serve

1 On a lightly floured surface, roll out the pastry to a 28cm/11in round less than 5mm/¼in thick. Transfer to a lightly floured baking sheet and chill.

2 Peel, halve and core the apples, sprinkle with lemon juice.

3 In a 25cm/10in *tarte tatin* tin, cook the butter, sugar and cinnamon until the butter has melted and the sugar has dissolved. Cook for 6–8 minutes until the mixture is a medium caramel colour. Remove from the heat and arrange the apple halves, standing on their edges, in the tin.

4 Return the tin to the heat and simmer for 20–25 minutes until the apples are tender and coloured. Remove from the heat and cool slightly.

5 Preheat the oven to 230°C/450°F/Gas 8. Place the pastry over the apples and tuck the edges inside the tin around the apples. Pierce the pastry in two or three places, then bake for 25–30 minutes until the pastry is golden and the filling is bubbling. Cool in the tin for 10–15 minutes.

6 To serve, run a sharp knife around the edge of the tin to loosen the pastry. Cover with a serving plate and carefully invert the tin and plate together. It is best to do this over a sink in case any caramel drips. Lift off the tin and loosen any apples that stick with a palette knife. Serve the tart warm with crème fraîche or whipped cream.

Rich Chocolate Pie

A delicious pie generously decorated with chocolate curls.

Serves 8

75g/3oz plain chocolate
50g/2oz/4 tbsp butter or margarine
45ml/3 tbsp golden syrup
3 eggs, beaten
150g/5oz/⅔ cup caster sugar
5ml/1 tsp vanilla essence
115g/4oz milk chocolate
475ml/16fl oz/2 cups whipping cream

For the pastry
165g/5½oz/1⅓ cups plain flour
2.5ml/½ tsp salt
115g/4oz/½ cup lard or vegetable fat
30–45ml/2–3 tbsp iced water

1 Preheat the oven to 220°C/425°F/Gas 7. For the pastry, sift the flour and salt into a bowl. Rub in the fat until the mixture resembles coarse breadcrumbs. Add water until the pastry forms a ball.

2 Roll out the pastry and use to line a 20–23cm/8–9in pie tin. Flute the edge. Prick the base and sides of the pastry case with a fork. Bake until lightly browned, 10–15 minutes. Cool in the tin on a wire rack.

3 Reduce the oven temperature to 180°C/350°F/Gas 4. In the top of a double boiler, melt the plain chocolate, the butter or margarine and syrup. Remove from the heat and stir in the eggs, sugar and vanilla. Pour the chocolate mixture into the pastry case. Bake until the filling is set, 35–40 minutes. Cool in the tin on a wire rack.

4 For the decoration, use the heat of your hands to soften the milk chocolate slightly. Use a swivel-headed vegetable peeler to shave off short, wide curls. Chill until needed.

5 Before serving, lightly whip the cream until soft peaks form. Spread the cream over the surface of the chocolate filling. Decorate with the milk chocolate curls.

Red Berry Tart with Lemon Cream

This flan is best filled just before serving so the pastry remains mouth-wateringly crisp.

Serves 6–8

150g/5oz/1¼ cups plain
  flour
25g/1oz/4 tbsp cornflour
30g/1½oz/scant ⅓ cup
  icing sugar
90g/3½oz/7 tbsp butter
5ml/1 tsp vanilla essence
2 egg yolks, beaten

For the filling
200g/7oz/scant 1 cup
  cream cheese, softened
45ml/3 tbsp lemon curd
grated rind and juice of
  1 lemon
icing sugar, to taste
  (optional)
225g/8oz/2 cups mixed
  red berry fruits
45ml/3 tbsp redcurrant
  jelly

1 Sift the flour, cornflour and icing sugar together. Rub in the butter until the mixture resembles fine breadcrumbs.

2 Beat the vanilla into the egg yolks, then stir into the flour mixture to make a firm dough. Add cold water if necessary.

3 Roll out the pastry and use it to line a 23cm/9in round flan tin. Trim the edges. Prick the base and leave to rest in the fridge for 30 minutes.

4 Preheat the oven to 200°C/400°F/Gas 6. Line the flan with greaseproof paper and fill with baking beans. Place on a baking sheet and bake for 20 minutes, removing the paper and beans after 15 minutes. Leave to cool, then remove the pastry case from the flan tin.

5 Cream the cheese, lemon curd and lemon rind and juice, adding icing sugar if you wish. Spread the mixture into the base of the flan. Top with the fruits. Warm the redcurrant jelly and trickle over the fruits just before serving.

Peach Tart with Almond Cream

Serves 8–10

4 large ripe peaches,
  peeled
115g/4oz blanched
  almonds
15g/½oz/2 tbsp plain
  flour
100g/3¾oz/scant ¼cup
  unsalted butter
115g/4oz/1 cup, plus
  2 tbsp caster sugar
1 egg, plus 1 egg yolk
1.5ml/¼ tsp vanilla
  essence, or
10ml/2 tsp rum

For the pastry
190g/6¼oz/generous
  1½ cups plain flour
2.5ml/½ tsp salt
100g/3¾oz/scant ¼cup
  cold unsalted butter,
  diced
1 egg yolk
10–45ml/2–3 tbsp iced
  water

1 Sift the flour and salt into a bowl. Rub in the butter until the mixture resembles coarse breadcrumbs. Stir in the egg yolk and enough water to bind the pastry. Gather into a ball, wrap and chill for at least 20 minutes. Preheat a baking sheet in the centre of a 200°C/400°F/Gas 6 oven.

2 Roll out the pastry 3mm/⅛in thick. Transfer to a 25cm/10in pie dish. Trim the edge, prick the base and chill.

3 Grind the almonds with the flour. With an electric mixer, cream the butter and 115g/4oz/scant ¾cup of the sugar until light and fluffy. Gradually beat in the egg and yolk. Stir in the almonds and vanilla or rum. Spread in the pastry case.

4 Halve the peaches and remove the stones. Cut crossways in thin slices and arrange on top of the almond cream like the spokes of a wheel. Keep the slices of each peach-half together. Fan out by pressing down gently at a slight angle.

5 Bake until the pastry browns, 10–15 minutes. Lower the heat to 180°C/350°F/Gas 4 and bake until the almond cream sets, about 15 minutes more. 10 minutes before the end of the cooking time, sprinkle with the remaining sugar.

Pear and Almond Cream Tart

This tart is equally successful made with nectarines, peaches, apricots or apples.

Serves 6

350g/12oz shortcrust or
  sweet shortcrust
  pastry
3 firm pears
lemon juice
15ml/1 tbsp peach
  brandy or cold water
60ml/4 tbsp peach jam,
  sieved

For the filling
90g/3½oz/generous
  ½ cup blanched whole
  almonds
50g/2oz/4 tbsp caster
  sugar
65g/2½oz/5 tbsp butter
1 egg, plus 1 egg white
few drops almond essence

1 Roll out the pastry and use to line a 23cm/9in flan tin. Chill. For the filling, put the almonds and sugar in a food processor or blender and pulse until finely ground but not pasty. Add the butter and process until creamy, then add the egg, egg white and almond essence and mix well.

2 Preheat a baking sheet in the oven at 190℃/375℉/Gas 5. Peel the pears, halve them, remove the cores and rub with lemon juice. Put the pear halves, cut-side down, on a board and slice thinly crossways, keeping the slices together.

3 Pour the filling into the pastry case. Slide a palette knife under one pear half and press the top to fan out the slices. Transfer to the tart, placing the fruit on the filling like spokes of a wheel.

4 Bake the tart on the baking sheet for 50–55 minutes, until the filling is set and well browned. Cool on a wire rack.

5 Heat the brandy or water with the jam. Brush over the top of the hot tart to glaze. Serve at room temperature.

Lemon Tart

This tart, a classic of France, has a refreshing tangy flavour.

Serves 8–10

350g/12oz shortcrust or
  sweet shortcrust
  pastry
grated rind of 2–
  3 lemons
150ml/¼ pint/⅔ cup
  freshly squeezed lemon
  juice

100g/3½oz/½ cup caster
  sugar
60ml/4 tbsp crème
  fraîche or double
  cream
4 eggs, plus 3 egg yolks
icing sugar, for dusting

1 Preheat the oven to 190℃/375℉/Gas 5. Roll out the pastry and use to line a 23cm/9in flan tin. Prick the base, line with foil and fill with baking beans. Bake for 15 minutes, or until the edges are dry. Remove the foil and beans, and bake for a further 5–7 minutes, until golden.

2 Beat together the lemon rind, juice and sugar, then gradually add the crème fraîche or double cream and beat until well blended. Beat in the eggs, one at a time, then beat in the egg yolks.

3 Pour the filling into the baked pastry case. Bake for about 15–20 minutes, until the filling is set. If the pastry begins to brown too much, cover the edges with foil. Leave to cool. Dust with icing sugar before serving.

Maple Walnut Tart

Makes sure you use 100 per cent pure maple syrup in this decadent tart.

Serves 8

3 eggs
1.5ml/¼ tsp salt
50g/2oz/4 tbsp caster
  sugar
50g/2oz/4 tbsp butter,
  melted
250ml/8fl oz/1 cup pure
  maple syrup
115g/4oz/1 cup chopped
  walnuts
whipped cream, to
  decorate

For the pastry

65g/2½oz/9 tbsp plain
  flour
65g/2½oz/½ cup
  wholemeal flour
1.5ml/¼ tsp salt
50g/2oz/4 tbsp cold
  butter, cut in pieces
40g/1½oz/3 tbsp cold
  vegetable fat or lard,
  cut in pieces
1 egg yolk

1 For the pastry, mix the flours and salt in a bowl. Add the fats and rub in until the mixture resembles coarse breadcrumbs. Stir in the egg yolk and 30–45ml/2–3 tbsp iced water to bind. Form into a ball, wrap and chill for 20 minutes.

2 Preheat the oven to 220°C/425°F/Gas 7. Roll out the pastry and use to line a 23cm/9in pie dish. Use the trimmings to stamp out heart shapes. Arrange on the pastry case rim with a little water.

3 Prick the pastry base, line with greaseproof paper and fill with baking beans. Bake for 10 minutes. Remove the paper and beans and bake until golden, 3–6 minutes more.

4 Whisk together the eggs, salt and sugar. Stir in the butter and maple syrup. Set the pastry case on a baking sheet. Pour in the filling, then sprinkle with the nuts.

5 Bake until just set, about 35 minutes. Cool on a wire rack. Decorate with piped whipped cream.

Pecan Tart

Serve this tart warm, accompanied by ice cream or whipped cream, if you wish.

Serves 8

3 eggs
pinch of salt
200g/7oz/generous 1 cup
  dark brown sugar
120ml/4fl oz/½ cup
  golden syrup
30ml/2 tbsp fresh lemon
  juice
75g/3oz/6 tbsp butter,
  melted
150g/5oz/1¼ cups
  chopped pecan nuts
50g/2oz/½ cup pecan nut
  halves

For the pastry

175g/6oz/1½ cups plain
  flour
15ml/1 tbsp caster sugar
5ml/1 tsp baking powder
2.5ml/½ tsp salt
75g/3oz/6 tbsp cold
  unsalted butter, cut in
  pieces
1 egg yolk
45–60ml/3–4 tbsp
  whipping cream

1 For the pastry, sift together the flour, sugar, baking powder and salt. Add the butter and rub in until the mixture resembles coarse breadcrumbs.

2 Blend the egg yolk and whipping cream, then stir into the flour mixture.

3 Form the pastry into a ball, then roll out and use to line a 23cm/9in pie dish. Flute the edge and chill for 20 minutes.

4 Preheat a baking sheet in the oven at 200°C/400°F/Gas 6. Lightly whisk the eggs and salt. Mix in the sugar, syrup, lemon juice and butter. Stir in the chopped nuts.

5 Pour into the pastry case and arrange the pecan nut halves in concentric circles on top.

6 Bake on the baking sheet for 10 minutes. Reduce the heat to 160°C/325°F/Gas 3 and bake for 25 minutes more.

Velvety Mocha Tart

A creamy smooth filling tops a dark light-textured base in this wondrous dessert.

Serves 8

10ml/2 tsp instant
  espresso coffee
30ml/2 tbsp hot water
175g/6oz plain chocolate
25g/1oz bitter cooking
  chocolate
350ml/12fl oz/1½ cups
  whipping cream,
  slightly warmed
120ml/4fl oz/½ cup
  whipped cream, to
  decorate

chocolate coated coffee
  beans, to decorate

For the base
150g/5oz/2½ cups
  crushed chocolate
  wafers
30ml/2 tbsp caster sugar
65g/2½oz/5 tbsp butter,
  melted

1 Combine the base ingredients. Press the mixture over the base and sides of a 23cm/9in pie dish. Chill.

2 Dissolve the coffee in the water. Set aside.

3 Melt the chocolates in the top of a double boiler. Set the base of the pan in cold water to cool.

4 Whip the cream until light and fluffy. Add the coffee and whip until the cream just holds its shape.

5 When the chocolate is at room temperature, fold it gently into the cream.

6 Pour into the biscuit base and chill until firm. Decorate with piped whipped cream and chocolate coated coffee beans just before serving.

Coconut Cream Tart

Serves 8

140g/5oz desiccated
  coconut
140g/5oz/¾ cup caster
  sugar
25g/1oz/4 tbsp cornflour
1.5ml/¼ tsp salt
625ml/1 pint/2½ cups
  milk
65ml/2fl oz whipping
  cream
2 egg yolks
30g/1oz/2 tbsp unsalted
  butter

10ml/2 tsp vanilla
  essence

For the pastry
140g/5oz/1¼ cups plain
  flour
1.5ml/¼ tsp salt
45g/1½oz/3 tbsp cold
  butter, cut in pieces
30g/1oz/3 tbsp cold
  vegetable fat or lard
30–45ml/2–3 tbsp iced
  water

1 Sift the flour and salt into a bowl, add the fats and rub in until it resembles coarse breadcrumbs. With a fork, stir in just enough water to bind the pastry. Gather into a ball, wrap and chill for 20 minutes. Preheat the oven to 220°C/425°F/Gas 7.

2 Roll out the pastry 3mm/⅛in thick. Line a 23cm/9in pie dish. Trim and flute the edges, prick the base, line with crumpled greaseproof paper and fill with baking beans. Bake for 10–12 minutes. Remove the paper and beans, reduce heat to 180°C/350°F/Gas 4 and bake until brown, 10–15 minutes.

3 Spread 55g/2oz of the coconut on a baking sheet and toast in the oven until golden, 6–8 minutes.

4 Put the sugar, cornflour and salt in a pan. In a bowl, whisk the milk, cream and yolks. Add the egg mixture to the pan.

5 Cook over a low heat, stirring, until the mixture comes to the boil. Boil for 1 minute, then remove from the heat. Add the butter, vanilla and remaining coconut.

6 Pour into the pre-baked pastry case. When cool, sprinkle toasted coconut in a ring in the centre.

Orange Tart

If you like oranges, this is the dessert for you!

Serves 8

200g/7oz/1 cup sugar	**For the pastry**
250ml/8fl oz/1 cup fresh	*210g/7½oz/scant 2 cups*
orange juice, strained	*plain flour*
2 large navel oranges	*2.5ml/½ tsp salt*
165g/5½oz/scant 1 cup	*50g/2oz/4 tbsp cold*
whole blanched	*butter, cut into pieces*
almonds	*40g/1½oz/3 tbsp cold*
50g/2oz/4 tbsp butter	*margarine, cut into*
1 egg	*pieces*
15ml/1 tbsp plain flour	*45 – 60ml/3 – 4 tbsp iced*
45ml/3 tbsp apricot jam	*water*

1 For the pastry, sift the flour and salt into a bowl. Add the butter and margarine and rub in until the mixture resembles coarse breadcrumbs. Stir in just enough water to bind the dough. Wrap and chill for 20 minutes. Roll out the pastry to a 5mm/¼in thickness. Use to line a 20cm/8in tart tin. Trim and chill until needed.

2 In a saucepan, combine 165g/5½oz/¾ cup of the sugar and the orange juice and boil until thick and syrupy. Cut the unpeeled oranges into 5mm/¼in slices. Add to the syrup. Simmer gently for 10 minutes. Put on a wire rack to dry. When cool, cut in half. Reserve the syrup. Place a baking sheet in the oven and heat to 200℃/400°F/Gas 6.

3 Grind the almonds finely in a blender or food processor. Cream the butter and remaining sugar until light and fluffy. Beat in the egg and 30ml/2 tbsp of the orange syrup. Stir in the almonds and flour.

4 Melt the jam over a low heat, then brush over the pastry case. Pour in the almond mixture. Bake on the baking sheet until set, about 20 minutes, then cool. Arrange overlapping orange slices on top. Boil the remaining syrup until thick and brush on top to gla .

Raspberry Tart

A luscious tart with a custard topped with juicy berries.

Serves 8

4 egg yolks	**For the pastry**
65g/2½oz/generous	*185g/6½oz/1⅔ cups plain*
4 tbsp caster sugar	*flour*
45ml/3 tbsp plain flour	*2.5ml/½ tsp baking*
300ml/10fl oz/1¼ cups	*powder*
milk	*1.5ml/¼ tsp salt*
1.5ml/¼ tsp salt	*15ml/1 tbsp sugar*
2.5ml/½ tsp vanilla	*grated rind of ½ orange*
essence	*75g/3oz/6 tbsp cold*
450g/1lb/2⅔ cups fresh	*butter, cut in pieces*
raspberries	*1 egg yolk*
75ml/5 tbsp redcurrant	*45 – 60ml/3 – 4 tbsp*
jelly	*whipping cream*
15ml/1 tbsp orange juice	

1 For the pastry, sift the flour, baking powder and salt into a bowl. Stir in the sugar and orange rind. Add the butter and rub in until the mixture resembles breadcrumbs. Stir in the egg yolk and cream to bind. Form into a ball, wrap and chill.

2 For the filling, beat the egg yolks and sugar until thick and creamy. Gradually stir in the flour. Bring the milk and salt just to the boil, then remove from the heat. Whisk into the egg yolk mixture, return to the pan and continue whisking over a moderately high heat until just bubbling. Cook for 3 minutes to thicken. Transfer to a bowl. Stir in the vanilla, then cover with greaseproof paper.

3 Preheat the oven to 200℃/400°F/Gas 6. Roll out the pastry and use to line a 25cm/10in pie dish. Prick the base, line with greaseproof paper and fill with baking beans. Bake for 15 minutes. Remove the paper and beans, and bake until golden, 6 – 8 minutes more. Leave to cool. Spread an even layer of the custard filling in the pastry case and arrange the raspberries on top. Melt the jelly and orange juice in a pan and brush on top to glaze.

Lattice Berry Pie

Choose any berries you like for this handsome pie.

Serves 8

450g/1lb/about 4 cups
berries, such as
bilberries, blueberries
and blackcurrants
115g/4oz/generous ½ cup
caster sugar
45ml/3 tbsp cornflour
30ml/2 tbsp fresh lemon
juice
25g/1oz/2 tbsp butter,
diced

For the pastry
275g/10oz/2½ cups plain
flour
4ml/¾ tsp salt
115g/4oz/½ cup cold
butter, diced
40g/1½oz/3 tbsp cold
vegetable fat or lard,
diced
75–90ml/5–6 tbsp iced
water
1 egg, beaten with
15ml/1 tbsp water, for
glazing

1 For the pastry, sift the flour and salt into a bowl. Add the butter and fat and rub in until the mixture resembles coarse breadcrumbs. Stir in just enough water to bind. Form into two balls, wrap and chill for 20 minutes. Roll out one ball and use to line a 23cm/9in pie dish, leaving a 1cm/½in overhang. Brush the base with egg.

2 Mix all the filling ingredients together, except the butter (reserve a few berries for decoration). Spoon into the pastry case and dot with the butter. Brush egg around the pastry rim.

3 Preheat a baking sheet at 220°C/425°F/Gas 7. Roll out the remaining pastry on a baking sheet lined with greaseproof paper. With a serrated pastry wheel, make 24 thin strips. Use the scraps to cut out leaf shapes, and mark veins. Weave the strips in a close lattice and transfer to the pie. Seal the edges and trim. Arrange the leaves around the rim. Brush with egg and bake for 10 minutes.

4 Reduce the heat to 180°C/350°F/Gas 4 and bake the pie for a further 40–45 minutes. Decorate with berries.

Plum Pie

Treat someone special with this lightly spiced plum pie.

Serves 8

900g/2lb red or purple
plums
grated rind of 1 lemon
15ml/1 tbsp fresh lemon
juice
115–175g/4–6oz/1–
1¼ cups caster sugar
45ml/3 tbsp quick-
cooking tapioca
1.5ml/¼ tsp salt
2.5ml/½ tsp ground
cinnamon
1.5ml/¼ tsp grated
nutmeg

For the pastry
275g/10oz/2½ cups plain
flour
5ml/1 tsp salt
75g/3oz/6 tbsp cold
butter, diced
50g/2oz/4 tbsp cold
vegetable fat or lard,
diced
50–120ml/2–4fl oz/
¼–½ cup iced water
milk, for glazing

1 For the pastry, sift the flour and salt into a bowl. Add the butter and fat and rub in until the mixture resembles coarse breadcrumbs. Stir in just enough water to bind the pastry. Form into two balls, wrap and chill for 20 minutes.

2 Preheat a baking sheet in the oven at 220°C/425°F/Gas 7. Roll out a pastry ball and use to line a 23cm/9in pie dish.

3 Halve and stone the plums, and chop roughly. Mix all the filling ingredients together, then transfer to the pastry case.

4 Roll out the remaining pastry, place on a baking sheet lined with greaseproof paper, and stamp out four hearts. Transfer the pastry lid to the pie using the paper.

5 Trim to leave a 2cm/¾in overhang. Fold this under the pastry base and pinch to seal. Arrange the hearts on top. Brush with milk and bake for 15 minutes. Reduce the heat to 180°C/350°F/Gas 4 and bake for a further 30–35 minutes.

Dorset Apple Cake

Serve this fruity apple cake warm, and spread with butter if liked.

Makes one 18cm/7in round cake

225g/8oz cooking apples, peeled, cored and chopped
juice of ½ lemon
225g/8oz/2 cups plain flour
7.5ml/1½ tsp baking powder
115g/4oz/½ cup butter, diced
165g/5½oz/scant 1 cup soft light brown sugar
1 egg, beaten
about 30–45ml/2–3 tbsp milk, to mix
2.5ml/½ tsp ground cinnamon

1 Preheat the oven to 180°C/350°F/Gas 4. Grease and line an 18cm/7in round cake tin.

2 Toss the apple with the lemon juice and set aside. Sift the flour and baking powder together, then rub in the butter, until the mixture resembles breadcrumbs.

3 Stir in 115g/4oz/¾ cup of the brown sugar, the apple and the egg, and mix well, adding sufficient milk to make a soft dropping consistency.

4 Transfer the dough to the prepared tin. In a bowl, mix together the remaining sugar and the cinnamon. Sprinkle over the cake mixture, then bake for 45–50 minutes, until golden. Leave to cool in the tin for 10 minutes, then transfer to a wire rack.

Parkin

The flavour of the cake will improve if it is stored in an air-tight container for several days or a week before serving.

Makes 16–20 squares

300ml/½ pint/1¼ cups milk
225g/8oz/5 tbsp golden syrup
225g/8oz/4 tbsp black treacle
115g/4oz/½ cup butter or margarine, diced
50g/2oz/scant ¼ cup dark brown sugar
450g/1lb/4 cups plain flour
2.5ml/½ tsp bicarbonate of soda
6.5ml/1¼ tsp ground ginger
350g/12oz/4 cups medium oatmeal
1 egg, beaten
icing sugar, for dusting

1 Preheat the oven to 180°C/350°F/Gas 4. Grease and line the base of a 20cm/8in square cake tin. Gently heat together the milk, syrup, treacle, butter or margarine and sugar, stirring until smooth. Do not allow the mixture to boil.

2 Stir together the flour, bicarbonate of soda, ginger and oatmeal. Make a well in the centre, pour in the egg, then slowly pour in the warmed mixture, stirring to make a smooth batter.

3 Pour the batter into the tin and bake for about 45 minutes, until firm to the touch. Cool slightly in the tin, then cool completely on a wire rack. Cut into squares and dust with icing sugar.

Banana Ginger Parkin

Parkin keeps well and really improves with keeping. Store it in a covered container for up to two months.

Makes 16–20 squares

200g/7oz/scant 2 cups
  plain flour
10ml/2 tsp bicarbonate of
  soda
10ml/2 tsp ground
  ginger
150g/5oz/1¼ cups
  medium oatmeal
50g/2oz/4 tbsp dark
  muscovado sugar

75g/3oz/6 tbsp sunflower
  margarine
150g/5oz/3 tbsp golden
  syrup
1 egg, beaten
3 ripe bananas, mashed
75g/3oz/¼ cup icing
  sugar
stem ginger, to decorate
  (optional)

1 Preheat the oven to 160°C/325°F/Gas 3. Grease and line an 18 x 28cm/7 x 11in cake tin.

2 Sift together the flour, bicarbonate of soda and ginger, then stir in the oatmeal. Melt the sugar, margarine and syrup in a saucepan, then stir into the flour mixture. Beat in the egg and mashed bananas.

3 Spoon into the tin and bake for about 1 hour, or until firm to the touch. Allow to cool in the tin, then turn out and cut into squares.

4 Sift the icing sugar into a bowl and stir in just enough water to make a smooth, runny icing. Drizzle the icing over each square and top with a piece of stem ginger, if you like.

Gooseberry Cake

This cake is delicious served warm with whipped cream.

Makes one 18cm/7in square cake

115g/4oz/½ cup butter
165g/5½oz/1⅓ cups self-
  raising flour
5ml/1 tsp baking powder
2 eggs, beaten
115g/4oz/generous ½ cup
  caster sugar
5–10ml/1–2 tsp rose
  water

pinch of freshly grated
  nutmeg
115g/4oz jar gooseberries
  in syrup, drained,
  juice reserved
caster sugar, to decorate
whipped cream, to serve

1 Preheat the oven to 180°C/350°F/Gas 4. Grease an 18cm/7in square cake tin, line the base and sides with greaseproof paper and grease the paper. Gently melt the butter, then transfer to a mixing bowl and allow to cool.

2 Sift together the flour and baking powder and add to the butter. Beat in the eggs, one at a time, the sugar, rose water and grated nutmeg, to make a smooth batter.

3 Mix in 15–30ml/1–2 tbsp of the reserved gooseberry juice, then pour half of the batter mixture into the prepared tin. Scatter over the gooseberries and pour over the remaining batter mixture.

4 Bake for about 45 minutes, or until a skewer inserted into the centre of the cake comes out clean.

5 Leave in the tin for 5 minutes, then turn out on a wire rack, peel off the lining paper and allow to cool for a further 5 minutes. Dredge with caster sugar and serve immediately with whipped cream, or leave the cake to cool completely before decorating.

Crunchy-topped Sponge Loaf

This light sponge makes a perfect tea-time treat.

Makes one 450g/1lb loaf

*200g/7oz/scant 1 cup
   butter, softened
finely grated rind of 1
   lemon
150g/5oz/5 tbsp caster
   sugar
3 eggs
75g/3oz/¾ cup plain
   flour, sifted
150g/5oz/1¼ cups self-
   raising flour, sifted*

For the topping
*45ml/3 tbsp clear honey
115g/4oz/¾ cup mixed
   peel
50g/2oz/½ cup flaked
   almonds*

1 Preheat the oven to 180°C/350°F/Gas 4. Grease and line a 450g/1lb loaf tin with greaseproof paper. Grease the paper.

2 Beat together the butter, lemon rind and sugar until light and fluffy. Blend in the eggs, one at a time.

3 Sift together the flours, then stir into the egg mixture. Fill the loaf tin.

4 Bake for 45 minutes, or until a skewer inserted into the centre comes out clean. Stand in the tin for 5 minutes. Turn the loaf out on to a wire rack, peel off the lining paper and leave to cool.

5 For the topping, melt the honey with the mixed peel and almonds. Remove from the heat, stir briefly, then spread over the cake top. Cool before serving.

Irish Whiskey Cake

Other whiskies could be used in this cake.

Makes one 23 x 13cm/9 x 5in cake

*175g/6oz/1½ cups
   chopped walnuts
75g/3oz/generous ½ cup
   raisins, chopped
75g/3oz/scant ½ cup
   currants
115g/4oz/1 cup plain
   flour
5ml/1 tsp baking powder
1.5ml/¼ tsp salt
115g/4oz/½ cup butter*

*225g/8oz/scant 1½ cups
   caster sugar
3 eggs, separated, at
   room temperature
5ml/1 tsp grated nutmeg
2.5ml/½ tsp ground
   cinnamon
85ml/5 tbsp Irish
   whiskey
icing sugar, for dusting*

1 Preheat the oven to 160°C/325°F/Gas 3. Base-line and grease a 23 x 13cm/9 x 5in loaf tin. Mix the nuts and dried fruit with 30ml/2 tbsp of the flour and set aside. Sift together the remaining flour, baking powder and salt.

2 Cream the butter and sugar until light and fluffy. Beat in the egg yolks.

3 Mix the nutmeg, cinnamon and whiskey. Fold into the butter mixture, alternating with the flour mixture.

4 Beat the egg whites until stiff. Fold into the whiskey mixture until just blended. Fold in the walnut mixture.

5 Fill the loaf tin and bake until a skewer inserted in the centre comes out clean, about 1 hour. Cool in the tin. To serve, dust with icing sugar over a template.

Autumn Dessert Cake

Greengages, plums or semi-dried prunes are delicious in this recipe.

Serves 6–8

115g/4oz/½ cup butter, softened	5ml/1 tsp baking powder
150g/5oz/5 tbsp caster sugar	2.5ml/½ tsp salt
3 eggs, beaten	675g/1½lb/3 cups stoned plums, greengages or semi-dried prunes
75g/3oz/¾ cup ground hazelnuts	60ml/4 tbsp lime marmalade
150g/5oz/1¼ cups shelled pecan nuts, chopped	15ml/1 tbsp lime juice
50g/2oz/½ cup plain flour	30ml/2 tbsp blanched almonds, chopped, to decorate

1 Preheat the oven to 180°C/350°F/Gas 4. Grease a 23cm/9in round, fluted tart tin.

2 Beat the butter and sugar until light and fluffy. Gradually beat in the eggs, alternating with the ground hazelnuts.

3 Stir in the pecan nuts, then sift and fold in the flour, baking powder and salt. Spoon into the tart tin.

4 Bake for 45 minutes, or until a skewer inserted into the centre comes out clean.

5 Arrange the fruit on the base. Return to the oven and bake for 10–15 minutes until the fruit has softened. Transfer to a wire rack to cool, then turn out.

6 Warm the marmalade and lime juice gently. Brush over the fruit, then sprinkle with the almonds. Allow to set, then chill before serving.

Apple Crumble Cake

In the autumn use windfall apples. Served warm with thick cream or custard, this cake doubles as a dessert.

Serves 8–10

For the topping

75g/3oz/⅔ cup self-raising flour	115g/4oz/1 cup self-raising flour, sifted
½ tsp ground cinnamon	2 cooking apples, peeled, cored and sliced
40g/1½oz/3 tbsp butter	50g/2oz/4 tbsp sultanas
25g/1oz/2 tbsp caster sugar	

To decorate

For the base

50g/2oz/4 tbsp butter, softened	1 red dessert apple, cored, thinly sliced and tossed in lemon juice
75g/3oz/6 tbsp caster sugar	25g/1oz/2 tbsp caster sugar, sifted
1 size 3 egg, beaten	pinch of ground cinnamon

1 Preheat the oven 180°C/350°F/Gas 4. Grease a deep 18cm/7in springform tin, line the base with greaseproof paper and grease the paper.

2 To make the topping, sift the flour and cinnamon into a mixing bowl. Rub the butter into the flour until it resembles breadcrumbs, then stir in the sugar. Set aside.

3 To make the base, put the butter, sugar, egg and flour into a bowl and beat for 1–2 minutes until smooth. Spoon into the prepared tin.

4 Mix together the apple slices and sultanas and spread them evenly over the top. Sprinkle with the topping.

5 Bake in the centre of the oven for about 1 hour. Cool in the tin for 10 minutes before turning out on to a wire rack and peeling off the lining paper. Serve warm or cool, decorated with slices of red dessert apple and caster sugar and cinnamon sprinkled over.

Light Fruit Cake

For the best flavour, wrap this cake in foil and store for a week before cutting.

Makes two 23 x 13cm/9 x 5in cakes

225g/8oz/1 cup prunes
225g/8oz/1⅓ cups dates
225g/8oz/1 cup currants
225g/8oz/generous 1½ cups sultanas
250ml/8fl oz/1 cup dry white wine
250ml/8fl oz/1 cup rum
350g/12oz/3 cups plain flour
10ml/2 tsp baking powder
5ml/1 tsp ground cinnamon
2.5ml/½ tsp grated nutmeg
225g/8oz/1 cup butter, at room temperature
225g/8oz/scant 1¼ cups caster sugar
4 eggs, lightly beaten
5ml/1 tsp vanilla essence

1 Stone the prunes and dates and chop finely. Place in a bowl with the currants and sultanas. Stir in the wine and rum and leave, covered, for 2 days. Stir occasionally.

2 Preheat the oven to 150°C/300°F/Gas 2 with a tray of hot water in the bottom. Line two 23 x 13cm/9 x 5in loaf tins with greaseproof paper and grease the paper.

3 Sift together the flour, baking powder, ground cinnamon and grated nutmeg.

4 Cream the butter and sugar together until light and fluffy. Gradually add the eggs and vanilla. Fold in the flour mixture in three batches. Fold in the dried fruit mixture and its liquid.

5 Divide the mixture between the tins and bake until a skewer inserted in the centre comes out clean, about 1½ hours. Stand for 20 minutes, then unmould on to a wire rack.

Rich Fruit Cake

Makes one 23 x 8cm/9 x 3in cake

140g/5oz/⅓ cup currants
170g/6oz/generous 1 cup raisins
50g/2oz/⅓ cup sultanas
55g/2oz/4 tbsp glacé cherries, halved
3 tbsp sweet sherry
170g/6oz/¾ cup butter
200g/7oz/scant 1 cup dark brown sugar
2 size 1 eggs, at room temperature
200g/7oz/1¼ cups plain flour
10ml/2 tsp baking powder
10ml/2 tsp each ground ginger, allspice, and cinnamon
15ml/1 tbsp golden syrup
15ml/1 tbsp milk
55g/2oz/5 tbsp cut mixed peel
115g/4oz/1 cup chopped walnuts

For the decoration
120ml/4fl oz/½ cup orange marmalade
crystallized citrus fruit slices
glacé cherries

1 A day in advance, combine the dried fruit and cherries in a bowl. Stir in the sherry, cover and soak overnight.

2 Preheat the oven to 150°C/300°F/Gas 2. Line and grease a 23 x 8cm/9 x 3in springform tin with greaseproof paper. Place a tray of hot water on the bottom of the oven.

3 Cream the butter and sugar. Beat in the eggs, 1 at a time. Sift the flour, baking powder and spices together three times. Fold into the butter mixture in three batches. Fold in the syrup, milk, dried fruit and liquid, mixed peel and nuts.

4 Spoon into the tin, spreading out so there is a slight depression in the centre. Bake for about 2½–3 hours. Cover with foil when the top is golden to prevent over-browning. Cool in the tin on a rack.

5 Melt the marmalade over a low heat, then brush over the top of the cake. Decorate with the crystallized citrus fruit slices and glacé cherries.

Creole Christmas Cake

Makes one 23cm/9in cake

450g/1lb/3 cups raisins
225g/8oz/1 cup currants
115g/4oz/¾ cup sultanas
115g/4oz/½ cup no-soak
 prunes, chopped
115g/4oz/1 cup candied
 orange peel, chopped
115g/4oz/1 cup chopped
 walnuts
60ml/4 tbsp dark
 brown sugar
5ml/1 tsp vanilla essence
5ml/1 tsp ground
 cinnamon
1.5ml/¼tsp each ground
 nutmeg and cloves

5ml/1 tsp salt
60ml/4 tbsp each rum,
 brandy and whisky
For the second stage
225g/8oz/2 cups plain
 flour
5ml/1 tsp baking powder
225g/8oz demerara sugar
225g/8oz/1 cup butter
4 eggs, beaten
For the topping
225g/8oz apricot
 jam, sieved
pecan halves and
 crystallized kumquat
 slices, to decorate

1 Put the first set of ingredients into a pan, mix and heat gently. Simmer over low heat for 15 minutes. Remove from the heat and cool. Transfer to a lidded jar and leave in the fridge for 7 days, stirring at least once a day.

2 Preheat the oven to 140°C/275°F/Gas 1. Line a 23cm/9in round cake tin with a double thickness of non-stick baking paper and grease it well. Beat the flour, baking powder, sugar and butter together until smooth, then gradually beat in the eggs until the mixture is well blended and smooth.

3 Fold in the fruit mixture and stir well to mix. Spoon the mixture into the prepared tin, level the surface and bake in the centre of the oven for 3 hours. Cover with foil and continue baking for 1 hour, until the cake feels springy. Cool on a wire rack then remove from the tin. Wrap in foil until needed. The cake will keep well for 1 year.

4 To decorate , heat the jam with 30ml/2 tbsp water, brush half over the cake. Arrange the nuts and fruit over the cake and brush with the remaining apricot glaze.

Light Jewelled Fruit Cake

If you want to cover this cake with marzipan and icing, omit the almond decoration.

Makes one 20cm/8in round or 18cm/7in square cake

115g/4oz/½ cup currants
115g/4oz/¾ cup sultanas
225g/8oz/1 cup mixed
 glacé cherries,
 quartered
50g/2oz/½ cup mixed
 peel, finely chopped
30ml/2 tbsp rum, brandy
 or sherry
225g/8oz/1 cup butter
225g/8oz/generous 1 cup
 caster sugar
finely grated rind of
 1 orange

grated rind of 1 lemon
4 eggs
50g/2oz/½ cup chopped
 almonds
50g/2oz/5 tbsp ground
 almonds
225g/8oz/2 cups plain
 flour

To decorate
50g/2oz/5 tbsp whole
 blanched almonds
 (optional)
15ml/1 tbsp apricot jam

1 A day in advance, soak the currants, sultanas, glacé cherries and mixed peel in the rum, brandy or sherry, cover and leave to soak overnight.

2 Grease and line a 20cm/8in round cake tin or an 18cm/7in square cake tin with a double thickness of greaseproof paper. Preheat the oven to 160°C/325°F/Gas 3. Beat the butter, sugar and orange and lemon rinds together until light and fluffy. Beat in the eggs, one at a time. Mix in the chopped almonds, ground almonds, soaked fruits (with the liquid) and the flour. Spoon into the cake tin and level the top. Bake for 30 minutes.

3 Arrange the almonds, if using, on top of the cake (do not press them into the cake or they will sink during cooking). Return the cake to the oven and cook for 1½–2 hours, or until the centre is firm to the touch. Let the cake cool in the tin for 30 minutes, then turn it out in its paper on to a wire rack. When cold, wrap foil over the paper and store in a cool place. To finish, warm, then sieve the jam and use to glaze the cake.

Angel Cake

This heavenly cake tastes simply divine!

Makes one 25cm/10in cake

130g/4½oz/generous
    1 cup sifted plain flour
30ml/2 tbsp cornflour
285g/10½oz/1½ cups
    caster sugar
10 – 11 egg whites
6.5ml/1¼ tsp cream of
    tartar

1.5ml/¼ tsp salt
5ml/1 tsp vanilla essence
1.5ml/¼ tsp almond
    essence
icing sugar, for dusting

1   Preheat the oven to 160°C/325°F/Gas 3. Sift the flours before measuring, then sift them four times together with 90g/3½oz/½ cup of the sugar.

2   Beat the egg whites until foamy. Sift over the cream of tartar and salt and continue to beat until the egg whites form soft peaks.

3   Add the remaining sugar in three batches, beating well after each addition. Stir in the vanilla and almond essences. Fold in the flour mixture in two batches.

4   Transfer to an ungreased 25cm/10in cake tin and bake until just browned on top, about 1 hour.

5   Turn the tin upside-down on to a wire rack and cool for 1 hour. Then invert on to a serving plate. Lay a star-shaped template on top of the cake, sift over some icing sugar and remove the template.

Spice Cake with Ginger Frosting

A rich three-layer cake with a creamy ginger frosting.

Makes one 20cm/8in round cake

300ml/10fl oz/1¼ cups
    milk
30ml/2 tbsp golden syrup
10ml/2 tsp vanilla
    essence
75g/3oz/¾ cup chopped
    walnuts
175g/6oz/¾ cup butter, at
    room temperature
285g/10½oz/1½ cups
    sugar
1 whole egg, plus 3 egg
    yolks
275g/10oz/2½ cups plain
    flour
15ml/1 tbsp baking
    powder
5ml/1 tsp grated nutmeg
5ml/1 tsp ground
    cinnamon

2.5ml/½ tsp ground
    cloves
1.5ml/¼ tsp ground
    ginger
1.5ml/¼ tsp mixed spice
stem ginger pieces, to
    decorate

For the frosting

175g/6oz/¾ cup cream
    cheese
25g/1oz/2 tbsp unsalted
    butter
200g/7oz/1⅓ cups icing
    sugar
30ml/2 tbsp finely
    chopped stem ginger
30ml/2 tbsp syrup from
    stem ginger

1   Preheat the oven to 180°C/350°F/Gas 4. Line and grease three 20cm/8in cake tins with greaseproof paper. In a bowl, combine the milk, golden syrup, vanilla and walnuts.

2   Cream the butter and sugar until light and fluffy. Beat in the egg and egg yolks. Add the milk mixture and stir well. Sift together the flour, baking powder and spices three times. Add to the butter mixture in four batches, folding in carefully.

3   Divide the cake mixture between the tins. Bake until the cakes spring back when touched lightly, about 25 minutes. Leave in the tins for 5 minutes, then cool on a wire rack. For the frosting, combine all the ingredients and beat until smooth. Spread the frosting between the layers and over the top. Decorate with pieces of stem ginger.

Lemon Coconut Layer Cake

Makes one 20cm/8in round cake

150g/5oz/1¼ cups plain
 flour, sifted with
 1.5ml/¼ tsp salt
8 eggs
370g/12¼oz/scant 2 cups
 caster sugar
15ml/1 tbsp grated
 orange rind
grated rind of 2 lemons
juice of 1 lemon
65g/2½oz/1¼ cups
 sweetened, shredded
 coconut
30ml/2 tbsp cornflour

250ml/8fl oz/1 cup water
75g/3oz/6 tbsp butter

For the frosting
115g/4oz/½ cup unsalted
 butter
115g/4oz/1 cup icing
 sugar
grated rind of 1 lemon
90–120ml/6–8 tbsp
 lemon juice
115g/4oz/2 cups
 sweetened shredded
 coconut

1 Preheat the oven to 180°C/350°F/Gas 4. Line and grease three 20cm/8in cake tins with greaseproof paper.

2 Place 6 of the eggs in a bowl set over hot water and beat until frothy. Beat in 165g/5½oz/¾ cup sugar until the mixture doubles in volume. Remove from the heat. Fold in the orange rind, half the lemon rind, 15ml/1 tbsp of the lemon juice and the coconut. Sift over the flour mixture and fold in well.

3 Divide the mixture between the cake tins. Bake until the cakes pull away from the sides of the tins, 25–30 minutes. Leave in the tins for 5 minutes, then cool on a wire rack.

4 Blend the cornflour with cold water to dissolve. Whisk in the remaining eggs until blended. In a pan, mix the remaining lemon rind and juice, water, remaining sugar and butter. Bring to the boil. Whisk in the cornflour, and return to the boil. Whisk until thick. Remove and cover with clear film.

5 Cream the butter and icing sugar. Stir in the lemon rind and enough lemon juice to obtain a spreadable consistency. Sandwich the cake layers with the lemon custard. Spread the frosting over the top and sides. Cover with the coconut.

Lemon Yogurt Ring

The glaze gives this dessert a refreshing finishing touch.

Serves 12

225g/8oz/1 cup butter, at
 room temperature
285g/10½oz/1½ cups
 caster sugar
4 eggs, separated
10ml/2 tsp grated lemon
 rind
90ml/6 tbsp lemon juice
250ml/8fl oz/1 cup
 natural yogurt
275g/10oz/2½ cups plain
 flour

10ml/2 tsp baking
 powder
5ml/1 tsp bicarbonate of
 soda
2.5ml/½ tsp salt

For the glaze
115g/4oz/1 cup icing
 sugar
30ml/2 tbsp lemon juice
45–60ml/3–4 tbsp
 natural yogurt

1 Preheat the oven to 180°C/350°F/Gas 4. Grease a 3-litre/5-pint/12½-cup *bundt* or fluted tube tin and dust with flour.

2 Cream the butter and caster sugar until light and fluffy. Add the egg yolks, one at a time, beating well after each addition. Add the lemon rind, juice and yogurt and stir .

3 Sift together the flour, baking powder and bicarbonate of soda. In another bowl, beat the egg whites and salt until they hold stiff peaks.

4 Fold the dry ingredients into the butter mixture, then fold in a dollop of egg whites. Fold in the remaining whites.

5 Pour into the tin and bake until a skewer inserted in the centre comes out clean, about 50 minutes. Leave in the tin for 15 minutes, then turn out and cool on a wire rack.

6 For the glaze, sift the icing sugar into a bowl. Stir in the lemon juice and just enough yogurt to make a smooth glaze.

7 Set the cooled cake on the wire rack over a sheet of greaseproof paper. Pour over the glaze and allow to set.

Carrot Cake with Geranium Cheese

Makes one 23 x 12cm/9 x 5in cake

115g/4oz/1 cup self-
    raising flour
5ml/1 tsp bicarbonate of
    soda
2.5ml/½ tsp ground
    cinnamon
2.5ml/½ tsp ground
    cloves
200g/7oz/generous 1 cup
    soft brown sugar
225g/8oz/generous
    1½ cups grated
    carrot
150g/5oz/1 cup sultanas
150g/5oz/½ cup finely
    chopped preserved
    stem ginger

150g/5oz/generous 1 cup
    pecan nuts
150ml/¼ pint/⅔ cup
    sunflower oil
2 eggs, lightly beaten

For the topping
2 – 3 lemon-scented
    geranium leaves
225g/8oz/2 cups icing
    sugar
60g/2¼oz/generous
    4 tbsp cream cheese
30g/1¼oz/generous
    2 tbsp softened butter
5ml/1 tsp grated lemon
    rind

1 For the topping, put the geranium leaves, torn into small pieces, in a small bowl and mix with the icing sugar. Leave in a warm place overnight for the sugar to take up the scent.

2 For the cake, sift the flour, bicarbonate of soda and spices together. Add the sugar, carrots, sultanas, ginger and pecan nuts. Stir well, then add the oil and beaten eggs. Mix with an electric mixer for 5 minutes.

3 Preheat the oven to 180°C/350°F/Gas 4. Then grease a 23 x 12cm/9 x 5in loaf tin, line the base with greaseproof paper, and grease the paper. Pour the mixture into the tin and bake for about 1 hour. Remove the cake from the oven, leave to stand for a few minutes, and then cool on a wire rack.

4 Meanwhile, make the cream cheese topping. Remove the pieces of geranium leaf from the icing sugar and discard. Place the cream cheese, butter and lemon rind in a bowl. Using an electric mixer, gradually add the icing sugar, beating well until smooth. Spread over the top of the cooled cake.

Carrot and Courgette Cake

If you can't resist the lure of a slice of iced cake, you'll love this spiced sponge with its delicious creamy topping.

Makes one 18cm/7in square cake

1 carrot
1 courgette
3 eggs, separated
115g/4oz/¼ cup soft light
    brown sugar
30ml/2 tbsp ground
    almonds
finely grated rind of
    1 orange
150g/5oz/1¼ cups
    self-raising wholemeal
    flour

5ml/1 tsp ground
    cinnamon
5ml/1 tsp icing sugar, for
    dusting
fondant carrots and
    courgettes, to decorate

For the topping
175g/6oz/¾ cup low-fat
    soft cheese
5ml/1 tsp clear honey

1 Preheat the oven to 180°C/350°F/Gas 4. Line an 18cm/7in square tin with non-stick baking paper. Coarsely grate the carrot and courgette.

2 Put the egg yolks, sugar, ground almonds and orange rind into a bowl and whisk until very thick and light. Sift together the flour and cinnamon and fold into the mixture together with the grated vegetables. Add any bran left in the sieve.

3 Whisk the egg whites until stiff and carefully fold them in, a half at a time. Spoon into the tin. Bake in the oven for 1 hour, covering the top with foil after 40 minutes. Leave to cool in the tin for 5 minutes, then turn out on to a wire rack and remove the lining paper.

4 For the topping, beat together the cheese and honey and spread over the cake. Dust with icing sugar and decorate with fondant carrots and courgettes.

Banana Coconut Cake

Slightly over-ripe bananas are best for this perfect coffee-morning cake.

Makes one 18cm/7in square cake

115g/4oz/½ cup butter, softened
115g/4oz/generous ½ cup caster sugar
2 eggs
115g/4oz/1 cup self-raising flour
50g/2oz/½ cup plain flour
5ml/1 tsp bicarbonate of soda
120ml/4fl oz/½ cup milk

2 large bananas, peeled and mashed
75g/3oz/1½ cups desiccated coconut, toasted

For the topping

25g/1oz/2 tbsp butter
30ml/2 tbsp clear honey
115g/4oz/2 cups shredded coconut

1 Preheat the oven to 190°C/375°F/Gas 5. Grease a deep 18cm/7in square cake tin, line with greaseproof paper and grease the paper.

2 Beat the butter and sugar until smooth and creamy. Beat in the eggs, one at a time. Sift together the flours and bicarbonate of soda, sift half into the butter mixture and stir to mix.

3 Combine the milk and mashed banana and beat half into the egg mixture. Stir in the remaining flour and banana mixtures and toasted coconut. Transfer to the cake tin and smooth the surface.

4 Bake for 1 hour, or until a skewer inserted into the centre of the cake comes out clean. Leave in the tin for 5 minutes, then turn out on to a wire rack, peel off the paper and cool.

5 For the topping, gently melt the butter and honey. Stir in the shredded coconut and cook, stirring, for 5 minutes or until lightly browned. Remove from the heat and allow to cool slightly. Spoon the topping over the cake and allow to cool.

St Clement's Cake

A tangy orange-and-lemon cake makes a spectacular centrepiece when decorated with fruits and flowers.

Makes one 23cm/9in ring cake

175g/6oz/¾ cup butter
75g/3oz/½ cup soft light brown sugar
3 eggs, separated
grated rind and juice of 1 orange and 1 lemon
150g/5oz/1¼ cups self-raising flour
75g/3oz/6 tbsp caster sugar

15g/½ oz/2 tbsp ground almonds
350ml/12fl oz/1½ cups double cream
15ml/1 tbsp Grand Marnier
16 crystallized orange and lemon slices, silver dragées, sugared almonds and fresh flowers, to decorate

1 Preheat the oven to 180°C/350°F/Gas 4. Grease and flour a 900ml/1½ pint/3¾ cup ring mould.

2 Cream half the butter and all of the brown sugar until pale and light. Beat in the egg yolks, orange rind and juice and fold in 75g/3oz/⅔ cup flour.

3 Cream the remaining butter and caster sugar. Stir in the lemon rind and juice and fold in the remaining flour and ground almonds. Whisk the egg whites until stiff, and fold in.

4 Spoon the two mixtures alternately into the prepared tin. Using a skewer or small spoon, swirl through the mixture to create a marbled effect. Bake for 45–50 minutes until risen, and a skewer inserted in the cake comes out clean. Cool in the tin for 10 minutes then transfer to a wire rack to cool.

5 Whip the cream and Grand Marnier together until lightly thickened. Spread over the cake and swirl a pattern over the icing with a palette knife. Decorate the ring with the crystallized fruits, dragées and sugared almonds to resemble a jewelled crown. Arrange a few fresh flowers in the centre.

Apple Cake

Makes one ring cake

675g/1½lb apples, peeled, cored and quartered
500g/1lb 2oz/generous 2⅓ cups caster sugar
15ml/1 tbsp water
350g/12oz/3 cups plain flour
9ml/1¾ tsp bicarbonate of soda
5ml/1 tsp ground cinnamon
5ml/1 tsp ground cloves
175g/6oz/generous 1 cup raisins
150g/5oz/1¼ cups chopped walnuts
225g/8oz/1 cup butter or margarine, at room temperature
5ml/1 tsp vanilla essence

For the icing

115g/4oz/1 cup icing sugar
1.5ml/¼ tsp vanilla essence
30–45ml/2–3 tbsp milk

1 Put the apples, 50g/2oz/4 tbsp of the sugar and the water in a saucepan and bring to the boil. Simmer for 25 minutes, stirring occasionally to break up any lumps. Leave to cool. Preheat the oven to 160°C/325°F/Gas 3. Thoroughly butter and flour a 1.75-litre/3-pint/7½-cup tube tin.

2 Sift the flour, bicarbonate of soda and spices into a bowl. Remove 30ml/2 tbsp of the mixture to another bowl and toss with the raisins and 115g/4oz/1 cup of the walnuts.

3 Cream the butter or margarine and remaining sugar together until light and fluffy. Fold in the apple mixture gently. Fold the flour mixture into the apple mixture. Stir in the vanilla and the raisin and walnut mixture. Pour into the tube tin. Bake until a skewer inserted in the centre comes out clean, about 1½ hours. Cool completely in the tin on a wire rack, then unmould on to the rack.

4 For the icing, put the sugar in a bowl and stir in the vanilla and 15ml/1 tbsp milk. Add more milk until the icing is smooth and has a thick pouring consistency. Transfer the cake to a serving plate and drizzle the icing on top. Sprinkle with the remaining nuts. Allow the icing to set.

Chocolate Amaretto Marquise

This light-as-air marquise is perfect for a special occasion, served with Amaretto cream.

Makes one heart-shaped cake

15ml/1 tbsp sunflower oil
75g/3oz/7–8 amaretti biscuits, crushed
25g/1oz/2 tbsp unblanched almonds, toasted and finely chopped
450g/1lb plain chocolate, broken into pieces
75ml/5 tbsp Amaretto liqueur
75ml/5 tbsp golden syrup
475ml/16fl oz/2 cups double cream
cocoa powder, to dust

For the Amaretto cream

350ml/12fl oz 1½ cups whipping or double cream
30–45 ml/2–3 tbsp Amaretto liqueur

1 Lightly oil a 23cm/9in heart-shaped or springform cake tin. Line the base with non-stick baking paper and oil the paper. In a small bowl, combine the crushed amaretti biscuits and the chopped almonds. Sprinkle evenly over the base of the tin.

2 Place the chocolate, Amaretto liqueur and golden syrup in a saucepan over very low heat. Stir frequently until the chocolate is melted and the mixture is smooth. Allow to cool for 6–8 minutes, until the mixture just feels warm.

3 Beat the cream until it just begins to hold its shape. Stir a large spoonful into the chocolate mixture, then quickly add the remaining cream and gently fold into the chocolate mixture. Pour into the prepared tin and tap the tin gently on the work surface to release any large air bubbles. Cover the tin with clear film and leave in the fridge overnight.

4 To unmould, run a thin-bladed sharp knife under hot water and dry carefully. Run the knife around the edge of the tin to loosen, place a serving plate over the tin, then invert to unmould. Carefully peel off the paper then dust with cocoa. Whip the cream and liqueur and serve separately.

Tangy Lemon Cake

The lemon syrup forms a crusty topping when completely cooled. Leave in the tin until ready to serve.

Makes one 900g/2lb loaf

175g/6oz/¾ cup butter
175g/6oz/scant 1 cup
   caster sugar
3 eggs, beaten
175g/6oz/1½ cups self-
   raising flour
grated rind of 1 orange
grated rind of 1 lemon

For the syrup
115g/4oz/generous ½ cup
   caster sugar
juice of 2 lemons

1 Preheat the oven to 180°C/350°F/Gas 4. Then grease a 900g/2lb loaf tin.

2 Beat the butter and sugar together until light and fluffy, then gradually beat in the eggs. Fold in the flour and the orange and lemon rinds.

3 Turn the cake mixture into the cake tin and bake for 1¼–1½ hours, until set in the centre, risen and golden. Remove the cake from the oven, but leave in the tin.

4 To make the syrup, gently heat the sugar in the lemon juice until melted, then boil for 15 seconds. Pour the syrup over the cake in the tin and leave to cool.

Pineapple and Apricot Cake

This is not a long-keeping cake, but it does freeze, well-wrapped in greaseproof paper and then foil.

Makes one 18cm/7in square or 20cm/8in round cake

175g/6oz/¾ cup unsalted
   butter
150g/5oz/generous ¾ cup
   caster sugar
3 eggs, beaten
few drops vanilla
   essence
225g/8oz/2 cups plain
   flour
1.5ml/¼ tsp salt
7.5ml/1½ tsp baking
   powder

225g/8oz/1¼ cups ready-
   to-eat dried apricots,
   chopped
115g/4oz/½ cup each
   chopped crystallized
   ginger and
   crystallized pineapple
grated rind and juice of
   ½ orange
grated rind and juice of
   ½ lemon
a little milk

1 Preheat the oven to 180°C/350°F/Gas 4. Double line an 18cm/7in square or 20cm/8in round cake tin. Cream the butter and sugar together until light and fluffy.

2 Gradually beat in the eggs with the vanilla essence, beating well after each addition. Sift together the flour, salt and baking powder, add a little with the last of the egg, then fold in the rest.

3 Gently fold in the apricots, ginger and pineapple and the fruit rinds, then add sufficient fruit juice and milk to give a fairly soft dropping consistency.

4 Spoon into the cake tin and smooth the top with a wet spoon. Bake for 20 minutes, then reduce the oven temperature to 160°C/325°F/Gas 3 and bake for a further 1½–2 hours, or until firm to the touch and a skewer comes out of the centre clean. Leave the cake to cool completely in the tin. Wrap in fresh paper before storing in an airtight tin.

Soured Cream Crumble Cake

The consistency of this cake, with its two layers of crumble, is sublime.

Makes one 23cm/9in square cake

115g/4oz/½ cup butter,
  at room temperature
130g/4½oz/scant ¼ cup
  caster sugar
3 eggs
210g/7½oz/scant 2 cups
  plain flour
5ml/1 tsp bicarbonate of
  soda
5ml/1 tsp baking powder
250ml/8fl oz/1 cup
  soured cream

For the topping
225g/8oz/1 cup dark
  brown sugar
10ml/2 tsp ground
  cinnamon
115g/4oz/1 cup finely
  chopped walnuts
50g/2oz/4 tbsp cold
  butter, cut into pieces

1 Preheat the oven to 180°C/350°F/Gas 4. Line the base of a 23cm/9in square cake tin with greaseproof paper and grease the paper and sides.

2 For the topping, place the brown sugar, cinnamon and walnuts in a bowl. Mix, then add the butter and rub in until the mixture resembles breadcrumbs.

3 To make the cake, cream the butter until soft. Add the sugar and beat until light and fluffy. Add the eggs, one at a time, beating well after each addition.

4 In another bowl, sift the flour, bicarbonate of soda and baking powder together three times. Fold the dry ingredients into the butter mixture in three batches, alternating with the soured cream. Fold until blended after each addition.

5 Pour half of the batter into the prepared tin and sprinkle over half of the topping. Pour the remaining batter on top and sprinkle over the remaining topping. Bake until browned, 60–70 minutes. Leave in the tin for 5 minutes, then turn out and cool on a wire rack.

Plum Crumble Cake

This cake can also be made with the same quantity of apricots or cherries.

Serves 8–10

150g/5oz/generous ½ cup
  butter or margarine,
  at room temperature
150g/5oz/¾ cup caster
  sugar
4 eggs, at room
  temperature
7.5ml/1½ tsp vanilla
  essence
150g/5oz/1¼ cups plain
  flour
5ml/1 tsp baking powder

675g/1½lb red plums,
  halved and stoned

For the topping
115g/4oz/1 cup plain
  flour
130g/4½oz/generous
  ¼ cup light brown
  sugar
7.5ml/1½ tsp ground
  cinnamon
75g/3oz/6 tbsp butter,
  cut in pieces

1 Preheat the oven to 180°C/350°F/Gas 4. Using greaseproof paper, line a 25 x 5cm/10 x 2in tin and grease the paper. For the topping, combine the flour, light brown sugar and cinnamon in a bowl. Add the butter and rub in until it resembles coarse breadcrumbs.

2 Cream the butter or margarine and sugar until light and fluffy. Beat in the eggs, one at a time. Stir in the vanilla. In three batches, sift, then fold in the flour and baking powder.

3 Pour the mixture into the tin. Arrange the plums on top and sprinkle with the topping.

4 Bake until a skewer inserted in the centre comes out clean, about 45 minutes. Cool in the tin.

5 To serve, run a knife around the inside edge and invert on to a plate. Invert again on to a serving plate so the topping is uppermost.

Pineapple Upside-down Cake

For an apricot cake, replace the pineapple slices with 225g/8oz/1¾ cups dried ready-to-eat apricots.

Makes one 25cm/10in round cake

115g/4oz/½ cup butter
200g/7oz/generous 1 cup
*   dark brown sugar*
450g/1lb canned
*   pineapple slices,*
*   drained*
4 eggs, separated
grated rind of 1 lemon
pinch of salt
115g/4oz/generous ½ cup
*   caster sugar*
75g/3oz/¾ cup plain
*   flour*
5ml/1 tsp baking powder

1 Preheat the oven to 180℃/350℉/Gas 4. Melt the butter in a 25cm/10in ovenproof cast-iron frying pan. Then reserve 15ml/1 tbsp butter. Add the brown sugar to the pan and stir to blend. Place the pineapple on top in one layer. Set aside.

2 Whisk together the egg yolks, reserved butter and lemon rind until well blended. Set aside.

3 Beat the egg whites and salt until stiff. Gradually fold in the caster sugar, then the egg yolk mixture.

4 Sift the flour and baking powder together. Carefully fold into the egg mixture in three batches.

5 Pour the mixture over the pineapple. Bake until a skewer inserted in the centre comes out clean, about 30 minutes.

6 While still hot, invert on to a serving plate. Serve hot or cold.

Upside-down Pear and Ginger Cake

This light spicy sponge, topped with glossy baked fruit and ginger, makes an excellent pudding.

Serves 6–8

900g/2lb can pear halves,
*   drained*
120ml/8 tbsp finely
*   chopped stem ginger*
120ml/8 tbsp ginger
*   syrup from the jar*
175g/6oz/1½ cups self-
*   raising flour*
2.5ml/½ tsp baking
*   powder*
5ml/1 tsp ground ginger
175g/6oz/1 cup soft light
*   brown sugar*
175g/6oz/¾ cup butter,
*   softened*
3 eggs, lightly beaten

1 Preheat the oven to 180℃/350℉/Gas 4. Base-line and grease a deep 20cm/8in round cake tin.

2 Fill the hollow in each pear with half the chopped stem ginger. Arrange, flat-sides down, in the base of the cake tin, then spoon over half the ginger syrup.

3 Sift together the flour, baking powder and ground ginger. Stir in the sugar and butter, add the eggs and beat until creamy, 1–2 minutes.

4 Spoon the mixture into the cake tin. Bake in the oven for 50 minutes, or until a skewer inserted in the centre of the cake comes out clean. Leave the cake in the tin for 5 minutes. Turn out on to a wire rack, peel off the lining paper and leave to cool completely.

5 Add the reserved ginger to the pear halves and drizzle over the remaining syrup.

Cranberry and Apple Ring

Tangy cranberries add an unusual flavour to this cake which is best eaten very fresh.

Makes one ring cake
225g/8oz/2 cups self-
  raising flour
5ml/1 tsp ground
  cinnamon
75g/3oz/⅓ cup light
  muscovado sugar
1 eating apple, cored and
  diced
75g/3oz/¾ cup fresh or
  frozen cranberries
60ml/4 tbsp sunflower oil
150ml/¼ pint/⅔ cup
  apple juice
cranberry jelly and apple
  slices, to decorate

1 Preheat the oven to 180°C/350°F/Gas 4. Lightly grease a 1-litre/1¾-pint/4-cup ring tin with oil.

2 Sift together the flour and ground cinnamon, then stir in the muscovado sugar.

3 Toss together the diced apple and cranberries. Stir into the dry ingredients, then add the oil and apple juice and beat together well.

4 Spoon the mixture into the prepared ring tin and bake for 35–40 minutes, or until the cake is firm to the touch. Turn out and leave to cool completely on a wire rack.

5 To serve, drizzle warmed cranberry jelly over the cake and decorate with apple slices.

Greek Honey and Lemon Cake

A wonderfully moist and tangy cake, you could ice it if you wished.

Makes one 19cm/7½in square cake
40g/1½oz/3 tbsp
  sunflower margarine
60ml/4 tbsp clear honey
finely grated rind and
  juice of 1 lemon
150ml/¼ pint/⅔ cup milk
150g/5oz/1¼ cups plain
  flour
7.5ml/1½ tsp baking
  powder
2.5ml/½ tsp grated
  nutmeg
50g/2oz/¼ cup semolina
2 egg whites
10ml/2 tsp sesame seeds

1 Preheat the oven to 200°C/400°F/Gas 6. Lightly oil and base-line a 19cm/7½in square deep cake tin.

2 Place the margarine and 45ml/3 tbsp of the honey in a saucepan and heat gently until melted. Reserve 15ml/1 tbsp lemon juice, then stir in the rest with the lemon rind and milk.

3 Sift together the flour, baking powder and nutmeg, then beat in with the semolina. Whisk the egg whites until they form soft peaks, then fold evenly into the mixture.

4 Spoon into the cake tin and sprinkle with sesame seeds. Bake for 25–30 minutes, until golden brown. Mix the reserved honey and lemon juice and drizzle over the cake while warm. Cool in the tin, then cut into fingers to serve.

Pear and Cardamom Spice Cake

Fresh pears and cardamoms – a classic combination – are used together in this moist fruit and nut cake.

Makes one 20cm/8in round cake

115g/4oz/½ cup butter
115g/4oz/generous ½ cup caster sugar
2 eggs, lightly beaten
225g/8oz/2 cups plain flour
15ml/1 tbsp baking powder
30ml/2 tbsp milk
crushed seeds from 2 cardamom pods
50g/2oz/½ cup walnuts, chopped
15ml/1 tbsp poppy seeds
500g/1¼lb dessert pears, peeled, cored and thinly sliced
3 walnut halves, to decorate
clear honey, to glaze

1 Preheat the oven to 180°C/350°F/Gas 4. Grease and base-line a 20cm/8in round, loose-based cake tin.

2 Cream the butter and sugar until pale and light. Gradually beat in the eggs. Sift over the flour and baking powder and fold in with the milk.

3 Stir in the cardamom seeds, chopped nuts and poppy seeds. Reserve one-third of the pear slices, and chop the rest. Fold into the creamed mixture.

4 Transfer to the cake tin. Smooth the surface, making a small dip in the centre. Place the walnut halves in the centre of the cake and fan the reserved pear slices around the walnuts, covering the cake mixture. Bake for 1¼–1½ hours, or until a skewer inserted in the centre comes out clean.

5 Remove the cake from the oven and brush with the honey. Leave in the tin for 20 minutes, then transfer to a wire rack to cool before serving.

Spiced Honey Nut Cake

A combination of ground pistachio nuts and breadcrumbs replaces flour in this recipe, resulting in a light, moist sponge cake.

Makes one 20cm/8in square cake

115g/4oz/generous ½ cup caster sugar
4 eggs, separated
grated rind and juice of 1 lemon
130g/4½oz/generous 1 cup ground pistachios
50g/2oz/scant 1 cup dried breadcrumbs

For the glaze
1 lemon
90ml/6 tbsp clear honey
1 cinnamon stick
15ml/1 tbsp brandy

1 Preheat the oven to 180°C/350°F/Gas 4. Grease and base-line a 20cm/8in square cake tin.

2 Beat the sugar, egg yolks, lemon rind and juice together until pale and creamy. Fold in 115g/4oz/1 cup of the ground pistachios and the breadcrumbs.

3 Whisk the egg whites until stiff and fold into the creamed mixture. Transfer to the cake tin and bake for 15 minutes, until risen and springy to the touch. Cool in the tin for 10 minutes, then transfer to a wire rack.

4 For the syrup, peel the lemon and cut the rind into very thin strips. Squeeze the juice into a small pan and add the honey and cinnamon stick. Bring to the boil, add the shredded rind, and simmer fast for 1 minute. Cool slightly and stir in the brandy.

5 Place the cake on a serving plate, prick all over with a skewer, and pour over the cooled syrup, lemon shreds and cinnamon stick. Sprinkle over the reserved pistachios.

Clare's American Carrot Cake

Makes one 20cm/8in round cake

*250ml/8fl oz/1 cup corn
    oil*
*175g/6oz/1¼ cups
    granulated sugar*
3 eggs
*175g/6oz/1½ cups plain
    flour*
*7.5ml/1½ tsp baking
    powder*
*7.5ml/1½ tsp bicarbonate
    of soda*
1.5ml/¼ tsp salt
*7.5ml/1½ tsp ground
    cinnamon*
*good pinch of grated
    nutmeg*
*1.5ml/¼ tsp ground
    ginger*

*115g/4oz/1 cup chopped
    walnuts*
*225g/8oz/generous
    1½ cups finely grated
    carrots*
5ml/1 tsp vanilla essence
*30ml/2 tbsp soured
    cream*
*8 tiny marzipan carrots,
    to decorate*

For the frosting
*175g/6oz/1 cup full fat
    soft cheese*
*25g/1oz/2 tbsp butter,
    softened*
*225g/8oz/2 cups icing
    sugar, sifted*

1 Preheat the oven to 180°C/350°F/Gas 4. Grease and line
two 20cm/8in loose-based round cake tins.

2 Put the corn oil and sugar into a bowl and beat well. Add
the eggs, one at a time, and beat thoroughly. Sift the flour,
baking powder, bicarbonate of soda, salt, cinnamon, nutmeg
and ginger into the bowl and beat well. Fold in the chopped
walnuts and grated carrots and stir in the vanilla essence and
soured cream.

3 Divide the mixture between the cake tins and bake in the
centre of the oven for about 65 minutes, or until a skewer
inserted into the centre of the cakes comes out clean. Leave to
cool in the tins on a wire rack. Meanwhile, beat all the frosting
ingredients together until smooth.

4 Sandwich the cakes together with a little frosting. Spread
the remaining frosting over the top and sides of the cake. Just
before serving, decorate with the marzipan carrots.

Passion Cake

**This cake is associated with Passion Sunday. The carrot and
banana give it a rich, moist texture.**

Makes one 20cm/8in round cake

*200g/7oz/1¾ cups self-
    raising flour*
*10ml/2 tsp baking
    powder*
5ml/1 tsp cinnamon
*2.5ml/½ tsp freshly
    grated nutmeg*
*150g/5oz/10 tbsp butter,
    softened, or sunflower
    margarine*
*150g/5oz/¾ cup soft
    brown sugar*
grated rind of 1 lemon
2 eggs, beaten
2 carrots, coarsely grated
1 ripe banana, mashed

115g/4oz/¾ cup raisins
*50g/2oz/½ cup chopped
    walnuts or pecan nuts*
30ml/2 tbsp milk
*6 – 8 walnuts, halved, to
    decorate*
*coffee crystal sugar, to
    decorate*

For the frosting
*200g/7oz/scant 1 cup
    cream cheese, softened*
*30g/1½oz/scant ⅓ cup
    icing sugar*
juice of 1 lemon
grated rind of 1 orange

1 Line and grease a deep 20cm/8in round cake tin. Preheat
the oven to 180°C/350°F/Gas 4. Sift the flour, baking powder
and spices into a bowl. In another bowl, cream the butter and
sugar with the lemon rind until it is light and fluffy, then beat
in the eggs. Fold in the flour mixture, then the carrots, banana,
raisins, chopped nuts and milk.

2 Spoon the mixture into the cake tin, level the top and bake
for about 1 hour, until risen and the top is springy to touch.
Turn the tin upside-down and allow the cake to cool in the tin
for 30 minutes. Then turn out on to a wire rack. When cold,
split the cake in half.

3 Cream the cheese with the icing sugar, lemon juice and
orange rind, then sandwich the two halves of the cake
together with half of the frosting. Spread the rest of the
frosting on top and decorate with walnut halves and sugar.

Caribbean Fruit and Rum Cake

Definitely a festive treat, this spicy cake contains both rum and sherry.

Makes one 25cm/10in round cake

450g/1lb/2 cups currants
450g/1lb/2¼ cups raisins
225g/8oz/1 cup prunes, stoned
115g/4oz/¾ cup mixed peel
400g/14oz/2⅔ cups dark soft brown sugar
5ml/1 tsp mixed spice
90ml/6 tbsp rum, plus more if needed

300ml/½ pint/1¼ cups sherry, plus more if needed
450g/1lb/4 cups self-raising flour
450g/1lb/2 cups butter, softened
10 eggs, beaten
5ml/1 tsp vanilla essence

1 Finely chop the dried fruits and peel in a food processor. Combine them in a bowl with 115g/4oz/generous ½ cup of the sugar, the mixed spice, rum and sherry. Cover and leave for 2 weeks. Stir daily and add more alcohol if you wish.

2 Preheat the oven to 160°C/325°F/Gas 3. Grease and then line a 25cm/10in round cake tin with a double layer of greaseproof paper.

3 Sift the flour, and set aside. Cream together the butter and remaining sugar and beat in the eggs until the mixture is smooth and creamy.

4 Add the fruit mixture, then gradually stir in the flour and vanilla essence. Mix well, adding more sherry if the mixture is too stiff; it should just fall off the back of the spoon.

5 Spoon the mixture into the prepared tin, cover loosely with foil and bake for about 2½ hours, until the cake is firm and springy. Leave to cool in the tin overnight.

Thai Rice Cake

A celebration gâteau made from fragrant Thai rice covered with a tangy cream icing and topped with fresh fruits.

Makes one 25cm/10in round cake

225g/8oz/1¼ cups Thai fragrant rice
1 litre/1¾ pints/4½ cups milk
115g/4oz/½ cup caster sugar
6 cardamom pods, crushed open
2 bay leaves
300ml/½ pint/1¼ cups whipping cream
6 eggs, separated

For the topping
300ml/½ pint/1¼ cups double cream
200g/7oz/scant 1 cup quark
5ml/1 tsp vanilla essence
grated rind of 1 lemon
30g/1½oz/scant ¼ cup caster sugar
soft berry fruits and sliced star or kiwi fruit, to decorate

1 Grease and line a deep 25cm/10in round cake tin. Boil the rice in unsalted water for 3 minutes, then drain.

2 Return the rice to the pan with the milk, sugar, cardamom pods and bay leaves. Bring to the boil, then simmer for 20 minutes, stirring occasionally.

3 Allow to cool, then remove the bay leaves and any cardamom husks. Turn into a bowl. Beat in the cream and then the egg yolks. Preheat the oven to 180°C/350°F/Gas 4.

4 Whisk the egg whites until they form soft peaks and fold into the rice mixture. Spoon into the cake tin and bake for 45–50 minutes, until risen and golden brown. The centre should be slightly wobbly – it will firm up as it cools.

5 Chill overnight in the tin. Turn out on to a large serving plate. Whip the double cream until stiff, then mix in the quark, vanilla essence, lemon rind and sugar. Cover the top and sides of the cake with the cream, swirling it attractively. Decorate with soft berry fruits and sliced star or kiwi fruit.

Luxurious Chocolate Cake

This delicious chocolate cake contains no flour and has a light mousse-like texture.

Makes one 20cm/8in round cake

175g/6oz/¾ cup butter, softened
130g/3½oz/⅔ cup caster sugar
9 x 25g/1oz squares plain chocolate, melted
225g/8oz/2 cups ground almonds
4 eggs, separated
4 x 25g/1oz squares white chocolate, melted, to decorate

1 Preheat the oven to 180°C/350°F/Gas 4. Grease and base-line a 20cm/8in springform cake tin. Beat 115g/4oz butter and all the sugar until light and fluffy. Add two-thirds of the plain chocolate, the almonds and egg yolks and beat well.

2 Whisk the egg whites in another clean, dry bowl until stiff. Fold them into the chocolate mixture, then transfer to the tin and smooth the surface. Bake for 50–55 minutes or until a skewer inserted into the centre comes out clean. Cool in the tin for 5 minutes, then remove from the tin and transfer to a wire rack. Remove the lining paper and cool completely.

3 Place the remaining butter and remaining melted chocolate in a saucepan. Heat very gently, stirring constantly, until melted. Place a large sheet of greaseproof paper under the wire rack to catch any drips. Pour the chocolate topping over the cake, allowing the topping to coat the top and sides. Leave to set for at least 1 hour.

4 To decorate, fill a paper piping bag with the melted white chocolate and snip the end. Drizzle the white chocolate around the edges. Use any remaining chocolate to make leaves. Allow to set then place on top of the cake.

One-stage Chocolate Sponge

For family teas, quick and easy favourites like this chocolate cake are invaluable.

Makes one 18cm/7in round cake

175g/6oz/¾ cup soft margarine, at room temperature
115g/4oz/½ cup caster sugar
50g/2oz/4 tbsp golden syrup
175g/6oz/1½ cups self-raising flour, sifted
45ml/3 tbsp cocoa powder, sifted
2.5ml/½ tsp salt
3 eggs, beaten
a little milk, as required
150ml/¼ pint/⅔ cup whipping cream
15–30ml/1–2 tbsp fine shred marmalade
icing sugar, for dusting

1 Preheat the oven to 180°C/350°F/Gas 4. Lightly grease or line two 18cm/7in sandwich tins. Place the margarine, sugar, syrup, flour, cocoa, salt and eggs in a large bowl, and cream together until well blended. If the mixture seems a little thick, stir in 15–30ml/1–2 tbsp milk, until you have a soft dropping consistency.

2 Spoon the mixture into the prepared sandwich tins and bake for about 30 minutes, changing shelves if necessary after 15 minutes, until the tops are just firm and the cakes are springy to the touch.

3 Leave the cakes to cool for 5 minutes, then remove from the tins and leave to cool completely on a wire rack.

4 Whip the cream and fold in the marmalade, then use to sandwich the two cakes together. Sprinkle the top with sifted icing sugar.

One-stage Victoria Sandwich

This versatile sponge recipe can be used for all sorts of cakes.

Makes one 18cm/7in round cake

175g/6oz/1½ cups self-raising flour	**To finish**
pinch of salt	60–90ml/4–6 tbsp raspberry jam
175g/6oz/¾ cup butter, softened	caster sugar or icing sugar
175g/6oz/scant 1 cup caster sugar	
3 eggs	

1 Preheat the oven to 180°C/350°F/Gas 4. Grease two 18cm/7in sandwich tins, line the bases with greaseproof paper and grease the paper.

2 Whisk all the cake ingredients together until smooth and creamy. Divide the mixture between the cake tins and smooth the surfaces. Bake for 25–30 minutes, or until a skewer inserted into the centre of the cakes comes out clean. Turn out on to a wire rack, peel off the lining paper and leave to cool.

3 Place one of the cakes on a serving plate and spread with the raspberry jam. Place the other cake on top.

4 Cut out paper star shapes, place on the cake and dredge with sugar. Remove the paper to reveal the pattern.

Mocha Victoria Sponge

A light coffee- and cocoa-flavoured sponge with a rich buttercream topping.

Makes one 18cm/7in round cake

175g/6oz/¼ cup butter	**For the coffee**
175g/6oz/generous ¾ cup caster sugar	**buttercream**
3 eggs	150g/5oz/generous ½ cup butter
175g/6oz/1½ cups self-raising flour, sifted	15ml/1 tbsp coffee essence or 10ml/2 tsp
15ml/1 tbsp strong black coffee	instant coffee powder dissolved in
15ml/1 tbsp cocoa powder mixed with	15–30ml/1–2 tbsp warm milk
15–30ml/1–2 tbsp boiling water	275g/10oz/2½ cups icing sugar

1 Preheat the oven to 180°C/350°F/Gas 4. Grease and base-line two 18cm/7in round sandwich tins. For the sponge, cream the butter and sugar until light and fluffy. Add the eggs, one at a time, beating well after each addition. Fold in the flour.

2 Divide the mixture into two bowls. Fold the coffee into one and the cocoa mixture into the other.

3 Place alternate spoonfuls of each mixture side by side in the cake tins. Bake for 25–30 minutes. Turn out on to a wire rack to cool.

4 For the buttercream, beat the butter until soft. Gradually beat in the remaining ingredients until smooth.

5 Sandwich the cakes, base-sides together, with a third of the buttercream. Cover the top and side with the rest.

Lemon and Apricot Cake

This cake is soaked in a tangy lemon syrup after baking to keep it really moist.

Makes one 23 x 13cm/9 x 5in loaf

175g/6oz/¾ cup butter, softened
175g/6oz/1½ cups self-raising flour
2.5ml/½ tsp baking powder
175g/6oz/¾ cup caster sugar
3 eggs, lightly beaten
finely grated rind of 1 lemon
175g/6oz/1½ cups ready-to-eat dried apricots, finely chopped

75g/3oz/¾ cup ground almonds
40g/1½oz/6 tbsp pistachio nuts, chopped
50g/2oz/½ cup flaked almonds
15g/½oz/2 tbsp whole pistachio nuts

For the syrup

45ml/3 tbsp caster sugar
freshly squeezed juice of 1 lemon

1 Preheat the oven to 180°C/350°F/Gas 4. Grease and line a 23 x 13cm/9 x 5in loaf tin with greaseproof paper and grease the paper.

2 Place the butter in a mixing bowl. Sift over the flour and baking powder, then add the sugar, eggs and lemon rind. Beat for 1–2 minutes until smooth and glossy, then stir in the apricots, ground almonds and chopped pistachio nuts.

3 Spoon the mixture into the loaf tin and smooth the surface. Sprinkle with the flaked almonds and the whole pistachio nuts. Bake for 1¼ hours, or until a skewer inserted into the centre of the cake comes out clean. Check the cake after 45 minutes and cover with a piece of foil when the top is nicely browned. Leave the cake to cool in the tin.

4 For the lemon syrup, gently dissolve the sugar in the lemon juice. Spoon the syrup over the cake. When the cake is completely cooled, turn it carefully out of the tin and peel off the lining paper.

Cherry Batter Cake

This colourful tray bake looks pretty cut into neat squares or fingers.

Makes one 33 x 23cm/13 x 9in cake

225g/8oz/2 cups self-raising flour
5ml/1 tsp baking powder
75g/3oz/6 tbsp butter, softened
150g/5oz/scant 1 cup soft light brown sugar
1 egg, lightly beaten
150ml/¼ pint/⅔ cup milk
icing sugar, for dusting
whipped cream, to serve (optional)

For the topping

675g/1½lb jar black cherries or blackcurrants, drained
175g/6oz/1 cup soft light brown sugar
50g/2oz/½ cup self-raising flour
50g/2oz/¼ cup butter, melted

1 Preheat the oven to 190°C/375°F/Gas 5. Grease and line a 33 x 23cm/13 x 9in Swiss roll tin with greaseproof paper and grease the paper.

2 To make the base, sift the flour and baking powder into a mixing bowl. Add the butter, sugar, egg and milk. Beat until the mixture becomes smooth, then turn into the prepared tin and smooth the surface.

3 Scatter the drained fruit evenly over the batter mixture.

4 Mix together the remaining topping ingredients and spoon evenly over the fruit. Bake for 40 minutes, or until golden brown and the centre is firm to the touch.

5 Leave to cool, then dust with icing sugar. Serve with whipped cream, if wished.

Fruit Salad Cake

You can use any combination of dried fruits in this rich, dark fruit cake.

Makes one 18cm/7in round cake

175g/6oz/1 cup roughly chopped mixed dried fruit, such as apples, apricots, prunes and peaches
250ml/8fl oz/1 cup hot tea
225g/8oz/2 cups wholemeal self-raising flour

5ml/1 tsp grated nutmeg
50g/2oz/⅓ cup dark muscovado sugar
45ml/3 tbsp sunflower oil
45ml/3 tbsp skimmed milk
demerara sugar, for sprinkling

1 Soak the dried fruits in the tea for several hours or overnight. Drain and reserve the liquid.

2 Preheat the oven to 180℃/350℉/Gas 4. Grease an 18cm/7in round cake tin and line the base with non-stick baking paper.

3 Sift the flour into a bowl with the nutmeg. Stir in the muscovado sugar, fruit and tea. Add the oil and milk, and mix well.

4 Spoon the mixture into the cake tin and sprinkle with demerara sugar. Bake for 50–55 minutes or until firm. Turn out on to a wire rack to cool.

Fairy Cakes with Blueberries

This luxurious treatment of fairy cakes means they will be as popular with adults as with children.

Makes 8–10

115g/4oz/½ cup soft margarine
115g/4oz/½ cup caster sugar
5ml/1 tsp grated lemon rind
pinch of salt
2 eggs, beaten

115g/4oz/1 cup self-raising flour, sifted
120ml/4fl oz/½ cup whipping cream
75–115g/3–4oz/¾– 1 cup blueberries
icing sugar, for dusting

1 Preheat the oven to 190℃/375℉/Gas 5. Cream the margarine, sugar, lemon rind and salt in a large bowl until pale and fluffy.

2 Gradually beat in the eggs, then fold in the flour until well mixed. Spoon the mixture into eight to ten paper cases on baking sheets and bake for 15–20 minutes, until just golden.

3 Leave the cakes to cool, then scoop out a circle of sponge from the top of each using the point of a small sharp knife, and set them aside.

4 Whip the cream and place a spoonful in each cake, plus a couple of blueberries. Replace the lids at an angle and sift over some icing sugar.

Jewel Cake

This pretty cake is excellent served as a tea-time treat.

Makes one 23 x 13cm/9 x 5in cake

115g/4oz/½ cup mixed
   glacé cherries, halved,
   washed and dried
50g/2oz/4 tbsp stem
   ginger in syrup,
   chopped, washed and
   dried
50g/2oz/5 tbsp chopped
   mixed peel
115g/4oz/1 cup self-
   raising flour
75g/3oz/¼ cup plain
   flour
25g/1oz/3 tbsp cornflour
175g/6oz/¾ cup butter

175g/6oz/scant 1 cup
   caster sugar
3 eggs
grated rind of 1 orange

To decorate

175g/6oz/1½ cups icing
   sugar, sifted
30–45ml/2–3 tbsp
   freshly squeezed
   orange juice
50g/2oz/¼ cup mixed
   glacé cherries, chopped
25g/1oz/2½ tbsp mixed
   peel, chopped

1 Preheat the oven to 180°C/350°F/Gas 4. Grease and line a 23 x 13cm/9 x 5in loaf tin and grease the paper.

2 Place the cherries, stem ginger and mixed peel in a polythene bag with 25g/1oz/4 tbsp of the self-raising flour and shake to coat evenly. Sift together the remaining flours and cornflour.

3 Beat together the butter and sugar until light and fluffy. Beat in the eggs, one at a time. Fold in the sifted flours with the orange rind, then stir in the dried fruit.

4 Transfer the mixture to the cake tin and bake for 1¼ hours, or until a skewer inserted into the centre comes out clean. Leave in the tin for 5 minutes, then cool on a wire rack.

5 For the decoration, mix the icing sugar with the orange juice until smooth. Drizzle the icing over the cake. Mix together the chopped glacé cherries and mixed peel, then use to decorate the cake. Allow the icing to set before serving.

Iced Paradise Cake

Makes one 23 x 13cm/9 x 5in cake

3 eggs
75g/3oz/scant ½ cup
   caster sugar
65g/12½oz/9 tbsp plain
   flour
15g/½oz/1 tbsp
   cornflour
90ml/6 tbsp dark rum
250g/9oz/1½ cups plain
   chocolate chips
30ml/2 tbsp golden syrup
30ml/2 tbsp water

400ml/14fl oz/1¾ cups
   double cream
115g/4oz/scant 1 cup
   desiccated coconut,
   toasted
25g/1oz/2 tbsp unsalted
   butter
30ml/2 tbsp single cream
50g/2oz/5 tbsp white
   chocolate chips, melted
coconut curls, to decorate
cocoa powder, for dusting

1 Preheat the oven to 200°C/400°F/Gas 6. Grease and flour two baking sheets. Line a 23 x 13cm/9 x 5in tin with clear film.

2 Whisk the eggs and sugar in a heatproof bowl until blended. Place over a pan of simmering water and whisk until pale and thick. Whisk off the heat until cool. Sift over the flour and cornflour and fold in. Pipe 30 8cm/3in sponge fingers on to the baking sheets. Bake for 8–10 minutes. Cool slightly on the sheets, then on a wire rack.

3 Line the base and sides of the loaf tin with sponge fingers. Brush with rum. Melt 75g/3oz/½ cup chocolate chips, syrup, water and 30ml/2 tbsp rum in a bowl over simmering water.

4 Whip the double cream until it holds its shape, stir in the chocolate mixture and toasted coconut. Pour into the tin and top with the remaining sponge fingers. Brush over the remaining rum. Cover with clear film and freeze until firm.

5 Melt the remaining chocolate, butter and cream as before, then cool slightly. Turn the cake out on to a wire rack. Pour over the icing to coat. Chill.

6 Drizzle the white chocolate in zigzags over the cake. Chill. Sprinkle with coconut curls and dust with cocoa powder.

Pound Cake with Red Fruit

This orange-scented cake is good for tea, or serve as a dessert with a fruit coulis.

Makes one 20 x 10cm/8 x 4in cake

450g/1lb/about 4 cups
fresh raspberries,
strawberries or stoned
cherries, or a
combination of any of
these
175g/6oz/¾ cup caster
sugar, plus
15 – 30ml/1 – 2 tbsp,
plus extra for
sprinkling

15ml/1 tbsp lemon juice
175g/6oz/1½ cups plain
flour
10ml/2 tsp baking
powder
pinch of salt
175g/6oz/¾ cup unsalted
butter, softened
3 eggs
grated rind of 1 orange
15ml/1 tbsp orange juice

1 Reserve a few whole fruits for decorating. In a blender or food processor, process the fruit until smooth. Add 15 – 30ml/1 – 2 tbsp sugar and the lemon juice, and process again. Strain the sauce and chill.

2 Grease the base and sides of a 20 x 10cm/8 x 4in loaf tin and line the base with non-stick baking paper. Grease the paper. Sprinkle with sugar and tip out any excess. Preheat the oven to 180°C/350°F/Gas 4.

3 Sift together the flour, baking powder and a pinch of salt. Beat the butter until creamy. Add the sugar and beat until light and fluffy. Add the eggs, one at a time, beating well after each addition. Beat in the orange rind and juice. Gently fold the flour mixture into the butter mixture in three batches, then spoon the mixture into the loaf tin and tap gently to release any air bubbles.

4 Bake for 35 – 40 minutes, until the top is golden and it is springy to the touch. Leave the cake in its tin on a wire rack for 10 minutes, then remove the cake from the tin and cool for 30 minutes. Remove the paper and serve slices of cake with a little of the fruit sauce, decorated with the reserved fruit.

Madeleine Cakes

These little tea cakes, baked in a special tin with shell-shaped cups, are best eaten on the day they are made.

Makes 12

165g/5½oz/generous
1¼ cups plain flour
5ml/1 tsp baking powder
2 eggs
75g/3oz/½ cup icing
sugar, plus extra for
dusting

grated rind of 1 lemon or
orange
15ml/1 tbsp lemon or
orange juice
75g/3oz/6 tbsp unsalted
butter, melted and
slightly cooled

1 Preheat the oven to 190°C/375°F/Gas 5. Generously grease a 12-cup madeleine cake tin. Sift together the flour and the baking powder.

2 Beat the eggs and icing sugar until the mixture is thick and creamy and leaves ribbon trails. Gently fold in the lemon or orange rind and juice.

3 Beginning with the flour mixture, alternately fold in the flour and melted butter in four batches. Leave to stand for 10 minutes, then spoon into the tin. Tap gently to release any air bubbles. Bake for 12 – 15 minutes, rotating the tin halfway through cooking, until a skewer inserted in the centre comes out clean. Tip out on to a wire rack to cool completely and dust with icing sugar before serving.

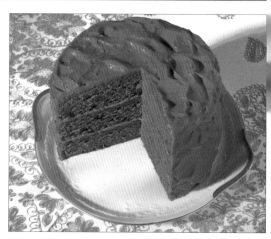

Chocolate-orange Battenburg Cake

A tasty variation on the traditional pink-and-white Battenburg cake.

Makes one 18cm/7in long rectangular cake

115g/4oz/½ cup soft
margarine
115g/4oz/½ cup caster
sugar
2 eggs, beaten
few drops vanilla essence
15g/½oz/1 tbsp ground
almonds
115g/4oz/1 cup self-
raising flour, sifted

grated rind and juice of
½ orange
15g/½oz/2 tbsp cocoa
powder, sifted
30 – 45ml/2 – 3 tbsp milk
1 jar chocolate and nut
spread
225g/8oz white almond
paste

1 Preheat the oven to 180°C/350°F/Gas 4. Grease and line an 18cm/7in square cake tin. Put a double piece of foil across the middle of the tin, to divide it into two equal oblongs.

2 Cream the margarine and sugar. Beat in the eggs, vanilla and almonds. Divide the mixture evenly into two halves. Fold half of the flour into one half, with the orange rind and enough juice to give a soft dropping consistency. Fold the rest of the flour and the cocoa into the other half, with enough milk to give a soft dropping consistency. Fill the tin with the two mixes and level the top.

3 Bake for 15 minutes, reduce the heat to 160°C/325°F/Gas 3 and cook for 20 – 30 minutes, until the top is just firm. Leave to cool in the tin for a few minutes. Turn out on to a board, cut each cake into two strips and trim evenly. Leave to cool.

4 Using the spread, sandwich the cakes together, Battenburg-style. Roll out the almond paste on a board lightly dusted with cornflour to a rectangle 18cm/7in wide and long enough to wrap around the cake. Wrap the paste around the cake, putting the join underneath. Press to seal.

Best-ever Chocolate Sandwich

A three-layered cake that would be ideal for a birthday party or a special high tea.

Makes one 20cm/8in round cake

115g/4oz/1cup plain
flour
50g/2oz/½ cup cocoa
powder
5ml/1 tsp baking powder
pinch of salt
6 eggs
225g/8oz/generous 1 cup
caster sugar
10ml/2 tsp vanilla
essence

115g/4oz/½ cup unsalted
butter, melted
225g/8oz plain chocolate,
chopped
75g/3oz/6 tbsp unsalted
butter
3 eggs, separated
250ml/8fl oz/1 cup
whipping cream
45ml/3 tbsp caster sugar

1 Preheat the oven to 180°C/350°F/Gas 4. Line three 20cm/8in round tins with greaseproof paper, grease the paper and dust with flour. Sift the flour, cocoa, baking powder and salt together three times.

2 Place the eggs and sugar in a heatproof bowl set over a pan of simmering water. Beat until doubled in volume, about 10 minutes. Add the vanilla. Fold in the flour mixture in three batches, then the butter.

3 Put the mixture in the tins. Bake until the cakes pull away from the tin sides, about 25 minutes. Transfer to a wire rack.

4 For the icing, melt the chocolate in the top of a double boiler. Off the heat, stir in the butter and egg yolks. Return to the heat and stir until thick.

5 Whip the cream until firm. In another bowl, beat the egg whites until stiff. Add the sugar and beat until glossy. Fold the cream, then the egg whites, into the chocolate mixture. Chill for about 20 minutes, then sandwich together and cover the cake with icing.

Chocolate Layer Cake

Makes one 23cm/9in cake

225g/8oz can cooked
  whole beetroot,
  drained and juice
  reserved
115g/4oz/½ cup unsalted
  butter, softened
550g/1lb 6oz/2½ cups
  light brown sugar
3 eggs
15ml/1 tbsp vanilla
  essence
75g/3oz unsweetened
  chocolate, melted
285g/10oz/2 cups plain
  flour

10ml/2 tsp baking
  powder
2.5ml/½ tsp salt
120ml/4fl oz/½ cup
  buttermilk
chocolate curls, to
  decorate (optional)

For the frosting

450ml/16fl oz/2 cups
  double cream
500g/1lb 2oz plain
  chocolate, chopped
15ml/1 tbsp vanilla
  essence

1 Preheat the oven to 180°C/350°F/Gas 4. Grease two 23cm/9in cake tins and dust with cocoa powder. Grate the beetroot and add it to its juice. Beat the butter, brown sugar, eggs and vanilla until pale and fluffy. Beat in the chocolate.

2 Sift together the flour, baking powder and salt. With the mixer on low speed and beginning and ending with flour mixture, alternately beat in flour and buttermilk. Add the beetroot and juice and beat for 1 minute. Fill the tins and bake for 30–35 minutes, until a skewer inserted in the centre comes out clean. Cool for 10 minutes, then unmould and cool.

3 To make the frosting, heat the cream until it just begins to boil, stirring occasionally to prevent scorching. Remove from the heat and stir in the chocolate, until melted and smooth. Stir in the vanilla. Strain into a bowl and chill, stirring every 10 minutes, for 1 hour.

4 Sandwich and cover the cake with frosting, and top with chocolate curls, if using. Allow to set for 20–30 minutes, then chill before serving.

Marbled Chocolate-peanut Cake

Serves 12–14

115g/4oz unsweetened
  chocolate, chopped
225g/8oz/1 cup unsalted
  butter, softened
225g/8oz/1 cup peanut
  butter
200g/6½oz/1 cup
  granulated sugar
220g/7oz/1 cup light
  brown sugar
5 eggs
285g/10oz/2 cups plain
  flour
10ml/2 tsp baking
  powder

2.5ml/½ tsp salt
125ml/4fl oz/½ cup milk
50g/2oz/5 tbsp chocolate
  chips

**For the chocolate-
peanut butter glaze**

25g/1oz/2 tbsp butter,
  diced
25g/1oz/2 tbsp smooth
  peanut butter
45ml/3 tbsp golden syrup
5ml/1 tsp vanilla essence
175g/6oz plain chocolate,
  broken into pieces

1 Preheat the oven to 180°C/350°F/Gas 4. Grease and flour a 3-litre/5-pint/12-cup tube tin or ring mould. In the top of a double boiler, melt the chocolate.

2 Beat the butter, peanut butter and sugars until light and creamy. Add the eggs, one at a time, beating well after each addition. Sift together the flour, baking powder and salt. Add to the butter mixture alternately with the milk.

3 Pour half the batter into another bowl. Stir the melted chocolate into one half and stir the chocolate chips into the other half. Drop alternate large spoonfuls of the two batters into the tin or mould. Using a knife, pull through the batters to create a swirled marbled effect; do not let the knife touch the side or base of the tin. Bake for 50–60 minutes, until the top springs back when touched. Cool in the tin on a wire rack for 10 minutes. Then unmould on to the wire rack.

4 Combine the glaze ingredients and 15ml/1 tbsp water in a small saucepan. Melt over a low heat, stirring. Cool slightly, then drizzle over the cake, allowing it to run down the side.

Chocolate Fairy Cakes

Makes 24

115g/4oz good-quality
   plain chocolate, cut
   into small pieces
15ml/1 tbsp water
300g/10oz/2½ cups plain
   flour
5ml/1 tsp baking powder
2.5ml/½ tsp bicarbonate
   of soda
pinch of salt
300g/10oz/scant 1½ cups
   caster sugar

170g/6oz/¾ cup butter or
   margarine, at room
   temperature
150ml/¼ pint/⅔ cup milk
5ml/1 tsp vanilla essence
3 eggs
1 recipe quantity
   buttercream, flavoured
   to taste

1 Preheat the oven to 180°C/350°F/Gas 4. Grease and flour 24 deep bun tins, about 6.5cm/2¾in in diameter, or use paper cases in the tins.

2 Put the chocolate and water in a bowl set over a pan of almost simmering water. Heat until melted and smooth, stirring. Remove from the heat and leave to cool.

3 Sift the flour, baking powder, bicarbonate of soda, salt and sugar into a large bowl. Add the chocolate mixture, butter or margarine, milk and vanilla essence.

4 With an electric mixer on medium-low speed, beat until smoothly blended. Increase the speed to high and beat for 2 minutes. Add the eggs and beat for 2 more minutes.

5 Divide the mixture evenly among the prepared bun tins and bake for 20–25 minutes, or until a skewer inserted into the centre of a cake comes out clean. Cool in the tins for 10 minutes, then turn out to cool completely on a wire rack.

6 Ice the top of each cake with buttercream, swirling it into a peak in the centre.

Chocolate Mint-filled Cupcakes

For extra mint flavour, chop eight thin mint cream-filled after-dinner mints and fold into the cake batter.

Makes 12

225g/8oz/2 cups plain
   flour
5ml/1 tsp bicarbonate of
   soda
pinch of salt
50g/2oz/½ cup cocoa
   powder
150g/5oz/10 tbsp
   unsalted butter,
   softened
300g/10½oz/1½ cups
   caster sugar
3 eggs
5ml/1 tsp peppermint
   essence

250ml/8fl oz/1 cup milk

For the filling
300ml/10fl oz/1¼ cups
   double or whipping
   cream
5ml/1 tsp peppermint
   essence

For the glaze
170g/6oz plain chocolate
115g/4oz/½ cup unsalted
   butter
5ml/1 tsp peppermint
   essence

1 Preheat the oven to 180°C/350°F/Gas 4. Line a 12-cup bun tray with paper cases. Sift together the flour, bicarbonate of soda, salt and cocoa powder. In another bowl, beat the butter and sugar until light and creamy. Add the eggs, one at a time, beating well after each addition; beat in the peppermint. On low speed, beat in the flour mixture alternately with the milk, until just blended. Spoon into the paper cases.

2 Bake for 12–15 minutes, until a skewer inserted in the centre of a cake comes out clean. Transfer to a wire rack to cool. When cool, remove the paper cases.

3 For the filling, whip the cream and peppermint until stiff. Spoon into a piping bag fitted with a small plain nozzle. Pipe about 15ml/1 tbsp into each cake through the base.

4 For the glaze, melt the chocolate and butter, stirring until smooth. Remove from the heat and stir in the peppermint essence. Cool, then spread on top of each cake.

Rich Chocolate Nut Cake

Use walnuts or pecan nuts for the cake sides if you prefer.

Makes one 23cm/9in round cake

225g/8oz/1 cup butter
225g/8oz plain chocolate
115g/4oz/1 cup cocoa
powder
350g/12oz/1¾ cups
caster sugar
6 eggs
85ml/3fl oz/5 tbsp
brandy

225g/8oz/2 cups finely
chopped hazelnuts

For the glaze
50g/2oz/4 tbsp butter
150g/5oz bitter cooking
chocolate
30ml/2 tbsp milk
5ml/1 tsp vanilla essence

1   Preheat the oven to 180°C/350°F/Gas 4. Line a 23 x 5cm/ 9 x 2in round tin with greaseproof paper and grease the paper. Melt the butter and chocolate in the top of a double boiler. Leave to cool.

2   Sift the cocoa into a bowl. Add the sugar and eggs and stir until just combined. Pour in the chocolate mixture and brandy. Fold in three-quarters of the nuts, then pour the mixture into the cake tin.

3   Set the tin in a roasting tin and pour 2.5cm/1in hot water into the outer tin. Bake until the cake is firm to the touch, about 45 minutes. Leave for 15 minutes, then unmould on to a wire rack. When cool, wrap in greaseproof paper and chill for at least 6 hours.

4   For the glaze, melt the butter and chocolate with the milk and vanilla in the top of a double boiler.

5   Place the cake on a wire rack over a plate. Drizzle the glaze over, letting it drip down the sides. Cover the cake sides with the remaining nuts. Transfer to a serving plate when set.

Multi-layer Chocolate Cake

For a change, sandwich the cake layers with softened vanilla ice cream. Freeze before serving.

Makes one 20cm/8in round cake

115g/4oz plain chocolate
175g/6oz/¾ cup butter
450g/1lb/2¼ cups caster
sugar
3 eggs
5ml/1 tsp vanilla essence
175g/6oz/1½ cups plain
flour
5ml/1 tsp baking powder

115g/4oz/1 cup chopped
walnuts

For the filling and topping
350ml/12fl oz/1½ cups
whipping cream
225g/8oz plain chocolate
15ml/1 tbsp vegetable oil

1   Preheat the oven to 180°C/350°F/Gas 4. Line two 20cm/8in round cake tins with greaseproof paper and grease the paper.

2   Melt the chocolate and butter in the top of a double boiler. Transfer to a bowl and stir in the sugar. Add the eggs and vanilla and mix well. Sift over the flour and baking powder. Stir in the walnuts.

3   Pour the mixture into the cake tins. Bake until a skewer inserted in the centre comes out clean, about 30 minutes. Stand for 10 minutes, then unmould on to a wire rack to cool.

4   Whip the cream until firm. Slice the cakes in half horizontally. Sandwich them together and cover the cake with the cream. Chill.

5   To make the chocolate curls, melt the chocolate and oil in the top of a double boiler. Spread on to a non-porous surface. Just before it sets, hold the blade of a knife at an angle to the chocolate and scrape across the surface to make curls. Use to decorate the cake.

Chocolate Frosted Layer Cake

The contrast between the frosting and the sponge creates a
dramatic effect when the cake is cut.

Makes one 20cm/8in round cake

225g/8oz/1 cup butter or margarine, at room temperature	10ml/2 tsp baking powder
285g/10½oz/1½ cups sugar	1.5ml/¼ tsp salt
4 eggs, separated	250ml/8fl oz/1 cup milk
10ml/2 tsp vanilla essence	**For the frosting**
385g/13½oz/3½ cups plain flour	150g/5oz plain chocolate
	120ml/4fl oz/½ cup soured cream
	1.5ml/¼ tsp salt

1 Preheat the oven to 180°C/350°F/Gas 4. Line two
20cm/8in round cake tins with greaseproof paper and grease
the paper. Dust the tins with flour. Tap to remove any excess.

2 Cream the butter or margarine until soft. Gradually add
the sugar and beat until light and fluffy. Beat the egg yolks,
then add to the butter mixture with the vanilla.

3 Sift the flour with the baking powder three times. Set
aside. Beat the egg whites with the salt until they peak stiffly.

4 Fold the dry ingredients into the butter mixture in three
batches, alternating with the milk. Add a dollop of the egg
white and fold in to lighten the mixture. Fold in the rest until
just blended.

5 Spoon into the cake tins and bake until the cakes pull
away from the sides, about 30 minutes. Leave in the tins for
5 minutes, then turn out on to a wire rack.

6 For the frosting, melt the chocolate in the top of a double
boiler. When cool, stir in the soured cream and salt. Sandwich
the layers with frosting, then spread on the top and side.

Devil's Food Cake with Orange

Makes one 23cm/9in round cake

50g/2oz/½ cup cocoa powder	120ml/4fl oz/½ cup soured cream
175ml/6fl oz/¾ cup boiling water	blanched orange rind shreds, to decorate
175g/6oz/¾ cup butter, at room temperature	**For the frosting**
350g/12oz/2 cups dark brown sugar	285g/10½oz/1½ cups caster sugar
3 eggs	2 egg whites
275g/10oz/2½ cups plain flour	60ml/4 tbsp frozen orange juice concentrate
7.5ml/1½ tsp bicarbonate of soda	15ml/1 tbsp lemon juice
1.5ml/¼ tsp baking powder	grated rind of 1 orange

1 Preheat the oven to 180°C/350°F/Gas 4. Line two
23cm/9in cake tins with greaseproof paper and grease the
paper. In a bowl, mix the cocoa and water until smooth.

2 Cream the butter and sugar until light and fluffy. Add the
eggs, one at a time, beating well after each addition. When the
cocoa mixture is lukewarm, add to the butter mixture. Sift
together the flour, soda and baking powder twice. Fold into
the cocoa mixture in three batches, alternating with the
soured cream. Pour into the tins and bake until the cakes pull
away from the sides, 30–35 minutes. Stand for 15 minutes,
then turn out on to a wire rack.

3 For the frosting, place all the ingredients in the top of a
double boiler. With an electric mixer, beat until the mixture
holds soft peaks. Continue beating off the heat until thick
enough to spread.

4 Sandwich the cake layers with frosting, then spread over
the top and side. Decorate with orange rind shreds.

French Chocolate Cake

This is typical of a French home-made cake – dense, dark and delicious. Serve with cream or a fruit coulis.

Makes one 24cm/9½in round cake

150g/5oz/5 tbsp caster sugar	*5 eggs, separated*
275g/10oz plain chocolate, chopped	*40g/1½oz/¼ cup plain flour, sifted*
175g/6oz/¾ cup unsalted butter, cut into pieces	*pinch of salt*
10ml/2 tsp vanilla essence	*icing sugar, for dusting*

1 Preheat the oven to 160°C/325°F/Gas 3. Butter a 24cm/9½in springform tin, sprinkle with sugar and tap out the excess.

2 Set aside 45ml/3 tbsp of the sugar. Place the chocolate, butter and remaining sugar in a heavy saucepan and cook over a low heat until melted. Remove from the heat, stir in the vanilla essence and leave to cool slightly.

3 Beat the egg yolks, one at a time, into the chocolate mixture, then stir in the flour.

4 Beat the egg whites with the salt until soft peaks form. Sprinkle over the reserved sugar and beat until stiff and glossy. Beat one-third of the whites into the chocolate mixture, then fold in the rest.

5 Pour the mixture into the tin and tap it gently to release any air bubbles.

6 Bake the cake for 35–45 minutes, until well risen and the top springs back when touched lightly. Transfer to a wire rack, remove the sides of the tin and leave to cool. Remove the tin base, dust the cake with icing sugar and transfer to a serving plate.

Almond Cake

Serve this wonderfully nutty cake with coffee, or, for a treat, with a glass of almond liqueur.

Makes one 23cm/9in round cake

225g/8oz/1⅓ cups blanched, toasted whole almonds	*2.5ml/½ tsp almond essence*
75g/3oz/5 tbsp icing sugar	*25g/1oz/4 tbsp plain flour*
3 eggs	*3 egg whites*
25g/1oz/2 tbsp butter, melted	*15ml/1 tbsp caster sugar*
	toasted whole almonds, to decorate

1 Preheat the oven to 160°C/325°F/Gas 3. Line a 23cm/9in round cake tin with greaseproof paper and grease the paper.

2 Coarsely chop the almonds and grind them with half the icing sugar in a blender or food processor. Transfer to a mixing bowl.

3 Beat in the whole eggs and remaining icing sugar until the mixture forms ribbon trails. Mix in the butter and almond essence. Sift over the flour and fold in.

4 Beat the egg whites until they peak softly. Add the caster sugar and beat until stiff and glossy. Fold into the almond mixture in four batches.

5 Spoon the mixture into the cake tin and bake until golden brown, 15–20 minutes. Decorate with toasted almonds.

Caramel Layer Cake

Makes one 20cm/8in round cake

275g/10oz/2½ cups plain flour
7.5ml/1½ tsp baking powder
175g/6oz/¾ cup butter, at room temperature
165g/5½oz/generous ⅔ cup caster sugar
4 eggs, beaten
5ml/1 tsp vanilla essence
120ml/4fl oz/½ cup milk
whipped cream, to decorate

caramel threads, to decorate (optional)

For the frosting
285g/10½oz/1⅓ cups dark brown sugar
250ml/8fl oz/1 cup milk
25g/1oz/2 tbsp unsalted butter
45 – 75ml/3 – 5 tbsp whipping cream

1 Preheat the oven to 180°C/350°F/Gas 4. Line two 20cm/8in cake tins with greaseproof paper and grease the paper. Sift the flour and baking powder together three times.

2 Cream the butter and caster sugar until light and fluffy. Slowly mix in the beaten eggs. Add the vanilla. Fold in the flour mixture, alternating with the milk. Divide the batter between the cake tins and spread evenly. Bake until the cakes pull away from the sides of the tin, about 30 minutes. Stand in the tins for 5 minutes, then turn out and cool on a wire rack.

3 For the frosting, bring the brown sugar and milk to the boil, cover and cook for 2 minutes. Uncover and continue to boil, without stirring, until the mixture reaches 119°C/238°F (soft ball stage) on a sugar thermometer.

4 Remove the pan from the heat and add the butter, but do not stir it in. Leave to cool until lukewarm, then beat until the mixture is smooth. Stir in enough cream to obtain a spreadable consistency.

5 Sandwich the cake together with frosting and then cover the top and sides. Decorate with whipped cream, and caramel threads if liked.

Marbled Spice Cake

You could bake this cake in a 20cm/8in round tin if you do not have a kugelhopf.

Makes one ring cake

75g/3oz/6 tbsp butter, softened
115g/4oz/generous ½ cup caster sugar
2 eggs, lightly beaten
few drops vanilla essence
130g/4½oz/generous 1 cup plain flour
7.5ml/1½ tsp baking powder

45ml/3 tbsp milk
45ml/3 tbsp black treacle
5ml/1 tsp mixed spice
2.5ml/½ tsp ground ginger
175g/6oz/1½ cups icing sugar, sifted, to decorate

1 Preheat the oven to 180°C/350°F/Gas 4. Grease and flour a 900g/2lb kugelhopf or ring mould.

2 Cream together the butter and sugar until light and fluffy. Beat in the eggs and vanilla.

3 Sift together the flour and baking powder, then fold into the butter mixture, alternating with the milk.

4 Add the treacle and spices to one-third of the mixture. Drop alternating spoonfuls of the two mixtures into the tin. Run a knife through them to give a marbled effect.

5 Bake for 50 minutes, or until a skewer inserted into the centre comes out clean. Leave in the tin for 10 minutes, then turn out on to a wire rack to cool.

6 To decorate, make a smooth icing with the icing sugar and some warm water. Drizzle over the cake and leave to set.

Raspberry Meringue Gâteau

A rich hazelnut meringue filled with cream and raspberries makes a delicious combination of textures and tastes.

Serves 8

4 egg whites
225g/8oz/1 cup caster
   sugar
few drops vanilla essence
5ml/1 tsp malt vinegar
115g/4oz/1 cup toasted
   chopped hazelnuts,
   ground
300ml/½ pint/1¼ cups
   double cream
350g/12oz /2 cups
   raspberries

icing sugar, for dusting
raspberries and mint
   sprigs, to decorate

For the sauce

225g/8oz/1⅓ cups
   raspberries
45ml/3 tbsp icing sugar
15ml/1 tbsp orange
   liqueur

1 Preheat the oven to 180°C/350°F/Gas 4. Grease two 20cm/8in cake tins and line the bases with greaseproof paper.

2 Whisk the egg whites in a large bowl until they hold stiff peaks, then gradually whisk in the caster sugar a tablespoon at a time, whisking well after each addition.

3 Continue whisking the meringue mixture for a minute or two until very stiff, then fold in the vanilla essence, vinegar and the ground hazelnuts. Divide the meringue mixture between the prepared tins and spread level. Bake for 50–60 minutes, until crisp. Remove the meringues from the tins and leave to cool on a wire rack.

4 Meanwhile, make the sauce. Purée the raspberries with the icing sugar and orange liqueur in a blender or food processor, then press the purée through a nylon sieve to remove any pips. Chill the sauce until ready to serve.

5 Whip the cream then fold in the raspberries. Sandwich the meringue rounds with the raspberry cream. Dust with icing sugar, decorate with fruit and mint and serve with the sauce.

Strawberry Mint Sponge

This combination of fruit, mint and ice cream will prove popular with everyone.

Makes one 20cm/8in round cake

6 – 10 fresh mint leaves,
   plus extra to decorate
175g/6oz/¾ cup caster
   sugar
175g/6oz/¾ cup butter
175g/6oz/1½ cups self-
   raising flour
3 eggs

1.2 litres/2 pints/5 cups
   strawberry ice cream,
   softened
600ml/1 pint/2½ cups
   double cream
30ml/2 tbsp mint liqueur
350g/12oz/2 cups fresh
   strawberries

1 Tear the mint into pieces, mix with the sugar, and leave overnight. (Remove the leaves from the sugar before use.)

2 Preheat the oven to 190°C/375°F/Gas 5. Grease and line a 20cm/8in deep springform cake tin. Cream the butter and sugar, add the flour, and then the eggs. Pour the mixture into the tin.

3 Bake for 20–25 minutes, or until a skewer inserted in the centre comes out clean. Turn out on to a wire rack to cool. When cool, split into two layers.

4 Wash the cake tin and line with clear film. Put the cake base back in the tin. Spread with the ice cream, then cover with the top half of the cake. Freeze for 3–4 hours.

5 Whip the cream with the liqueur. Turn the cake out on to a serving plate and quickly spread a layer of whipped cream all over it, leaving a rough finish. Freeze until 10 minutes before serving. Decorate the cake with the strawberries and place fresh mint leaves around it.

Chestnut Cake

This rich, moist cake can be made up to 1 week in advance and kept, undecorated and wrapped, in an airtight tin.

Serves 8–10

150g/5oz/1¼ cups plain flour	*425g/15oz can chestnut purée*
pinch of salt	*9 eggs, separated*
225g/8oz/1 cup butter, softened	*105ml/7 tbsp dark rum*
150g/5oz/¾ cup caster sugar	*300ml/½ pint/1¼ cups double cream*
	marron glacés and icing sugar, to decorate

1 Preheat the oven to 180℃/350℉/Gas 4. Grease and line a 20cm/8in springform cake tin.

2 Sift the flour and salt and set aside. Beat the butter and sugar together until light and fluffy. Fold in two-thirds of the chestnut purée, with the egg yolks. Fold in the flour and salt.

3 Whisk the egg whites in a clean, dry bowl until stiff.Beat a little of the egg whites into the chestnut mixture, until evenly blended, then fold in the remainder. Transfer the cake mixture to the tin and smooth the surface. Bake in the centre of the oven for about 1¼ hours, or until a skewer comes out clean. Leave in the tin and place on a wire rack.

4 Using a skewer, pierce holes over the cake. Sprinkle with 60ml/4 tbsp of rum, then cool. Remove the cake from the tin, peel off the lining paper and cut horizontally into two layers. Place bottom layer on a serving plate. Whisk the cream with the remaining rum, sugar and chestnut purée until smooth.

5 To assemble, spread two-thirds of the chestnut cream mixture over the bottom layer and place other layer on top. Spread some chestnut cream over the top and sides of the cake, pipe the remainder in large swirls round the edge of the cake. Decorate with chopped marron glacés and icing sugar.

Marbled Ring Cake

Glaze this cake with running icing if you prefer.

Makes one 25cm/10in ring cake

115g/4oz plain chocolate	*15ml/1 tbsp vanilla essence*
350g/12oz/3 cups plain flour	*10 eggs, at room temperature*
5ml/1 tsp baking powder	*icing sugar, for dusting*
450g/1lb/2 cups butter, at room temperature	
725g/1lb 10oz/3¾ cups caster sugar	

1 Preheat the oven to 180℃/350℉/Gas 4. Line a 25 x 10cm/10 x 4in ring mould with greaseproof paper and grease the paper. Dust with flour. Melt the chocolate in the top of a double boiler, stirring occasionally. Set aside.

2 Sift together the flour and baking powder. In another bowl, cream the butter, sugar and vanilla essence until light and fluffy. Add the eggs, two at a time, then gradually blend in the flour mixture.

3 Spoon half of the mixture into the ring mould. Stir the chocolate into the remaining mixture, then spoon into the tin. With a palette knife, swirl the mixtures for a marbled effect.

4 Bake until a skewer inserted in the centre comes out clean, about 1¼ hours. Cover with foil halfway through baking. Stand for 15 minutes, then unmould and transfer to a wire rack. To serve, dust with icing sugar.

Chocolate and Nut Gâteau

Hazelnuts give an interesting crunchy texture to this delicious iced dessert.

Serves 6–8

75g/3oz/½ cup shelled
  hazelnuts
about 32 sponge fingers
150ml/¼ pint/¾ cup cold
  strong black coffee
30ml/2 tbsp brandy
450ml/¾ pint/1¾ cups
  double cream

75g/3oz/6 tbsp icing
  sugar, sifted
150g/5oz plain chocolate
icing sugar and cocoa
  powder, for dusting

1 Preheat the oven to 200°C/400°F/Gas 6. Spread out the hazelnuts on a baking sheet and toast them in the oven for 5 minutes until golden. Transfer the nuts to a clean dish towel and rub off the skins while still warm. Cool, then chop finely.

2 Line a 1.2 litre/2 pint/5 cup loaf tin with clear film and cut enough sponge fingers to fit the base and sides. Reserve the remaining fingers.

3 Mix the coffee and brandy in a shallow dish. Dip the sponge fingers briefly into the coffee mixture and return to the tin, sugary side down.

4 Whip the cream with the icing sugar until it forms soft peaks. Roughly chop 75g/3oz of the chocolate, and fold into the cream with the hazelnuts. Melt the remaining chocolate in a bowl set over a pan of barely simmering water. Cool, then fold into the cream mixture. Spoon into the tin.

5 Moisten the remaining biscuits in the coffee mixture and lay over the filling. Wrap and freeze until firm.

6 Remove from the freezer 30 minutes before serving. Turn out on to a serving plate and dust with icing sugar and cocoa.

Chocolate and Orange Angel Cake

This light-as-air sponge with its fluffy icing is the answer to a cake-lover's prayer.

Makes one 20cm/8in ring cake

25g/1oz/¼ cup plain
  flour
15g/½oz/2 tbsp cocoa
  powder
15g/½oz/2 tbsp cornflour
pinch of salt
5 egg whites
2.5ml/½ tsp cream of
  tartar

115g/4oz/scant ½ cup
  caster sugar
blanched and shredded
  rind of 1 orange, to
  decorate

For the icing

200g/7oz/1 cup caster
  sugar
1 egg white

1 Preheat the oven to 180°C/350°F/Gas 4. Sift the flour, cocoa powder, cornflour and salt together three times. Beat the egg whites in a large bowl until foamy. Add the cream of tartar, then whisk until soft peaks form.

2 Add the caster sugar to the egg whites a spoonful at a time, whisking after each addition. Sift a third of the flour and cocoa mixture over the meringue and gently fold in. Repeat twice more.

3 Spoon the mixture into a non-stick 20cm/8in ring mould and level the top. Bake for 35 minutes, or until springy when lightly pressed. Turn upside-down on to a wire rack and leave to cool in the tin. Carefully ease out of the tin.

4 For the icing, put the sugar in a pan with 75ml/5 tbsp cold water. Stir over a low heat until dissolved. Boil until the syrup reaches soft ball stage (119°C/238°F on a sugar thermometer). Remove from the heat. Whisk the egg white until stiff. Add the syrup in a thin stream, whisking all the time, until the mixture is very thick and fluffy.

5 Spread the icing over the top and sides of the cooled cake. Sprinkle the orange rind over the top of the cake and serve.

Chocolate Date Cake

A stunning cake that tastes wonderful. Rich and gooey –
it's a chocoholic's delight!

Serves 8

200g/7oz/scant 1 cup
  fromage frais
200g/7oz/scant 1 cup
  mascarpone
5ml/1 tsp vanilla essence,
  plus few extra drops
icing sugar, to taste
4 egg whites
115g/4oz/½ cup caster
  sugar

200g/7oz plain chocolate
175g/6oz/scant 1 cup
  Medjool dates, stoned
  and chopped
175g/6oz/1½ cups
  walnuts or pecan
  nuts, chopped

1 Preheat the oven to 180°C/350°F/Gas 4. Grease and base-line a 20cm/8in springform cake tin.

2 To make the frosting, mix together the fromage frais and mascarpone, add a few drops of vanilla essence and icing sugar to taste, then set aside.

3 Whisk the egg whites until they form stiff peaks. Whisk in 30ml/2 tbsp of the caster sugar until the meringue is thick and glossy, then fold in the remainder.

4 Chop 175g/6oz of the chocolate. Carefully fold into the meringue with the dates, nuts and 5ml/1 tsp of the vanilla essence. Pour into the prepared tin, spread level and bake for about 45 minutes, until risen around the edges.

5 Allow to cool in the tin for about 10 minutes, then unmould, peel off the lining paper and leave until completely cold. Swirl the frosting over the top of the cake.

6 Melt the remaining chocolate in a bowl over hot water. Spoon into a small paper piping bag and drizzle the chocolate over the cake. Chill before serving.

Warm Lemon and Syrup Cake

This delicious cake is the perfect winter dessert for both children and adults.

Serves 8

3 eggs
175g/6oz/¾ cup butter,
  softened
175g/6oz/¾ cup caster
  sugar
175g/6oz/1½ cups self-
  raising flour
50g/2oz/½ cup ground
  almonds
1.25ml/¼ tsp freshly
  grated nutmeg

50g/2oz/5 tbsp candied
  lemon peel, finely
  chopped
grated rind of 1 lemon
30ml/2 tbsp lemon juice
poached pears, to serve

For the syrup
175g/6oz/¾ cup caster
  sugar
juice of 3 lemons

1 Preheat the oven to 180°C/350°F/Gas 4. Grease and base-line a deep, round 20cm/8in cake tin.

2 Place all the cake ingredients in a large bowl and beat well for 2–3 minutes, until light and fluffy.

3 Tip the mixture into the prepared tin, spread level and bake for 1 hour, or until golden and firm to the touch.

4 Meanwhile, make the syrup. Put the sugar, lemon juice and 75ml/5 tbsp water in a pan. Heat gently, stirring, until the sugar has dissolved, then boil, without stirring, for a further 1–2 minutes.

5 Turn out the cake on to a plate with a rim. Prick the surface of the cake all over with a fork, then pour over the hot syrup. Leave to soak for about 30 minutes. Serve the cake warm with thin wedges of poached pears.

Strawberry Shortcake Gâteau

A light biscuit-textured sponge forms the base of this summertime dessert.

Makes one 20cm/8in round cake

225g/8oz/2 cups fresh strawberries, hulled	40g/1½oz/3 tbsp caster sugar
30ml/2 tbsp ruby port	1 egg, lightly beaten
225g/8oz/2 cups self-raising flour	15–30ml/1–2 tbsp milk melted butter, for brushing
10ml/2 tsp baking powder	250ml/8fl oz/1 cup double cream
75g/3oz/6 tbsp unsalted butter, diced	icing sugar, for dusting

1 Preheat the oven to 220°C/425°F/Gas 7. Grease and base-line two 20cm/8in round, loose-based cake tins. Reserve 5 strawberries, slice the rest and marinate in the port for about 1–2 hours. Strain, reserving the port.

2 Sift the flour and baking powder into a bowl. Rub in the butter until the mixture resembles fine breadcrumbs and stir in the sugar. Work in the egg and 15ml/1 tbsp of the milk to form a soft dough, adding more milk if needed.

3 Knead on a lightly floured surface and divide in two. Roll out each half, mark one half into eight wedges, and transfer to the cake tins. Brush with a little melted butter and bake for 15 minutes until risen and golden. Cool in the tins for 10 minutes, then transfer to a wire rack.

4 Cut the marked cake into wedges. Reserving a little cream for decoration, whip the rest until it holds its shape, and fold in the reserved port and strawberry slices. Spread over the cake. Place the wedges on top and dust with icing sugar.

5 Whip the remaining cream and use to pipe swirls on each wedge. Halve the reserved strawberries and use to decorate the cake.

Almond and Raspberry Swiss Roll

A light and airy sponge cake is rolled up with a fresh cream and raspberry filling for a decadent tea-time treat.

Makes one 23cm/9in long roll

3 eggs	caster sugar, for dusting
75g/3oz/⅓ cup caster sugar	250ml/8fl oz/1 cup double cream
50g/2oz/½ cup plain flour	225g/8oz/generous 1 cup fresh raspberries
30ml/2 tbsp ground almonds	16 flaked almonds, toasted, to decorate

1 Preheat the oven to 200°C/400°F/Gas 6. Grease a 33 x 23cm/13 x 9in Swiss roll tin and line with greaseproof and grease the paper.

2 Whisk the eggs and sugar in a heatproof bowl until blended. Place over a pan of simmering water and whisk until thick and pale. Whisk off the heat until cool. Sift over the flour and almonds and fold in gently.

3 Transfer to the prepared tin and bake for 10–12 minutes, until risen and springy to the touch. Invert the cake in its tin on to greaseproof paper dusted with caster sugar. Leave to cool, then remove the tin and lining paper.

4 Reserve a little cream, then whip the rest until it holds its shape. Fold in all but 8 raspberries and spread the mixture over the cooled cake, leaving a narrow border. Roll the cake up and sprinkle with caster sugar.

5 Whip the reserved cream until it just holds its shape, and spoon along the cake centre. Decorate with the reserved raspberries and toasted flaked almonds.

Orange and Walnut Swiss Roll

This unusual cake is tasty enough to serve alone, but you could also pour over some single cream.

Makes one 24cm/9½in long roll

4 eggs, separated
115g/4oz/generous ½ cup
*   caster sugar*
115g/4oz/1 cup very
*   finely chopped*
*   walnuts*
pinch of cream of tartar
pinch of salt
icing sugar, for dusting

For the filling
300ml/10fl oz/1¼ cups
*   whipping cream*
15ml/1 tbsp caster sugar
grated rind of 1 orange
15ml/1 tbsp orange-
*   flavour liqueur*

1 Preheat the oven to 180°C/350°F/Gas 4. Line a 30 x 24cm/12 x 9½in Swiss roll tin with greaseproof paper and grease the paper.

2 Beat the egg yolks and sugar until thick. Stir in the walnuts. Beat the egg whites with the cream of tartar and salt until stiffly peaking. Fold into the walnut mixture.

3 Pour the mixture into the prepared tin and level. Bake for 15 minutes. Invert the cake on to greaseproof paper dusted with icing sugar. Peel off the lining paper. Roll up the cake with the sugared paper. Leave to cool.

4 For the filling, whip the cream until softly peaking. Fold in the caster sugar, orange rind and liqueur.

5 Unroll the cake. Spread with the filling, then re-roll. Chill. To serve, dust with icing sugar.

Chocolate Swiss Roll

Makes one 33cm/13in long roll

225g/8oz plain chocolate
45ml/3 tbsp water
30ml/2 tbsp rum, brandy
*   or strong coffee*
7 eggs, separated
170g/6oz/scant 1 cup
*   caster sugar*

1.5ml/¼ tsp salt
350ml/12fl oz/1½ cups
*   whipping cream*
icing sugar, for dusting

1 Preheat the oven to 180°C/350°F/Gas 4. Line and grease a 38 x 33cm/15 x 13in Swiss roll tin with greaseproof paper.

2 Combine the chocolate, water and rum or other flavouring in the top of a double boiler, or in a heatproof bowl set over simmering water. Heat until melted. Set aside.

3 With an electric mixer, beat the egg yolks and sugar until thick. Stir in the melted chocolate.

4 In another bowl, beat the egg whites and salt until they hold stiff peaks. Fold a large dollop of egg whites into the yolk mixture to lighten it, then carefully fold in the rest of the egg whites.

5 Pour the mixture into the tin and smooth evenly with a palette knife. Bake for 15 minutes. Remove from the oven, cover with greaseproof paper and a damp cloth. Leave to stand for 1–2 hours. With an electric mixer, whip the cream until stiff. Set aside.

6 Run a knife along the inside edge of the tin to loosen the cake, then invert the cake on to a sheet of greaseproof paper that has been dusted with icing sugar.

7 Peel off the lining paper. Spread with an even layer of whipped cream, then roll up the cake with the help of the sugared paper. Chill for several hours. Before serving, dust with an even layer of icing sugar.

Apricot Brandy-snap Roulade

A magnificent combination of soft and crisp textures, this cake looks impressive and is easy to prepare.

Makes one 33cm/13in long roll

4 eggs, separated
7.5ml/1½ tsp fresh
   orange juice
115g/4oz/generous ½ cup
   caster sugar
175g/6oz/1½ cups
   ground almonds
4 brandy snaps, crushed,
   to decorate

For the filling
150g/5oz canned
   apricots, drained
300ml/½ pint/1¼ cups
   double cream
25g/1oz/¼ cup icing
   sugar

1 Preheat the oven to 190°C/375°F/Gas 5. Base-line and grease a 33 x 23cm/13 x 9in Swiss roll tin. Beat together the egg yolks, orange juice and sugar until thick and pale, about 10 minutes. Fold in the ground almonds.

2 Whisk the egg whites until they hold stiff peaks. Fold into the almond mixture, then transfer to the Swiss roll tin and smooth the surface. Bake for 20 minutes, or until a skewer inserted into the centre comes out clean. Leave to cool in the tin, covered with a just-damp dish towel.

3 For the filling, process the apricots in a blender or food processor until smooth. Whip the cream and icing sugar until it holds soft peaks. Fold in the apricot purée.

4 Spread the crushed brandy snaps on a sheet of greaseproof paper. Spread one-third of the cream mixture over the cake, then invert on to the brandy snaps. Peel off the lining paper.

5 Use the remaining cream mixture to cover the whole cake, then roll up the roulade from a short end. Transfer to a serving dish.

Apricot and Orange Roulade

This sophisticated dessert is very good served with a spoonful of Greek yogurt or crème fraîche.

Makes one 33cm/13in long roll

For the roulade
4 egg whites
115g/4oz/½ cup golden
   caster sugar
50g/2oz/½ cup plain
   flour
finely grated rind of 1
   small orange
45ml/3 tbsp orange juice

For the filling
115g/4oz/½ cup ready-
   to-eat dried apricots
150ml/¼ pint/⅔ cup
   orange juice

To decorate
10ml/2 tsp icing sugar
shredded orange rind

1 Preheat the oven to 200°C/400°F/Gas 6. Base-line and grease a 33 x 23cm/13 x 9in Swiss roll tin.

2 To make the roulade, place the egg whites in a large bowl and whisk until they hold soft peaks. Gradually add the sugar, whisking hard between each addition. Fold in the flour, orange rind and juice. Spoon the mixture into the tin and spread it evenly.

3 Bake for 15–18 minutes, or until the sponge is firm and light golden in colour. Turn out on to a sheet of greaseproof paper and roll it up loosely from one short side. Leave to cool.

4 Roughly chop the apricots and place them in a pan with the orange juice. Cover and leave to simmer until most of the liquid has been absorbed. Purée the apricots in a food processor or blender.

5 Unroll the roulade and spread with the apricot mixture. Roll up, arrange strips of paper diagonally across the roll, sprinkle lightly with icing sugar, remove the paper and scatter with orange rind.

Classic Cheesecake

Dust the top of the cheesecake with icing sugar to decorate, if you wish.

Serves 8

50g/2oz/⅔ cup digestive
    biscuits, crushed
900g/2lb/4 cups cream
    cheese, at room
    temperature
245g/8¾oz/generous
    1¼ cups sugar

grated rind of 1 lemon
45ml/3 tbsp lemon juice
5ml/1 tsp vanilla essence
4 eggs

1 Preheat the oven to 160°C/325°F/Gas 3. Grease a 20cm/8in springform tin. Place on a 30cm/12in circle of foil. Press it up the sides to seal tightly. Press the crushed biscuits into the base of the tin.

2 Beat the cream cheese until smooth. Add the sugar, lemon rind and juice, and vanilla, and beat until blended. Beat in the eggs, one at a time.

3 Pour into the prepared tin. Set the tin in a larger baking tray and place in the oven. Pour enough hot water in the outer tray to come 2.5cm/1in up the side of the tin.

4 Bake until the top is golden brown, about 1½ hours. Cool in the tin.

5 Run a knife around the edge to loosen, then remove the rim of the tin. Chill for at least 4 hours before serving.

Chocolate Cheesecake

Substitute digestive biscuits for the base to create a slightly different pudding.

Serves 10–12

275g/10oz plain
    chocolate
1.1kg/2½lb/5 cups cream
    cheese, at room
    temperature
200g/7oz/1 cup sugar
10ml/2 tsp vanilla
    essence
4 eggs
15ml/1 tbsp cocoa
    powder

175ml/6fl oz/¾ cup
    soured cream

For the base
200g/7oz/2⅓ cups
    chocolate biscuits,
    crushed
75g/3oz/6 tbsp butter,
    melted
2.5ml/½ tsp ground
    cinnamon

1 Preheat the oven to 180°C/350°F/Gas 4. Grease the base and sides of a 23 x 7.5cm/9 x 3in springform tin.

2 For the base, mix the biscuits with the butter and cinnamon. Press into the base of the tin.

3 Melt the chocolate in the top of a double boiler. Set aside.

4 Beat the cream cheese until smooth, then beat in the sugar and vanilla. Add the eggs, one at a time.

5 Stir the cocoa powder into the soured cream. Add to the cream cheese mixture. Stir in the melted chocolate.

6 Pour over the crust. Bake for 1 hour. Cool in the tin, then remove the rim. Chill before serving.

Marbled Cheesecake

Serves 10

900g/2lb/4 cups cream
    cheese, at room
    temperature
200g/7oz/1 cup
    caster sugar
4 eggs

5ml/1 tsp vanilla essence
50g/2oz/½ cup cocoa
    powder, dissolved in
    75ml/5 tbsp hot water
70g/2½oz/1 cup digestive
    biscuits, crushed

1 Preheat the oven to 180°C/350°F/Gas 4. Grease and base-line a 20 x 7.5cm/8 x 3in cake tin.

2 With an electric mixer, beat the cheese until smooth and creamy. Add the sugar and beat to incorporate. Beat in the eggs, one at a time. Do not overmix.

3 Divide the mixture between two bowls. Stir the vanilla into one, then add the chocolate mixture to the other. Pour a cupful of the vanilla mixture into the centre of the tin to make an even layer. Slowly pour over a cupful of chocolate mixture in the centre. Repeat, alternating cupfuls of the batter in a circular pattern until both are used up.

4 Set the tin in a larger baking tray and pour in hot water to come 3cm/1½in up the sides of the cake tin. Bake until the top of the cake is golden, about 1½ hours. It will rise during baking but will sink later. Leave to cool in the tin on a rack.

5 To turn out, run a knife around the inside edge. Place a flat plate, bottom-side up, over the tin and invert on to the plate.

6 Sprinkle the crushed biscuits evenly over the base, gently place another plate over them, and invert again. Cover and chill for at least 3 hours, or overnight. To serve, cut slices with a sharp knife dipped in hot water.

Baked Cheesecake with Fresh Fruits

Vary the fruit decoration to suit the season for this rich, creamy dessert.

Serves 12

175g/6oz/2 cups
    digestive biscuits,
    crushed
50g/2oz/¼ cup unsalted
    butter, melted
450g/1lb/2 cups curd
    cheese
150ml/¼ pint/⅔ cup
    soured cream
115g/4oz/generous ½ cup
    caster sugar
3 eggs, separated
grated rind of 1 lemon

30ml/2 tbsp Marsala
2.5ml/½ tsp almond
    essence
50g/2oz/½ cup ground
    almonds
50g/2oz/scant ½ cup
    sultanas
450g/1lb prepared mixed
    fruits, such as figs,
    cherries, peaches and
    strawberries, to
    decorate

1 Preheat the oven to 180°C/350°F/Gas 4. Grease and line the sides of a 25cm/10in round springform tin. Combine the biscuits and butter and press into the base of the tin. Chill for 20 minutes.

2 For the cake mixture, beat together the cheese, cream, sugar, egg yolks, lemon rind, Marsala and almond essence until smooth and creamy.

3 Whisk the egg whites until stiff and fold into the cheese mixture with all the remaining ingredients, except the fruit, until evenly combined. Pour over the biscuit base and bake for 45 minutes, until risen and just set in the centre.

4 Leave in the tin until completely cold. Carefully remove the tin and peel away the lining paper.

5 Chill the cheesecake for at least 1 hour before decorating with the prepared fruits, just before serving.

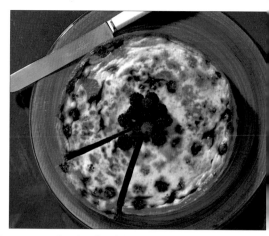

Tofu Berry "Cheesecake"

Strictly speaking, this summery "cheesecake" is not a cheese-cake at all, as it's based on tofu – but who would guess?

Serves 6

For the base
50g/2oz/4 tbsp margarine
30ml/2 tbsp apple juice
115g/4oz/1 cup bran flakes

For the filling
275g/10oz/1½ cups tofu or low fat soft cheese
200g/7oz/scant 1 cup natural yogurt
15ml/1 tbsp/1 sachet powdered gelatine

60ml/4 tbsp apple juice

For the topping
175g/6oz/1½ cups mixed summer soft fruit, such as strawberries, raspberries, redcurrants, blackberries
30ml/2 tbsp redcurrant jelly
30ml/2 tbsp hot water

1 For the base, place the margarine and apple juice in a pan and heat gently until melted. Crush the cereal and stir it into the pan. Tip into a 23cm/9in round flan tin and press down firmly. Leave to set.

2 For the filling, place the tofu or cheese and yogurt in a food processor or blender and process until smooth. Dissolve the gelatine in the apple juice and stir into the tofu mixture.

3 Spread the tofu mixture over the chilled base, smoothing it evenly. Chill until set.

4 Remove the flan tin and place the "cheesecake" on a serving plate. Arrange the fruits over the top. Melt the redcurrant jelly with the hot water. Let it cool, and then spoon over the fruit to serve.

Baked Blackberry Cheesecake

This light cheesecake is best made with wild blackberries; if they're not available, use cultivated ones.

Serves 6
175g/6oz/¾ cup cottage cheese
150g/5oz/¾ cup natural yogurt
15ml/1 tbsp plain wholemeal flour
25g/1oz/2 tbsp golden caster sugar

1 egg
1 egg white
finely grated rind and juice of ½ lemon
200g/7oz/scant 2 cups fresh or frozen and thawed blackberries

1 Preheat the oven to 180°C/350°F/Gas 4. Lightly grease and base-line an 18cm/7in sandwich tin.

2 Place the cottage cheese in a food processor or blender and process until smooth. Place in a bowl, then add the yogurt, flour, sugar, egg and egg white, and mix. Add the lemon rind, juice and blackberries, reserving a few.

3 Tip the mixture into the tin and bake for 30–35 minutes, or until just set. Turn off the oven and leave the cake in it for a further 30 minutes.

4 Run a knife around the edge of the cheesecake and turn it out. Remove the lining paper and place the cheesecake on a warm serving plate.

5 Decorate the cheesecake with the reserved blackberries and serve warm.

Coffee, Peach and Almond Daquoise

Makes one 23cm/9in gâteau

5 eggs, separated
425g/15oz/scant 2 cups
  caster sugar
15ml/1 tbsp cornflour
175g/6oz/1½ cups
  ground almonds,
  toasted
135ml/4½fl oz/generous
  ½ cup milk
275g/10oz/1¼ cups
  unsalted butter, diced

45–60ml/3–4 tbsp
  coffee essence
2 x 400g/14oz cans peach
  halves in juice,
  drained
65g/2½oz/generous
  ½ cup flaked almonds,
  toasted
icing sugar, for dusting
few fresh mint leaves, to
  decorate

1 Preheat the oven to 150°C/300°F/Gas 2. Draw three 23cm/9in circles on to some greaseproof paper and place on baking sheets.

2 Whisk the egg whites until stiff. Gradually whisk in 275g/10oz/scant 1½ cups of the sugar until thick and glossy. Fold in the cornflour and almonds. Using a 1cm/½in plain nozzle, pipe circles of the mixture on to the paper. Bake for 2 hours. Turn on to wire racks to cool.

3 For the buttercream, beat together the egg yolks and remaining sugar until thick and pale. Heat the milk to boiling point and beat into the egg mixture. Return to the pan and heat until the mixture coats the back of a spoon. Strain into a large bowl and beat until lukewarm. Gradually beat in the butter until glossy. Beat in the coffee essence.

4 Trim the meringues and crush the trimmings. Reserve 3 peach halves, chop the rest and fold into half the buttercream with the crushed meringue. Use to sandwich the meringues together and place on a serving plate.

5 Ice the cake with the plain buttercream. Cover the top with flaked almonds and dust generously with icing sugar. Thinly slice the reserved peaches and use to decorate the cake edge with some mint leaves.

Mocha Brazil Layer Torte

Makes one 20cm/8in round cake

For the meringue	**For the icing**
3 egg whites	175g/6oz/1 cup plain
115g/4oz/generous ½ cup	chocolate chips
caster sugar	30ml/2 tbsp coffee
15ml/1 tbsp coffee	essence
essence	30ml/2 tbsp water
75g/3oz/¾ cup Brazil	600ml/1 pint/2½ cups
nuts, toasted and	double cream, whipped
finely ground	
20cm/8in chocolate	**To decorate**
sponge cake	12 chocolate triangles
	12 chocolate-coated coffee
	beans

1 Preheat the oven to 150°C/300°F/Gas 2. Draw two 20cm/8in circles on greaseproof paper and place on a baking sheet. Grease, base-line and flour a 20cm/8in round springform tin.

2 For the meringue, whisk the egg whites until stiff. Whisk in the sugar until glossy. Fold in the coffee essence and nuts. Using a 1cm/½in plain nozzle, pipe circles of the mixture on to the paper. Bake for 2 hours. Cool. Increase the oven temperature to 180°C/350°F/Gas 4.

3 For the icing, melt the chocolate chips, coffee essence and water in a bowl over a pan of simmering water. Remove from the heat and fold in the whipped cream.

4 Cut the cake into three equal layers. Trim meringue discs to the same size and assemble the cake with a layer of sponge, a little icing and a meringue disc, ending with sponge.

5 Reserve a little of the remaining icing, use the rest to cover the cake completely, forming a swirling pattern over the top. Using the reserved icing, and a piping bag with a star nozzle, pipe 24 small rosettes on top of the cake. Top alternately with the coffee beans and the chocolate triangles.

Fresh Fruit Genoese

This Italian classic can be made with any selection of seasonal fruits.

Serves 8–10

For the sponge
175g/6oz/1½ cups plain flour
pinch of salt
4 eggs
115g/4oz/½ cup caster sugar
90ml/6 tbsp orange-flavoured liqueur

For the filling and topping
600ml/1 pint/2½ cups double cream
60ml/4 tbsp vanilla sugar
450g/1lb mixed fresh fruits
150g/5oz/1¼ cups pistachio nuts, chopped
60ml/4 tbsp apricot jam, warmed and sieved

1 Preheat the oven to 180°C/350°F/Gas 4. Grease and line the base of a 20cm/ 8in springform cake tin.

2 Sift the flour and salt together three times, then set aside. Using an electric mixer, beat the eggs and sugar together for 10 minutes until thick and pale.

3 Fold the flour mixture gently into the egg and sugar mixture. Transfer the cake mixture to the prepared tin and bake for 30–35 minutes. Leave the cake in the tin for about 5 minutes, then transfer to a wire rack, remove paper and cool.

4 Cut the cake horizontally in to two layers, place the bottom layer on a plate. Sprinkle both layers with liqueur.

5 Add the vanilla sugar to the cream and whisk until the cream holds peaks. Spread two-thirds of the cream over the bottom layer and top with half of the fruit. Top with the second layer and spread the top and sides with the remaining cream. Press the nuts around the sides, arrange remaining fruit on top and brush with the apricot jam.

Fruit Gâteau with Heartsease

This gâteau would be lovely to serve as a dessert at a summer lunch party in the garden.

Makes one ring cake
90g/3½oz/½ cup soft margarine
100g/3½oz/scant ½ cup sugar
10ml/2 tsp clear honey
150g/5oz/1¼ cups self-raising flour
2.5ml/½ tsp baking powder
30ml/2 tbsp milk
2 eggs
15ml/1 tbsp rose water
15ml/1 tbsp Cointreau

To decorate
16 heartsease pansy flowers
1 egg white, lightly beaten
caster sugar
icing sugar
450g/1lb/4 cups strawberries
strawberry leaves

1 Preheat the oven to 190°C/375°F/Gas 5. Grease and lightly flour a ring mould. Put the soft margarine, sugar, honey, flour, baking powder, milk and eggs into a mixing bowl and beat well for 1 minute. Add the rose water and the Cointreau and mix well.

2 Pour the mixture into the mould and bake for 40 minutes. Allow to stand for a few minutes, and then turn out on to a serving plate.

3 Crystallize the heartsease pansies by painting them with the lightly beaten egg white and sprinkling with caster sugar. Leave to dry.

4 Sift icing sugar over the cake. Fill the centre of the ring with strawberries – if they will not all fit, place some around the edge. Decorate with the crystallized heartsease flowers and some strawberry leaves.

Nut and Apple Gâteau

Makes one 23cm/9in round cake

115g/4oz/1 cup pecan
    nuts or walnuts,
    toasted
50g/2oz/½ cup plain
    flour
10ml/2 tsp baking
    powder
1.5ml/¼ tsp salt

2 large cooking apples
3 eggs
225g/8oz/scant 1¼ cups
    caster sugar
5ml/1 tsp vanilla essence
175ml/6fl oz/¾ cup
    whipping cream

1 Preheat the oven to 160°C/325°F/Gas 3. Line two 23cm/9in cake tins with greaseproof paper and grease the paper.

2 Finely chop the nuts. Reserve 25ml/1½ tbsp of them and place the rest in a mixing bowl. Sift over the flour, baking powder and salt and stir.

3 Peel and core the apples. Cut into 3mm/⅛in dice, then stir into the flour mixture.

4 Beat the eggs until frothy. Gradually add the sugar and vanilla and beat until ribbon trails form, about 8 minutes. Fold in the flour mixture.

5 Pour into the cake tins and bake until a skewer inserted in the centre comes out clean, about 35 minutes. Leave to stand for 10 minutes, then turn out on to a wire rack to cool.

6 Whip the cream until firm. Use half for the filling. Pipe rosettes on the top and sprinkle over the reserved nuts.

Chocolate Pecan Nut Torte

This torte uses finely ground nuts instead of flour. Toast, then cool the nuts before grinding finely in a processor.

Makes one 20cm/8in round cake

200g/7oz plain chocolate,
    chopped
150g/5oz/10 tbsp
    unsalted butter, cut
    into pieces
4 eggs
100g/3½oz/½ cup caster
    sugar
10ml/2 tsp vanilla
    essence
115g/4oz/1 cup ground
    pecan nuts
10ml/2 tsp ground
    cinnamon

24 toasted pecan nut
    halves, to decorate
    (optional)

**For the chocolate
honey glaze**
115g/4oz plain chocolate,
    chopped
60g/2oz/¼ cup unsalted
    butter, cut into pieces
30ml/2 tbsp honey
pinch of ground
    cinnamon

1 Preheat the oven to 180°C/350°F/Gas 4. Grease a 20cm/8in springform tin, line with greaseproof paper, then grease the paper. Wrap the tin with foil.

2 Melt the chocolate and butter over a low heat, stirring until smooth. Set aside. Beat the eggs, sugar and vanilla until frothy. Stir in the melted chocolate and butter, ground nuts and cinnamon. Pour into the tin. Place in a large roasting tin and pour boiling water into the roasting tin, to come 2cm/¾in up the side of the springform tin. Bake for 25–30 minutes, until the edge of the cake is set, but the centre soft. Remove the foil and set on a wire rack.

3 For the glaze, melt the chocolate, butter, honey and cinnamon, stirring until smooth. Remove from the heat. If using, dip toasted pecan halves halfway into the glaze and place on greaseproof paper to set. Remove the cake from its tin and invert on to a wire rack. Remove the paper. Pour the glaze over the cake, tilting the rack to spread it. Use a palette knife to smooth the sides. Arrange the nuts on top.

Coconut Lime Gâteau

Makes one 23cm/9in round cake

225g/8oz/2 cups plain
  flour
12.5ml/2½ tsp baking
  powder
1.5ml/¼ tsp salt
225g/8oz/1 cup butter, at
  room temperature
225g/8oz/generous 1 cup
  caster sugar
grated rind of 2 limes
4 eggs
60ml/4 tbsp fresh lime
  juice

75g/3oz/1½ cups
  desiccated coconut

For the frosting
450g/1lb/generous 2 cups
  granulated sugar
60ml/4 tbsp water
pinch of cream of tartar
1 egg white, whisked
  stiffly

1 Preheat the oven to 180°C/350°F/Gas 4. Grease and base-line two 23cm/9in sandwich tins. Sift together the flour, baking powder and salt.

2 Beat the butter until soft. Add the sugar and lime rind and beat until pale and fluffy. Beat in the eggs, one at a time.

3 Gradually fold in the dry ingredients, alternating with the lime juice, then stir in two-thirds of the coconut.

4 Divide the mixture between the cake tins, even the tops and bake for 30–35 minutes. Cool in the tins on a wire rack for 10 minutes, then turn out and peel off the lining paper.

5 Bake the remaining coconut until golden brown, stirring occasionally. For the frosting, heat the sugar, water and cream of tartar until dissolved, stirring. Boil to reach 120°C/250°F on a sugar thermometer. Remove from the heat and, when the bubbles subside, whisk in the egg white until thick.

6 Sandwich and cover the cake with the frosting. Sprinkle over the toasted coconut. Leave to set.

Exotic Celebration Gâteau

Use any tropical fruits you can find to make a spectacular display of colours and tastes.

Makes one 20cm/8in ring gâteau

175g/6oz/¾ cup butter,
  softened
175g/6oz/scant 1 cup
  caster sugar
3 eggs, beaten
250g/9oz/2¼ cups self-
  raising flour
30–45ml/2–3 tbsp milk
90–120ml/6–8 tbsp
  light rum
425ml/14fl oz/scant
  2 cups double cream
25g/1oz/¼ cup icing
  sugar, sifted

To decorate
450g/1lb mixed fresh
  exotic and soft fruits,
  such as figs,
  redcurrants, star fruit
  and kiwi fruit
90ml/6 tbsp apricot jam,
  warmed and sieved
30ml/2 tbsp warm water
icing sugar

1 Preheat the oven to 190°C/375°F/Gas 5. Grease and flour a deep 20cm/8in ring mould.

2 Beat together the butter and sugar until light and fluffy. Gradually beat in the eggs, then fold in the flour and milk.

3 Spoon the mixture into the ring mould. Bake the cake for 45 minutes, or until a skewer inserted into the centre comes out clean. Turn out on to a wire rack and leave to cool.

4 Place the cake on a serving plate. Make holes randomly over the cake with a skewer. Drizzle over the rum and allow to soak in.

5 Beat together the cream and icing sugar until the mixture holds soft peaks. Spread all over the cake. Arrange the fruits in the hollow centre of the cake. Mix the apricot jam and water, then brush over the fruit. Sift over some icing sugar.

Chocolate and Fresh Cherry Gâteau

Makes one 20cm/8in round cake

115g/4oz/½ cup butter
150g/5oz/⅔ cup caster
  sugar
3 eggs, lightly beaten
175g/6oz/1 cup plain
  chocolate chips, melted
60ml/4 tbsp kirsch
150g/5oz/1¼ cups self-
  raising flour
5ml/1 tsp ground
  cinnamon
2.5ml/½ tsp ground
  cloves
350g/12oz fresh cherries,
  stoned and halved
45ml/3 tbsp morello
  cherry jam, warmed

5ml/1 tsp lemon juice

For the frosting
115g/4oz/⅔ cup plain
  chocolate chips
50g/2oz/¼ cup unsalted
  butter
60ml/4 tbsp double cream

To decorate
75g/3oz/½ cup white
  chocolate chips, melted
18 fresh cherries
few rose leaves, washed
  and dried

1 Preheat the oven to 160°C/325°F/Gas 3. Grease, base-line and flour a 20cm/8in round springform tin.

2 Cream the butter and 115g/4oz/½ cup of the sugar until pale. Beat in the eggs. Stir in the chocolate and half the kirsch. Fold in the flour and spices. Transfer to the tin and bake for 55–60 minutes, or until a skewer inserted in the centre comes out clean. Cool for 10 minutes then transfer to a wire rack.

3 For the filling, bring the cherries, remaining kirsch and sugar to the boil, cover, and simmer for 10 minutes. Uncover for a further 10 minutes until syrupy. Leave to cool.

4 Halve the cake horizontally. Cut a 1cm/½in deep circle from the base, leaving a 1cm/½in edge. Crumble into the filling and stir to form a paste. Fill and cover the cake base.

5 Sieve the jam and lemon juice. Brush all over the cake. For the frosting, melt all the ingredients. Cool, pour over the cake. Decorate with chocolate-dipped cherries and leaves.

Coffee Almond Flower Gâteau

This delicious cake can be made quite quickly. Ring the changes by using a coffee-flavoured sponge.

Makes one 20cm/8in round cake

475g/1lb 2oz/2¼ cups
  coffee-flavour butter
  icing
2 x 20cm/8in round
  sponge cakes with
  chopped nuts

75g/3oz plain chocolate
20 blanched almonds
4 chocolate-coated coffee
  beans

1 Reserve 60ml/4 tbsp of the butter icing for piping and use the rest to sandwich the sponges together and cover the top and side of the cake. Smooth the top with a palette knife and serrate the side with a scraper.

2 Melt the chocolate in a heatproof bowl over a pan of hot water. Remove from the heat, then dip in half of each almond at a slight angle. Leave to dry on greaseproof paper. Return the chocolate to the pan of hot water (off the heat) so it does not set. Remove and allow to cool slightly.

3 Arrange the almonds on top of the cake to represent flowers. Place a chocolate-coated coffee bean in the flower centres. Spoon the remaining melted chocolate into a greaseproof paper piping bag. Cut a small piece off the end in a straight line. Pipe the chocolate in wavy lines over the top of the cake and in small beads around the top edge.

4 Transfer the cake to a serving plate. Place the reserved buttercream in a fresh piping bag fitted with a No 2 writing nozzle. Pipe beads of icing all around the bottom of the cake, then top with small beads of chocolate.

Vegan Chocolate Gâteau

A rare treat for vegans, this gâteau tastes really delicious.

Makes one 20cm/8in gâteau

275g/10oz/2½ cups self-
  raising wholemeal
  flour
50g/2oz/½ cup cocoa
  powder
15ml/1 tbsp baking
  powder
250g/9oz/1¼ cups caster
  sugar
a few drops of vanilla
  essence
135ml/9 tbsp sunflower
  oil
350ml/12fl oz/1½ cups
  water

sifted cocoa powder, to
  decorate
25g/1oz/¼ cup chopped
  nuts, to decorate

For the chocolate fudge
50g/2oz/¼ cup soya
  margarine
45ml/3 tbsp water
250g/9oz/2¼ cups icing
  sugar
30ml/2 tbsp cocoa
  powder

1 Preheat the oven to 160°C/325°F/Gas 3. Grease and line a deep 20cm/8in round cake tin, and grease the paper.

2 Sift the flour, cocoa and baking powder into a large mixing bowl. Add the sugar and vanilla, then gradually beat in the oil and water to make a smooth batter. Pour the mixture into the cake tin and smooth the surface. Bake for 45 minutes, or until a skewer inserted into the centre of the cake comes out clean. Leave in the tin for 5 minutes, then turn out on to a wire rack and leave to cool. Cut the cake in half.

3 For the chocolate fudge, gently melt the margarine with the water. Remove from the heat, add the icing sugar and cocoa, and beat until smooth and shiny. Allow to cool until firm enough to spread and pipe.

4 Place a layer of cake on a serving plate and spread over two-thirds of the chocolate fudge. Top with the other layer of cake. Using a star nozzle, pipe chocolate fudge stars over the cake. Sprinkle with cocoa powder and chopped nuts.

Black Forest Gâteau

A perfect gâteau for a special tea party, or for serving as a sumptuous dinner-party dessert.

Makes one 20cm/8in gâteau

5 eggs
175g/6oz/scant 1 cup
  caster sugar
50g/2oz/½ cup plain
  flour
50g/2oz/½ cup cocoa
  powder
75g/3oz/6 tbsp butter,
  melted

For the filling
75 – 90ml/5 – 6 tbsp
  kirsch

600ml/1 pint/2½ cups
  double cream
425g/15oz can black
  cherries, drained,
  stoned and chopped

To decorate
chocolate curls
15 – 20 fresh cherries,
  preferably with stems
icing sugar

1 Preheat the oven to 180°C/350°F/Gas 4. Base-line and grease two deep 20cm/8in round cake tins.

2 Beat together the eggs and sugar for 10 minutes, or until thick and pale. Sift over the flour and cocoa, and fold in gently. Trickle in the melted butter and fold in gently.

3 Transfer the mixture to the cake tins. Bake for 30 minutes, or until springy to the touch. Leave in the tins for 5 minutes, then turn out on to a wire rack, peel off the lining paper and leave to cool. Cut each cake in half horizontally and sprinkle with the kirsch.

4 Whip the cream until softly peaking. Combine two-thirds of the cream with the chopped cherries. Place a layer of cake on a serving plate and spread with one-third of the filling. Repeat twice, and top with a layer of cake. Use the reserved cream to cover the top and sides of the gâteau.

5 Decorate the gâteau with chocolate curls, fresh cherries and dredge with icing sugar.

Walnut Coffee Gâteau

Serves 8–10

140g/5oz/1¼ cups
   walnuts
150g/5½oz/generous
   ¾ cup caster sugar
5 eggs, separated
55g/2oz/scant 1 cup dry
   breadcrumbs
15ml/1 tbsp cocoa powder
15ml/1 tbsp instant coffee
30ml/2 tbsp rum or
   lemon juice

1.5ml/¼ tsp salt
90ml/6 tbsp redcurrant
   jelly, warmed
chopped walnuts, for
   decorating

For the frosting
225g/8oz plain chocolate
750ml/1¼ pint/3 cups
   whipping cream

1 For the frosting, combine the chocolate and cream in the top of a double boiler until the chocolate melts. Cool, then cover and chill overnight, or until the mixture is firm.

2 Preheat the oven to 180°C/350°F/Gas 4. Line and grease a 23 x 5cm/9 x 2in cake tin. Grind the nuts with 45ml/3 tbsp of the sugar in a food processor, blender or coffee grinder.

3 With an electric mixer, beat the egg yolks and remaining sugar until thick and lemon-coloured. Fold in the walnuts. Stir in the breadcrumbs, cocoa, coffee and rum or lemon juice.

4 In another bowl, beat the egg whites with the salt until they hold stiff peaks. Fold carefully into the walnut mixture. Pour the meringue batter into the tin and bake until the top of the cake springs back when touched, about 45 minutes. Allow the cake to stand for 5 minutes, then turn out and cool, before slicing the cake in half horizontally.

5 With an electric mixer, beat the chocolate frosting mixture on low speed until it becomes lighter, about 30 seconds. Brush some of the jelly over the cut cake layer. Spread with some of the chocolate frosting, then sandwich with the remaining cake layer. Brush the top of the cake with jelly, then cover the side and top with the remaining frosting. Make a starburst pattern with a knife and sprinkle chopped walnuts around the edge.

Sachertorte

A rich cake, ideal to serve as a treat for anyone who is a self-confessed chocoholic.

Makes one 23cm/9in round cake

115g/4oz plain chocolate
90g/3oz/⅓ cup unsalted
   butter, at room
   temperature
50g/2oz/¼ cup sugar
4 eggs, separated, plus 1
   egg white
1.5ml/¼ tsp salt
65g/2½oz/9 tbsp plain
   flour, sifted

For the topping
75ml/5 tbsp apricot jam
250ml/8fl oz/1 cup plus
   15ml/1 tbsp water
15g/½oz/1 tbsp unsalted
   butter
175g/6oz plain chocolate
75g/3oz/⅓ cup sugar
ready-made chocolate
   decorating icing

1 Preheat the oven to 160°C/325°F/Gas 3. Line and grease a 23cm/9in cake tin. Melt the chocolate in the top of a double boiler and set aside.

2 Cream the butter and sugar until light and fluffy. Stir in the chocolate, then beat in the egg yolks, one at a time.

3 Beat the egg whites with the salt until stiff. Fold a dollop of whites into the chocolate mixture to lighten it. Fold in the remaining whites in three batches, alternating with the sifted flour. Pour into the tin and bake until a skewer comes out clean, about 45 minutes. Turn out on to a wire rack.

4 Meanwhile, melt the jam with 15ml/1 tbsp of the water, then strain for a smooth consistency. For the frosting, melt the butter and chocolate in the top of a double boiler. In a heavy saucepan, dissolve the sugar in the remaining water, then boil until it reaches 107°C/225°F (thread stage) on a sugar thermometer. Plunge the base of the pan into cold water for 1 minute. Stir into the chocolate. Cool for a few minutes.

5 Brush the warm jam over the cake. Pour over the frosting and spread over the top and sides. Leave to set overnight. Decorate with chocolate icing.

Dundee Cake

This is the perfect recipe for a festive occasion when a lighter fruit cake is required.

Makes one 20cm/8in round cake

175g/6oz/¾ cup butter
175g/6oz/1 cup light
  soft brown sugar
3 eggs
225g/8oz/2 cups plain
  flour
10ml/2 tsp baking
  powder
5ml/1 tsp ground
  cinnamon
2.5ml/½ tsp ground
  cloves
1.5ml/¼ tsp grated
  nutmeg
225g/8oz/generous
  1½ cups sultanas

175g/6oz/generous 1 cup
  raisins
175g/6oz/¾ cup glacé
  cherries, halved
115g/4oz/¾ cup chopped
  mixed peel
50g/2oz/½ cup blanched
  almonds, chopped
grated rind of 1 lemon
30ml/2 tbsp brandy
115g/4oz/1 cup whole
  blanched almonds,
  to decorate

1 Preheat the oven to 160°C/325°F/Gas 3. Grease and line a 20cm/8in round deep cake tin. Cream the butter and sugar until pale and light. Add the eggs, 1 at a time, beating well after each addition.

2 Sift together the flour, baking powder and spices. Fold into the egg mixture alternately with the remaining ingredients, until evenly combined. Transfer to the cake tin. Smooth the surface, then make a small dip in the centre.

3 Decorate the top of the cake by pressing the blanched almonds in decreasing circles over the entire surface. Bake for 2–2¼ hours, until a skewer inserted in the centre of the cake comes out clean.

4 Leave to cool in the tin for 30 minutes then transfer the cake to a wire rack.

Vegan Dundee Cake

As it contains neither eggs nor dairy products, this cake is suitable for vegans.

Makes one 20cm/8in square cake

350g/12oz/scant 2½ cups
  wholemeal flour
5ml/1 tsp mixed spice
175g/6oz/¾ cup soya
  margarine
175g/6oz/1 cup dark
  muscovado sugar, plus
  30ml/2 tbsp
175g/6oz/generous 1 cup
  sultanas
175g/6oz/1 cup currants
175g/6oz/generous 1 cup
  raisins
75g/3oz/½ cup chopped
  mixed peel
150g/5oz/generous ½ cup
  glacé cherries, halved
finely grated rind of
  1 orange

30ml/2 tbsp ground
  almonds
25g/1oz/¼ cup blanched
  almonds, chopped
5ml/1 tsp bicarbonate
  of soda
120ml/4fl oz/½ cup soya
  milk
75ml/3fl oz/⅓ cup
  sunflower oil
30ml/2 tbsp malt vinegar

To decorate
mixed nuts, such as
  pistachios, pecan nuts
  and macadamia nuts
glacé cherries
angelica
60ml/4 tbsp clear honey,
  warmed

1 Preheat the oven to 150°C/300°F/Gas 2. Grease and double-line a deep 20cm/8in square loose-based cake tin.

2 Sift together the flour and mixed spice. Rub in the soya margarine. Stir in the sugar, dried fruits, mixed peel, cherries, orange rind, ground almonds and blanched almonds.

3 Dissolve the bicarbonate in a little of the milk. Warm the remaining milk with the oil and vinegar and add the bicarbonate mixture. Stir into the flour mixture.

4 Spoon into the tin and smooth. Bake for 2½ hours. Leave in the tin for 5 minutes, then cool on a rack. Decorate with the nuts, cherries and angelica and brush with the honey.

Panforte

This rich, spicy nougat-type cake is a Christmas speciality of Siena in Italy.

Makes one 20cm/8in round cake

275g/10oz/1⅔ cups
    mixed chopped exotic
    peel, to include lemon
    orange, citron, papaya
    and pineapple
115g/4oz/1 cup
    unblanched almonds
50g/2oz/½ cup walnut
    halves
50g/2oz/½ cup plain
    flour

5ml/1 tsp ground
    cinnamon
1.5ml/¼ tsp each grated
    nutmeg, ground
    cloves and ground
    coriander
175g/6oz/1 cup caster
    sugar
60ml/4 tbsp water
icing sugar, for dusting

1 Preheat the oven to 180℃/350℉/Gas 4. Grease and base-line a 20cm/8in round loose-based cake tin with rice paper. Put the mixed peel and nuts in a bowl. Sift in the flour and spices and mix well.

2 Dissolve the caster sugar and water in a small saucepan, then boil until the mixture reaches 107℃/225℉ on a sugar thermometer (thread stage). Pour on to the fruit mixture, stirring to coat well. Transfer to the cake tin, pressing into the sides with a metal spoon.

3 Bake for 25–30 minutes, until the mixture is bubbling. Cool in the tin for 5 minutes.

4 Use a lightly oiled palette knife to work around the edges of the cake to loosen it. Remove the cake from the tin, leaving the base in place. Leave to go cold, then remove the base and dust generously with icing sugar.

Kulich

This Russian yeast cake is traditionally made at Eastertime.

Makes two cakes

15ml/1 tbsp easy-blend
    dried yeast
90ml/6 tbsp lukewarm
    milk
75g/3oz/scant ½ cup
    caster sugar
500g/1¼lb/5 cups plain
    flour
pinch of saffron strands
30ml/2 tbsp dark rum
2.5ml/½ tsp ground
    cardamom seeds
2.5ml/½ tsp ground
    cumin
50g/2oz/4 tbsp unsalted
    butter
2 eggs plus 2 egg yolks

½ vanilla pod, finely
    chopped
25g/1oz/2 tbsp each
    crystallized ginger,
    mixed peel, almonds
    and currants, chopped

To decorate

75g/3oz/¾ cup icing
    sugar, sifted
7.5–10ml/1½–2 tsp
    warm water
drop of almond essence
2 candles
blanched almonds
mixed peel

1 Blend together the yeast, milk, 25g/1oz/2 tbsp sugar and 50g/2oz/½ cup flour. Leave in a warm place for 15 minutes, until frothy. Soak the saffron in the rum for 15 minutes.

2 Sift together the remaining flour and spices and rub in the butter. Stir in the rest of the sugar. Add the yeast mixture, saffron liquid and remaining ingredients. Knead until smooth. Put in an oiled bowl, cover and leave until doubled in size.

3 Preheat the oven to 190℃/375℉/Gas 5. Grease, line and flour two 500g/1¼lb coffee tins or 15cm/6in clay flowerpots.

4 Punch down the dough and form into two rounds. Press into the tins or pots, cover and leave for 30 minutes. Bake for 35 minutes for the pots or 50 minutes for the tins. Cool.

5 Mix together the icing sugar, water and almond essence. Pour over the cakes. Decorate with the candles, nuts and peel.

Yule Log

This rich seasonal treat could provide an economical alternative to a traditional iced fruit cake.

Makes one 28cm/11in long roll

4 eggs, separated
150g/5oz/¾ cup caster
    sugar
5ml/1 tsp vanilla essence
pinch of cream of tartar
    (optional)
115g/4oz/1 cup plain
    flour, sifted

250ml/8fl oz/1 cup
    whipping cream
300g/11oz plain
    chocolate, chopped
30ml/2 tbsp rum or
    Cognac
icing sugar, for dusting

1 Preheat the oven to 190°C/375°F/Gas 5. Grease, line and flour a 40 x 28cm/16 x 11in Swiss roll tin.

2 Whisk the egg yolks with all but 25g/1oz/2 tbsp of the sugar until pale and thick. Add the vanilla essence.

3 Whisk the egg whites (with the cream of tartar if not using a copper bowl) until they form soft peaks. Add the reserved sugar and continue whisking until stiff and glossy.

4 Fold half the flour into the yolk mixture. Add a quarter of the egg whites and fold in to lighten the mixture. Fold in the remaining flour, then the remaining egg whites.

5 Spread the mixture in the tin. Bake for 15 minutes. Turn on to paper sprinkled with caster sugar. Roll up and leave to cool.

6 Bring the cream to the boil. Put the chocolate in a bowl and add the cream. Stir until the chocolate has melted, then beat until it is fluffy and has thickened to a spreading consistency. Mix a third of the chocolate cream with the rum or Cognac.

7 Unroll the cake and spread with the rum mixture. Re-roll and cut off about a quarter, at an angle. Arrange to form a branch. Spread the chocolate cream over the cake. Mark with a fork, add Christmas decorations and dust with icing sugar.

Chocolate Chestnut Roulade

A traditional version of Bûche de Nôel, the delicious French Christmas gâteau.

Makes one 33cm/13in long roll

225g/8oz plain chocolate
50g/2oz white chocolate
4 eggs, separated
115g/4oz/generous ½ cup
    caster sugar

For the chestnut filling
150ml/¼ pint/⅔ cup
    double cream

225g/8oz can chestnut
    purée
50–65g/2–2½oz/
    4–5 tbsp icing sugar,
    plus extra for dusting
15–30ml/1–2 tbsp
    brandy

1 Preheat the oven to 180°C/350°F/Gas 4. Line and grease a 23 x 33cm/9 x 13in Swiss roll tin.

2 For the chocolate curls, melt 50g/2oz of the plain and all of the white chocolate in separate bowls set over saucepans of hot water. When melted, spread on a non-porous surface and leave to set. Hold a long sharp knife at a 45-degree angle to the chocolate and push it along the chocolate, turning the knife in a circular motion. Put the curls on greaseproof paper.

3 Melt the remaining plain chocolate. Beat the egg yolks and caster sugar until thick and pale. Stir in the chocolate.

4 Whisk the whites until they form stiff peaks, then fold into the mixture. Turn into the tin and bake for 15–20 minutes. Cool, covered with a just-damp dish towel, on a wire rack.

5 Sprinkle a sheet of greaseproof paper with caster sugar. Turn the roulade out on to it. Peel off the lining paper and trim the edges of the roulade. Cover with the dish towel.

6 For the filling, whip the cream until softly peaking. Beat together the chestnut purée, icing sugar and brandy until smooth, then fold in the cream. Spread over the roulade and roll it up. Top with chocolate curls and dust with icing sugar.

Chocolate Christmas Cups

To crystallize cranberries for decoration, beat an egg white until frothy. Dip each berry in egg white then in sugar.

Makes about 35 cups

70–80 foil or paper sweet cases

275g/10oz plain chocolate, broken into pieces

175g/6oz cooked, cold Christmas pudding

75ml/3fl oz/⅓ cup brandy or whisky

chocolate leaves and a few crystallized cranberries, to decorate

1 Place the chocolate in a bowl over a saucepan of hot water. Heat gently until the chocolate is melted, stirring until the chocolate is smooth.

2 Using a pastry brush, brush or coat the base and sides of about 35 sweet cases. Allow to set, then repeat, reheating the melted chocolate if necessary, and apply a second coat. Leave to cool and set completely, 4 – 5 hours or overnight. Reserve the remaining chocolate.

3 Crumble the Christmas pudding in a small bowl, sprinkle with the brandy or whisky and allow to stand for 30 – 40 minutes, until the spirit is absorbed.

4 Spoon a little of the pudding mixture into each cup, smoothing the top. Reheat the remaining chocolate and spoon over the top of each cup to cover the surface of each cup to the edge. Leave to set.

5 When completely set, carefully peel off the cases and place in clean foil cases. Decorate with chocolate leaves and crystallized cranberries.

Eggless Christmas Cake

This simple cake contains a wealth of fruit and nuts to give it that traditional Christmas flavour.

Makes one 18cm/7in square cake

75g/3oz/½ cup sultanas

75g/3oz/½ cup raisins

75g/3oz/½ cup currants

75g/3oz/scant ½ cup glacé cherries, halved

50g/2oz/¼ cup mixed peel

250ml/8fl oz/1 cup apple juice

25g/1oz/scant ¼ cup toasted hazelnuts

30ml/2 tbsp pumpkin seeds

2 pieces stem ginger in syrup, chopped

finely grated rind of 1 lemon

120ml/4fl oz/½ cup milk

50ml/2fl oz/¼ cup sunflower oil

225g/8oz/2 cups wholemeal self-raising flour

10ml/2 tsp mixed spice

45ml/3 tbsp brandy or dark rum

apricot jam, for brushing

glacé fruits, to decorate

1 Soak the sultanas, raisins, currants, cherries and mixed peel in the apple juice overnight.

2 Preheat the oven to 150℃/300°F/Gas 2. Grease and line an 18cm/7in square cake tin.

3 Add the hazelnuts, pumpkin seeds, ginger and lemon rind to the fruit. Stir in the milk and oil. Sift the flour and spice, then stir in with the brandy or rum.

4 Spoon into the cake tin and bake for about 1½ hours, or until the cake is golden brown and firm to the touch.

5 Turn out and cool on a wire rack. Brush with sieved apricot jam and decorate with glacé fruits.

Flourless Fruit Cake

This makes the perfect base for a birthday cake for anyone who needs to avoid eating flour.

Makes one 25cm/10in round cake

450g/1lb/1⅓ cups
  mincemeat
350g/12oz/2 cups dried
  mixed fruit
115g/4oz/½ cup ready-to-
  eat dried apricots,
  chopped
115g/4oz/⅔cup ready-to-
  eat dried figs, chopped
115g/4oz/½ cup glacé
  cherries, halved
115g/4oz/1 cup walnut
  pieces
225g/8oz/8 – 10 cups
  cornflakes, crushed
4 eggs, lightly beaten
410g/14½oz can
  evaporated milk
5ml/1 tsp mixed spice
5ml/1 tsp baking powder
mixed glacé fruits,
  chopped, to decorate

1 Preheat the oven to 150°C/300°F/Gas 2. Grease a 25cm/10in round cake tin, line the base and sides with a double thickness of greaseproof paper and grease the paper.

2 Put all the ingredients into a large mixing bowl. Beat together well.

3 Turn into the cake tin and smooth the surface.

4 Bake for about 1¾ hours or until a skewer inserted in the centre of the cake comes out clean. Allow the cake to cool in the tin for 10 minutes, then turn out on to a wire rack, peel off the lining paper and leave to cool completely. Decorate with the chopped glacé fruits.

Glazed Christmas Ring

Makes one 25cm/10in ring cake

225g/8oz/generous 1½
  cups sultanas
175g/6oz/generous 1 cup
  raisins
175g/6oz/generous 1 cup
  currants
175g/6oz/1 cup dried
  figs, chopped
90ml/6 tbsp whisky
45ml/3 tbsp orange juice
225g/8oz/1 cup butter
225g/8oz/1cup dark soft
  brown sugar
5 eggs
250g/9oz/2¼ cups plain
  flour
15ml/1 tbsp baking
  powder
15ml/1 tbsp mixed spice
115g/4oz/⅔ cup glacé
  cherries, chopped
115g/4oz/1 cup brazil
  nuts, chopped
50g/2oz/⅓ cup chopped
  mixed peel
50g/2oz/½ cup ground
  almonds
grated rind and juice
  1 orange
30ml/2 tbsp thick-cut
  orange marmalade

To decorate

150ml/¼ pint/⅔ cup
  thick-cut orange
  marmalade
15ml/1 tbsp orange juice
175g/6oz/1 cup glacé
  cherries
115g/4oz/⅔cup dried
  figs, halved
75g/3oz/½ cup whole
  brazil nuts

1 Put the dried fruits in a bowl, pour over 60ml/4 tbsp of the whisky and all the orange juice and marinate overnight.

2 Preheat the oven to 160°C/325°F/Gas 3. Grease and line a 25cm/10in ring mould. Cream the butter and sugar. Beat in the eggs. Sift together the remaining flour, baking powder and mixed spice. Fold into the egg mixture, alternating with the rest of the ingredients, except the whisky. Transfer to the tin and bake for 1 hour, then reduce the oven temperature to 150°C/300°F/Gas 2 and bake for a further 1¾–2 hours.

3 Prick the cake all over and pour over the reserved whisky. Cool in the tin for 30 minutes, then transfer to a wire rack. Boil the marmalade and orange juice for 3 minutes. Stir in the fruit and nuts. Cool, then spoon over the cake and leave to set.

Noel Christmas Cake

If you like a traditional royal-iced cake, this is a simple design using only one icing and easy-to-pipe decorations.

Makes one 20cm/8in round cake

20cm/8in round rich fruit cake
30ml/2 tbsp apricot jam, warmed and sieved
750g/1¼lb/5¼ cups marzipan
900g/2lb/6 cups royal icing
red and green food colouring

Materials/equipment
23cm/9in round silver cake board
3 greaseproof paper piping bags
No 1 writing nozzle bags
2 x No 0 writing nozzles
44 large gold dragées
2.5m/2½yd gold ribbon, 2cm/¾in wide
2.5m/2½yd red ribbon, 5mm/¼in wide

1 Brush the fruit cake with apricot jam, cover with the marzipan and place on the cake board.

2 Flat-ice the top of the cake with two layers of royal icing and leave to dry. Ice the sides of the cake and peak the royal icing, leaving a space around the centre for the ribbon. Leave to dry. Reserve the remaining royal icing.

3 Pipe beads of icing around the top edge of the cake and place a gold dragée on alternate beads. Using a No 1 writing nozzle, write "NOEL" across the cake and pipe holly leaves, stems and berries around the top.

4 Secure the ribbons around the side of the cake. Tie a red bow and attach to the front of the cake. Use the remaining ribbon for the board. Leave to dry overnight.

5 Tint 30ml/2 tbsp of the royal icing bright green and 15ml/1 tbsp bright red. Using a No 0 writing nozzle, over-pipe "NOEL" in red, then the edging beads and berries. Overpipe the holly in green. Leave to dry.

Christmas Tree Cake

No piping is involved in this bright and colourful cake, making it an easy choice.

Makes one 20cm/8in round cake

45ml/3 tbsp apricot jam
20cm/8in round rich fruit cake
900g/2lb/6 cups marzipan
green, red, yellow and purple food colouring

225g/8oz/1½ cups royal icing
edible silver balls

Materials/equipment
25cm/10in round cake board

1 Warm, then sieve the apricot jam and brush the cake with it. Colour 675g/1½lb/4½ cups of the marzipan green. Use to cover the cake. Leave to dry overnight.

2 Secure the cake to the board with royal icing. Spread the icing halfway up the cake side. Press the flat side of a palette knife into the icing, then pull away sharply to form peaks.

3 Make three different-size Christmas tree templates. Tint half the remaining marzipan a deeper green than the top. Using the templates, cut out three tree shapes and arrange them on the cake.

4 Divide the remaining marzipan into three and colour red, yellow and purple. Use a little of each marzipan to make five 9cm/3in rolls. Loop them alternately around the top edge of the cake. Make small red balls and press on to the loop ends.

5 Use the remaining marzipan to make the tree decorations. Arrange on the trees, securing with water, if necessary. Finish the cake by adding silver balls to the Christmas trees.

Christmas Stocking Cake

A bright and happy cake that is sure to delight children at Christmas time.

Makes one 20cm/8in square cake

20cm/8in square rich fruit cake	red and green food colouring
45ml/3 tbsp apricot jam, warmed and sieved	
900g/2lb/6 cups marzipan	**Materials/equipment**
	25cm/10in square silver cake board
1.2kg/2½lb/7½ cups sugarpaste icing	1.25m/1½yd red ribbon, 2cm/¾in wide
15ml/1 tbsp royal icing	1m/1yd green ribbon, 2cm/¾in wide

1 Brush the cake with the apricot jam and place on the cake board. Cover with marzipan.

2 Set aside 225g/8oz/1½ cups of the sugarpaste icing. Cover the cake with the rest. Leave to dry. Secure the red ribbon around the board and the green ribbon around the cake with royal icing.

3 Divide the icing in half and roll out one half. Using a template, cut out two sugarpaste stockings, one 5mm/¼in larger all round. Put the smaller one on top of the larger one.

4 Divide the other half of the sugarpaste into two and tint one red and the other green. Roll out and cut each colour into seven 1cm/½in strips. Alternate the strips on top of the stocking. Roll lightly to fuse and press the edges together. Leave to dry.

5 Shape the remaining white sugarpaste into four parcels. Trim with red and green sugarpaste ribbons. Use the remaining red and green sugarpaste to make thin strips to decorate the cake sides. Secure in place with royal icing. Stick small sugarpaste balls over the joins. Arrange the stocking and parcels on the cake top.

Marbled Cracker Cake

Here is a Christmas cake that is decorated in a most untraditional way!

Makes one 20cm/8in round cake

20cm/8in round rich fruit cake	**Materials /equipment**
	wooden cocktail sticks
45ml/3 tbsp apricot jam, warmed and sieved	25cm/10in round cake board
675g/1½lb/4½ cups marzipan	red, green and gold thin gift-wrapping ribbon
750g/1¾lb/5¼ cups sugarpaste icing	3 red and 3 green ribbon bows
red and green food colouring	
edible gold balls	

1 Brush the cake with the jam. Roll out the marzipan and use to cover the cake. Leave to dry overnight.

2 Form a roll with 500g/1¼lb/3¾ cups of the sugarpaste icing. With a cocktail stick, dab a few drops of red colouring on to the icing. Repeat with the green. Knead lightly. Roll out the icing until marbled. Brush the marzipan with water and cover with the icing. Position the cake on the cake board.

3 Colour half of the remaining sugarpaste icing red and the rest green. Use half of each colour to make five crackers, about 6cm/2½in long. Decorate each with a gold ball. Leave to dry on greaseproof paper.

4 Roll out the remaining red and green icings, and cut into 1cm/½in wide strips. Then cut into 12 red and 12 green diamonds. Attach them alternately around the top and base of the cake with water.

5 Cut the ribbons into 10cm/4in lengths. Arrange them with the crackers on the cake top. Attach the bows with softened sugarpaste icing, between the diamonds at the top cake edge.

Greek New Year Cake

A "good luck", foil-wrapped gold coin is traditionally baked into this cake.

Makes one 23cm/9in square cake

275g/10oz/2½ cups plain
  flour
10ml/2 tsp baking
  powder
50g/2oz/½ cup ground
  almonds
225g/8oz/1 cup butter,
  softened
175g/6oz/generous ¾ cup
  caster sugar, plus
  extra for sprinkling

4 eggs
150ml/¼ pint/⅔ cup
  fresh orange juice
50g/2oz/½ cup blanched
  almonds
15g/½oz/1 tbsp sesame
  seeds

1 Preheat the oven to 180°C/350°F/Gas 4. Grease a 23cm/9in square cake tin, line with greaseproof paper and grease the paper.

2 Sift together the flour and baking powder and stir in the ground almonds.

3 Cream the butter and sugar until light and fluffy. Beat in the eggs, 1 at a time. Fold in the flour mixture, alternating with the orange juice.

4 Spoon the mixture into the cake tin. Arrange the blanched almonds on top, then sprinkle over the sesame seeds. Bake for 50 minutes, or until a skewer inserted in the centre comes out clean. Leave in the tin for 5 minutes, then turn out on to a wire rack and peel off the lining paper. Sprinkle with caster sugar before serving.

Starry New Year Cake

Makes one 23cm/9in round cake

23cm/9in round Madeira
  cake
675g/1½lb/3 cups butter
  icing
750g/1¾lb/5¼ cups
  sugarpaste icing
grape violet and
  mulberry food
  colouring
gold, lilac shimmer and
  primrose sparkle
  powdered food
  colouring

Materials/equipment
fine paintbrush
star-shaped cutter
florist's wire, cut into
  short lengths
28cm/11in round
  cake board
purple ribbon with
  gold stars

1 Cut the cake into three layers. Sandwich together with three-quarters of the butter icing. Spread the rest thinly over the top and sides of the cake.

2 Tint 500g/1¼lb/3¼ cups of the sugarpaste icing purple with the grape violet and mulberry food colouring. Roll out and use to cover the cake. Leave to dry overnight.

3 Place the cake on a sheet of greaseproof paper. Water down some gold and lilac food colouring. Use a paintbrush to flick each colour in turn over the cake. Leave to dry.

4 For the stars, divide the remaining sugarpaste icing into three pieces. Tint one portion purple with the grape violet food colouring, one with the lilac shimmer and one with the primrose sparkle. Roll out each colour to 3mm/⅛in thick. Cut out ten stars in each colour and highlight the stars by flicking on the watered-down gold and lilac colours.

5 While the icing is soft, push the florist's wire through the middle of 15 of the stars. Leave to dry overnight. Put the cake on the board. Arrange the stars on top of the cake. Secure the unwired ones with water. Secure the ribbon around the base.

Simnel Cake

This is a traditional cake to celebrate Easter, but it is delicious at any time of the year.

Makes one 20cm/8in round cake

225g/8oz/1 cup butter, softened
225g/8oz/generous 1 cup caster sugar
4 eggs, beaten
500g/1¼lb/3⅓ cups mixed dried fruit
115g/4oz/½ cup glacé cherries
45ml/3 tbsp sherry (optional)

275g/10oz/2½ cups plain flour
15ml/1 tbsp mixed spice
5ml/1 tsp baking powder
675g/1½lb/4½ cups yellow marzipan
1 egg yolk, beaten
ribbons, sugared eggs and sugarpaste animals, to decorate

1 Preheat the oven to 160°C/325°F/Gas 3. Grease a deep 20cm/8in round cake tin, line with a double thickness of greaseproof paper and grease the paper.

2 Beat together the butter and sugar until light and fluffy. Gradually beat in the eggs. Stir in the dried fruit, glacé cherries and sherry, if using. Sift over the flour, mixed spice and baking powder, then fold in.

3 Roll out half the marzipan to a 20cm/8in round. Spoon half of the cake mixture into the cake tin and place the round of marzipan on top. Add the other half of the cake mixture and smooth the surface.

4 Bake for 2½ hours, or until golden and springy to the touch. Leave in the tin for 15 minutes, then turn out on to a wire rack, peel off the lining paper and leave to cool.

5 Roll out the reserved marzipan to fit the cake. Brush the cake top with egg yolk and place the marzipan on top. Flute the edges and make a pattern on top with a fork. Brush with more egg yolk. Put the cake on a baking sheet and grill for 5 minutes to brown the top lightly. Cool before decorating.

Easter Sponge Cake

This light lemon quick-mix sponge cake is decorated with lemon butter icing and cut-out marzipan flowers.

Makes one 20cm/8in round cake

3-egg quantity lemon-flavour quick-mix sponge cake
675g/1½lb/3 cups lemon-flavour butter icing
50g/2oz/½ cup flaked almonds, toasted

To decorate
50g/2oz/⅓ cup homemade or commercial white marzipan
green, orange and yellow food colouring

1 Preheat the oven to 160°C/325°F/Gas 3. Bake the cakes in two lined and greased 20cm/8in round sandwich tins for 35–40 minutes until they are golden brown and spring back when lightly pressed in the centre. Loosen the edges of the cakes with a palette knife, turn out, remove the lining paper and cool on a wire rack.

2 Sandwich the cakes together with one-quarter of the butter icing. Spread the side of the cake evenly with another one-quarter of butter icing.

3 Press the almonds on to the sides to cover evenly. Spread the top of the cake evenly with another one-quarter of icing. Finish with a palette knife dipped in hot water, spreading backwards and forwards to give an even lined effect.

4 Place the remaining icing into a nylon piping bag fitted with a medium-size gâteau nozzle and pipe a scroll edging.

5 Using the marzipan and food colouring, make six cut-out daffodils and ten green and eight orange cut-out marzipan flowers. Arrange them on the cake and leave the icing to set.

Easter Egg Nest Cake

Celebrate Easter with this colourfully adorned, fresh-tasting lemon sponge cake.

Makes one 20cm/8in ring cake

20cm/8in lemon sponge ring cake
350g/12oz/1½ cups lemon-flavour butter icing
225g/8oz/1½ cups marzipan

pink, green and purple food colouring
small foil-wrapped chocolate eggs

Materials/equipment
25cm/10in cake board

1 Cut the cake in half horizontally and sandwich together with one-third of the butter icing. Place on the cake board. Use the remaining icing to cover the cake. Smooth the top and swirl the side with a palette knife.

2 For the marzipan plaits, divide the marzipan into three and tint pink, green and purple. Cut each portion in half. Using one-half of each colour, roll thin sausages long enough to go around the base. Pinch the ends together, then twist the strands into a rope. Pinch the other ends to seal.

3 Place the coloured marzipan rope on the cake board around the cake.

4 For the nests, take the remaining portions of coloured marzipan and divide each into five. Roll each piece into a 16cm/6½in rope. Take a rope of each colour, pinch the ends together, twist to form a multi-coloured rope and pinch the other ends. Form into a circle. Repeat to make five nests.

5 Space the nests evenly on the cake. Place small chocolate eggs in the nests.

Mother's Day Bouquet

A piped bouquet of flowers can bring as much pleasure as a fresh one for a Mother's Day treat.

Makes one 18cm/7in round cake

675g/1½lb/3 cups butter icing
2 x 18cm/7in round sponge cakes
green, blue, yellow and pink food colouring

Materials/equipment
serrated scraper
No 3 writing and petal nozzles
5 greaseproof paper piping bags

1 Reserve one-third of the butter icing for decorating. Sandwich together the two sponges with butter icing and place on a serving plate. Cover the top and side with the rest of the butter icing, smoothing the top with a palette knife and serrating the side using a scraper.

2 Divide the remaining butter icing into four bowls. Tint them green, blue, yellow and pink.

3 Decorate the top of the cake first. Use No 3 writing nozzles for the blue and green icing and petal nozzles for the yellow and pink. Pipe on the vase and flowers.

4 For the side decoration, spoon the remaining yellow icing into a fresh piping bag fitted with a No 3 writing nozzle. Pipe the stems, then the flowers and flower centres. Finish by piping green beads at the top and base edges of the cake.

Mother's Day Basket

Makes one 15cm/6in cake

175g/6oz/1½ cups self-
  rising flour, sifted
175g/6oz/scant 1 cup
  caster sugar
175g/6oz/¾ cup soft
  margarine
3 eggs
900g/2lb/4 cups orange-
  flavour butter icing

Materials/equipment
thin 15cm/6in round
  silver cake board
greaseproof paper piping
  bag
basketweave nozzle
foil
1m/1yd mauve ribbon,
  1cm/½in wide
fresh flowers
0.5m/½yd spotted mauve
  ribbon, 3mm/⅛in
  wide

1 Preheat the oven to 160°C/325°F/Gas 3. Lightly grease and base-line a 15cm/6in brioche mould. Place all the cake ingredients in a bowl, mix together then beat for 1–2 minutes until smooth. Transfer to the prepared mould and bake for about 1¼ hours, or until risen and golden.

2 Place the cooled cake upside-down on the board. Cover the sides with one-third of the butter icing. Using a basketweave nozzle, pipe the sides with a basketweave pattern.

3 Invert the cake on the board and spread the top with butter icing. Pipe a shell edging with the basketweave nozzle. Pipe the basketweave pattern over the cake top, starting at the edge. Leave to set.

4 Fold a strip of foil several layers thick. Wrap the plain ribbon around the strip and bend up the ends to secure the ribbon. Form the foil into a handle and press into the icing.

5 Finish by tying a posy of fresh flowers with the spotted ribbon and making a mixed ribbon bow for the handle.

Basket Cake

This is a perfect cake for a retirement gathering or other special occasion.

Makes one basket-shaped cake

20cm/8in round
  Madeira cake
450g/1lb/2 cups coloured
  butter icing
chocolates or sweets and
  ribbon for decoration

Materials/equipment
pastillage (gum paste)
2 greaseproof paper
  piping bags, fitted
  with a plain tube and
  a basketweave tube
powder food colour

1 Cut a template from card to the same size as the top of the cake, fold it in half and cut along the fold. Roll out pastillage fairly thinly and cut out two pieces for the lid, using the templates as a guide. Leave to dry.

2 Coat the top of the cake with butter icing. Fill both piping bags with butter icing and on the side of the cake and about 2.5cm/1in on to the top of the cake, pipe a plain vertical line, then pipe short lengths of basketweave across the line. Pipe another plain line along the ends of the basketweave strips. Pipe the next row of basketweave strips in the spaces left between the existing strips and over the new plain line. Continue until the side of the cake and the area on the top is completely covered.

3 Brush the underside of the pastillage lid with powder food colour, then pipe a basketweave on top of the lid.

4 Divide the top of the cake in half and pipe a line of basketweave along this central line. Use two or three pieces of pastillage to support each lid half in an open position on the cake. Fill the area under each lid half with chocolates or sweets and decorate with ribbon

Valentine's Heart Cake

This cake could also be used to celebrate a special birthday or anniversary.

Makes one 20cm/8in square cake

	Materials/equipment
20cm/8in square light fruit cake	25cm/10in square cake board
45ml/3 tbsp apricot jam, warmed and sieved	5cm/2in heart-shaped cutter
900g/2lb/6 cups marzipan	2.5cm/1in heart-shaped cutter
1.5kg/3lb/9 cups royal icing	4 greaseproof paper piping bags
115g/4oz/¼ cup sugarpaste icing	No 1 and No 2 writing and No 42 star nozzles
red food colouring	heart-patterned ribbon

1 Brush the cake with the apricot jam. Roll out the marzipan and use to cover the cake. Leave to dry overnight.

2 Secure the cake on the cake board with a little royal icing. Flat-ice the cake with three or four layers of smooth icing. Set aside some royal icing in an airtight container for piping.

3 Tint the sugarpaste icing red. Roll it out and cut 12 hearts with the larger cutter. Stamp out the middles with the smaller cutter. Cut four extra small hearts. Dry on greaseproof paper.

4 Using a No 1 writing nozzle, pipe wavy lines in royal icing around the four small hearts. Leave to dry. Using a fresh bag and a No 42 nozzle, pipe swirls around the top and base of the cake. Colour 15ml/1 tbsp of the remaining royal icing red and pipe red dots on top of each white swirl with the No 1 nozzle.

5 Secure the ribbon in place. Using a No 2 writing nozzle, pipe beads down each corner, avoiding the ribbon. Decorate the cake with the hearts, using royal icing to secure them.

Valentine's Box of Chocolates Cake

This cake would also make a wonderful surprise for Mother's Day.

Makes one 20cm/8in heart-shaped cake

	Materials/equipment
20cm/8in heart-shaped chocolate sponge cake	23cm/9in square piece of stiff card
275g/10oz/generous 2 cups marzipan	pencil and scissors
120ml/8 tbsp apricot jam, warmed and sieved	23cm/9in square cake board
900g/2lb/6 cups sugarpaste icing	piece of string
red food colouring	small heart-shaped cutter
225g/8oz/about 16–20 hand-made chocolates	length of ribbon and a pin
	small paper sweet cases

1 Place the cake on the card, draw around it and cut the heart shape out. It will be used to support the box lid. Cut through the cake horizontally just below the dome. Place the top section on the card and the base on the board.

2 Use the string to measure around the outside of the base. Roll the marzipan into a long sausage to the measured length. Place on the cake around the outside edge. Brush both sections of the cake with apricot jam. Tint the sugarpaste icing red and cut off one-third. Cut another 50g/2oz/8 tbsp portion from the larger piece. Set aside. Use the large piece to cover the base section of cake.

3 Stand the lid on a raised surface. Use the reserved one-third of sugarpaste icing to cover the lid. Roll out the remaining piece of icing and stamp out small hearts with the cutter. Stick them around the edge of the lid with water. Tie the ribbon in a bow and secure on top of the lid with the pin.

4 Place the chocolates in the paper cases and arrange in the cake base. Position the lid slightly off-centre, to reveal the chocolates. Remove the ribbon and pin before serving.

Double Heart Engagement Cake

For a celebratory engagement party, these sumptuous cakes make the perfect centrepiece.

Makes two 20cm/8in heart-shaped cakes

350g/12oz plain chocolate
2 x 20cm/8in heart-shaped chocolate sponge cakes
675g/1½lb/3 cups coffee-flavour butter icing

icing sugar, for dusting
fresh raspberries, to decorate

Materials/equipment
2 x 23cm/9in heart-shaped cake boards

1 Melt the chocolate in a heatproof bowl over a saucepan of hot water. Pour the chocolate on to a smooth, non-porous surface and spread it out with a palette knife. Leave to cool until just set, but not hard.

2 To make the chocolate curls, hold a large sharp knife at a 45-degree angle to the chocolate and push it along the chocolate in short sawing movements. Leave to set on greaseproof paper.

3 Cut each cake in half horizontally. Use one-third of the butter icing to sandwich the cakes together. Use the remaining icing to coat the tops and sides of the cakes.

4 Place the cakes on the cake boards. Generously cover the tops and sides of the cakes with the chocolate curls, pressing them gently into the butter icing.

5 Sift a little icing sugar over the top of each cake and decorate with raspberries. Chill until ready to serve.

Sweetheart Cake

Makes one 20cm/8in heart-shaped cake

20cm/8in heart-shaped light fruit cake
30ml/2 tbsp apricot jam, warmed and sieved
900g/2lb/6 cups marzipan
900g/2lb/6 cups sugarpaste icing
red food colouring
225g/8oz/1½ cups royal icing

large and medium heart-shaped plunger cutters
1m/1yd red ribbon, 2.5cm/1in wide
1m/1yd looped red ribbon, 1cm/½in wide
0.5m/½yd red ribbon, 5mm/¼in wide
greaseproof paper piping bag
medium star nozzle
fresh red rosebud

Materials/equipment
25cm/10in silver heart-shaped cake board

1 Brush the cake with apricot jam, place on the cake board and cover with marzipan. Cover the cake and board with sugarpaste icing. Leave to dry overnight.

2 Tint the sugarpaste icing red. Cut out 18 large and 21 medium-size hearts. Leave to dry on greaseproof paper.

3 Secure the wide ribbon around the cake board. Secure a band of the looped ribbon around the side of the cake with a bead of icing. Tie a bow with long tails and attach to the side of the cake with a bead of icing.

4 Using the star nozzle, pipe a row of royal icing stars around the base of the cake and attach a medium-size heart to every third star. Pipe stars around the cake top, and arrange large red hearts on each one.

5 Tie a bow on to the rosebud stem and place on the cake top just before serving.

Cloth-of-Roses Cake

This cake simply says "congratulations". It is a very pretty cake that is bound to impress your guests.

Makes one 20cm/8in round cake

*20cm/8in round light
fruit cake
45ml/3 tbsp apricot jam,
warmed and sieved
675g/1½lb/4½ cups
marzipan
900g/2lb/6 cups
sugarpaste icing
yellow, orange and green
food colouring*

*115g/4oz/¼ cup royal
icing*

Materials/equipment
*25cm/10in cake board
5.5cm/2¼in plain cutter
petal cutter
thin yellow ribbon*

1 Brush the cake with apricot jam. Cover with marzipan and leave to dry overnight.

2 Cut off 675g/1½lb/4½ cups of the sugarpaste icing and divide in half. Colour pale yellow and pale orange.

3 Make a greaseproof paper template for the orange icing by drawing a 25cm/10in circle round the cake board then, using the plain cutter, draw scallops around the circle.

4 Cover the cake side with yellow sugarpaste icing. Place the cake on the board. Using the template, cut out the orange sugarpaste icing. Place on the cake and bend the scallops slightly. Leave to dry overnight.

5 For the roses and leaves, cut off three-quarters of the remaining sugarpaste icing and divide into four. Tint pale yellow, deep yellow, orange, and marbled yellow and orange. Make 18 roses. Tint the remaining icing green. Cut out 24 leaves with a petal cutter. Dry on greaseproof paper.

6 Secure the leaves and roses with royal icing. Decorate the cake with the ribbon.

Rose Blossom Wedding Cake

Serves 80

*23cm/9in square rich
fruit cake
15cm/6in square rich
fruit cake
75ml/5 tbsp apricot jam,
warmed and sieved
1.5kg/3⅓lb/10½ cups
marzipan
1.5kg/3⅓lb/10½ cups
royal icing, to coat
675g/1½lb/4½ cups royal
icing, to pipe
pink and green food
colouring*

Materials/equipment
*28cm/11in square
cake board
20cm/8in square
cake board
No 1 writing and No 42
nozzles
greaseproof paper piping
bags
thin pink ribbon
8 pink bows
3–4 cake pillars
12 miniature roses
few fern sprigs*

1 Brush the cakes with the jam and cover with marzipan. Leave to dry overnight, then secure to their boards with icing. Flat-ice the cakes with three or four layers, allowing each to dry overnight. Dry for several days.

2 For the sugar pieces, use the No 1 writing nozzle to pipe the double-triangle design in white icing on greaseproof paper. You will need 40 pieces, but make extra. Tint some icing pale pink and some very pale green. Using No 1 writing nozzles, pipe pink dots on the corners of the top triangles and green on the corners of the lower triangles. Leave to dry.

3 Use a pin to mark out the triangles on the tops and sides of each cake. Using a No 1 writing nozzle, pipe double white lines over the pin marks, then pipe cornelli inside all the triangles. With a No 42 nozzle, pipe white shells around the top and base edges of each cake, between the triangles.

4 Using No 1 writing nozzles, pipe pink and green dots on the cake corners. Secure the sugar pieces to the cakes and boards with icing. Attach the ribbons and bows. Assemble the cake with the pillars and decorate with roses and fern sprigs.

Basketweave Wedding Cake

This wonderful wedding cake can be made in any flavour.

Serves 150

25cm/10in, 20cm/8in
  and 15cm/6in square
  Madeira cakes
2.75kg/6lb/12 cups
  butter icing

Materials/equipment

30cm/12in square silver
  cake board
20cm/8in and 15cm/6in
  thin silver cake board
smooth scraper

12 small greaseproof
  piping bags
No 4 writing and
  basketweave nozzles
1.5m/1½yd pale lilac
  ribbon, 2.5cm/1in
  wide
2.5m/2½yd deep lilac
  ribbon, 5mm/¼in
  wide
30 fresh lilac-coloured
  freesias

1   Level the cake tops, then invert the cakes on to the boards and cover with butter icing. Use a smooth scraper on the sides and a palette knife to smooth the top. Leave to set for 1 hour.

2   Pipe a line of icing with the No 4 writing nozzle on to the corner of the large cake, from the base to the top. Using the basketweave nozzle, pipe a basketweave pattern (see above photograph). Pipe all around the side of the cake and neaten the top edge with a shell border, using the basketweave nozzle. Repeat for the second cake.

3   To decorate the top of the small cake, start at the edge with a straight plain line, then pipe across with the basketweave nozzle, spacing the lines equally apart. When the top is complete, work the design around the sides, making sure the top and side designs align. Leave the cakes overnight to set.

4   Fit the wide and narrow lilac ribbons around the board. Use the remaining narrow ribbon to tie eight small bows with long tails. Trim off the flower stems.

5   Assemble the cakes. Decorate with the bows and flowers.

Chocolate-iced Anniversary Cake

This attractive cake is special enough to celebrate any wedding anniversary.

Makes one 20cm/8in round cake

20cm/8in round Madeira
  cake
475g/1lb 2oz/2¼ cups
  chocolate-flavour
  butter icing

For the chocolate icing

175g/6oz plain chocolate
150ml/¼ pint/⅔ cup
  single cream
2.5ml/½ tsp instant
  coffee powder

To decorate

chocolate buttons,
  quartered

selection of fresh fruits,
  such as kiwi fruit,
  nectarines, peaches,
  apricots and Cape
  gooseberries, peeled
  and sliced as necessary

Materials/equipment

No 22 star nozzle
greaseproof paper
  piping bag
gold ribbon, about
  5mm/¼in wide
florist's wire

1   Cut the cake horizontally into three and sandwich together with three-quarters of the butter icing. Place on a wire rack over a baking sheet.

2   To make the satin chocolate icing, put all of the ingredients in a saucepan and melt over a very low heat until smooth. Immediately pour over the cake to coat completely. Use a palette knife, if necessary. Allow to set.

3   Transfer the cake to a serving plate. Using a No 22 star nozzle, pipe butter icing scrolls around the top edge. Decorate with chocolate button pieces and fruit.

4   Make seven ribbon decorations. For each one, make two small loops from ribbon and secure the ends with a twist of florist's wire . Cut the wire to the length you want and use to position the decoration in the fruit. Remove before serving.

Silver Wedding Cake

Makes one 25cm/10in round cake

25cm/10in round rich or
 light fruit cake
60ml/4 tbsp apricot jam,
 warmed and sieved
1.2kg/2½lb/7½ cups
 marzipan
1.5kg/3lb/9 cups royal
 icing

For the petal paste
10ml/2 tsp gelatine
75ml/5 tbsp cold water
10ml/2 tsp liquid glucose
10ml/2 tsp white
 vegetable fat
450g/1lb/4 cups icing
 sugar, sifted
5ml/1 tsp gum
 tragacanth, sifted
1 egg white

Materials/equipment
30cm/12in round silver
 cake board
1.5m/1½yd white ribbon,
 2.5cm/1in wide
2m/2yd silver ribbon,
 2.5cm/1in wide
club cocktail cutter
tiny round cutter
greaseproof piping bag
No 1 writing nozzle
50 large silver dragées
1.5m/1½yd silver ribbon,
 5mm/¼in wide
7 silver leaves
"25" silver cake
 decoration

1 Brush the cake with apricot jam and cover with marzipan. Place on the board. Flat-ice the top and side of the cake with three or four layers of royal icing. Leave to dry overnight, then ice the board. Reserve the remaining royal icing. Secure the wider ribbons around the board and cake with icing.

2 For the petal paste, melt the first four ingredients in a pan set over a bowl of hot water. Mix the sugar, gum tragacanth, egg white and gelatine mixture to a paste and knead until smooth. Leave for 2 hours, then re-knead. Make 65 cut-outs using the two cutters. Leave to dry overnight.

3 Arrange 25 cut-outs around the top and secure with icing beads piped with a No 1 writing nozzle. Repeat at the base. Pipe icing beads between and press a dragée in each. Leave to dry. Thread the thin ribbon through. Arrange seven cut-outs and seven dragées in the centre. Position the leaves and "25".

Golden Wedding Heart Cake

Makes one 23cm/9in round cake

60ml/4 tbsp apricot jam
23cm/9in round rich
 fruit cake
900g/2lb/6 cups
 marzipan
900g/2lb/6 cups
 sugarpaste icing
cream food colouring
115g/4oz/¾ cup royal
 icing

Materials/equipment
28cm/11in round cake
 board

crimping tool
pins
small heart-shaped
 plunger tool
7.5cm/3in plain cutter
dual large and small
 blossom cutter
stamens
frill cutter
wooden cocktail stick
foil-wrapped chocolate
 hearts

1 Warm, then sieve the apricot jam and brush over the cake. Cover with marzipan and leave to dry overnight.

2 Tint 675g/1½lb/4½ cups of the sugarpaste icing very pale cream and cover the cake. Put on the board. Crimp the top edge. With pins, mark eight equidistant points around the top edge. Crimp slanting lines to the base. Emboss the base edge with the plunger. Use the plain cutter to emboss a circle on top.

3 Divide the remaining sugarpaste icing into two and tint cream and pale cream. Using half of each colour, make flowers with the blossom cutter. Make pinholes in the large flowers. Leave to dry then secure the stamens in the holes with royal icing.

4 Make eight frills with the rest of the sugarpaste icing using the frill cutter, and a cocktail stick to trim and fill the edges. Attach the frills with water next to the crimped lines on the cake side. Crimp the edges of the deeper coloured frills.

5 Secure the flowers on the top and side of the cake with royal icing. Place the chocolate hearts in the centre.

Marzipan Bell Cake

This cake can be easily adapted to make a christening cake if you leave out the holly decorations.

Makes one 18cm/7in round cake

18cm/7in round rich or
   light fruit cake
30ml/2 tbsp apricot jam,
   warmed and sieved
900g/2lb/6 cups
   marzipan
green, yellow and red
   food colouring

Materials/equipment
20cm/8in round silver
   cake board
crimping tool
bell and holly leaf cutter
1m/1yd red ribbon,
   2cm/¾in wide
1m/1yd green ribbon,
   5mm/¼in wide
0.25m/¼yd red ribbon,
   5mm/¼in wide

1 Brush the cake with apricot jam and place on the cake board. Tint two-thirds of the marzipan pale green. Use to cover the cake. Crimp the top edge of the cake to make a scalloped pattern.

2 Tint a small piece of remaining marzipan bright yellow, another bright red and the rest bright green. Make two yellow bells and clappers, 11 green holly leaves (veins marked with the back of a knife), two green bell ropes, 16 red holly berries and two bell-rope ends. Leave to dry.

3 Secure the wide red and fine green ribbons around the side of the cake with a pin. Tie a double bow from red and green fine ribbon and attach to the side with a pin.

4 Arrange the bells, clappers, bell ropes, holly leaves and berries on top of the cake and secure with apricot jam.

Christening Sampler

Serves 30

20cm/8in square rich
   fruit cake
45ml/3 tbsp apricot jam,
   warmed and sieved
450g/1lb/3cups marzipan
675g/1½lb/4½ cups
   sugarpaste icing
brown, yellow, orange,
   purple, cream, blue,
   green and pink food
   colouring

Materials/equipment
25cm/10in square
   cake board
fine paintbrush
small heart-shaped
   biscuit cutter

1 Brush the cake with apricot jam. Roll out the marzipan, cover the cake and leave to dry overnight. Roll out 150g/5oz/1 cup of the sugarpaste icing to fit the cake top. Brush the top with water and cover with the icing.

2 Colour 300g/10oz/2 cups of the icing brown and roll out four pieces to the length and about 1cm/½in wider than the cake sides. Brush the sides with water and cover with icing, folding over the extra width at the top and cutting the corners at an angle to make the picture frame. Place on a cake board. With a fine paintbrush, paint over the sides with watered-down brown food colouring to represent wood grain.

3 Take the remaining icing and colour small amounts yellow, orange, brown, purple and cream and two shades of blue, green and pink. Leave a little white. Use these colours to shape the ducks, teddy bear, bulrushes, water, branch and leaves. Cut out a pink heart and make the baby's initial from white icing.

4 Mix the white and pink icings together for the apple blossom flowers. Make the shapes for the border. Attach the decorations to the cake with a little water.

5 Use the leftover colours to make "threads". Arrange in loops around the base of the cake on the board.

Teddy Bear Christening Cake

To personalize the cake, make a simple plaque for the top and pipe on the name of the new baby.

Makes one 20cm/8in square cake

20cm/8in square light
   fruit cake
45ml/3 tbsp apricot jam,
   warmed and sieved
900g/2lb/6 cups
   marzipan
800g/1¾lb/5¼ cups
   sugarpaste icing
   peach, yellow, blue and
   brown food colouring
115g/4oz/¾ cup royal
   icing

Materials/equipment
25cm/10in square cake
   board
crimping tool
cornflour, for dipping
fine paintbrush
wooden cocktail stick
peach ribbon
small blue ribbon bow

1 Brush the cake with the apricot jam. Roll out the marzipan and use to cover the cake. Leave to dry overnight.

2 Colour 500g/1¼lb/3¼ cups of the sugarpaste icing peach, then roll it out. Brush the marzipan with water and cover the cake with the icing. Place the cake on the board. Using a crimping tool dipped in cornflour, crimp the top and base edges of the cake.

3 Divide the remaining sugarpaste into three. Leave one-third white and tint one-third yellow. Divide the last third in two, tint one half peach and the other blue.

4 Make flowers from the peach and blue sugarpaste. Leave to dry. Reserve the blue trimmings. Make a yellow teddy bear. Paint on its face with brown food colouring. Give it a blue button. Leave to dry. Make a blue blanket. Frill the white edge with a cocktail stick. Secure the frill to the blanket with water.

5 Decorate the cake with the ribbon, place the bear on top under its blanket, securing with royal icing. Secure the flowers and the bear's bow-tie in the same way.

Daisy Christening Cake

A ring of daisies sets off this pretty pink christening cake.

Makes one 20cm/8in round cake

20cm/8in round rich
   fruit cake
45ml/3 tbsp apricot jam,
   warmed and sieved
675g/1½lb/4½ cups
   marzipan
900g/2lb/6 cups royal
   icing
115g/4oz/¾ cup
   sugarpaste icing
pink and yellow food
   colouring

Materials/equipment
25cm/10in round cake
   board
fine paintbrush
5cm/2in fluted cutter
wooden cocktail stick
2 greaseproof paper
   piping bags
No 42 nozzle
pink and white ribbon

1 Brush the cake with the apricot jam. Roll out the marzipan and use to cover the cake. Leave to dry overnight.

2 Use a little royal icing to secure the cake to the board. Tint three-quarters of the royal icing pink. Flat-ice the cake with three or four layers, using white for the top and pink for the side. Allow each layer to dry overnight before applying the next. Set aside a little of both icings in airtight containers.

3 Make 28 daisies. For each daisy, shape a small piece of sugarpaste icing to look like a golf tee. Snip the edges and curl them slightly. Dry on greaseproof paper. Trim the stems and paint the edges pink and the centres yellow.

4 To make the plaque, roll out the remaining sugarpaste icing and cut out a circle with the fluted cutter. Roll a cocktail stick around the edge until it frills. Dry on greaseproof paper, then paint the name and the edges with pink food colouring.

5 Pipe twisted ropes around the top and base of the cake with the reserved white royal icing. Then pipe a row of stars around the top of the cake. Stick the plaque in the centre with royal icing. Stick on the daisies and decorate with the ribbons.

Birthday Parcel

Serves 10

15cm/6in square Madeira cake

275g/10oz/1⅓ cup orange-flavour butter icing

45ml/3 tbsp apricot jam, warmed and sieved

450g/1lb/3 cups sugarpaste icing

blue, orange and green food colouring

icing sugar, for dusting

Materials/equipment

15 – 18cm/7 – 8in square cake board

small triangular and round cocktail cutters

1 Cut the cake in half horizontally and sandwich together with the butter icing. Brush the cake with apricot jam. Colour three-quarters of the sugarpaste icing blue. Divide the remaining sugarpaste icing in half and colour one half orange and the other half green. Wrap the orange and green sugarpaste separately in clear film and set aside. Roll out the blue icing on a work surface lightly dusted with icing sugar and use it to cover the cake. Position on the cake board.

2 While the sugarpaste covering is still soft, use the cocktail cutters to cut out triangles and circles from the blue icing, lifting out the shapes to expose the cake.

3 Roll out the orange and green icings and cut out circles and triangles to fill the exposed holes in the blue icing. Roll out the trimmings and cut three orange strips, 2cm/¾in wide and long enough to go over the corner of the cake and 3 very thin green strips the same length as the orange ones. Place the strips next to each other to make three striped ribbons, and secure the pieces together with a little water.

4 Place one striped ribbon over one corner of the cake, securing with a little water. Place a second strip over the opposite corner. Cut the remaining ribbon in half. Bend each half to make loops and attach both to one corner of the cake with water to form a loose bow.

Chocolate Fruit Birthday Cake

The marzipan fruits on this moist chocolate Madeira cake make an eye-catching decoration.

Makes one 18cm/7in square cake

18cm/7in square deep chocolate Madeira cake

45ml/3 tbsp apricot jam, warmed and sieved

450g/1lb/3 cups marzipan

450g/1lb/2cups chocolate fudge icing

red, yellow, orange, green and purple food colouring

whole cloves

angelica strips

Materials/equipment

20cm/8in square silver cake board

medium gâteau nozzle

nylon piping bag

0.75m/¾yd yellow ribbon, 1cm/½in wide

1 Level the cake top and invert. Brush with apricot jam.

2 Use two-thirds of the marzipan to cover the cake. Reserve the trimmings.

3 Place the cake on a wire rack over a tray and pour three-quarters of the chocolate fudge icing over, spreading with a palette knife. Leave for 10 minutes, then place on the board.

4 Using the reserved icing and a medium-size gâteau nozzle, pipe stars around the top edge and base of the cake. Leave to set.

5 Using the reserved marzipan, food colouring, cloves and angelica strips, model a selection of fruits.

6 Secure the ribbon around the sides of the cake. Decorate the top with the marzipan fruits.

Eighteenth Birthday Cake

A really striking cake for an eighteenth birthday. Change the shape if you don't have the tin.

Serves 80

33.5 x 20cm/13½ x 8in
  diamond-shaped deep
  rich or light fruit cake
45ml/3 tbsp apricot jam,
  warmed and sieved
1.1kg/2½lb/7½ cups
  marzipan
1.6kg/3½lb/10½ cups
  sugarpaste
black food colouring
30ml/2 tbsp royal icing

Materials/equipment
38 x 23cm/15 x 9in
  diamond-shaped cake
  board
"18" template
small greaseproof paper
  piping bag
No 1 writing nozzle
2m/2yd white ribbon,
  2.5cm/1in wide
2m/2yd black ribbon,
  3mm/⅛in wide

1 Make the cake using quantities for a 23cm/9in round cake. Brush with apricot jam. Cover in marzipan. Place on the cake board. Cover the cake using 1.2kg/2½lb/7½ cups sugarpaste icing. Knead the trimmings into the remaining sugarpaste and tint black.

2 Use two-thirds of the black sugarpaste to cover the board.

3 Use a quarter of the remaining sugarpaste to cut out a number "18" using a template. Use the rest to cut out a variety of bow ties, wine glasses and music notes. Leave to dry on greaseproof paper.

4 Tint the royal icing black. Using a No 1 writing nozzle, attach the cut-outs to the cake top and sides.

5 Tie four small bows with the black ribbon. Secure with icing to the top corners. Position and secure black ribbon around the cake base and white ribbon around the board.

Flickering Birthday Candle Cake

Flickering stripy candles are ready to blow out on this birthday cake for all ages.

Makes one 20cm/8in square cake

20cm/8in square Madeira
  cake
350g/12oz/1½ cups
  butter icing
45ml/3 tbsp apricot jam,
  warmed and sieved
800g/1¾lb/5¼ cups
  sugarpaste icing
pink, yellow, purple and
  jade food colouring
edible silver balls

Materials/equipment
23cm/9in square cake
  board
small round cutter
pink and purple food
  colouring pens
5mm/¼in wide jade-
  coloured ribbon

1 Cut the cake into three layers. Sandwich together with the butter icing and brush the cake with the apricot jam. Roll out 500g/1¼lb/3¾ cups of the sugarpaste icing and use to cover the cake. Position on the cake board.

2 Divide the remaining sugarpaste into four pieces and tint them pink, yellow, pale purple and jade.

3 Make the candles from jade and the flames from yellow icing. Press a silver ball into their bases. Position the candles and flames on the cake with a little water. Mould strips in yellow and purple icing to go round the candles. Secure with water. Cut small wavy pieces from the pink and purple icing for smoke, and arrange them, using water, above the candles.

4 Cut out yellow circles with the cutter for the side decorations. Mould small pink balls and press a silver ball into their centres. Attach using water.

5 Using food colouring pens, draw wavy lines and dots coming from the purple and pink wavy icings. Decorate the sides of the cake board with the ribbon, securing at the back with a little softened sugarpaste.

Flower Birthday Cake

A simple birthday cake decorated with piped yellow and white flowers and ribbons.

Makes one 18cm/7in round cake

18cm/7in round light
  fruit cake
30ml/2 tbsp apricot jam,
  warmed and sieved
675g/1½lb/4½ cups
  marzipan
1.2kg/2½lb/7½ cups royal
  icing
yellow and orange food
  colouring

petal nozzle, No 1 and
  2 writing nozzles, and
  medium star nozzle
greaseproof paper piping
  bags
1m/1yd white ribbon,
  2cm/¾in wide
2m/2yd coral ribbon,
  1cm/½in wide
25cm/10in coral ribbon,
  5mm/¼in wide

Materials/equipment

23cm/9in round silver
  cake board

1   Brush the cake with apricot jam and cover with marzipan. Place on the board.

2   Flat-ice the top and side of the cake with three layers of royal icing. Leave to dry, then ice the board. Reserve the remaining royal icing.

3   Tint one-third of the reserved royal icing yellow and 15ml/1 tbsp of it orange. Using the petal nozzle for the petals and No 1 writing nozzle for the centres, make four white narcissi with yellow centres and nine yellow narcissi with orange centres. Make nine plain white flowers with a snipped piping bag with yellow centres. When dry, secure to the top.

4   Use the star nozzle to pipe shell edgings to the cake top and base. Pipe "Happy Birthday" using the No 2 writing nozzle. Overlay in orange using the No 1 writing nozzle.

5   Secure the ribbons around the board and cake side. Finish with a coral bow.

Jazzy Chocolate Gâteau

This cake is made with Father's Day in mind, though you can make it for anyone who loves chocolate.

Serves 12–15

2 x quantity chocolate-
  flavour quick-mix
  sponge cake mix
75g/3oz/3 squares plain
  chocolate
75g/3oz/3 squares white
  chocolate
175g/6oz fudge frosting
115g/4oz/1 cup glacé
  icing

5ml/1 tsp weak coffee
8 tbsp chocolate hazelnut
  spread

Materials/equipment

2 x 20cm/8in round cake
  tins
greaseproof paper piping
  bag
No 1 writing nozzle

1   Preheat the oven to 160°C/325°F/Gas 3. Grease the cake tins, line the bases with greaseproof paper and grease the paper. Divide the cake mixture evenly between the tins and smooth the surfaces. Bake in the centre of the oven for about 20–30 minutes, or until firm to the touch. Turn out on to a wire rack, peel off the lining paper and leave to cool.

2   Melt the chocolates in two separate bowls, pour on to baking paper and spread evenly. As it begins to set, place another sheet of baking paper on top and turn the chocolate "sandwich" over. When set, peel off the paper and turn the chocolate sheets over. Cut out haphazard shapes of chocolate and set aside.

3   Sandwich the two cakes together using the fudge frosting. Place the cake on a stand or plate. Colour the glacé icing using the weak coffee and add enough water to form a spreading consistency. Spread the icing on top of the cake almost to the edges. Cover the side of the cake with chocolate hazelnut spread.

4   Press the chocolate pieces around the side of the cake and, using a piping bag fitted with a No 1 nozzle, decorate the top of the cake with "jazzy" lines over the glacé icing.

Petal Retirement Cake

Makes one 20cm/8in petal-shaped cake

20cm/8in petal-shaped
  deep light fruit cake
45ml/3 tbsp apricot jam,
  warmed and sieved
900g/2lb/6 cups
  marzipan
mulberry and pink food
  colouring
900g/2lb/6 cups
  sugarpaste icing
275g/10oz petal paste
15ml/1 tbsp royal icing

foam sponge
large and small blossom
  plunger cutters
2m/2yd white ribbon,
  2cm/¾in wide
2m/2yd fuchsia ribbon,
  1cm/½in wide
2m/2yd fuchsia ribbon,
  3mm/⅛in wide
greaseproof paper piping
  bag
No 1 writing nozzle
pink food colouring pen
fresh flowers

Materials/equipment

23cm/9in petal-shaped
  silver cake board

1 Brush the cake with jam and put on the board. Cover with marzipan. Knead mulberry colouring into the sugarpaste icing. Use to cover the cake and board. Dry overnight.

2 Tint the petal paste with pink colouring. Roll and cut out a 5 x 2.5cm/2 x 1in rectangle. Fold in half and dry over a foam sponge to make the card. Make holes in the top edges of the fold for the ribbon. Cut out 30 large and four small plunger blossom flowers. Leave to dry.

3 Using the royal icing and a No 1 writing nozzle, secure the white and narrow fuchsia ribbons around the board and the medium ribbon around the cake base. Tie six small bows from the narrow ribbon for the base.

4 Attach the large flowers to the side of the cake with icing. Secure the small flowers to the board. Draw a design and write a message inside the card with the pen. Thread ribbon through the holes and tie a bow. Place on the cake top with the fresh flowers.

Pansy Retirement Cake

You can use other edible flowers such as nasturtiums, roses or tiny daffodils for this cake, if you prefer.

Makes one 20cm/8in round cake

20cm/8in round light
  fruit cake
45ml/3 tbsp apricot jam,
  warmed and sieved
675g/1½lb/4½ cups
  marzipan
1.1kg/2½lb/7½ cups royal
  icing
orange food colouring
about 7 sugar-frosted
  pansies (orange and
  purple)

Materials/equipment

25cm/10in round cake
  board
2 greaseproof paper
  piping bags
No 19 star and No 1
  writing nozzles
2cm/¾in wide purple
  ribbon
3mm/⅛in wide dark
  purple ribbon

1 Brush the cake with the apricot jam. Roll out the marzipan and use to cover the cake. Leave to dry overnight.

2 Secure the cake to the cake board with a little royal icing. Tint a quarter of the royal icing pale orange. Flat-ice the cake with three layers of smooth icing. Use the orange icing for the top and the white for the side. Set aside a little of both icings in airtight containers for decoration.

3 Spoon the reserved white royal icing into a greaseproof paper piping bag fitted with a No 19 star nozzle. Pipe a row of scrolls around the cake top. Pipe a second row directly underneath the first row in the reverse direction. Pipe another row of scrolls around the base of the cake.

4 Spoon the reserved orange icing into a fresh piping bag fitted with a No 1 writing nozzle. Pipe around the outline of the top of each scroll. Pipe a row of single orange dots below the lower row of reverse scrolls at the top and a double row of dots above the base row of scrolls. Arrange the sugar-frosted pansies on top of the cake. Decorate the side with the ribbons.

Hallowe'en Pumpkin Patch Cake

Celebrate Hallowe'en with this autumn-coloured cake, colourfully decorated with sugarpaste pumpkins.

Makes one 20cm/8in round cake

175g/6oz/generous 1 cup sugarpaste icing	**Materials/equipment**
brown and orange food colouring	*wooden cocktail stick*
2 x 20cm/8in round chocolate sponge cakes	*fine paintbrush*
675g/1¹/₂lb/3 cups orange-flavour butter icing	*23cm/9in round cake board*
chocolate chips	*serrated scraper*
angelica	*No 7 writing nozzle*
	greaseproof paper piping bag

1 For the pumpkins, tint a very small piece of the sugarpaste icing brown, and the rest orange. Shape some balls of the orange icing the size of walnuts and some a bit smaller. Make ridges with a cocktail stick. Make stems from the brown icing and secure with water. Paint highlights on the pumpkins in orange. Leave to dry on greaseproof paper.

2 Cut both cakes in half horizontally. Use one-quarter of the butter icing to sandwich the cakes together. Place the cake on the board. Use two-thirds of the remaining icing to cover the cake. Texture the icing with a serrated scraper.

3 Using a No 7 writing nozzle, pipe a twisted rope pattern around the top and base edges of the cake with the remaining butter icing. Decorate with chocolate chips.

4 Cut the angelica into diamond shapes and arrange on the cake with the pumpkins.

Fudge-frosted Starry Roll

Whether it's for a birthday or another occasion, this sumptuous-looking cake is sure to please.

Makes one 33cm/13in long roll

23 x 33cm/9 x 13in Swiss roll sponge	*75g/3oz/6 tbsp butter or margarine*
175g/6oz/³/₄ cup chocolate butter icing	*65ml/4¹/₂ tbsp milk or single cream*
50g/2oz white chocolate	*7.5ml/1¹/₂ tsp vanilla essence*
50g/2oz plain chocolate	

For the fudge frosting

75g/3oz plain chocolate, broken into pieces	**Materials/equipment**
350g/12oz/3 cups icing sugar, sifted	*small star cutter*
	several greaseproof paper piping bags
	No 19 star nozzle

1 Unroll the sponge and spread with the butter icing. Re-roll and set aside.

2 For the decorations, melt the white chocolate in a bowl set over a pan of hot water and spread on to a non-porous surface. Leave to firm, then cut out stars with the cutter. Leave to set on greaseproof paper. To make lace curls, melt the plain chocolate and then cool slightly. Cover a rolling pin with greaseproof paper. Pipe zigzags on the paper and leave on the rolling pin until cool.

3 For the frosting, stir all the ingredients over a low heat until melted. Remove from the heat and beat frequently until cool and thick. Cover the cake with two-thirds of the frosting, swirling with a palette knife.

4 With a No 19 star nozzle, use the remaining frosting to pipe diagonal lines on the cake.

5 Position the lace curls and stars. Transfer the cake to a serving plate and decorate with more stars.

Lucky Horseshoe Cake

This horseshoe-shaped cake, made to wish "good luck", is made from a round cake and the shape is then cut out.

Makes one 25cm/10in horseshoe cake

25cm/10in rich fruit cake
60ml/4 tbsp apricot jam, warmed and sieved
800g/1¾lb/5¼ cups marzipan
1kg/2¼lb/6¼ cups sugarpaste icing
peach and blue food colouring
edible silver balls
115g/4oz/¼ cup royal icing

Materials/equipment
30cm/12in round cake board
crimping tool
pale blue ribbon, 3mm/⅛in wide
scalpel
large and small blossom cutters

1 Make a horseshoe template and use to shape the cake. Brush the cake with the apricot jam. Roll out 350g/12oz/2¼ cups of the marzipan to a 25cm/10in circle. Using the template, cut out the shape and place on the cake. Measure the inside and outside of the cake. Cover with the remaining marzipan. Place the cake on the board and leave overnight.

2 Tint 800g/1¾lb/5¼ cups of the sugarpaste icing peach. Cover the cake in the same way. Crimp the top edge.

3 Draw and measure the ribbon insertion on the template. Cut 13 pieces of ribbon fractionally longer than each slit. Make the slits through the template with a scalpel. Insert the ribbon with a painted tool. Leave to dry overnight.

4 Make a small horseshoe template. Tint half the remaining sugarpaste icing pale blue. Using the template, cut out nine blue shapes. Mark each horseshoe with a sharp knife. Cut out 12 large and 15 small blossoms. Press a silver ball into the centres of the larger blossoms. Leave to dry. Repeat with the white icing. Decorate the cake and board with the ribbon, horseshoes and blossoms, securing with royal icing.

Bluebird Bon-voyage Cake

This cake is sure to see someone off on an exciting journey in a very special way.

Makes one 20cm/8in round cake

450g/1lb/3 cups royal icing
blue food colouring
800g/1¾lb/5¼ cups sugarpaste icing
20cm/8in round Madeira cake
350g/12oz/1½ cups butter icing
45ml/3 tbsp apricot jam, warmed and sieved

edible silver balls

Materials/equipment
No 1 writing nozzle
greaseproof paper piping bags
25cm/10in round cake board
thin pale blue ribbon

1 Make two-thirds of the royal icing softer to use for the run-outs. Make the rest stiffer for the outlines and further piping. Tint the softer icing bright blue. Cover and leave overnight.

2 Make two different-size bird templates, and use to pipe the run-outs on greaseproof paper. Using a No 1 writing nozzle, pipe the outlines, and then fill in. You need four large and five small birds. Leave to dry for at least 2 days.

3 Tint two-thirds of the sugarpaste icing blue. Form all the icing into small rolls and place them alternately together on a work surface. Form into a round and lightly knead to marble.

4 Cut the cake horizontally into three and sandwich together with the butter icing. Place the cake on the board, flush with an edge, and brush with apricot jam. Roll out the marbled icing and use to cover the cake and board.

5 Using the No 1 writing nozzle and the stiffer royal icing, pipe a wavy line around the edge of the board. Position the balls evenly in the icing. Secure the birds to the cake with royal icing. Pipe beads of white icing for eyes and stick on a ball. Drape the ribbon between the beaks, securing with icing.

Ghost Cake

This children's cake is really simple to make yet very effective. It is ideal for a Hallowe'en party.

Serves 15–20
900g/2lb/6 cups
    sugarpaste icing
black food colouring
2 Madeira cakes, baked in
    an 18cm/7in square
    cake tin and a
    300ml/½ pint/1¼ cup
    pudding basin

350g/12oz/1½ cups
    butter icing

Materials/equipment
23cm/9in round cake
    board
fine paintbrush

1 Tint 115g/4oz/¾ cup of the sugarpaste icing dark grey and use to cover the cake board.

2 Cut two small corners off the large cake. Cut two larger wedges off the other two corners, then stand the cake on the board. Divide the larger trimmings in half and wedge around the base of the cake.

3 Secure the small cake to the top of the larger cake with butter icing. Completely cover both of the cakes with the remaining butter icing.

4 Roll out the remaining sugarpaste icing to an oval shape 50 x 30cm/20 x 12in. Lay it over the cake, letting the icing fall into folds around the sides. Gently smooth the icing over the top half of the cake and trim off any excess.

5 Using black food colouring and a fine paintbrush, paint two oval eyes on to the head.

Cat-in-a-Basket Cake

Makes one 15cm/6in round cake
800g/1¾lb/5¼ cups
    marzipan
red, green, yellow and
    brown food colouring
15cm/6in round deep
    sponge cake
30ml/2 tbsp apricot jam,
    warmed and sieved
50g/2oz/4 tbsp butter
    icing

50g/2oz/4 tbsp white
    sugarpaste icing

Materials/equipment
20cm/8in round cake
    board
fine paintbrush

1 Tint 350g/12oz/2 cups of the marzipan pink. Divide the rest in half and tint one half green and the other yellow. Brush the cake with the apricot jam and place it on the board.

2 Roll out the pink marzipan to a rectangle measuring 15 x 25cm/6 x 10in. Cut five 1cm/½in wide strips, about 24cm/9½in long, keeping them attached to the rectangle at one end. Roll out the green marzipan and cut it into 7.5cm/3in lengths of the same width. Fold back alternate pink strips and lay a green strip across widthways. Bring the pink strips over the green strip to form the weave. Keep repeating the process until the entire length is woven. Press lightly to join. Repeat with the rest of the rectangle and more strips of green marzipan.

3 Press the two pieces of basketweave on to the side of cake, joining them neatly. Model a yellow marzipan cat about 7.5cm/3in across. Leave to dry overnight.

4 Roll out the sugarpaste icing and place on the centre of the cake. Put the cat on top and arrange the icing in folds around it. Trim the edges neatly.

5 Make long ropes from any leftover pink and green marzipan. Twist together and press on to the top edge of the cake. Paint the cat's features in brown food colouring.

Fish-shaped Cake

A very easy, but colourful cake, perfect for a small child's birthday party.

Makes one fish-shaped cake

450g/1lb/3 cups
  sugarpaste icing
blue, orange, red, mauve
  and green food
  colouring
sponge cake, baked in a
  3.5 litre/6 pint/15 cup
  ovenproof mixing
  bowl
350g/12oz/1½ cups
  butter icing

1 blue Smartie

Materials/equipment
large oval cake board
2.5cm/1in plain biscuit
  cutter
greaseproof paper piping
  bag

1 Tint two-thirds of the sugarpaste icing blue, roll out very thinly and use to cover the dampened cake board.

2 Invert the cake and trim into the fish shape. Slope the sides. Place on the cake board.

3 Tint all but 15ml/1 tbsp of the butter icing orange. Use to cover the cake, smoothing with a palette knife. Score curved lines for scales, starting from the tail end.

4 Tint half the remaining sugarpaste icing red. Shape and position two lips. Cut out the tail and fins. Mark with lines using a knife and position on the fish. Make the eye from white sugarpaste and the blue Smartie.

5 Tint a little sugarpaste mauve, cut out crescent-shaped scales using a biscuit cutter and place on the fish. Tint the remaining sugarpaste green and cut into long thin strips. Twist each strip and arrange around the board.

6 To make the bubbles around the fish, place the reserved butter icing in a piping bag, snip off the end and pipe small circles on to the board.

Pink Monkey Cake

This cheeky little monkey could be made in any colour icing you wish.

Makes one 20cm/8in cake

20cm/8in round sponge
  cake
115g/4oz/½ cup butter
  icing
45ml/3 tbsp apricot jam,
  warmed and sieved
450g/1lb/3 cups
  marzipan
500g/1¼lb/scant 3¼ cups
  sugarpaste icing

red, blue and black food
  colouring

Materials/equipment
25cm/10in round cake
  board
2 candles and holders

1 Trace the outline and paws of the monkey from the photograph. Enlarge to fit the cake and cut a template.

2 Split and fill the cake with butter icing. Place on the cake board and use the template to cut out the basic shape of the monkey. Use the trimmings to shape the nose and tummy. Brush with apricot jam and cover with a layer of marzipan.

3 Tint 450g/1lb/3 cups of the sugarpaste icing pale pink and use to cover the cake. Leave to dry overnight.

4 Mark the position of the face and paws. Tint a little of the sugarpaste icing blue and use for the eyes. Tint a little icing black and cut out the pupils and tie.

5 Tint the remaining sugarpaste icing dark pink and cut out the nose, mouth, ears and paws. Stick all the features in place with water. Roll the trimmings into balls and place on the board to hold the candles.

Porcupine Cake

Melt-in-the-mouth strips of chocolate flake give this porcupine its spiky coating.

Serves 15–20

2 chocolate sponge cakes,
  baked in a 1.2 litre/
  2 pint/5 cup and a
  600ml/1 pint/2½ cup
  pudding basin
500g/1¼lb/2½ cups
  chocolate-flavour
  butter icing
cream, black, green,
  brown and red food
  colouring

5–6 chocolate flakes
50g/2oz/⅓ cup white
  marzipan

Materials/equipment
36cm/14in long
  rectangular cake board
wooden cocktail stick
fine paintbrush

1 Use the smaller cake for the head and shape a pointed nose at one end. Reserve the trimmed wedges.

2 Place the cakes side-by-side on the board, inverted, and use the trimmings to fill in the sides and top where they meet. Secure with butter icing.

3 Cover the cake with the remaining butter icing and mark the nose with a cocktail stick.

4 Make the spikes by breaking the chocolate flakes into thin strips and sticking them into the butter icing all over the body part of the porcupine.

5 Reserve a small portion of marzipan. Divide the remainder into three and tint cream, black and green. Tint a tiny portion of the reserved marzipan brown. Shape cream ears and feet, black-and-white eyes, and black claws and nose. Arrange all the features on the cake. Make green apples and highlight in red with a fine paintbrush. Make the stalks from the brown marzipan and push them in to the apples.

Mouse-in-Bed Cake

This cake is suitable for almost any age. Make the mouse well in advance to give it time to dry.

Makes one 20 x 15cm/8 x 6in cake

20cm/8in square sponge
  cake
115g/4oz/½ cup butter
  icing
45ml/3 tbsp apricot jam
  warmed and sieved
450g/1lb/3 cups
  marzipan
675g/1½lb/4½ cups
  sugarpaste icing

blue and red food
  colouring

Materials/equipment
25cm/10in square cake
  board
flower cutter
blue and red food
  colouring pens

1 Cut 5cm/2in off one side of the cake. Split and fill the main cake with butter icing. Place on the cake board, brush with apricot jam and cover with a layer of marzipan. With the cake off-cut, shape a hollowed pillow, the torso and the legs of the mouse. Cover with marzipan and leave to dry overnight.

2 Cover the cake and pillow with white sugarpaste icing. Lightly frill the edge of the pillow with a fork. To make the valance, roll out 350g/12oz/2¼ cups of sugarpaste icing and cut into four 7.5cm/3in wide strips. Attach to the bed with water. Arrange the pillow and mouse body on the cake.

3 For the quilt, tint 75g/3oz/½ cup of sugarpaste icing blue and roll out to an 18cm/7in square. Mark with a diamond pattern and the flower cutter. Cover the mouse with the quilt.

4 Cut a 2.5 x 19cm/1 x 7½in white sugarpaste icing strip for the sheet, mark the edge and place over the quilt, tucking it under at the top edge.

5 Tint 25g/1oz/2 tbsp of marzipan pink and make the head and paws of the mouse. Put the head on the pillow, tucked under the sheet, and the paws over the edge of the sheet. Use food colouring pens to draw on the face of the mouse.

Teddy's Birthday

After the pieces have been assembled and stuck into the cake, an icing smoother is useful to flatten the design.

Makes one 20cm/8in round cake

20cm/8in round cake	**Materials/equipment**
115g/4oz/½ cup butter icing	25cm/10in round cake board
45ml/3 tbsp apricot jam, warmed and sieved	small greaseproof paper piping bags
350g/12oz/2 cups marzipan	No 7 shell and No 7 star nozzle
450g/1lb/3 cups sugarpaste icing	1.5m/1½yd red ribbon
brown, red, blue and black food colouring	2 candles and holders
115g/4oz/¼ cup royal icing	
edible silver balls	

1 Split and fill the cake with butter icing. Place on the cake board and brush with apricot jam. Cover with a layer of marzipan then a layer of sugarpaste icing. Using a template, mark the design on top of the cake.

2 Colour one-third of the remaining sugarpaste icing pale brown. Colour a piece pink, a piece red, some blue and a tiny piece black. Using the template, cut out the pieces and place in position on the cake. Stick down by lifting the edges carefully and brushing the undersides with a little water. Roll small ovals for the eyes and stick in place with the nose and eyebrows. Cut out a mouth and press flat.

3 Tie the ribbon around the cake. Colour the royal icing blue and pipe the border around the base of the cake with the shell nozzle and tiny stars around the small cake with the star nozzle, inserting silver balls. Put the candles on the cake.

Party Teddy Bear Cake

The teddy on this cake is built up with royal icing and coloured coconut.

Makes one 20cm/8in square cake

20cm/8in square sponge cake	115g/4oz/¼ cup royal icing
115g/4oz/½ cup butter icing	
45ml/3 tbsp apricot jam, warmed and sieved	**Materials/equipment**
450g/1lb/3 cups marzipan	25cm/10in square cake board
350g/12oz/2 cups white sugarpaste icing	2 small greaseproof paper piping bags
25g/1oz/½ cup desiccated coconut	small red bow
blue and black food colouring	No 7 shell nozzle
	1.5m/1½yd red ribbon
	6 candles and holders

1 Cut the cake in half and sandwich together with butter icing. Place on the cake board and brush with apricot jam. Cover with a thin layer of marzipan and then white sugarpaste icing. Leave to dry overnight. Using a template, carefully mark the position of the teddy on to the cake.

2 Put the coconut into a bowl and mix in a drop of blue colouring to colour it pale blue. Spread a thin layer of royal icing within the outline of the teddy. Before the icing dries, sprinkle on some pale blue coconut and press it down lightly.

3 Roll out the sugarpaste trimmings and cut out a nose, ears and paws. Stick in place with a little royal icing. Tint some royal icing black and pipe on the eyes, nose and mouth. Use the bow as a tie and stick it in place. Pipe a white royal icing border around the base of the cake, tie the ribbon around the cake and position the candles on top.

Iced Fancies

These cakes are ideal for a children's tea-party. Ready-made cake decorating products may be used instead, if preferred.

Makes 16
115g/4oz/½ cup butter,
  at room temperature
225g/8oz/generous 1 cup
  caster sugar
2 eggs, at room
  temperature
175g/6oz/1½ cups plain
  flour
1.5ml/¼ tsp salt
7.5ml/1½ tsp baking
  powder
120ml/4fl oz/½ cup milk
5ml/1 tsp vanilla essence

For the icing
2 large egg whites
400g/14oz/3½ cups sifted
  icing sugar
1–2 drops glycerine
juice of 1 lemon
food colourings
coloured vermicelli, to
  decorate
crystallized lemon and
  orange slices, to
  decorate

1 Preheat the oven to 190°C/375°F/Gas 5. Line a 16-bun tray with paper cases.

2 Cream the butter and sugar until light and fluffy. Add the eggs, 1 at a time, beating well after each addition. Sift over and stir in the flour, salt and baking powder, alternating with the milk. Add the vanilla essence.

3 Half-fill the cups and bake for about 20 minutes, or until the tops spring back when touched. Stand in the tray to cool for 5 minutes, then unmould on to a wire rack.

4 For the icing, beat the egg whites until stiff. Gradually add the sugar, glycerine and lemon juice, and beat for 1 minute.

5 Tint the icing with different food colourings. Ice the cakes.

6 Decorate the cakes with coloured vermicelli and crystallized lemon and orange slices. Make freehand decorations using a paper piping bag.

Fairy Castle Cake

If the icing on this cake dries too quickly, dip a palette knife into hot water to help smooth the surface.

Makes one castle-shaped cake
20cm/8in round sponge
  cake
115g/4oz/½ cup butter
  icing
45ml/3 tbsp apricot jam,
  warmed and sieved
675g/1½lb/4½ cups
  marzipan
8 mini Swiss rolls
675g/1½lb/4½ cups royal
  icing
red, blue and green food
  colouring

jelly diamonds
4 ice cream cones
2 ice cream wafers
50g/2oz/1 cup desiccated
  coconut
8 marshmallows

Materials/equipment
30cm/12in square cake
  board
wooden cocktail stick

1 Split and fill the cake with butter icing, place in the centre of the board and brush with apricot jam. Cover with a layer of marzipan. Cover each of the Swiss rolls with marzipan. Stick four of them around the cake and cut the other four in half.

2 Tint two-thirds of the royal icing pale pink and cover the cake. Ice the extra pieces of Swiss roll and stick them around the top of the cake. Use a cocktail stick to score the walls with a brick pattern. Make windows on the corner towers from jelly diamonds. Cut the ice cream cones to make the tower spires and stick them in place. Leave to dry overnight.

3 Tint half the remaining royal icing pale blue and cover the cones. Use a fork to pattern the icing. Shape the wafers for the gates, stick to the cake and cover with blue icing. Use the back of a knife to mark planks.

4 Tint the coconut with a few drops of green colouring. Spread the board with the remaining royal icing and sprinkle over the coconut. Stick on the marshmallows with a little royal icing to make the small turrets.

Sailing Boat

For chocoholics, make this cake using chocolate sponge.

Makes one boat-shaped cake

20cm/8in square sponge cake	**Materials/equipment**
225g/8oz/1 cup butter icing	25cm/10in square cake board
15ml/1 tbsp cocoa powder	rice paper
4 large chocolate flakes	blue and red powder tints
115g/4oz/¾ cup royal icing	paint brush
blue food colouring	plastic drinking straw
	wooden cocktail stick
	2 small cake ornaments

1 Split and fill the cake with half of the butter icing. Cut 7cm/2¾in from one side of the cake. Shape the larger piece to resemble the hull of a boat. Place diagonally across the cake board. Mix the cocoa powder into the remaining butter icing and spread evenly over the top and sides of the boat.

2 Make the rudder and tiller from short lengths of flake and place them at the stern of the boat. Split the rest of the flakes lengthways and press on to the sides of the boat, horizontally, to resemble planks of wood. Sprinkle the crumbs over the top.

3 Cut two rice paper rectangles, one 14 x 16cm/5¼ x 6½in and the other 15 x 7.5cm/6 x 3in. Cut the bigger one in a gentle curve to make the large sail and the smaller one into a triangle. Brush a circle of blue powder tint on to the large sail. Wet the edges of the sails and stick on to the straw. Make a hole for the straw 7.5cm/3in from the bow of the boat and push into the cake.

4 Cut a rice paper flag and brush with red powder tint. Stick the flag on to a cocktail stick and insert into the top of the straw. Tint the royal icing blue and spread on the board in waves. Place the small ornaments on the boat.

Spiders' Web Cake

A spooky cake for any occasion, fancy dress or otherwise.

Makes one 900g/2lb cake

900g/2lb dome-shaped lemon sponge cake	cocoa powder, for dusting
225g/8oz/¾ cup lemon-flavour glacé icing	chocolate vermicelli
black and yellow food colouring	2 – 3 liquorice wheels, sweet centres removed
	15g/½oz/2 tbsp sugarpaste icing

For the spiders

115g/4oz plain chocolate, broken into pieces	**Materials/equipment**
150ml/¼ pint/⅔ cup double cream	greaseproof paper
45ml/3 tbsp ground almonds	small greaseproof paper piping bag
	wooden skewer
	20cm/8in cake board

1 Place the cake on greaseproof paper. Tint 45ml/3 tbsp of the glacé icing black. Tint the rest yellow and pour it over the cake, letting it run down the side.

2 Fill a piping bag with the black icing and, starting at the centre top, drizzle it round the cake in an evenly-spaced spiral. Finish the web by drawing downwards through the icing with a skewer. When set, place on the cake board.

3 For the spiders, gently melt the chocolate with the cream, stirring frequently. Transfer to a bowl, allow to cool, then beat the mixture for 10 minutes, or until thick and pale. Stir in the ground almonds, then chill until firm enough to handle. Dust your hands with a little cocoa, then make walnut-size balls with the mixture. Roll the balls in chocolate vermicelli.

4 For the legs, cut the liquorice into 4cm/1½in lengths. Make holes in the sides of the spiders and insert the legs. For the spiders' eyes, tint a piece of sugarpaste icing black and form into tiny balls. Make larger balls with white icing. Stick on using water. Arrange the spiders on and around the cake.

Toy Telephone Cake

The child's name could be piped in a contrasting colour of icing, if you wish.

Makes one telephone-shaped cake

15cm/6in square sponge cake
50g/2oz/¼ cup butter icing
30ml/2 tbsp apricot jam, warmed and sieve
275g/10oz/2 cups marzipan
350g/12oz/2 cups sugarpaste icing
yellow, blue, red and black food colouring
liquorice strips

115g/4oz/¼ cup royal icing

Materials/equipment
20cm/8in square cake board
piping nozzle
small greaseproof paper piping bag
No 1 writing nozzle

1 Split and fill the cake with butter icing. Trim to the shape of a telephone. Round off the edges and cut a shallow groove where the receiver rests on the telephone. Place the cake on the board and brush with apricot jam.

2 Cover the cake with marzipan then sugarpaste icing. Tint half the remaining sugarpaste icing yellow, a small piece blue and the rest of the icing red. To make the dial, cut out an 8cm/3½in diameter circle in yellow and a 4cm/1½in diameter circle in blue. Stamp out 12 red discs for the numbers with the end of a piping nozzle and cut out a red receiver. Position on the cake with water.

3 Twist the liquorice around to form a curly cord and use royal icing to stick one end to the telephone and the other end to the receiver. Tint the royal icing black and pipe the numbers on the discs and the child's name on the telephone.

Bumble Bee Cake

The edible sugar flowers that are used to decorate this cake were bought ready-made.

Makes one bee-shaped cake

20cm/8in round sponge cake
115g/4oz/½ cup butter icing
45ml/3 tbsp apricot jam, warmed and sieved
350g/12oz/2¼ cups marzipan
500g/1¼ lb/3¾ cups sugarpaste icing
yellow, black, blue and red food colouring

115g/4oz/¼ cup royal icing
50g/2oz/1 cup desiccated coconut

Materials/equipment
25cm/10in square cake board
6 sugarpaste daisies
1 paper doily
sticky tape
1 pipe cleaner

1 Split and fill the cake with butter icing. Cut in half to make semicircles, sandwich the halves together and stand upright on the cake board. Trim the ends to shape the head and tail. Brush with apricot jam and cover with a layer of marzipan. Tint 350g/12oz/2¼ cups of the sugarpaste icing yellow and use to cover the cake.

2 Tint 115g/4oz/¾ cup of the sugarpaste icing black. Roll out and cut three stripes, each 2.5 x 25cm/1 x 10in. Space evenly on the cake and stick on with water. Use the remaining icing to make the eyes and mouth, tinting the icing blue for the pupils and pink for the mouth. Stick on with water.

3 Tint the coconut with a drop of yellow colouring. Cover the cake board with royal icing then sprinkle with coconut. Place the daisies on the board.

4 To make the wings, cut the doily in half, wrap each half into a cone shape and stick together with sticky tape. Cut the pipe cleaner in half and stick the pieces into the cake, just behind the head. Place the wings over the pipe cleaners.

Toy Car Cake

You can add a personalized number plate with the child's name and age to the back of this car.

Makes one car-shaped cake

20cm/8in round sponge cake	red and green sweets
115g/4oz/½ cup butter icing	**Materials/equipment**
45ml/3 tbsp apricot jam, warmed and served	25cm/10in round cake board
450g/1lb/3 cups marzipan	wooden cocktail stick cutters, 4cm/1½in and 2.5cm/1in
500g/1¼lb/3¼ cups sugarpaste icing	small greaseproof paper piping bag
yellow, red and black food colouring	No 1 writing nozzle
30ml/2 tbsp royal icing	2 candles and holders

1 Split and fill the cake with the butter icing. Cut in half and sandwich the halves together. Stand upright and slice off pieces to create the windscreen and bonnet. Place on the cake board and brush with apricot jam.

2 Cut a strip of marzipan to cover the top of the cake to level the joins. Then cover the cake all over with marzipan. Tint 450g/1lb/3 cups of the sugarpaste icing yellow and use to cover the cake. Leave to dry overnight.

3 Mark the outlines of the doors and windows on to the car with a cocktail stick.

4 Tint the remaining sugarpaste icing red. Cut out four wheels with the larger cutter. Stick in place with water. Mark the hubs in the centre of each wheel with the smaller cutter.

5 Tint the royal icing black and pipe over the outline marks of the doors and windows. Stick on sweets for headlights with royal icing. Press the candles into sweets and stick to the board with royal icing.

Fire Engine Cake

This jolly fire engine is simplicity itself as the decorations are mainly bought sweets and novelties.

Makes one 20 x 10cm/8 x 4in cake

20cm/8in square sponge cake	115g/4oz/4 tbsp royal icing
115g/4oz/½ cup butter icing	sweets
45ml/3 tbsp apricot jam, warmed and sieved	50g/2oz/1 cup desiccated coconut
350g/12oz/2¼ cups marzipan	**Materials/equipment**
450g/1lb/3 cups sugarpaste icing	25cm/10in round cake board
red, black and green food colouring	small greaseproof paper piping bag
liquorice strips	No 2 plain nozzle
	2 silver bells
	3 candles and holders

1 Split and fill the cake with the butter icing. Cut in half and sandwich one half on top of the other. Place on the cake board and brush with apricot jam.

2 Trim a thin wedge off the front edge to make a sloping windscreen. Cover with marzipan. Tint 350g/12oz/2¼ cups of the sugarpaste icing red and use to cover the cake.

3 For the ladder, cut the liquorice into two strips and some short pieces for the rungs. Tint half the royal icing black and use some to stick the ladder to the top of the cake. Roll out the remaining sugarpaste icing, cut out windows and stick them on with a little water.

4 Pipe around the windows in black royal icing. Stick sweets in place for headlights, lamps and wheels and stick the silver bells on the roof. Tint the coconut green, spread a little royal icing over the cake board and sprinkle with the coconut. Stick sweets to the board with royal icing and press the candles into the sweets.

Sandcastle Cake

Clown Face Cake

Crushed digestive biscuits make convincing-looking sand when used to cover this fun cake.

Children love this happy clown whose frilly collar is surprisingly simple to make.

Makes one 15cm/6in round cake

*2 x 15cm/6in round
 sponge cakes
115g/4oz/½ cup butter
 icing
45ml/3 tbsp apricot jam,
 warmed and sieved
115g/4oz/¾ cup digestive
 biscuits
115g/4oz/¾ cup royal
 icing*

*blue food colouring
shrimp-shaped sweets*

Materials/equipment
*25cm/10in square cake
 board
rice paper
plastic drinking straw
4 candles and holders*

Makes one 20cm/8in cake

*20cm/8in round
 sponge cake
115g/4oz/½ cup
 butter icing
45ml/3 tbsp apricot jam,
 warmed and sieved
450g/1lb/3 cups
 marzipan
450g/1lb/3 cups
 sugarpaste icing
115g/4oz/¾ cup
 royal icing
edible silver balls*

*red, green, blue and black
 food colouring*

Materials/equipment
*25cm/10in round
 cake board
small greaseproof paper
 piping bag
No 8 star nozzle
wooden cocktail stick
cotton wool
two candles and holders*

1 Split both of the cakes, then sandwich all the layers together with the butter icing. Place in the centre of the cake board. Cut 3cm/1¼in off the top just above the filling and set aside. Shape the rest of the cake with slightly sloping sides.

2 Cut four 3cm/1¼in cubes from the reserved piece of cake. Stick on the cubes for the turrets and brush with apricot jam.

3 Crush the digestive biscuits and press through a sieve to make the "sand". Press some crushed biscuits on to the cake, using a palette knife to get a smooth finish.

4 Colour some royal icing blue and spread on the board around the sandcastle to make a moat. Spread a little royal icing on the board around the outside edge of the moat and sprinkle on some crushed biscuit.

5 To make the flag, cut a small rectangle of rice paper and stick on to half a straw with water. Push the end of the straw into the cake. Stick candles into each turret and arrange the shrimp-shaped sweets on the board.

1 Split and fill the cake with butter icing. Place on the cake board and brush with apricot jam. Cover with a thin layer of marzipan then with white sugarpaste icing. Mark the position of the features. Pipe stars around the base of the cake with some royal icing, placing silver balls as you work, and leave to dry overnight.

2 Make a template for the face and features. Tint half the remaining sugarpaste icing pink and cut out the face base. Tint and cut out all the features, rolling a sausage to make the mouth. Cut thin strands for the hair. Stick all the features and hair in place with a little water.

3 Tint the remaining sugarpaste icing green. Cut three strips 4cm/1½in wide. Give each a scalloped edge and stretch by rolling a cocktail stick along it to make the frill. Stick on with water and arrange the frills, holding them in place with cotton wool until dry. Place the candles at the top of the head.

Pinball Machine

Serves 8–10

25cm/10in square sponge
    cake
225g/8oz/1½ cups butter
    icing
45ml/3 tbsp apricot jam,
    warmed and sieved
450g/1lb/3 cups
    marzipan
115g/4oz/¼ cup royal
    icing
450g/1lb/3 cups
    sugarpaste icing

yellow, blue, green and
    red food colouring
sweets
2 ice cream fan wafers

Materials/equipment
20cm/8in round cake tin
30cm/12in square cake
    board
small greaseproof paper
    piping bag
No 1 writing nozzle

1 Split and fill the sponge cake with butter icing. Cut off a
5cm/2in strip from one side and reserve. Cut a thin wedge off
the top of the cake, diagonally along its length, to end just
above the halfway mark. This will give a sloping table.

2 Using the cake tin as a guide, cut the reserved strip of cake
to make a rounded back for the pinball table. Brush the back
and table with apricot jam, then cover separately with
marzipan and place on the board. Stick them together with
royal icing. Leave to dry overnight.

3 Cover with a layer of sugarpaste icing and leave to dry.
Use a template to mark out the pinball design on the top of
the cake. Colour the remaining sugarpaste icing yellow, blue,
green and pink. Roll out the colours and cut to fit the design.
Stick on the pieces with water and smooth the joins carefully.

4 Using royal icing, stick sweets on the cake as buffers,
flippers, lights and knobs. Roll some blue sugarpaste icing
into a long sausage and edge the pinball table and divider.
Cut zig-zags for the sides and a screen for the back. Stick on
with water. Stick the ice cream fans at the back of the screen.
Load the pinball sweets. Add the child's name on the screen
with run-out letters or piping.

Pirate's Hat

**If you prefer, buy ready-made black sugarpaste icing rather
than tinting it yourself.**

Serves 8–10

25cm/10in round sponge
    cake
225g/8oz/1 cup butter
    icing
45ml/3 tbsp apricot jam,
    warmed and sieved
450g/1lb/3 cups
    marzipan
500g/1¼lb/3¾ cups
    sugarpaste icing

black and gold food
    colouring
chocolate money
jewel sweets

Materials/equipment
30cm/12in square cake
    board
fine paint brush

1 Split and fill the cake with butter icing. Cut in half and
sandwich the halves together. Stand upright diagonally across
the cake board and cut shallow dips from each end to create
the brim of the hat. Brush with apricot jam.

2 Cut a strip of marzipan to lay over the top of the cake.
Then cover the whole of the cake with a layer of marzipan.
Tint 450g/1lb/3 cups of the sugarpaste icing black. Use to
cover the cake.

3 Roll out the remaining sugarpaste icing and cut some
1cm/½in strips. Stick the strips in place with a little water
around the brim of the pirate's hat and mark with the prongs
of a fork to make a braid.

4 Make a skull and crossbones template and mark on to the
hat. Cut the shapes out of the white sugarpaste icing and stick
in place with water. Paint the braid strip gold and arrange the
chocolate money and jewel sweets on the board.

Noah's Ark Cake

This charming cake is decorated with small animals, about 4cm/1½in high, available from cake decorating shops.

Makes one 20 x 13cm/8 x 5in cake

20cm/8in square sponge cake	115g/4oz/¾ cup royal icing
115g/4oz/½ cup butter icing	chocolate mint stick
45ml/3 tbsp apricot jam, warmed and sieved	**Materials/equipment**
450g/1lb/3 cups marzipan	25cm/10in square cake board
450g/1lb/3 cups sugarpaste icing	skewer
brown, yellow and blue food colouring	rice paper flag
	small animal cake ornaments

1 Split and fill the cake with butter icing. Cut off and set aside a 7.5cm/3in strip. Shape the remaining piece of cake to form the hull of the boat. Place diagonally on the cake board.

2 Use the set-aside piece of cake, to cut a rectangle 10 x 6cm/4 x 2½in for the cabin and a triangular piece for the roof. Sandwich together with butter icing or apricot jam.

3 Cover the three pieces with a layer of marzipan. Tint the sugarpaste icing brown and use most of it to cover the hull and cabin. Use the remaining brown icing to make a long sausage. Stick around the edge of the hull with water. Mark planks with the back of a knife. Leave to dry overnight.

4 Tint one-third of the royal icing yellow and spread it over the cabin roof with a palette knife. Roughen it with a skewer to create a thatch effect.

5 Tint the remaining royal icing blue and spread over the cake board, making rough waves. Stick a rice paper flag on to the chocolate mint stick and press on the back of the boat. Stick the small animals on to the boat with a dab of icing.

Balloons Cake

This is a simple yet effective cake design that can be adapted to suit any age.

Makes one 20cm/8in round cake

20cm/8in round cake	**Materials/equipment**
115g/4oz/½ cup butter icing	25cm/10in round cake board
45ml/3 tbsp apricot jam, warmed and sieved	2 small greaseproof paper piping bags
450g/1lb/3 cups marzipan	No 2 plain and No 7 star nozzles
450g/1lb/3 cups sugarpaste icing	1.5m/1½yd blue ribbon
red, blue, green and yellow food colouring	3 candles and holders
115g/4oz/¾ cup royal icing	

1 Split and fill the cake with butter icing. Place on the cake board and brush with apricot jam. Cover with a layer of marzipan then sugarpaste icing.

2 Divide the remaining sugarpaste icing into three pieces and tint pink, blue and green. Make a balloon template, roll out the coloured sugarpaste and cut out one balloon from each colour. Stick on to the cake with water and rub the edges gently to round them off.

3 Tint the royal icing yellow. With a plain nozzle, pipe on the balloon strings and a number on each balloon. Using the star nozzle, pipe a border around the base of the cake.

4 Tie the ribbon round the cake and place the candles on top.

Horse Stencil Cake

Use a fairly dry brush when painting the design on this cake and allow each colour to dry before adding the next.

Makes one 20cm/8in round cake

	Materials/equipment
20cm/8in round sponge cake	25cm/10in round cake board
115g/4oz/½ cup butter icing	spoon with decorative handle
45ml/3 tbsp apricot jam, warmed and sieved	fine paintbrush
450g/1lb/3 cups marzipan	horse and letter stencils
450g/1lb/3 cups sugarpaste icing	1.5m/1½yd blue ribbon
yellow, brown, black, red, orange and blue food colouring	7 candles and holders

1 Split and fill the cake with butter icing. Place on the cake board and brush with apricot jam. Cover with a layer of marzipan. Tint the sugarpaste icing yellow, roll out and use to cover the cake. Roll the trimmings into two thin ropes, long enough to go halfway round the cake. Brush water in a thin band around the base of the cake, lay on the ropes and press together. Pattern the border with the decorative spoon handle. Leave to dry overnight.

2 If you do not have a stencil, make one by tracing a simple design on to a thin piece of card and cutting out the shape with a craft knife. Place the horse stencil in the centre of the cake. With a fairly dry brush, gently paint over the parts you want to colour first. Allow these to dry completely before adding another colour, otherwise the colours will run into each other. Clean the stencil between colours.

3 When the horse picture is finished carefully paint on the lettering. Tie the ribbon around the side of the cake and place the candles on top.

Doll's House Cake

Serves 8–10

	Materials/equipment
25cm/10in square sponge cake	30cm/12in square cake board
225g/8oz/1 cup butter icing	pastry wheel
45ml/3 tbsp apricot jam, warmed and sieved	large and fine paintbrushes
450g/1lb/3 cups marzipan	wooden cocktail stick
450g/1lb/3 cups sugarpaste icing	small greaseproof paper piping bags
red, yellow, blue, black, green and gold food colouring	No 2 writing nozzle
115g/4oz/¼ cup royal icing	flower decorations

1 Split and fill the cake with butter icing. Cut triangles off two corners and use the pieces to make a chimney. Place on the cake board and brush with apricot jam. Cover with a layer of marzipan then sugarpaste icing.

2 Mark the roof with a pastry wheel and the chimney with the back of a knife. Paint the chimney red and the roof yellow.

3 Tint 25g/1oz/2 tbsp of sugarpaste icing red and cut out a 7.5 x 12cm/3 x 4½in door. Tint enough sugarpaste icing blue to make a fanlight. Stick to the cake with water. Mark windows, 6cm/2½in square, with a cocktail stick. Paint on curtains with blue food colouring. Tint half the royal icing black and pipe around the windows and the door.

4 Tint the remaining royal icing green. Pipe the flower stems and leaves under the windows and the climber up on to the roof. Stick the flowers in place with a little icing and pipe green flower centres. Pipe the house number or child's age, the knocker and handle on the door. Leave to dry for 1 hour, then paint with gold food colouring.

Treasure Chest Cake

Allow yourself a few days before the party to make this cake as the lock and handles need to dry for 48 hours.

Makes one 20 x 10cm/8 x 4in cake

20cm/8in square sponge cake
115g/4oz/½ cup butter icing
45ml/3 tbsp apricot jam, warmed and sieved
350g/12oz/2cups marzipan
400g/14oz/2½ cups sugarpaste icing
brown and green food colouring
50g/2oz/1 cup desiccated coconut
115g/4oz/¾ cup royal icing
edible gold dusting powder
edible silver balls
chocolate money

Materials/equipment
30cm/12in round cake board
fine paintbrush

1 Split and fill the cake with butter icing. Cut the cake in half and sandwich the halves on top of each other with butter icing. Place on the cake board.

2 Shape the top into a rounded lid and brush with apricot jam. Cover with a layer of marzipan. Tint 350g/12oz/2¼ cups of the sugarpaste icing brown and use to cover the cake.

3 Use the brown sugarpaste trimmings to make strips. Stick on to the chest with water. Mark the lid with a sharp knife.

4 Tint the coconut with a few drops of green colouring. Spread a little royal icing over the cake board and press the green coconut lightly into it to make the grass.

5 From the remaining sugarpaste icing, cut out the padlock and handles. Cut a keyhole shape from the padlock and shape the handles over a small box. Leave to dry. Stick the padlock and handles in place with royal icing and paint them gold. Stick silver balls on to look like nails. Arrange the chocolate money on the board.

Lion Cake

For an animal lover or a celebration cake for a Leo horoscope sign, this cake is ideal.

Makes one 28 x 23cm/11 x 9in oval cake

25 x 30cm/10 x 12in sponge cake
350g/12oz/1½ cups orange flavour butter icing
orange and red food colouring
675g/1½lb/4½ cups yellow marzipan
50g/2oz/generous 4 tbsp sugarpaste icing
red and orange liquorice bootlaces
long and round marshmallows

Materials/equipment
30cm/12in square cake board
cheese grater
small heart-shaped cutter

1 With the flat side of the cake uppermost, cut it to make an oval shape with an uneven scallop design around the edge. Turn the cake over and trim the top level.

2 Place the cake on the cake board. Tint the butter icing orange and use it to cover the cake.

3 Roll 115g/4oz/¾ cup of marzipan to a 15cm/6in square. Place in the centre of the cake for the lion's face.

4 Grate the remaining marzipan and use to cover the sides and the top of the cake up to the face panel.

5 Tint the sugarpaste icing red. Use the heart-shaped cutter to stamp out the lion's nose and position on the cake with water. Roll the remaining red icing into two thin, short strands to make the lion's mouth, and stick on with water.

6 Cut the liquorice into graduated lengths, and place on the cake for the whiskers. Use two flattened round marshmallows for the eyes and two snipped long ones for the eyebrows.

Train Cake

This cake is made in a train-shaped tin, so all you need to do is decorate it.

Makes one train-shaped cake

train-shaped sponge cake,
    about 35cm/14in long
675g/1½lb/3 cups butter
    icing
yellow food colouring
red liquorice bootlaces
90–120ml/6–8 tbsp
    coloured vermicelli
4 liquorice wheels

Materials/equipment
25 x 38cm/10 x 15in cake
    board
2 fabric piping bags
small round and small
    star nozzles
pink and white cotton
    wool balls

1 Slice off the top surface of the cake to make it flat. Place diagonally on the cake board.

2 Tint the butter icing yellow. Use half of it to cover the cake.

3 Using a round nozzle and a quarter of the remaining butter icing, pipe a straight double border around the top edge of the cake.

4 Place the red liquorice bootlaces on the piped border. Snip the bootlaces around the curves on the train.

5 Using a small star nozzle and the remaining butter icing, pipe small stars over the top of the cake. Add extra liquorice and piping, if you like. Use a palette knife to press on the coloured vermicelli all around the sides of the cake.

6 Pull a couple of balls of cotton wool apart for the steam and stick on the cake board with butter icing. Press the liquorice wheels in place for the wheels.

Number 7 Cake

Any combination of colours will work well for this cake with its marbled effect.

Makes one 30cm/12in long cake

23 x 30cm/9 x 12in
    sponge cake
350g/12oz/1½ cups
    orange-flavour butter
    icing
60ml/4 tbsp apricot jam,
    warmed and sieved
675g/1½lb/4½ cups
    sugarpaste icing

blue and green food
    colouring
rice paper sweets

Materials /equipment
25 x 33cm/10 x 13in cake
    board
small "7" cutter

1 Place the cake flat-side up and cut out the number seven. Slice the cake horizontally, sandwich together with the butter icing and place on the board.

2 Brush the cake evenly with apricot jam. Divide the sugarpaste icing into three and tint one of the pieces blue and another green. Set aside 50g/2oz/scant ½cup from each of the coloured icings. Knead together the large pieces of blue and green icing with the third piece of white icing to marble. Use to cover the cake.

3 Immediately after covering, use the cutter to remove sugarpaste shapes in a random pattern from the covered cake.

4 Roll out the reserved blue and green sugarpaste icing and stamp out shapes with the same cutter. Use these to fill the stamped-out shapes from the cake. Decorate the board with some rice paper sweets.

Musical Cake

Creating a sheet of music on a cake requires very delicate piping work, so it is best to practise first.

Makes one 20 x 25cm/8 x 10in cake

25cm/10in square sponge cake
225g/8oz/1 cup butter icing
45ml/3 tbsp apricot jam, warmed and sieved
450g/1lb/3 cups marzipan
450g/1lb/3 cups sugarpaste icing
115g/4oz/¾ cup royal icing
black food colouring

Materials/equipment
25 x 30cm/10 x 12in cake board
wooden cocktail stick
2 small greaseproof paper piping bags
No 0 writing and No 7 shell nozzles
1.5m/1½yd red ribbon

1 Split and fill the cake with a little butter icing. Cut a 5cm/2in strip off one side of the cake. Place the cake on the cake board and brush with apricot jam. Cover with a layer of marzipan then sugarpaste icing. Leave to dry overnight.

2 Make a template and mark out the sheet of music and child's name with a cocktail stick.

3 Using white royal icing and a No 0 nozzle, begin by piping the lines and bars. Leave to dry.

4 Tint the remaining icing black and pipe the clefs, name and notes. With the shell nozzle, pipe a royal icing border around the base of the cake and tie a ribbon around the side.

Magic Rabbit Cake

Makes one 15cm/6in tall round cake

2 x 15cm/6in round cakes
225g/8oz/1 cup butter icing
115g/4oz/¾ cup royal icing
45ml/3 tbsp apricot jam, warmed and sieved
675g/1½lb/4½ cups marzipan
675g/1½lb/4½ cups sugarpaste icing
black and pink food colouring
edible silver balls

Materials/equipment
25cm/10in square cake board
2 small greaseproof paper piping bags
star nozzle
1.5m/1½yd pink ribbon

1 Split and fill the cakes with butter icing, then sandwich them one on top of the other. Stick on the centre of the cake board with a little royal icing. Brush with apricot jam. Use 450g/1lb/3 cups of the marzipan to cover the cake.

2 Tint the sugarpaste icing grey. Use about two-thirds of it to cover the cake. Roll out the rest to a 20cm/8in round. Cut a 15cm/6in circle from its centre. Lower the brim over the cake. Shape the brim sides over wooden spoon handles until dry.

3 Cut a cross in the 15cm/6in grey circle and place on the hat. Curl the triangles over a wooden spoon handle to shape. Smooth the join at the top and sides of the hat.

4 Tint the remaining marzipan pink and make the rabbit's head, about 5cm/2in wide with a pointed face. Mark the position of the eyes, nose and mouth. Leave to dry overnight.

5 Stick the rabbit in the centre of the hat with a little royal icing. Pipe a border of royal icing around the top and base of the hat and decorate with silver balls while still wet. Tint the remaining royal icing black and pipe the rabbit's eyes and mouth. Tie the ribbon round the hat.

Nurse's Kit Cake

The box is easy to make and is simply filled with toy kit.

Makes one 20 x 17cm/8 x 6½in cake

35 x 20cm/14 x 8in	**Materials/equipment**
chocolate sponge cake	*25cm/10in square cake*
120ml/4fl oz/½ cup	*board*
apricot jam, warmed	*selection of toy medical*
and sieved	*equipment*
675g/1½lb/4½ cups	
sugarpaste icing	
red food colouring	

1 Place the cake dome-side down and cut in half widthways.

2 To make the base of the nurse's box, turn one cake half dome-side up and hollow out the centre to a depth of 1cm/½in, leaving a 1cm/½in border on the three uncut edges. Brush the tops and sides of both halves with jam.

3 Tint 150g/5oz/generous ½ cup sugarpaste icing deep pink. Use a little to make a small handle for the box. Wrap in clear film and set aside. Cover the cake board with the rest of the pink icing. Tint 25g/1oz/2 tbsp of the sugarpaste icing red. Cover with clear film and set aside.

4 Tint the remaining icing light pink and divide into two portions, one slightly bigger than the other. Roll out the bigger portion and use to cover the base of the box, easing it into the hollow and along the edges. Trim, then position the base on the cake board.

5 Roll out the other portion and use to cover the lid of the box. Trim, then place on top of the base at a slight angle.

6 Stick the handle to the base of the box using water. Cut a small cross out of red icing and stick it on the lid. Place a few toy items under the lid, protruding slightly. Arrange some more items around the board and cake.

Ballerina Cake

Use flower cutters with ejectors to make the tiny flowers.

Makes one 20cm/8in round cake

20cm/8in round sponge	**Materials/equipment**
cake	*25cm/10in round cake*
115g/4oz/½ cup butter	*board*
icing	*small flower cutter*
45ml/3 tbsp apricot jam,	*small circle cutter*
warmed and sieved	*wooden cocktail stick*
450g/1lb/3 cups	*cotton wool*
marzipan	*fine paintbrush*
450g/1lb/3 cups	*3 small greaseproof paper*
sugarpaste icing	*piping bags*
pink, yellow, blue and	*No 7 shell nozzle*
green food colouring	*1.5m/1½yd pink ribbon*
115g/4oz/¼ cup royal	
icing	

1 Split and fill the cake with butter icing. Place on the board and brush with apricot jam. Cover with marzipan then sugarpaste icing. Leave to dry overnight. Divide the rest of the sugarpaste into three. Tint flesh tone, light pink and dark pink. Stamp out 15 pale pink flowers. Leave to dry.

2 Make a template of the ballerina. Mark her position on the cake. Cut out a flesh-tone body and dark pink bodice. Stick on with water, rounding off the edges.

3 Cut two dark pink underskirts, a pale pink top skirt and a dark pink bodice extension to make the tutu. Stamp out hollow, fluted circles, divide the circles into four and frill the fluted edges with a cocktail stick. Stick the tutu in place, supported with cotton wool. Cut out and stick on pale pink shoes. Leave to dry overnight.

4 Paint the ballerina's face and hair. Position 12 hoop and three headdress flowers. Tint some royal icing green and dark pink to complete the flowers and ballet shoes. Pipe a border around the base with the shell nozzle. Tie round the ribbon.

Monsters on the Moon

A great cake for little monsters! This cake is best eaten on the day of making.

Serves 12–15

1 quantity quick-mix
  sponge cake
500g/1¼lb/3¼ cups
  sugarpaste icing
225g/8oz/1½ cups
  marzipan
black food colouring
edible silver glitter
  powder (optional)
375g/12oz/¾ cups
  caster sugar

2 egg whites
60ml/4 tbsp water

Materials/equipment
ovenproof wok
various sizes of plain
  round and star cutters
30cm/12in round cake
  board
small monster toys

1 Preheat the oven to 180ºC/350ºF/Gas 4. Grease and line the wok. Spoon in the cake mixture and smooth the surface. Bake in the centre of the oven for 35–40 minutes. Leave for 5 minutes, then turn out on to a rack and peel off the paper.

2 With the cake dome-side up, use the round cutters to cut out craters. Press in the cutters to about 2.5cm/1in deep, then remove and cut the craters out of the cake with a knife.

3 Use 115g/4oz/¾ cup of the sugarpaste icing to cover the cake, pulling off small pieces and pressing them in uneven strips around the edges of the craters. Tint the remaining sugarpaste icing black. Roll out and cover the board. Stamp out stars and replace with marzipan stars of the same size. Dust with glitter powder, if using and place on the board.

4 Put the sugar, egg whites and water in a heatproof bowl over a pan of simmering water. Beat until thick and peaky. Spoon the icing over the cake, swirling it into the craters and peaking it unevenly. Sprinkle over the silver glitter powder, if using, then position the monsters on the cake.

Circus Cake

This colourful design is easy to achieve and is sure to delight young children.

Makes one 20cm/8in cake

20cm/8in round sponge
  cake
115g/4oz/½ cup butter
  icing
45ml/3 tbsp apricot jam,
  warmed and sieved
450g/1lb/3 cups
  marzipan
450g/1lb/3 cups
  sugarpaste icing
red and blue food
  colouring

115g/4oz/¾ cup royal
  icing
edible silver balls
3 digestive biscuits

Materials/equipment
25cm/10in round cake
  board
small greaseproof paper
  piping bag
No 5 star nozzle
5cm/2in plastic circus
  ornaments

1 Split and fill the cake with butter icing. Place on the cake board and brush with apricot jam. Cover with a layer of marzipan then sugarpaste icing.

2 Tint 115g/4oz/¾ cup sugarpaste icing pink, then roll into a rope and stick around the top edge of the cake with a little water.

3 Tint half the remaining sugarpaste icing red and half blue. Roll out each colour and cut into twelve 2.5cm/1in squares. Stick the squares alternately at an angle around the side of the cake with a little water. Pipe stars around the base of the cake with royal icing and stick in the edible silver balls.

4 Crush the digestive biscuits by pressing through a sieve to make the "sand" for the circus ring. Scatter over the top of the cake and place small circus ornaments on top.

Frog Prince Cake

Serves 8–10

20cm/8in round sponge
  cake
115g/4oz/½ cup butter
  icing
45ml/3 tbsp apricot jam,
  warmed and sieved
450g/1lb/3 cups
  marzipan
cornflour, for dusting
400g/1¼lb/3¾ cups
  sugarpaste icing

115g/4oz/¾ cup royal
  icing
green, red, black and gold
  food colouring

Materials/equipment
25cm/10in square cake
  board
glass
fine paintbrush

1   Split and fill the cake with butter icing. Cut in half and sandwich the halves together with apricot jam. Stand upright diagonally across the cake board. Brush the cake with apricot jam and cover with marzipan.

2   Tint 450g/1lb/3 cups of the sugarpaste icing green and cover the cake. Roll the remaining green sugarpaste icing into 1cm/½in diameter sausages. You will need two folded 20cm/8in lengths for the back legs and 14 10cm/4in lengths for the front legs and feet. Stick in place with a little royal icing. Roll balls for the eyes and stick in place.

3   Roll out the reserved sugarpaste icing and cut a 5 x 19cm/2 x 7½in strip. Cut out triangles along one edge to make the crown shape. Wrap around a glass dusted with cornflour and moisten the edges to join. Leave to dry.

4   Cut a 10cm/4in circle for the white shirt. Stick in place and trim the base edge. Cut white circles and stick to the eyes. Tint a little sugarpaste pink, roll into a sausage and stick on for the mouth. Tint the rest black and use for the pupils and the bow tie. Stick in place.

5   Paint the crown with gold food colouring, leave to dry, then stick into position with royal icing.

Ladybird Cake

Children will love this colourful and appealing ladybird, and it is very simple to make.

Serves 10–12

3-egg quantity quick-mix
  sponge cake
175g/6oz butter icing
60ml/4 tbsp lemon
  curd, warmed
icing sugar, for dusting

1kg/2¼ lb sugarpaste
  icing
food colourings
5 marshmallows
50g/2oz marzipan
2 pipe cleaners

1   Preheat the oven to 180°C/350°F/Gas 4. Grease and line the base of a 1.2 litre/2 pint/5 cup ovenproof bowl. Spoon in the cake mixture and smooth the surface. Bake for 55–60 minutes until a skewer comes out clean. Cool.

2   Cut the cake in half crossways and sandwich together with the butter icing. Cut vertically through the cake, about a third of the way in. Brush both pieces with the lemon curd.

3   Colour 450g/1lb of the sugarpaste icing red. Dust a work surface with icing sugar and roll out the icing to about 5mm/¼ in thick. Use to cover the larger piece of cake to make the body. Using a wooden skewer, make an indentation down the centre for the wings. Colour 350g/12oz of icing black, roll out three-quarters and use to cover the smaller piece of cake for the head. Place both cakes on a cakeboard, press together.

4   Roll out 50g/2oz icing and cut out two 5cm/2in circles for the eyes, stick to the head with water. Roll out the remaining black icing and cut out eight 4cm/1½ in circles. Use two of these for the eyes and stick the others on to the body.

5   Colour some icing green and squeeze through a garlic crusher to make grass. Flatten the marshmallows and stick a marzipan round in the centre of each. Colour pipe cleaners black and press a ball of black icing on to the end of each. Arrange grass on board, with the ladybird and decorations.

Spaceship Cake

Serves 10–12

25cm/10in square sponge cake
225g/8oz/1 cup butter icing
60ml/4 tbsp apricot jam, warmed and sieved
350g/12oz/2¼ cups marzipan
450g/1lb/3 cups sugarpaste icing

blue, red and black food colouring

Materials/equipment
30cm/12in square cake board
4 silver candles and holders
gold paper stars

1 Split and fill the sponge cake with butter icing. Cut a 10cm/4in wide piece diagonally across the middle of the cake, about 25cm/10in long. Shape the nose end and straighten the other end.

2 From the off-cuts make three 7.5cm/3in triangles for the wings and top of the ship. Cut two smaller triangles for the booster jets. Position the main body, wings and top of the cake diagonally across the board. Add extra pieces of cake in front of the top triangle. Brush the cake and booster jets with apricot jam, then cover with a layer of marzipan and sugarpaste icing.

3 Divide the remaining sugarpaste icing into three. Tint blue, pink and black. Roll out the blue icing and cut it into 1cm/½in strips. Stick around the base of the cake with water and outline the boosters. Cut a 2.5cm/1in strip and stick down the centre of the spaceship.

4 Roll out the pink and black sugarpaste icing separately and cut shapes, numbers and the child's name to finish the design. When complete, position the boosters.

5 Make small cubes with the off-cuts of sugarpaste icing and use to stick the candles to the cake board. Decorate the board with gold stars.

Racing Track Cake

This cake will delight eight-year-old racing car enthusiasts.

Serves 10–12

2 x 15cm/6in round sponge cakes
115g/4oz/½ cup butter icing
60ml/4 tbsp apricot jam, warmed and sieved
450g/1lb/3 cups marzipan
500g/1¼lb/3¼ cups sugarpaste icing
blue and red food colouring
115g/4oz/¾ cup royal icing

Materials/equipment
25 x 35cm/10 x 14in cake board
5cm/2in fluted cutter
2 small greaseproof paper piping bags
No 8 star and No 2 plain nozzles
8 candles and holders
2 small racing cars

1 Split and fill the cakes with a little butter icing. Cut off a 1cm/½in piece from the side of each cake and place the cakes on the cake board, cut edges together.

2 Brush the cake with apricot jam and cover with a layer of marzipan. Tint 450g/1lb/3 cups of the sugarpaste icing pale blue and use to cover the cake.

3 Mark a 5cm/2in circle in the centre of each cake. Roll out the remaining white sugarpaste icing and cut out two fluted 5cm/2in circles and stick them in the marked spaces.

4 Tint the royal icing red. Pipe a shell border around the base of the cake using the star nozzle. Pipe a track for the cars on the cake using the plain nozzle and stick the candles into the two white circles. Place the cars on the track.

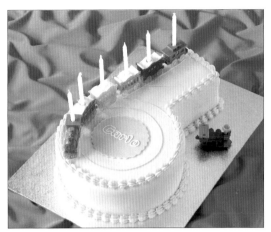

Floating Balloons Cake

Makes one 20cm/8in round cake

20cm/8in round sponge
  or fruit cake, covered
  with 800g/1¾lb/
  5½ cups marzipan, if
  liked
900g/2lb/6 cups
  sugarpaste icing
red, green and yellow
  food colouring
3 eggs
2 egg whites
450g/1lb/4 cups icing
  sugar

Materials/equipment
25cm/10in round cake
  board
3 bamboo skewers,
  25cm/10in, 24cm/
  9½in and 23cm/9in
  long
small star cutter
greaseproof paper piping
  bags
fine writing nozzle
1m/1yd fine coloured
  ribbon
8 candles

1 Place the cake on the board. Tint 50g/2oz/scant ½ cup of the sugarpaste icing red, 50g/2oz/scant ½ cup green and 115g/4oz/1 cup yellow. Cover the cake with the remaining icing. Use just under half the yellow icing to cover the board.

2 Using a skewer, pierce the eggs and carefully empty the contents. Wash and dry the shells. Cover them carefully with the tinted sugarpaste and insert a bamboo skewer in each. Use the trimmings to stamp out a star shape of each colour. Thread on to the skewers for the balloon knots.

3 Trace 16 balloon shapes on to baking paper. Beat the egg whites with the icing sugar until smooth and divide among four bowls. Leave one white and tint the others red, green and yellow. With the fine writing nozzle and white icing, trace round the balloon shapes. Thin the tinted icings with water. Fill the run-outs using snipped piping bags. Dry overnight.

4 Stick the run-outs around the side of the cake with icing. Pipe white balloon strings. Push the large balloons into the centre and decorate with the ribbon. Push the candles into the icing around the edge.

Number 6 Cake

Use the round cake tin as a guide to cut the square cake to fit neatly around the round cake.

Serves 10–12

15cm/6in round and
  15cm/6in square
  sponge cakes
115g/4oz/½ cup butter
  icing
60ml/4 tbsp apricot jam,
  warmed and sieved
450g/1lb/3 cups
  marzipan
500g/1¼lb/3¼ cups
  sugarpaste icing
yellow and green food
  colouring

115g/4oz/¾ cup royal
  icing

Materials/equipment
25 x 35cm/10 x 14in cake
  board
2 small greaseproof paper
  piping bags
7.5cm/3in fluted cutter
No 1 plain and No 8 star
  nozzles
plastic train set with 6
  candles

1 Split and fill the cakes with butter icing. Cut the square cake in half and cut, using the round cake tin as a guide, a rounded end from one rectangle to fit around the round cake. Trim the cakes to the same depth and assemble the number on the cake board. Brush with apricot jam and cover with a thin layer of marzipan.

2 Tint 450g/1lb/3 cups of the sugarpaste icing yellow and the rest green. Cover the cake with the yellow icing. With the cutter, mark a circle in the centre of the round cake. Cut out a green sugarpaste icing circle. Stick in place with water and leave to dry overnight.

3 Mark a track the width of the train on the top of the cake. Tint the royal icing yellow and pipe the track with the plain nozzle. Use the star nozzle to pipe a border around the base and top of the cake. Pipe the name on the green circle and attach the train and candles with royal icing.

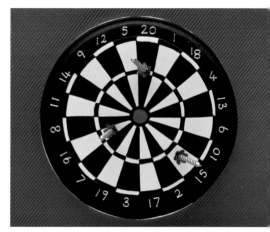

Spider's Web Cake

Make the marzipan spider several days before you need the cake to give it time to dry.

Makes one 20cm/8in round cake

20cm/8in round deep
    sponge cake
225g/8oz/1 cup butter
    icing
45ml/3 tbsp apricot jam,
    warmed and sieved
30ml/2 tbsp cocoa
    powder
chocolate vermicelli
40g/1½oz/4 tbsp
    marzipan
yellow, red, black and
    brown food colouring

225g/8oz/1½ cups icing
    sugar
15 – 30ml/1 – 2 tbsp
    water

Materials/equipment
25cm/10in round cake
    board
2 small greaseproof paper
    piping bags
wooden cocktail stick
star nozzle
8 candles and holders

1 Split and fill the cake with half the butter icing. Brush the sides with apricot jam, add the cocoa to the remaining butter icing then smooth a little over the sides of the cake. Roll the sides of the cake in chocolate vermicelli. Place on the board.

2 For the spider, tint the marzipan yellow. Roll half of it into two balls for the head and body. Tint a small piece red and make three balls and a mouth. Tint a tiny piece black for the eyes. Roll the rest of the marzipan into eight legs and two smaller feelers. Stick together.

3 Gently heat the icing sugar and water over a pan of hot water. Use two-thirds of the glacé icing to cover the cake top.

4 Tint the remaining glacé icing brown and use it to pipe concentric circles on to the cake. Divide the web into eighths by drawing lines across with a cocktail stick. Leave to set.

5 Put the rest of the chocolate butter icing into a piping bag fitted with a star nozzle and pipe a border around the web. Put candles around the border and the spider in the centre.

Dart Board Cake

Makes one 25cm/10in round cake

25cm/10in round sponge
    cake
175g/6oz/¾ cup butter
    icing
5ml/3 tbsp apricot jam,
    warmed and sieved
450g/1lb/3 cups
    marzipan
450g/1lb/3 cups
    sugarpaste icing
115g/4oz/¾ cup royal
    icing

black, red, yellow and
    silver food colouring

Materials/equipment
30cm/12in round cake
    board
icing smoother
1cm/½in plain circle
    cutter
small greaseproof paper
    piping bag
No 1 writing nozzle
3 candles and holders

1 Split and fill the cake with butter icing and put on to the board. Brush with jam and cover with marzipan. Colour some of the sugarpaste icing black, a small piece red and the remaining yellow. Cover the cake with black sugarpaste icing. Cut a 20cm/8in circular template out of greaseproof paper. Fold it in quarters, then divide each quarter into fifths.

2 Using the template, mark the centre and wedges on the top of the cake with a sharp knife. Cut out ten wedges from the yellow sugarpaste, using the template as a guide. Place on alternate sections but do not stick in place yet. Repeat with the black sugarpaste. Cut 3mm/⅛in off each wedge and swop the colours. Mark a 13cm/5in circle in the centre of the board and cut out 3mm/⅛in pieces to swop with adjoining colours. Stick in place and use an icing smoother to flatten.

3 Use the cutter to remove the centre for the bull's eye. Replace with a circle of red sugarpaste, cut with the same cutter. Surround it with a strip of black sugarpaste. Roll the remaining black sugarpaste into a long sausage to fit round the base of the cake and stick in place with a little water. Mark numbers on the board and pipe on with royal icing. Leave to dry then paint with silver food colouring. Stick candles in at an angle to resemble darts.

Camping Tent Cake

Makes one 20 x 10cm/8 x 4in cake

20cm/8in square sponge
  cake
115g/4oz/½ cup butter
  icing
45ml/3 tbsp apricot jam,
  warmed and sieved
450g/1lb/3 cups
  marzipan
500g/1¼lb/3¼ cups
  sugarpaste icing
brown, orange, green,
  red and blue food
  colouring
115g/4oz/¼ cup royal
  icing

50g/2oz/1 cup desiccated
  coconut
chocolate mint sticks

Materials/equipment
25cm/10in square cake
  board
wooden cocktail sticks
fine paintbrush
4 small greaseproof paper
  piping bags
No 1 basketweave and
  plain nozzles

1 Split and fill the cake with butter icing. Cut the cake in half. Cut one half in two diagonally from the top right edge to the bottom left edge to form the roof of the tent. Stick the two wedges, back-to-back, on top of the rectangle with jam. Trim to 10cm/4in high and use the trimmings on the base. Place the cake diagonally on the board and brush with jam.

2 Cover with marzipan, reserving some for modelling. Tint 50g/2oz/scant ½ cup of the sugarpaste icing brown and cover one end of the tent. Tint the rest orange and cover the rest of the cake. Cut a semicircle for the tent opening and a central 7.5cm/3in slit. Lay over the brown end. Secure the flaps with royal icing. Put halved cocktail sticks in the corners and ridge.

3 Tint the coconut green. Spread the board with a thin layer of royal icing and sprinkle with the coconut.

4 Tint the reserved marzipan flesh-colour and use to make a model of a child. Paint on a blue T-shirt and leave to dry. Tint some royal icing brown and pipe on the hair with a basketweave nozzle. Tint the icing and pipe on the mouth and eyes. Make a bonfire with broken chocolate mint sticks.

Army Tank Cake

Create an authentic camouflaged tank by combining green and brown sugarpaste icing.

Makes one 25 x 15cm/10 x 6in cake

25cm/10in square sponge
  cake
225g/8oz/1 cup butter
  icing
45ml/3 tbsp apricot jam,
  warmed and sieved
450g/1lb/3 cups
  marzipan
450g/1lb/3 cups
  sugarpaste icing

brown, green and black
  food colouring
chocolate flake
liquorice strips
60ml/4 tbsp royal icing
round biscuits
sweets

Materials/equipment
25 x 35cm/10 x 14in
  cake board

1 Split and fill the sponge cake with butter icing. Cut off a 10cm/4in strip from one side of the cake. Use the off-cut to make a 15 x 7.5cm/6 x 3in rectangle, and stick on the top.

2 Shape the sloping top and cut a 2.5cm/1in piece from both ends between the tracks. Shape the rounded ends for the wheels and tracks. Place on the cake board and brush with apricot jam. Cover with a layer of marzipan.

3 Tint a quarter of the sugarpaste icing brown and the rest green. Roll out the green to a 25cm/10in square. Break small pieces of brown icing and place all over the green. Flatten and roll out together to give a camouflage effect. Turn the icing over and repeat.

4 Continue to roll out until the icing is 3mm/⅛in thick. Lay it over the cake and gently press to fit. Cut away the excess. Cut a piece into a 6cm/2½in disc and stick on the top with a little water. Cut a small hole in it for the gun and insert the chocolate flake. Stick liquorice on for the tracks, using a little black royal icing. Stick on biscuits for the wheels and sweets for the lights and portholes.

Computer Game Cake

Making a cake look like a computer is easier than you think. This cake is ideal for a computer game fanatic.

Makes one 14 x 13cm/5½ x 5in cake

15cm/6in square sponge cake
115g/4oz/½ cup butter icing
45ml/3 tbsp apricot jam, warmed and sieved
225g/8oz/1½ cups marzipan
275g/10oz/scant 2 cups sugarpaste icing

black, blue, red and yellow food colouring
royal icing, to decorate

Materials/equipment
20cm/8in square cake board
wooden cocktail stick
fine paintbrush
small greaseproof paper piping bag

1 Split and fill the cake with a little butter icing. Cut 2.5cm/1in off one side of the cake and 1cm/½in off the other side. Round the corners slightly. Place on the cake board and brush with apricot jam. Cover with a layer of marzipan.

2 Tint 225g/8oz/1½ cups of the sugarpaste black. Use to cover the cake. Reserve the trimmings. With a cocktail stick, mark the speaker holes and position of the screen and knobs.

3 Tint half the remaining sugarpaste pale blue, roll out and cut out a 6cm/2½in square for the screen. Stick in the centre of the game with a little water. Tint a small piece of sugarpaste red and the rest yellow. Use to cut out the switch and controls. Stick them in position with water. Roll the reserved black sugarpaste icing into a long, thin sausage and edge the screen and base of the cake. .

4 With a fine paintbrush, draw the game on to the screen with a little blue colouring. Pipe letters on to the buttons with royal icing.

Chessboard Cake

To make this cake look most effective, ensure that the squares have very sharp edges.

Makes one 25cm/10in square cake

25cm/10in square sponge cake
225g/8oz/1 cup butter icing
60ml/4 tbsp apricot jam, warmed and sieved
800g/1¾lb/5¼ cups marzipan
500g/1¼lb/3¾ cups sugarpaste icing

black and red food colouring
edible silver balls
115g/4oz/¾ cup royal icing

Materials/equipment
30cm/12in square cake board
small greaseproof paper piping bag
No 8 star nozzle

1 Split and fill the cake with butter icing. Place on the board and brush with jam. Roll out 450g/1lb/3 cups of marzipan and use to cover the cake. Then cover with 450g/1lb/3 cups of the sugarpaste icing. Leave to dry overnight.

2 Divide the remaining marzipan into two, and tint black and red. To shape the chess pieces, roll 50g/2oz/4 tbsp of each colour into a sausage and cut into eight equal pieces. Shape into pawns.

3 Divide 75g/3oz/generous 4 tbsp of each colour into six equal pieces and use to shape into two castles, two knights and two bishops.

4 Divide 25g/1oz/2 tbsp of each colour marzipan in half and shape a queen and a king. Decorate with silver balls. Leave to dry overnight.

5 Cut 1cm/½in black strips of marzipan to edge the board and stick in place with water. Pipe a border round the base of the cake with royal icing. Place the chess pieces in position.

Kite Cake

The happy face on this cheerful kite is a great favourite with children of all ages.

Serves 10–12

25cm/10in square sponge cake
225g/8oz/1 cup butter icing
45ml/3 tbsp apricot jam, warmed and sieved
675g/1½lb/4½ cups sugarpaste icing
yellow, red, green, blue and black food colouring
450g/1lb/3 cups marzipan
115g/4oz/¾ cup royal icing

Materials/equipment

30cm/12in square cake board
wooden cocktail stick
small greaseproof paper piping bag
No 8 star nozzle
6 candles and holders

1 Trim the cake into a kite shape, then split and fill with butter icing. Place diagonally on the cake board and brush with apricot jam. Cover with a layer of marzipan

2 Tint 225g/8oz/1½ cups of the sugarpaste icing pale yellow and cover the cake. Make a template of the face, tie and buttons and mark on to the cake with a cocktail stick. Divide the rest of the sugarpaste icing into four and tint red, green, blue and black. Cut out the features and stick on with water.

3 Pipe a royal icing border around the base of the cake.

4 For the kite's tail, roll out each colour separately and cut two 4 x 1cm/1½ x ½in lengths in blue, red and green. Pinch each length to shape into a bow.

5 Roll the yellow into a long rope and lay it on the board in a wavy line from the narrow end of the kite. Stick the bows in place with water. Roll balls of yellow sugarpaste, stick on the board with a little royal icing and press in the candles.

Hotdog Cake

Makes one 23cm/9in long cake

23 x 33cm/9 x 13in Swiss roll sponge
175g/6oz/¾ cup coffee flavour butter icing
90ml/6 tbsp apricot jam, warmed and sieved
450g/1lb/3 cups sugarpaste icing
brown and red food colouring
15–30ml/1–2 tbsp toasted sesame seeds
115g/4oz/¾ cup glacé icing

Filling

175g/6oz sponge cake pieces
50g/2oz/¼ cup dark brown sugar
45ml/3tbsp orange juice
75ml/5tbsp honey

Materials/equipment

fine paintbrush
2 small greaseproof paper piping bags
napkin, plate, knife and fork

1 Unroll the Swiss roll, spread with butter icing, then roll up again. Slice the Swiss roll along the centre lengthways, almost to the base and ease the two halves apart.

2 Mix all the filling ingredients in a food processor or blender until smooth. Shape the mixture with your hands to a 23cm/9in sausage shape.

3 Tint all the sugarpaste icing brown. Set aside 50g/2oz/scant ½ cup and use the rest to cover the cake.

4 Paint the top of the "bun" with diluted brown food colouring to give a toasted effect. Position the "sausage".

5 Divide the glacé icing in half. Tint one half brown and the other red. Pipe red icing along the sausage, then overlay with brown icing. Sprinkle the sesame seeds over the "bun".

6 Cut the reserved brown sugarpaste icing into thin strips. Place on the cake with the joins under the "sausage". Place the cake on a napkin on a serving plate, with a knife and fork.

Drum Cake

This is a colourful cake for very young children. It even comes complete with drumsticks.

Makes one 15cm/6in round cake

15cm/6in round sponge cake
50g/2oz/4 tbsp butter icing
45ml/3 tbsp apricot jam, warmed and served
350g/12oz/2cups marzipan
450g/1lb/3 cups sugarpaste icing

red, blue and yellow food colouring
royal icing, for sticking

Materials/equipment
20cm/8in round cake board

1 Split and fill the cake with a little butter icing. Place on the cake board and brush with apricot jam. Cover with a layer of marzipan and leave to dry overnight.

2 Tint half of the sugarpaste icing red and roll it out to 25 x 30cm/10 x 12in. Cut in half and stick to the side of the cake with water.

3 Roll out a circle of white sugarpaste icing to fit the top of the cake and divide the rest in half. Tint one half blue and the other yellow. Divide the blue into four pieces and roll into sausages long enough to go halfway round the cake. Stick around the base and top of the cake with a little water.

4 Mark the cake into six around the top and base. Roll the yellow sugarpaste icing into 12 strands long enough to cross diagonally from top to base to form the drum strings. Roll the rest of the yellow icing into 12 small balls and stick where the strings join the drum.

5 Knead together the red and white sugarpaste icing until streaky, then roll two balls and sticks 15cm/6in long. Leave to dry overnight. Stick together with royal icing to make the drumsticks and place on top of the cake.

Ice Cream Cones

Individual cakes make a change for a party. Put a candle in the special person's one.

Makes 9

115g/4oz/¾ cup marzipan
9 ice cream cones
9 sponge fairy cakes
350g/12oz/1½ cups butter icing
red, green and brown food colouring

coloured and chocolate vermicelli, wafers and chocolate sticks
sweets

Materials/equipment
3 12-egg egg boxes
foil

1 Make the stands for the cakes by turning the egg boxes upside down and pressing three balls of marzipan into evenly spaced holes in each box. Wrap the boxes in foil. Pierce the foil above the marzipan balls and insert the cones, pressing them in gently.

2 Gently push a fairy cake into each cone. If the bases of the cakes are too large, trim them down with a small, sharp knife. The cakes should be quite secure in the cones.

3 Divide the butter icing into three bowls and tint them pale red, green and brown.

4 Using a small palette knife, spread each cake with some of one of the icings, making sure that the finish on the icing is a little textured so it looks like ice cream.

5 To insert a wafer or chocolate stick into an ice cream, use a small, sharp knife to make a hole through the icing and into the cake, then insert the wafer or stick. Add the finishing touches to the cakes by sprinkling over some coloured and chocolate vermicelli. Arrange sweets around the cones.

Treasure Map

Makes one 20 x 25cm/8 x 10in cake

*25cm/10in square sponge
    cake
225g/8oz/1½ cups butter
    icing
45ml/3 tbsp apricot jam,
    warmed and sieved
450g/1lb/3 cups
    marzipan
675g/1½lb/4½ cups
    sugarpaste icing
yellow, brown, paprika,
    green, black and red
    food colouring*

*115g/4oz/¾ cup
    royal icing*

Materials/equipment
*25 x 35cm/10 x 14in cake
    board
fine paintbrush
kitchen paper
4 small greaseproof paper
    piping bags
No 7 shell and No 1
    writing nozzles
6 candles and holders*

1 Split and fill the cake with butter icing, cut it into a 20 x 25cm/8 x 10in rectangle and place on the cake board. Brush with apricot jam. Cover with a layer of marzipan then with 450g/1lb/3cups sugarpaste icing.

2 Colour the remaining sugarpaste icing yellow and cut out with an uneven outline. Stick on to the cake with water and leave to dry overnight. Mark the island, river, lake, mountains and trees on the map.

3 With brown and paprika colours and a fine paintbrush, paint the edges of the map to look old, smudging the colours together with kitchen paper. Paint the island pale green and the water around the island, the river and the lake pale blue. Dry overnight before painting on the other details, otherwise the colours will run.

4 Pipe a border of royal icing around the base of the cake with a shell nozzle. Colour a little royal icing red and pipe the path to the treasure, marked with an "X". Colour some icing green and pipe on grass and trees. Finally colour some icing black and pipe on a North sign with the writing nozzle.

Royal Crown Cake

This regal cake is sure to delight any prince or princess.

Serves 16–20

*20cm/8in and 15cm/6in
    round sponge cake
175g/6oz/¾ cup butter
    icing
45ml/3 tbsp apricot jam,
    warmed and sieved
450g/1lb/3 cups
    marzipan
500g/1¼lb/3¾ cups
    sugarpaste icing
red food colouring*

*450g/1lb/3 cups royal
    icing
small black jelly sweets
4 ice cream fan wafers
edible silver balls
jewel sweets*

Materials/equipment
*30cm/12in square cake
    board
wooden cocktail sticks*

1 Split and fill the cakes with butter icing. Sandwich one on top of the other and place on the board. Shape the top cake into a dome.

2 Brush the cake with apricot jam and cover with marzipan. Set aside 115g/4oz/¾ cup of the sugarpaste icing and use the rest to cover the cake.

3 Tint the reserved sugarpaste icing red, and use to cover the dome of the cake. Trim away the excess.

4 Spoon rough mounds of royal icing around the base of the cake and stick a black jelly sweet on each mound.

5 Cut the ice cream wafers in half. Spread both sides of the wafers with royal icing and stick to the cake, smoothing the icing level with the sides of the cake.

6 Use cocktail sticks to support the wafers until they are dry. Put silver balls on top of each point and stick jewel sweets around the side of the crown with a little royal icing.

Box of Chocolates Cake

This sophisticated cake is perfect for an adult's birthday and will delight chocolate lovers.

Makes one 15cm/6in square cake

15cm/6in square sponge
  cake
50g/2oz/4 tbsp butter
  icing
30ml/2 tbsp apricot jam,
  warmed and sieved
350g/12oz/2¼ cups
  marzipan
350g/12oz/2¼ cups
  sugarpaste icing
red food colouring

wrapped chocolates

Materials/equipment
20cm/8in square cake
  board
small paper sweet cases
1.30m/1½yd x
  4cm/1½in-wide gold
  and red ribbon

1 Split and fill the cake with butter icing. Cut a shallow square from the top of the cake, leaving a 1cm/¼in border around the edge. Place on the cake board and brush with apricot jam. Cover with a layer of marzipan.

2 Roll out the sugarpaste icing and cut an 18cm/7in square. Ease it into the hollow dip and trim. Tint the remaining sugarpaste icing red and use to cover the sides.

3 Put the chocolates into paper cases and arrange in the box. Tie the ribbon around the sides and tie a big bow.

Strawberry Cake

Makes one 900g/2lb cake
650g/1lb 7oz/scant
  4½ cups marzipan
green, red and yellow
  food colouring
30ml/2 tbsp apricot jam,
  warmed and sieved
900g/2lb heart-shaped
  sponge cake

caster sugar, for dusting

Materials/equipment
30cm/12in round cake
  board
icing smoother
teaspoon

1 Tint 175g/6oz/generous 1 cup of the marzipan green. Brush the cake board with apricot jam, roll out the green marzipan and use to cover the board. Trim the edges. Use an icing smoother to flatten and smooth the marzipan.

2 Brush the remaining apricot jam over the top and sides of the cake. Position the cake on the cake board. Tint 275g/10oz/scant 2 cups of the remaining marzipan red. Roll it out to 5mm/¼in thick and use to cover the cake, smoothing down the sides. Trim the edges. Use the handle of a teaspoon to indent the "strawberry" evenly and lightly all over.

3 For the stalk, tint 175g/6oz/generous 1 cup of the marzipan bright green. Cut it in half and roll out one portion into a 10 x 15cm/4 x 6in rectangle. Cut "V" shapes out of the rectangle, leaving a 2.5cm/1in border across the top, to form the calyx. Position on the cake, curling the "V" shapes to make them look realistic.

4 Roll the rest of the green marzipan into a sausage shape 13cm/5in long. Bend it slightly, then position it on the board to form the stalk.

5 For the strawberry pips, tint the remaining marzipan yellow. Pull off tiny pieces and roll them into tear-shaped pips. Place them in the indentations all over the strawberry. Dust the cake and board with sifted caster sugar.

Gift-wrapped Parcel

If you don't have a tiny flower cutter for the "wrapping paper" design, then press a small decorative button into the icing while still soft to create a pattern.

Makes one 15cm/6in square cake

15cm/6in square cake	red and green food
50g/2oz/4 tbsp butter	colouring
icing	30ml/2 tbsp royal icing
45ml/3 tbsp apricot jam,	
warmed and served	**Materials/equipment**
450g/1lb/3 cups	20cm/8in square cake
marzipan	board
350g/12oz/2¼ cups pale	small flower cutter
lemon yellow fondant	(optional)
icing	

1 Split and fill the cake with butter icing. Place on the cake board and brush with jam. Cover with half the marzipan, then yellow fondant and mark with a small flower cutter.

2 Divide the remaining marzipan in half, colour one half pink and the other pale green. Roll out the pink marzipan and cut into four 2.5 x 18cm/1 x 7in strips. Roll out the green marzipan and cut into four 1cm/½in strips the same length. Centre the green strips on top of the pink strips and stick on to the cake with a little water. Cut two 5cm/2in strips from each colour and cut a "V" from the ends to form the ends of the ribbon. Stick in place and leave to dry overnight.

3 Cut the rest of the green into four 2.5 x 7.5cm/1 x 3in lengths and the pink into four 1 x 7.5cm/½ x 3in lengths. Centre the pink on top of the green, fold in half, stick ends together and slip over the handle of a wooden spoon, dusted with cornflour. Leave to dry overnight.

4 Cut the ends in "V" shapes to fit neatly together on the cake. Cut two pieces for the join in the centre. Remove the bows from the spoon and stick in position with royal icing.

Sweetheart Cake

The heart-shaped run-outs can be made a week before the cake is made to ensure that they are completely dry.

Makes one 20cm/8in round cake

20cm/8in round sponge	**Materials/equipment**
cake	25cm/10in round cake
115g/4oz/½ cup butter	board
icing	spoon with decorative
45ml/3 tbsp apricot jam,	handle
warmed and served	small greaseproof paper
450g/1lb/3 cups	piping bag
marzipan	No 1 writing no. le
675g/1½lb/4½ cups	8 candles and hol'ers
sugarpaste icing	1.5m/1½yd x 2.5cm/1in
red food colouring	wide ribbon
115g/4oz/¾ cup royal	
icing	

1 Split and fill the cake with butter icing. Place on the cake board and brush with apricot jam. Cover with a layer of marzipan. Tint the sugarpaste icing pale pink and cover the cake and board. Mark the edge with the decorative handle of a spoon.

2 Tint the royal icing dark pink. Make a heart-shaped template and use to pipe the run-outs on greaseproof paper. Using a No 1 writing nozzle, pipe the outlines in a continuous line. Then fill in until the hearts are rounded. You will need eight for the cake top. Leave to dry for at least 2 days.

3 Arrange the hearts on top of the cake and place the candles in the centre. Tie the ribbon round the cake.

Rosette Cake

This cake is quick to decorate and looks truly professional.

Makes one 20cm/8in square cake

20cm/8in square sponge
  cake
450g/1lb/2 cups butter
  icing
60ml/4 tbsp apricot jam,
  warmed and sièved
mulberry red food
  colouring
crystallized violets

Materials/equipment
25cm/10in square cake
  board
serrated scraper
piping bag
No 8 star nozzle
4 candles and holders

1 Split and fill the cake with a little butter icing. Place in the centre of the cake board and brush with apricot jam. Tint the remaining butter icing dark pink. Spread the top and sides with butter icing.

2 Using the serrated scraper, hold it against the cake and move it from side to side across the top to make waves. Hold the scraper against the side of the cake, resting the flat edge on the board and draw it along to give straight ridges along each side.

3 Put the rest of the butter icing into a piping bag fitted with a No 8 star nozzle. Mark a 15cm/6in circle on the top of the cake and pipe stars around it and around the base of the cake. Place the candles and violets in the corners.

Number 10 Cake

This is a very simple cake to decorate. If you can't master the shell edge, pipe stars instead.

Makes one 20cm/8in tall round cake

20cm/8in and 15cm/6in
  round sponge cakes
450g/1lb/2 cups butter
  icing
75ml/5 tbsp apricot jam,
  warmed and sieved
coloured vermicelli
cream food colouring

Materials/equipment
25cm/10in round cake
  board
wooden cocktail stick
plastic "10" cake
  decoration
small greaseproof paper
  piping bag
No 7 shell and No 7 star
  nozzles
10 candles and holders

1 Split and fill both cakes with a little butter icing. Brush the sides with apricot jam. When cold, spread a layer of butter icing on the sides then roll in coloured vermicelli to cover.

2 Tint the rest of the icing cream, spread over the top of each cake. Place the small cake on top of the large cake. Using a cocktail stick, make a pattern in the icing on top of the cake.

3 Using the remaining icing, pipe around the base of the cakes and around the edge. Stick the "10" decoration in the centre of the top tier and two candles on either side. Arrange the other candles evenly around the base cake.

Shirt and Tie Cake

Makes one 19 x 26.5cm/7½ x 10½in cake

*coffee sponge cake, baked
    in a 19 x 26.5cm/
    7½ x 5in loaf tin
350g/12oz/1½ cups
    coffee-flavour butter
    icing
90ml/6 tbsp apricot jam,
    warmed and sieved
good 1kg/2lb 6oz/7 cups
    sugarpaste icing
blue food colouring
125g/4oz/1 cup icing
    sugar, sifted*

45–60ml/3–4 tbsp water

Materials/equipment
*30 x 39cm/15½ x 12in
    cake board
steel ruler
small greaseproof paper
    piping bag
small round nozzle
card collar template
"Happy Birthday"
    decoration
tissue paper (optional)*

1 Cut the cake in half horizontally and sandwich together with the butter icing. Brush the cake with apricot jam. Colour 675g/1½lb/4½ cups sugarpaste icing light blue and roll out to about 5mm/¼in thick. Use to cover the whole cake. Trim away any excess icing. Place the cake on the cake board.

2 Using a steel ruler, make grooves down the length and sides of the cake, about 2.5cm/1in apart. Mix the icing sugar and water to make a glacé icing to pipe into the grooves.

3 To make the collar, roll out 225g/8oz/1½ cups sugarpaste icing to a 40.5 x 10cm/16½ x 4in rectangle. Lay the piece of card for the collar on top. Brush water around the edges, then carefully lift one edge over the card to encase it completely. Trim the two short ends to match the angles of the card. Lift the collar and gently bend it round and position on the cake.

4 Colour 175g/6oz/1 cup sugarpaste icing dark blue. Cut off one-third and shape into a tie knot. Position the knot. Roll out the rest to about 5mm/¼in thick. Cut out a tie piece to fit under the knot and long enough to hang over the edge of the cake. Position the tie piece, tucking it under the knot and securing in place with a little water. Finish the cake with the "Happy Birthday" decoration and tissue paper, if using.

Mobile Phone Cake

Makes one 23 x 13cm/9 x 5in cake

*sponge cake, baked in a 23
    x 13cm/9 x 5in loaf tin
30ml/2 tbsp apricot jam,
    warmed and sieved
375g/13oz/2¼ cups
    sugarpaste icing
black food colouring
10 small square sweets
2 striped liquorice sweets
30–45ml/2–3 tbsp icing
    sugar
2.5–5ml/½–1 tsp water*

Materials/equipment
*25 x 18cm/10 x 7in cake
    board
diamond-shaped biscuit
    cutter
small piece of foil
small greaseproof paper
    piping bag
small round nozzle*

1 Turn the cake upside-down. Make a 2.5cm/1in diagonal cut 2.5cm/1in from one end. Cut down vertically to remove the wedge. Remove the middle of the cake to the wedge depth up to 4cm/1½in from the other end.

2 Place the cake on the board and brush with apricot jam. Tint 275g/10oz/1¼ cups of the sugarpaste icing black. Use to cover the cake, smoothing it over the carved shape. Reserve the trimmings.

3 Tint 75g/3oz/ ½ cup of the sugarpaste icing grey. Cut a piece to fit the hollowed centre, leaving a 1cm/½in border, and another piece 2.5cm/1in square. Stamp out the centre of the square with the cutter. Secure all the pieces on the cake with water.

4 Position the sweets and the foil for the display pad. For the glacé icing, mix the icing sugar with the water and tint black. With the small round nozzle, pipe border lines around the edges of the phone, including the grey pieces of sugarpaste. Pipe the numbers on the keys.

5 Roll a sausage shape from the reserved black sugarpaste for the aerial. Indent one side of the top with a knife and secure the aerial with water.

Heart Cake

Makes one 20cm/8in heart-shaped cake

3 egg whites
350g/12oz/1¼ cups
  caster sugar
30ml/2 tbsp cold water
30ml/2 tbsp fresh lemon
  juice
1.5ml/¼ tsp cream of
  tartar
red food colouring
20cm/8in heart-shaped
  sponge cake

85–115g/3–4oz/¾–1 cup
  icing sugar

Materials/equipment
30cm/12in square cake
  board
small greaseproof piping
  bag
small nozzle

1 Make the icing by combining 2 of the egg whites, the caster sugar, water, lemon juice and cream of tartar in the top of a double boiler or in a bowl set over simmering water. With an electric mixer, beat until thick and holding soft peaks, about 7 minutes. Remove from the heat and continue beating until the mixture is thick enough to spread. Colour the icing pale pink.

2 Put the cake on the cake board and spread the icing evenly on the cake. Smooth the top and sides. Leave to set for 3–4 hours, or overnight.

3 Place 1 tbsp of the remaining egg white in a bowl and whisk until frothy. Gradually beat in enough icing sugar to make a stiff mixture suitable for piping.

4 Spoon the white icing into a piping bag and pipe the decorations on the top and sides of the cake as shown in the photograph above.

Bowl-of-Strawberries Cake

The strawberry theme of the painting is carried on into the moulded decorations on this summery birthday cake.

Makes one 20cm/8in petal-shaped cake

350g/12oz/1½ cups
  butter icing
red, yellow, green and
  claret food colouring
20cm/8in petal-shaped
  Madeira cake
45ml/3 tbsp apricot jam,
  warmed and sieved
675g/1½lb/4½ cups
  sugarpaste icing
yellow powder tint

Materials/equipment
25cm/10in petal-shaped
  cake board
paint palette or small
  saucers
fine paintbrushes
thin red and green
  ribbons

1 Tint the butter icing pink. Cut the cake horizontally into three. Sandwich together with the butter icing. Brush the cake with apricot jam. Use 500g/1¼lb/3¾ cups of the sugarpaste icing to cover the cake. Place on the cake board and leave to dry overnight.

2 For the strawberries, tint three-quarters of the remaining sugarpaste icing red, and equal portions of the rest yellow and green. Make the strawberries, securing with water if necessary. Leave to dry on greaseproof paper.

3 Put the red, green, yellow and claret food colouring in a palette and water them down slightly. Paint the bowl and strawberries, using yellow powder tint to highlight the bowl.

4 Decorate the cake with the ribbons. Secure two strawberries to the top of the cake, and arrange the others around the base.

Barley Twist Cake

Makes one 20cm/8in round cake

20cm/8in round sponge
  cake
115g/4oz/½ cup butter
  icing
45ml/3 tbsp apricot jam,
  warmed and sieved
450/1lb/3 cups marzipan
450g/1lb/3 cups pale
  yellow sugarpaste
  icing
115g/4oz/¼ cup white
  sugarpaste icing
115g/4oz/¾ cup royal
  icing

blue food colouring
pink dusting powder

Materials/equipment

25cm/10in round cake
  board
wooden cocktail stick
fine paintbrush
No 1 plain nozzle
small greaseproof paper
  piping bags
6 small blue bows

1 Split and fill the cake with butter icing. Place on the board and brush with jam. Cover with marzipan, then yellow sugarpaste icing, extending it over the board. Mark six equidistant points around the cake with a cocktail stick.

2 Colour 40g/½oz/1 tbsp of white sugarpaste icing pale blue and roll out thinly. Moisten a paintbrush with water and brush lightly over it. Roll out the same quantity of white icing, lay on top and press together. Roll out to a 20cm/8in square.

3 Cut 5mm/¼in strips, carefully twist each one, moisten the six marked points around the cake with water and drape each barley twist into place, pressing lightly to stick to the cake.

4 Cut out a jersey shape from white icing and stick on with water. Roll some icing into a ball and colour a small amount dark blue. Roll into two tapering 7.5cm/3in needles with a small ball at the end. Dry overnight. Stick the needles and ball in position. Using royal icing and a No 1 nozzle, pipe the stitches and wool in position. Pipe a white border around the base of the cake. Stick small bows around the edge of the cake with a little royal icing and carefully brush the knitting with red powder tint.

Tablecloth Cake

Makes one 20cm/8in round cake

20cm/8in round sponge
  cake
115g/4oz/½ cup butter
  icing
45ml/3 tbsp apricot jam,
  warmed and sieved
450g/1lb/3 cups
  marzipan
675g/1½lb/4½ cups
  sugarpaste icing
115g/4oz/¾ cup royal
  icing
red food colouring

Materials/equipment

25cm/10in round cake
  board
spoon with decorative
  handle
8 wooden cocktail sticks
sharp needle
skewer
8 red ribbon bows
small greaseproof paper
  piping bags
No 2 and No 0 plain
  nozzles

1 Split and fill the cake with butter icing. Place on the board and brush with apricot jam. Cover with a layer of marzipan. Tint 450g/1lb/3 cups of the sugarpaste icing red and cover the cake and board. Roll the rest of the red fondant into a thin rope long enough to go round the cake. Stick around the base of the cake with water. Mark with the decorative handle of a spoon. Leave to dry overnight.

2 Roll out the remaining icing to a 25cm/10in circle and trim. Lay this icing over the cake and drape the "cloth" over the wooden cocktail sticks set at equidistant points.

3 Mark a 10cm/4in circle in the centre of the cake. Make a template of the flower design and transfer to the cake with a needle. Use a skewer to make the flowers; the red colour should show through.

4 Remove the cocktail sticks and stick on the bows with royal icing. With a No 2 plain nozzle and white royal icing pipe around the circle in the centre. With a No 0 plain nozzle, pipe small dots around the edge of the cloth. Colour some royal icing red and pipe a name in the centre.

Pizza Cake

Quick and easy, this really is a definite winner for pizza fanatics everywhere.

Makes one 23cm/9in round cake

23cm/9in shallow sponge cake
350g/12oz/1½ cups butter icing
red and green food colouring
175g/6oz/generous 1 cup yellow marzipan

25g/1oz/4 tbsp sugarpaste icing
15ml/1 tbsp desiccated coconut

Materials/equipment
25cm/10in pizza plate
cheese grater
leaf cutter

1 Place the cake on the pizza plate. Tint the butter icing red and spread evenly over the cake, leaving a 1cm/½in border.

2 Knead the marzipan for a few minutes, to soften slightly, then grate it like cheese, and sprinkle all over the top of the red butter icing.

3 Tint the sugarpaste icing green. Use the leaf cutter to cut out two leaf shapes. Mark the veins with the back of a knife and place on the pizza cake.

4 For the chopped herbs, tint the desiccated coconut dark green. Then scatter over the pizza cake.

Flowerpot Cake

Makes one round cake

Madeira cake, baked in a 1.2-litre/2-pint/5-cup pudding basin
175g/6oz/½ cup jam
175g/6oz/¾ cup butter icing
30ml/2 tbsp apricot jam, warmed and sieved
575g/1¼lb/4¼ cups sugarpaste icing
125g/4oz/¾ cup royal icing

dark orange-red, red, silver, green, purple and yellow food colouring
2 chocolate flakes, coarsely crushed

Materials/equipment
fine paintbrush
wooden spoon

1 Slice the cake into three layers and stick together again with jam and butter icing. Cut out a shallow circle from the cake top, leaving a 1cm/½in rim. Brush the outside of the cake and rim with apricot jam. Tint 400g/14oz/2¼ cups of the sugarpaste orange-red and cover the cake, moulding it over the rim. Reserve the trimmings. Leave to dry.

2 Use the trimmings to make decorations and handles for the flowerpot. Leave to dry on greaseproof paper. Sprinkle the chocolate flakes into the pot for soil.

3 Tint a small piece of sugarpaste very pale orange-red. Use to make a seed bag. When dry, paint on a pattern in food colouring. Tint two small pieces of icing red and silver. Make a trowel and dry over a wooden spoon handle.

4 Tint the remaining icing green, purple and a small piece yellow. Use to make the flowers and leaves, attaching together with royal icing. Score leaf veins with the back of a knife. Leave to dry on greaseproof paper.

5 Attach all the decorations to the flowerpot and arrange the plant, seed bag and trowel with soil, seeds and grass made from leftover tinted sugarpaste.

Glittering Star Cake

With a quick flick of a paintbrush you can give a sparkling effect to this glittering cake.

Makes one 20cm/8in round cake

20cm/8in round rich
  fruit cake
40ml/2½ tbsp apricot
  jam, warmed and
  sieved
675g/1½lb/4½ cups
  marzipan
450g/1lb/4 cups
  sugarpaste icing
115g/4oz/¾ cup royal
  icing

silver, gold, lilac
  shimmer, red sparkle,
  glitter green and
  primrose sparkle food
  colouring and powder
  tints

Materials/equipment
paintbrush
25cm/10in round cake
  board

1 Brush the cake with the apricot jam. Use two-thirds of the marzipan to cover the cake. Leave to dry overnight.

2 Cover the cake with the sugarpaste icing. Leave to dry.

3 Place the cake on a large sheet of greaseproof paper. Dilute a little powdered silver food colouring and, using a loaded paintbrush, flick it all over the cake to give a spattered effect. Allow to dry.

4 Make templates of two different-size moon shapes and three irregular star shapes. Divide the remaining marzipan into six pieces and tint silver, gold, lilac, pink, green and yellow. Cut into stars and moons using the templates as a guide, cutting some of the stars in half.

5 Place the cut-outs on greaseproof paper, brush each with its own colour powder tint. Allow to dry.

6 Secure the cake on the board with royal icing. Arrange the stars and moons at different angles all over the cake, attaching with royal icing, and position the halved stars upright as though coming out of the cake. Allow to set.

Racing Ring Cake

Serves 12

ring mould sponge cake
350g/12oz/1½ cups
  butter icing
500g/1lb 2oz/4⅓ cups
  sugarpaste icing
125g/4oz/¾ cup royal
  icing, for fixing
black, blue, yellow, green,
  orange, red, purple
  food colouring
selection of liquorice
  sweets, dolly mixtures
  and teddy bears

113g/4½oz packet
  liquorice Catherine
  wheels

Materials/equipment
25cm/10in round cake
  board
wooden kebab skewer
fine paintbrush

1 Cut the cake in half horizontally and fill with some butter icing. Cover the outside with the remaining butter icing.

2 Use 350g/12oz/2¼ cups of sugarpaste icing to coat the top and inside of the cake. Use the trimmings to roll an oblong for the flag. Cut the skewer to 12.5cm/5in and fold one end of the flag around it, securing with water. Paint on the pattern with black food colouring. Colour a ball of icing black, and stick on top of the skewer. Make a few folds and leave to dry.

3 Colour the remaining sugarpaste icing blue, yellow, green, orange, red and a very small amount purple. Shape each car in two pieces, attaching in the centre with royal icing where the seat joins the body of the car. Add decorations and headlights and attach dolly mixture wheels with royal icing. Place a teddy bear in each car and leave to set.

4 Unwind the Catherine wheels and remove the centre sweets. Fix them to the top of the cake with royal icing. Secure one strip round the bottom. Cut some of the liquorice into small strips and attach round the middle of the outside of the cake with royal icing. Arrange small liquorice sweets around the bottom of the cake. Position the cars on top of the cake on the tracks and attach the flag to the outside with royal icing.

Artist's Cake

Making cakes is an art in itself, and this cake proves it!

Makes one 20cm/8in square cake

20cm/8in square rich
  fruit cake
45ml/3 tbsp apricot jam,
  warmed and sieved
450g/1lb/3 cups
  marzipan
800g/1¾lb/5¼ cups
  sugarpaste icing
115g/4oz/¾ cup royal
  icing

chestnut, yellow, blue,
  black, silver, paprika,
  green and mulberry
  food colouring

Materials/equipment
25cm/10in square cake
  board
fine paintbrush

1 Brush the cake with the apricot jam. Cover in marzipan and leave to dry overnight.

2 Make a template of a painter's palette that will fit the cake top. Tint 175g/6oz/generous 1 cup of the sugarpaste very pale chestnut. Cut out the palette shape, place on greaseproof paper and leave to dry overnight.

3 Tint 450g/1lb/3 cups of the sugarpaste icing dark chestnut. Use to cover the cake. Secure the cake on the board with royal icing. Leave to dry.

4 Divide half the remaining sugarpaste icing into seven equal parts and tint yellow, blue, black, silver, paprika, green and mulberry. Make all the decorative pieces for the box and palette, using the remaining white sugarpaste for the paint tubes. Leave to dry on greaseproof paper.

5 Paint black markings on the paint tubes and chestnut wood markings on the box.

6 Position all the sugarpaste pieces on the cake and board using royal icing. Leave to dry.

Liquorice Sweet Cake

Makes one 20cm/8in square cake

20cm/8in and 15cm/6in
  square Madeira cakes
675g/1½lb/3 cups butter
  icing
45ml/3 tbsp apricot jam,
  warmed and sieved
350g/12oz/2¼ cups
  marzipan
800g/1¾lb/5¼ cups
  sugarpaste icing

egg-yellow, black, blue
  and mulberry food
  colouring

Materials/equipment
25cm/10in square cake
  board
4.5cm/1¾in round cutter

1 Cut both cakes horizontally into three. Fill with butter icing, reserving a little to coat the smaller cake. Wrap and set aside the smaller cake. Brush the larger cake with apricot jam. Cover with marzipan and secure on the cake board with butter icing. Leave to dry overnight.

2 Tint 350g/12oz/2¼ cups of the sugarpaste icing yellow. Take 115g/4oz/¾ cup of the sugarpaste icing and tint half black and leave the other half white. Cover the top and one-third of the sides of the cake with yellow sugarpaste icing.

3 Use the white icing to cover the lower third of the sides of the cake. Use the black icing to fill the central third.

4 Cut the smaller cake into three equal strips. Divide two of the strips into three squares each. Cut out two circles from the third strip, using a cutter as a guide.

5 Tint 115g/4oz/¾ cup of the remaining sugarpaste black. Divide the rest into four equal portions, leave one white and tint the others blue, pink and yellow.

6 Coat the outsides of the cake cut-outs with the reserved butter icing. Use the tinted and white sugarpaste to cover the pieces to resemble sweets. Make small rolls from the trimmings. Arrange on and around the cake.

Sun Cake

Makes one 20cm/8in star-shaped cake

2 x 20 x 5cm/8 x 2in
   sponge cakes
25g/1oz/2 tbsp unsalted
   butter
450g/1lb/4 cups sifted
   icing sugar
120ml/4fl oz/½ cup
   apricot jam
30ml/2 tbsp water
2 large egg whites
1–2 drops glycerine
juice of 1 lemon
yellow and orange food
   colouring

Materials/equipment
40cm/16in square cake
   board
fabric piping bag
small star nozzle

1 Cut one of the cakes into eight wedges. Trim the outsides to fit round the other cake. Make butter icing with the butter and 25g/1oz/2 tbsp of the icing sugar. Place the whole cake on a 40cm/16in board and attach the sunbeams with the butter icing.

2 Melt the jam with the water and brush over the cake.

3 For the icing, beat the egg whites until stiff. Gradually add the icing sugar, glycerine and lemon juice, and beat for 1 minute. Tint yellow and spread over the cake. Tint the remaining icing bright yellow and orange. Pipe the details on to the cake.

Strawberry Basket Cake

Makes one small rectangular cake

sponge cake baked in a
   450g/1lb/3 cup loaf tin
45ml/3 tbsp apricot jam,
   warmed and sieved
675g/1½lb/4½ cups
   marzipan
350g/12oz/1½cups
   chocolate-flavour
   butter icing
red food colouring
50g/2oz/4 tbsp caster
   sugar

Materials/equipment
small star nozzle
small greaseproof paper
   piping bag
10 plastic strawberry
   stalks
30 x 7.5cm/12 x 3in strip
   foil
30cm/12in thin red
   ribbon

1 Level the top of the cake and make it perfectly flat. Score a 5mm/¼in border around the edge and scoop out the inside to make a shallow hollow.

2 Brush the sides and border edges of the cake with apricot jam. Roll out 275g/10oz/scant 2 cups of the marzipan, cut into rectangles and use to cover the sides of the cake, overlapping the borders. Press the edges together to seal.

3 Using the star nozzle, pipe vertical lines 2.5cm/1in apart all around the sides of the cake. Pipe short horizontal lines of butter icing alternately crossing over and then stopping at the vertical lines to give a basketweave effect. Pipe a decorative line of icing around the top edge of the basket to finish.

4 Tint the remaining marzipan red and mould it into ten strawberry shapes. Roll in the caster sugar and press a plastic stalk into each top. Arrange in the "basket".

5 For the basket handle, fold the foil into a thin strip and wind the ribbon around it to cover. Bend up the ends and then bend into a curve. Push the ends into the sides of the cake. Decorate with bows made from the ribbon.

Banana Gingerbread Slices

Bananas make this spicy bake delightfully moist. The flavour develops on keeping, so store the gingerbread for a few days before cutting, if possible.

Makes 20 slices

275g/10oz/2¹/₂ cups plain flour
20ml/4 tsp ground ginger
10ml/2 tsp mixed spice
5ml/1 tsp bicarbonate of soda
115g/4oz/¹/₂ cup soft light brown sugar

60ml/4 tbsp corn oil
30ml/2 tbsp molasses or black treacle
30ml/2 tbsp malt extract
2 eggs, beaten
60ml/4 tbsp orange juice
3 ripe bananas
115g/4oz/scant 1 cup raisins or sultanas

1 Preheat the oven to 180°C/350°F/Gas 4. Line and grease a 28 x 18cm/11 x 7in baking tin.

2 Sift the flour, spices and bicarbonate of soda into a mixing bowl. Spoon some of the mixture back into the sieve, add the brown sugar and sift the mixture back into the bowl.

3 Make a well in the centre of the dry ingredients and add the oil, molasses or treacle, malt extract, eggs, and orange juice. Mix thoroughly.

4 Mash the bananas in a bowl. Add to the gingerbread mixture with the raisins or sultanas. Mix well.

5 Scrape the mixture into the prepared tin. Bake for 35–40 minutes or until the centre springs back when the surface of the cake is lightly pressed.

6 Leave the gingerbread in the tin to cool for 5 minutes, then turn onto a wire rack, remove the lining paper and leave to cool completely. Cut into 20 slices to serve.

Banana and Apricot Chelsea Buns

Old favourites get a new twist with a delectable filling.

Serves 9

225g/8oz/2 cups strong plain flour
10ml/2 tsp mixed spice
2.5ml/¹/₂ tsp salt
25g/1oz/2 tbsp soft margarine
7.5ml/1¹/₂ tsp easy-blend dried yeast
50g/2oz/¹/₄ cup caster sugar
90ml/6 tbsp hand-hot milk
1 egg, beaten

For the filling
1 large ripe banana
175g/6oz/1 cup ready-to-eat dried apricots
30ml/2tbsp soft light brown sugar

For the glaze
30ml/2tbsp caster sugar
30ml/2tbsp water

1 Grease an 18cm/7in square cake tin. Prepare the filling. Mash the banana in a bowl. Using kitchen scissors, snip in the apricots, then stir in the brown sugar. Mix well.

2 Sift the flour, spice and salt into a mixing bowl. Rub in the margarine, then stir in the yeast and sugar. Make a well in the centre and pour in the milk and the egg. Mix to a soft dough, adding a little extra milk if necessary.

3 Turn the dough onto a floured surface and knead for 5 minutes until smooth and elastic. Roll out to a 30 x 23cm/ 12 x 9in rectangle. Spread the filling over the dough and roll up lengthways like a Swiss roll, with the join underneath. Cut into 9 pieces and place cut side downwards in the prepared tin. Cover and leave in a warm place until doubled in size.

4 Preheat the oven to 200°C/400°F/Gas 6. Bake the buns for 20–25 minutes until golden brown. Meanwhile make the glaze: mix the caster sugar and water in a small saucepan. Heat, stirring, until dissolved, then boil for 2 minutes. Brush the glaze over the buns while still hot, then remove from the tin and cool on a wire rack.

Lemon Sponge Fingers

These sponge fingers are perfect for serving with fruit salads or light, creamy desserts.

Makes about 20

2 eggs
75g/3oz/6 tbsp caster
   sugar
grated rind of 1 lemon

50g/2oz/½ cup plain
   flour, sifted
caster sugar, for
   sprinkling

1 Preheat the oven to 190°C/375°F/Gas 5. Line two baking sheets with non-stick baking paper. Whisk the eggs, sugar and lemon rind together with a hand-held electric whisk until thick and mousse-like: when the whisk is lifted, a trail should remain on the surface of the mixture for at least 30 seconds.

2 Carefully fold in the flour with a large metal spoon using a figure-of-eight action.

3 Place the mixture in a piping bag fitted with a 1cm/½in plain nozzle. Pipe into finger lengths on the prepared baking sheets, leaving room for spreading.

4 Sprinkle the fingers with caster sugar. Bake for 6–8 minutes until golden brown, then remove to a wire rack to cool completely.

Variation
To make Hazelnut Fingers, omit the lemon rind and fold in 25g/1oz/¼ cup toasted ground hazelnuts and 5ml/1 tsp mixed spice with the flour.

Apricot and Almond Fingers

These delicious almond fingers will stay moist for several days, thanks to the addition of apricots.

Makes 18

225g/8oz/2 cups self-
   raising flour
115g/4oz/½ cup soft light
   brown sugar
50g/2oz/⅓ cup semolina
175g/6oz/1 cup ready-to-
   eat dried apricots,
   chopped
30ml/2 tbsp clear honey

30ml/2 tbsp malt extract
2 eggs, beaten
60ml/4 tbsp skimmed
   milk
60ml/4 tbsp sunflower oil
few drops of almond
   essence
30ml/2 tbsp flaked
   almonds

1 Preheat the oven to 160°C/325°F/Gas 3. Grease and line a 28 x 18cm/11 x 7in baking tin. Sift the flour into a bowl and stir in the sugar, semolina and apricots. Make a well in the centre and add the honey, malt extract, eggs, milk, oil and almond essence. Mix well until combined.

2 Turn the mixture into the prepared tin, spread to the edges and sprinkle with the flaked almonds.

3 Bake for 30–35 minutes or until the centre springs back when lightly pressed. Invert the cake on a wire rack to cool. Remove the lining paper if necessary and cut into 18 slices with a sharp knife.

Cook's Tip
If you cannot find ready-to-eat dried apricots, soak chopped dried apricots in boiling water for 1 hour, then drain them and add to the mixture. This works well with other dried fruit too. Try ready-to-eat dried pears or peaches for a change.

Raspberry Muffins

Unlike English muffins, which are made from a yeast mixture and cooked on a griddle, these American muffins are baked, giving them a light and spongy texture.

Makes 10–12

275g/10oz/2¹/₂ cups plain
    flour
15ml/1 tbsp baking
    powder
115g/4oz/¹/₂ cup caster
    sugar

1 egg
250ml/8fl oz/1 cup
    buttermilk
60ml/4 tbsp sunflower oil
150g/5oz/1 cup
    raspberries

1 Preheat the oven to 200°C/400°F/Gas 6. Arrange 12 paper cases in a deep muffin tin. Sift the flour and baking powder into a mixing bowl, stir in the sugar, then make a well in the centre.

2 Mix the egg, buttermilk and oil together in a jug, pour into the bowl and mix quickly until just combined.

3 Add the raspberries and lightly fold in with a metal spoon. Spoon into the paper cases to within a third of the top.

4 Bake the muffins for 20–25 minutes until golden brown and firm in the middle. Remove to a wire rack and serve while still warm.

Cook's Tip
This is a fairly moist mixture which should only be lightly mixed. Over-mixing toughens the muffins and breaks up the fruit. Use blackberries, blueberries or blackcurrants instead of raspberries if you prefer.

Date and Apple Muffins

These tasty muffins are delicious with morning coffee or breakfast. You will only need one or two per person as they are very filling.

Makes 12

150g/5oz/1¹/₄ cups self-
    raising wholemeal
    flour
150g/5oz/1¹/₄ cups self-
    raising white flour
5ml/1 tsp ground
    cinnamon
5ml/1 tsp baking powder
25g/1oz/2 tbsp soft
    margarine
75g/3oz/6 tbsp soft light

brown sugar
250ml/8fl oz/1 cup apple
    juice
30ml/2 tbsp pear and
    apple spread
1 egg, lightly beaten
1 eating apple
75g/3oz/¹/₂ cup chopped
    dates
15ml/1 tbsp chopped
    pecan nuts

1 Preheat the oven to 200°C/400°F/Gas 6. Arrange 12 paper cases in a deep muffin tin. Put the wholemeal flour in a mixing bowl. Sift in the white flour with the cinnamon and baking powder. Rub in the margarine until the mixture resembles breadcrumbs, then stir in the brown sugar.

2 In a bowl, stir a little of the apple juice with the pear and apple spread until smooth. Add the remaining juice, mix well, then add to the rubbed-in mixture with the egg. Peel and core the apple, chop the flesh finely and add it to the bowl with the dates. Mix quickly until just combined.

3 Divide the mixture among the muffin cases. Sprinkle with the chopped pecans.

4 Bake the muffins for 20–25 minutes until golden brown and firm in the middle. Turn onto a wire rack and serve while still warm.

Filo and Apricot Purses

Filo pastry is very easy to use and is low in fat. Always keep a packet in the freezer ready for rustling up a speedy teatime treat.

Makes 12

115g/4oz/1 cup ready-to-
  eat dried apricots
45ml/3 tbsp apricot
  compôte
3 amaretti biscuits,
  crushed

3 sheets of filo pastry
20ml/4 tsp soft
  margarine, melted
icing sugar, for dusting

1 Preheat the oven to 180℃/350℉/Gas 4. Grease two baking sheets. Chop the apricots, put them in a bowl and stir in the apricot compôte. Mix in the amaretti biscuits.

2 Cut the filo pastry into 24 13cm/5in squares, pile the squares on top of each other and cover with a clean dish towel to prevent the pastry from drying out.

3 Lay one pastry square on a flat surface, brush lightly with melted margarine and lay another square diagonally on top. Brush the top square with melted margarine. Spoon a small mound of apricot mixture in the centre of the pastry, bring up the edges and pinch together in a money-bag shape. The margarine will help to make the pastry stick.

4 Repeat with the remaining filo squares and filling to make 12 purses in all. Arrange on the prepared baking sheets and bake for 5–8 minutes until golden brown. Dust with icing sugar and serve warm.

Cook's Tip
The easiest way to crush the amaretti biscuits is to put them in a plastic bag and roll with a rolling pin.

Filo Scrunchies

Quick and easy to make, these are ideal to serve at teatime. Eat them warm or they will lose their crispness.

Makes 6

5 apricots or plums
4 sheets of filo pastry
20ml/4 tsp soft
  margarine, melted

50g/2oz/¼ cup demerara
  sugar
30ml/2 tbsp flaked
  almonds
icing sugar, for dusting

1 Preheat the oven to 190℃/375℉/Gas 5. Cut the apricots or plums in half, remove the stones and slice the fruit thinly.

2 Cut the filo pastry into 12 18cm/7in squares. Pile the squares on top of each other and cover with a clean dish towel to prevent the pastry from drying out. Remove one square and brush it with melted margarine. Lay a second filo square on top, then, using your fingers, mould the pastry into neat folds.

3 Lay the scrunched filo square on a baking sheet. Make five more scrunchies in the same way, working quickly so that the pastry does not dry out.Arrange a few slices of fruit in the folds of each scrunchie, then sprinkle generously with demerara sugar and almonds.

4 Bake the scrunchies for 8–10 minutes until golden brown, then loosen from the baking sheet with a palette knife. Place on a platter, dust with icing sugar and serve immediately.

Cook's Tip
Filo pastry dries out very quickly. Keep it covered as much as possible with clear film or a dry cloth to limit exposure to the air, or it will become too brittle to use.

Coffee Sponge Drops

These light biscuits are delicious on their own, but taste even better with a filling made by mixing low-fat soft cheese with chopped stem ginger.

Makes about 24

50g/2oz/¹/₂ cup plain
flour
15ml/1 tbsp instant
coffee powder
2 eggs
75g/3oz/6 tbsp caster
sugar

For the filling (optional)
115g/4oz/¹/₂ cup low fat
soft cheese
40g/1¹/₂oz/¹/₄ cup
chopped stem ginger

1 Preheat the oven to 190°C/375°F/Gas 5. Line two baking sheets with non-stick paper. Sift the flour and coffee powder together.

2 Combine the eggs and caster sugar in a heatproof bowl. Place over a saucepan of simmering water. Beat with a hand-held electric whisk until thick and mousse-like: when the whisk is lifted a trail should remain on the surface of the mixture for at least 30 seconds.

3 Carefully fold in the sifted flour mixture with a large metal spoon, being careful not to knock out any air.

4 Spoon the mixture into a piping bag fitted with a 1cm/¹/₂in plain nozzle and pipe 4cm/1¹/₂in rounds on the prepared baking sheets. Bake for 12 minutes. Cool on a wire rack. Sandwich together in pairs with a ginger-cheese filling (above) or a coffee icing, if you like.

Variation
To make Chocolate Sponge Drops, replace the coffee with 30ml/2 tbsp reduced-fat cocoa powder.

Oaty Crisps

These biscuits are very crisp and crunchy – ideal to serve with morning coffee.

Makes 18

175g/6oz/1¹/₂ cups rolled
oats
75g/3oz/6 tbsp soft light
brown sugar

1 egg
60ml/4 tbsp sunflower oil
30ml/2 tbsp malt extract

1 Preheat the oven to 190°C/375°F/Gas 5. Grease two baking sheets. Mix the oats and brown sugar in a bowl, breaking up any lumps in the sugar.

2 Add the egg, oil and malt extract, mix well, then leave to soak for 15 minutes.

3 Using a teaspoon, place small heaps of the mixture on the prepared baking sheets, leaving room for spreading. Press into 7.5cm/3in rounds with a dampened fork.

4 Bake the biscuits for 10–15 minutes until golden brown. Leave to cool for 1 minute, then remove with a palette knife and cool on a wire rack.

Variation
Add 50g/2oz/¹/₂ cup chopped almonds or hazelnuts to the mixture. You can also add some jumbo oats to give a coarser texture.

Snowballs

These light and airy morsels make a good accompaniment to yogurt ice cream.

Makes about 20
2 egg whites
115g/4oz/¹/₂ cup caster sugar
15ml/1 tbsp cornflour, sifted
5ml/1 tsp white wine vinegar
1.5ml/¹/₄ tsp vanilla essence

1 Preheat the oven to 150°C/300°F/Gas 2 and line two baking sheets with non-stick baking paper. Whisk the egg whites in a grease-free bowl, using a hand-held electric whisk, until very stiff.

2 Add the caster sugar, a little at a time, whisking until the meringue is very stiff. Whisk in the cornflour, vinegar and vanilla essence.

3 Using a teaspoon, mound the mixture into snowballs on the prepared baking sheets. Bake for 30 minutes.

4 Cool on the baking sheets, then remove the snowballs from the paper with a palette knife.

Variation
Make Pineapple Snowballs by lightly folding about 50g/2oz/¹/₃ cup finely chopped semi-dried pineapple into the meringue.

Caramel Meringues

Muscovado sugar gives these meringues a marvellous caramel flavour. Take care not to overcook them, so that they stay chewy in the middle.

Makes about 20
115g/4oz/¹/₂ cup muscovado sugar
2 egg whites
5ml/1 tsp finely chopped walnuts

1 Preheat the oven to 160°C/325°F/Gas 3. Line two baking sheets with non-stick paper. Press the sugar through a metal sieve into a bowl. Whisk the egg whites in a grease-free bowl until very stiff and dry, then add the sieved brown sugar, about 15ml/1 tbsp at a time, whisking it in the meringue until it is thick and glossy.

2 Spoon small mounds of the mixture onto the prepared baking sheets. Sprinkle with the walnuts.

3 Bake for 30 minutes, then leave to cool for 5 minutes on the baking sheets. Transfer the meringues to a wire rack to cool completely.

Cook's Tip
For an easy sophisticated filling, mix 115g/4oz/¹/₂ cup low-fat soft cheese with 15ml/1 tbsp icing sugar. Chop 2 slices of fresh pineapple and add to the mixture. Sandwich the meringues together in pairs.

Chocolate Banana Cake

A delicious sticky chocolate cake, moist enough to eat without the icing if you want to cut down on the calories.

Serves 8

225g/8oz/2 cups self-
    raising flour
45ml/3 tbsp fat-reduced
    cocoa powder
115g/4oz/½ cup soft light
    brown sugar
30ml/2 tbsp malt extract
30ml/2 tbsp golden syrup
2 eggs, beaten
60ml/4 tbsp skimmed
    milk

60ml/4 tbsp sunflower oil
2 large ripe bananas

For the icing
175g/6oz/1½ cups icing
    sugar, sifted
30ml/2 tbsp fat-reduced
    cocoa powder, sifted
15 – 30ml/1 – 2 tbsp
    warm water

1 Preheat the oven to 160°C/325°F/Gas 3. Line and grease a deep 20cm/8in round cake tin. Sift the flour into a mixing bowl with the cocoa powder. Stir in the sugar.

2 Make a well in the centre and add the malt extract, golden syrup, eggs, milk and oil. Mix well. Mash the bananas thoroughly and stir them into the mixture until thoroughly combined.

3 Spoon the mixture into the prepared tin and bake for 1 – 1¼ hours or until the centre of the cake springs back when lightly pressed. Remove the cake from the tin and turn on to a wire rack to cool.

4 Make the icing: put the icing sugar and cocoa in a mixing bowl and gradually add enough water to make a mixture thick enough to coat the back of a wooden spoon. Pour over the top of the cake and ease to the edges, allowing the icing to dribble down the sides.

Spiced Apple Cake

Grated apple and dates give this cake a natural sweetness. It may not be necessary to add all the sugar.

Serves 8

225g/8oz/2 cups self-
    raising wholemeal
    flour
5ml/1 tsp baking powder
10ml/2 tsp ground
    cinnamon
175g/6oz/1 cup chopped
    dates
75g/3oz/scant ½ cup soft
    light brown sugar

15ml/1 tbsp pear and
    apple spread
120ml/4fl oz/½ cup
    apple juice
2 eggs, beaten
90ml/6 tbsp sunflower oil
2 eating apples, cored
    and grated
15ml/1 tbsp chopped
    walnuts

1 Preheat the oven to 180°C/350°F/Gas 4. Line and grease a 20cm/8in deep round cake tin. Sift the flour, baking powder and cinnamon into a mixing bowl, then mix in the dates and make a well in the centre.

2 Mix the sugar with the pear and apple spread in a small bowl. Gradually stir in the apple juice. Add to the dry ingredients with the eggs, oil and apples. Mix thoroughly.

3 Spoon into the prepared cake tin, sprinkle with the walnuts and bake for 60 – 65 minutes or until a skewer inserted into the centre of the cake comes out clean. Invert on a wire rack, remove the lining paper and leave to cool.

Cook's Tip
It is not necessary to peel the apples – the skin adds extra fibre and softens on cooking.

Irish Whiskey Cake

This moist rich fruit cake is drizzled with whiskey as soon as it comes out of the oven.

Serves 10

115g/4oz/scant 1 cup sultanas	300ml/½ pint/1¼ cups cold tea
115g/4oz/scant 1 cup raisins	1 egg, beaten
115g/4oz/½ cup currants	300g/11oz/2½ cups self-raising flour, sifted
115g/4oz/½ cup glacé cherries	45ml/3 tbsp Irish whiskey
175g/6oz/1 cup soft light brown sugar	

1 Mix the dried fruit, cherries, sugar and tea in a large bowl. Leave to soak overnight until the tea has been absorbed.

2 Preheat the oven to 180℃/350℉/Gas 4. Line and grease a 1kg/2¼lb loaf tin. Add the egg and flour to the fruit mixture and beat thoroughly until well mixed.

3 Pour into the prepared tin and bake for 1½ hours or until a skewer inserted into the centre comes out clean.

4 Prick the top of the cake with a skewer and drizzle over the whiskey while still hot. Allow to stand for 5 minutes, then remove from the tin and cool on a wire rack.

Cook's Tip
If time is short use hot tea and soak the fruit for two hours instead of overnight.

Fruit and Nut Cake

A rich fruit cake that matures with keeping.

Serves 12–14

175g/6oz/1½ cups self-raising wholemeal flour	90ml/6 tbsp sunflower oil
175g/6oz/1½ cups self-raising white flour	175ml/6fl oz/¾ cup orange juice
10ml/2 tsp mixed spice	2 eggs, beaten
15ml/1 tbsp apple and apricot spread	675g/1½lb/4 cups luxury mixed fruit
45ml/3 tbsp clear honey	115g/4oz/½ cup glacé cherries, halved
15ml/1 tbsp molasses	45ml/3 tbsp split almonds

1 Preheat the oven to 160℃/325℉/Gas 3. Line and grease a deep 20cm/8in cake tin. Tie a band of newspaper around the outside of the tin and stand it on a pad of newspaper on a baking sheet.

2 Combine the flours in a mixing bowl. Stir in the mixed spice and make a well in the centre.

3 Put the apple and apricot spread in a small bowl. Gradually stir in the honey and molasses. Add to the bowl with the oil, orange juice, eggs and mixed fruit. Stir with a wooden spoon to mix thoroughly.

4 Scrape the mixture into the prepared tin and smooth the surface. Arrange the cherries and almonds in a decorative pattern over the top. Bake for 2 hours or until a skewer inserted into the centre of the cake comes out clean. Turn on to a wire rack to cool, then remove the lining paper.

Cook's Tip
For a less elaborate cake, omit the cherries, chop the almonds roughly and sprinkle them over the top.

Angel Cake

Served with fromage frais and fresh raspberries, this makes a light dessert.

Serves 10

*40g/1¹/₂oz/scant ¹/₂ cup
cornflour
40g/1¹/₂oz/scant ¹/₂ cup
plain flour
8 egg whites*

*225g/8oz/1 cup caster
sugar, plus extra for
sprinkling
5ml/1 tsp vanilla essence
icing sugar, for dusting*

1 Preheat the oven to 180°C/350°F/Gas 4. Sift both flours into a bowl.

2 Whisk the egg whites in a large grease-free bowl until very stiff, then gradually add the sugar and vanilla essence, whisking until the mixture is thick and glossy.

3 Fold in the flour mixture with a large metal spoon. Spoon into an ungreased 25cm/10in angel cake tin, smooth the surface and bake for 40–45 minutes.

4 Sprinkle a piece of greaseproof paper with caster sugar and set an egg cup in the centre. Invert the cake tin over the paper, balancing it carefully on the egg cup. When cold, the cake will drop out of the tin. Transfer it to a plate, dust generously with icing sugar and serve.

Variation

Make a lemon icing by mixing 175g/6oz/1¹/₂ cups icing sugar with 15–30ml/1–2 tbsp lemon juice. Drizzle the icing over the cake and decorate with lemon slices and mint sprigs or physalis.

Peach Swiss Roll

This is the perfect cake for a summer afternoon tea in the garden.

Serves 6–8

*3 eggs
115g/4oz/¹/₂ cup caster
sugar
75g/3oz/³/₄ cup plain
flour, sifted*

*15ml/1 tbsp boiling
water
90ml/6 tbsp peach jam
icing sugar, for dusting
(optional)*

1 Preheat the oven to 200°C/400°F/Gas 6. Line and grease a 30 x 20cm/12 x 8in Swiss roll tin. Combine the eggs and sugar in a bowl. Beat with a hand-held electric whisk until thick and mousse-like: when the whisk is lifted a trail should remain on the surface of the mixture for at least 30 seconds.

2 Carefully fold in the flour with a large metal spoon, then add the boiling water in the same way.

3 Spoon into the prepared tin, spread evenly to the edges and bake for 10–12 minutes until the cake springs back when lightly pressed.

4 Spread a sheet of greaseproof paper on a flat surface, sprinkle it with caster sugar, then invert the cake on top. Peel off the lining paper.

5 Make a neat cut two-thirds of the way through the cake, about 1 cm/¹/₂ in from the short edge nearest you – this will make it easier to roll. Trim the remaining edges.

6 Spread the cake with the peach jam and roll up quickly from the partially-cut end. Hold in position for a minute, making sure the join is underneath. Cool on a wire rack. Dust with icing sugar before serving, if you like.

Pear and Sultana Tea Bread

This is an ideal tea bread to make when pears are plentiful.
There's no better use for autumn windfalls.

Serves 6–8

25g/1oz/3 cups rolled
   oats
50g/2oz/¼ cup soft light
   brown sugar
30ml/2 tbsp pear or apple
   juice
30ml/2 tbsp sunflower oil
1 large or 2 small pears

115g/4oz/1 cup self-
   raising flour
115g/4oz/scant 1 cup
   sultanas
2.5ml/½ tsp baking
   powder
10ml/2 tsp mixed spice
1 egg

1 Preheat the oven to 180°C/350°F/Gas 4. Line a 450g/1lb
loaf tin with non-stick paper. Put the oats in a bowl with the
sugar, pour over the pear or apple juice and oil, mix well and
leave to stand for 15 minutes.

2 Quarter, core and grate the pear(s). Add to the bowl with
the flour, sultanas, baking powder, spice and egg. Using a
wooden spoon, mix thoroughly.

3 Spoon the tea bread mixture into the prepared loaf tin.
Bake for 55–60 minutes or until a skewer inserted into the
centre comes out clean.

4 Invert the tea bread on a wire rack and remove the lining
paper. Leave to cool.

Cook's Tip
*Health-food shops sell concentrated pear juice, ready
for diluting as required.*

Banana and Ginger Tea Bread

The bland creaminess of banana is given a delightful lift
with chunks of stem ginger in this tasty tea bread. If you
like a strong ginger flavour add 5ml/1 tsp ground ginger
with the flour.

Serves 6–8

175g/6oz/1½ cups
   self-raising flour
5ml/1 tsp baking powder
40g/1½oz/3 tbsp soft
   margarine
50g/2oz/¼ cup soft light
   brown sugar

50g/2oz/⅓ cup drained
   stem ginger, chopped
60ml/4 tbsp skimmed
   milk
2 ripe bananas, mashed

1 Preheat the oven to 180°C/350°F/Gas 4. Line and grease a
450g/1lb loaf tin. Sift the flour and baking powder into a
mixing bowl.

2 Rub in the margarine until the mixture resembles
breadcrumbs, then stir in the sugar.

3 Add the ginger, milk and mashed bananas and mix to a
soft dough.

4 Spoon into the prepared tin and bake for 40–45 minutes.
Run a palette knife around the edges to loosen them, turn the
tea bread onto a wire rack and leave to cool.

Variation
*To make Banana and Walnut Tea Bread, add 5ml/1 tsp
mixed spice and omit the chopped stem ginger. Stir in
50g/2oz/½ cup chopped walnuts and add
50g/2oz/scant ½ cup sultanas.*

Olive and Oregano Bread

This is an excellent accompaniment to all salads and is very good with grilled goat's cheese.

Serves 8–10

15ml/1 tbsp olive oil
1 onion, chopped
450g/1lb/4 cups strong
    white flour
10ml/2 tsp easy-blend
    dried yeast
5ml/1 tsp salt
1.5ml/¼ tsp black pepper
50g/2oz/⅓ cup pitted
    black olives, roughly
    chopped
15ml/1 tbsp black olive
    paste
15ml/1 tbsp chopped
    fresh oregano
15ml/1 tbsp chopped
    fresh parsley
300ml/½ pint/1¼ cups
    hand-hot water

1   Lightly oil a baking sheet. Heat the olive oil in a frying pan and fry the onion until golden brown.

2   Sift the flour into a mixing bowl. Add the yeast, salt and pepper. Make a well in the centre. Add the fried onion (with the oil), the olives, olive paste, herbs and water. Gradually incorporate the flour and mix to a soft dough, adding a little extra water if necessary.

3   Turn the dough onto a floured surface and knead for 5 minutes until smooth and elastic. Shape into a 20cm/8in round and place on the prepared baking sheet. Using a sharp knife, make criss-cross cuts over the top, cover and leave in a warm place until doubled in size. Preheat the oven to 220°C/425°F/Gas 7.

4   Bake the olive and oregano loaf for 10 minutes, then lower the oven temperature to 200°C/400°F/Gas 6. Bake for 20 minutes more, or until the loaf sounds hollow when tapped underneath. Cool on a wire rack.

Sun-dried Tomato Plait

This makes a marvellous centrepiece for a summer buffet.

Serves 8–10

225g/8oz/2 cups
    wholemeal flour
225g/8oz/2 cups strong
    white flour
5ml/1 tsp salt
1.5ml/¼ tsp black pepper
10ml/2 tsp easy-blend
    dried yeast
pinch of sugar
300ml/½ pint/1¼ cups
    hand-hot water
115g/4oz/¾ cup drained
    sun-dried tomatoes in
    oil, chopped, plus
15ml/1 tbsp oil from
    the jar
25g/1oz/¼ cup freshly
    grated Parmesan
    cheese
30ml/2 tbsp red pesto
2.5ml/½ tsp coarse
    sea salt

1   Lightly oil a baking sheet. Put the wholemeal flour in a mixing bowl. Sift in the white flour, salt and pepper. Add the yeast and sugar. Make a well in the centre and add the water, the sun-dried tomatoes, oil, Parmesan and pesto. Gradually incorporate the flour and mix to a soft dough, adding a little extra water if necessary.

2   Turn the dough onto a floured surface and knead for 5 minutes until smooth and elastic. Shape into 3 33cm/13in long sausages.

3   Dampen the ends of the three sausages. Press them together at one end, plait them loosely, then press them together at the other end. Place on the baking sheet, cover and leave in a warm place until doubled in size. Preheat the oven to 220°C/425°F/Gas 7.

4   Sprinkle the plait with coarse sea salt. Bake for 10 minutes, then lower the oven temperature to 200°C/400°F/Gas 6 and bake for a further 15–20 minutes, or until the loaf sounds hollow when tapped underneath. Cool on a wire rack.

Cheese and Onion Herb Stick

An extremely tasty bread which is very good with soup or salads. Use a strong cheese to give plenty of flavour.

Makes 2 sticks, each serving 4–6

15ml/1 tbsp sunflower oil
1 red onion, chopped
450g/1lb/4 cups strong
  white flour
5ml/1 tsp salt
5ml/1 tsp mustard
  powder
10ml/2 tsp easy-blend
  dried yeast

45ml/3 tbsp chopped
  fresh herbs, such as
  thyme, parsley,
  marjoram or sage
75g/3oz/¾ cup grated
  reduced-fat Cheddar
  cheese
300ml/½ pint/1¼ cups
  hand-hot water

1 Lightly oil two baking sheets. Heat the oil in a frying pan and fry the onion until well browned.

2 Sift the flour, salt and mustard powder into a mixing bowl. Stir in the yeast and herbs. Set aside 30ml/2 tbsp of the cheese. Add the rest to the flour mixture and make a well in the centre. Add the water with the fried onions and oil; gradually incorporate the flour and mix to a soft dough, adding a little extra water if necessary.

3 Turn the dough onto a floured surface and knead for 5 minutes until smooth and elastic. Divide the mixture in half and roll each piece into a stick 30cm/12in in length.

4 Place each bread stick on a baking sheet, make diagonal cuts along the top and sprinkle with the reserved cheese. Cover and leave until doubled in size. Preheat the oven to 220°C/425°F/Gas 7.

5 Bake the loaves for 25 minutes or until the bread sounds hollow when tapped underneath.

Focaccia

This Italian flatbread is best served warm. It makes a delicious snack with olives and feta cheese.

Serves 8

450g/1lb/4 cups strong
  white flour
5ml/1 tsp salt
1.5ml/¼ tsp freshly
  ground black pepper
10ml/2 tsp easy-blend
  dried yeast
300ml/½ pint/1¼ cups
  hand-hot water
pinch of sugar
15ml/1 tbsp pesto

115g/4oz/⅔ cup pitted
  black olives, chopped
25g/1oz/3 tbsp drained
  sun-dried tomatoes in
  oil, chopped, plus
  15ml/1 tbsp oil from
  the jar
5ml/1 tsp coarse sea salt
5ml/1 tsp chopped fresh
  rosemary

1 Lightly oil a 30 x 20cm/12 x 8in Swiss roll tin. Sift the flour, salt and pepper into a bowl. Add the yeast and sugar and make a well in the centre.

2 Add the water with the pesto, olives and sun-dried tomatoes (reserve the oil). Mix to a soft dough, adding a little extra water if necessary.

3 Turn the dough onto a floured surface and knead for 5 minutes until smooth and elastic. Roll into a rectangle measuring 33 x 23cm/13 x 9in. Lop over the rolling pin and place in the prepared tin. Leave to rise until doubled in size. Preheat the oven to 220°C/425°F/Gas 7.

4 Using your fingertips, make indentations all over the dough. Brush with the oil from the sun-dried tomatoes, then sprinkle with the salt and rosemary. Bake for 20–25 minutes until golden. Remove to a wire rack and serve warm.

Spinach and Bacon Bread

This bread is so good that it is a good idea to make double the quantity and freeze one of the loaves.

Makes 2 loaves, each serving 8

15ml/1 tbsp olive oil	1 sachet easy-blend dried
1 onion, chopped	yeast
115g/4oz rindless smoked	475ml/16fl oz/2 cups
bacon rashers,	hand-hot water
chopped	225g/8oz chopped
675g/1¹/₂lb/6 cups plain	spinach, thawed if
flour	frozen
7.5ml/1¹/₂ tsp salt	25g/1oz/¹/₄ cup grated
2.5ml/¹/₂ tsp grated	reduced-fat Cheddar
nutmeg	cheese

1 Lightly oil two 23cm/9in cake tins. Heat the oil in a frying pan and fry the onion and bacon for 10 minutes until golden brown.

2 Sift the flour, salt and nutmeg into a mixing bowl, add the yeast and make a well in the centre. Add the water. Tip in the fried bacon and onion, with the oil, then add the well-drained spinach. Gradually incorporate the flour and mix to a soft dough.

3 Turn the dough onto a floured surface and knead for 5 minutes until smooth and elastic. Divide the mixture in half. Shape each half into a ball, flatten slightly and place in a tin, pressing the dough so that it extends to the edges.

4 Mark each loaf into six wedges and sprinkle with the cheese. Cover loosely with a plastic bag and leave in a warm place until each loaf has doubled in size. Preheat the oven to 200°C/400°F/Gas 6.

5 Bake the loaves for 25–30 minutes or until they sound hollow when tapped underneath. Cool on a wire rack.

Parma Ham and Parmesan Bread

This nourishing bread can be made very quickly, and is a meal in itself when served with a tomato and feta salad.

Serves 8

225g/8oz/2 cups self-	30ml/2 tbsp chopped
raising wholemeal	fresh parsley
flour	25g/1oz/2 tbsp freshly
225g/8oz/2 cups self-	grated Parmesan
raising plain flour	cheese
5ml/1 tsp salt	45ml/3 tbsp Meaux
5ml/1 tsp freshly ground	mustard
black pepper	350ml/12fl oz/1¹/₂ cups
75g/3oz Parma ham,	buttermilk
chopped	skimmed milk, to glaze

1 Preheat the oven to 200°C/400°F/Gas 6. Flour a baking sheet. Put the wholemeal flour in a bowl and sift in the plain flour, salt and pepper. Stir in the ham and parsley. Set aside about half of the grated Parmesan and add the rest to the flour mixture. Make a well in the centre.

2 Mix the mustard and buttermilk in a jug, pour into the bowl and quickly mix to a soft dough.

3 Turn onto a well-floured surface and knead very briefly. Shape into an oval loaf and place on the baking sheet.

4 Brush the loaf with milk, sprinkle with the reserved Parmesan and bake for 25–30 minutes until golden brown. Cool on a wire rack.

Cook's Tip
When chopping the ham, sprinkle it with flour so that it does not stick together. Do not knead the mixture as for a yeast dough, or it will become tough. It should be mixed quickly and kneaded very briefly before shaping.

Austrian Three-Grain Bread

A mixture of grains gives this close-textured bread a delightful nutty flavour.

Makes 1 large loaf

225g/8oz/2 cups strong
  white flour
7.5ml/1½ tsp salt
225g/8oz/2 cups malted
  brown flour
225g/8oz/2 cups rye flour
75g/3oz/¾ cup medium
  oatmeal

1 sachet easy-blend dried
  yeast
45ml/3 tbsp sunflower
  seeds
30ml/2 tbsp linseeds
475ml/16fl oz/2 cups
  hand-hot water
30ml/2 tbsp malt extract

1 Sift the plain flour and salt into a mixing bowl and add the remaining flours, oatmeal, yeast and sunflower seeds. Set aside 5ml/1 tsp of the linseeds and add the rest to the flour mixture. Make a well in the centre.

2 Add the water to the bowl with the malt extract. Gradually incorporate the flour and mix to a soft dough, adding extra water if necessary.

3 Flour a baking sheet. Turn the dough onto a floured surface and knead for 5 minutes until smooth and elastic. Divide it in half. Roll each half into a sausage, about 30cm/12in in length. Twist the two pieces together, dampen each end and press together firmly.

4 Lift the loaf onto the prepared baking sheet. Brush with water, sprinkle with the remaining linseeds and cover loosely with a large plastic bag (balloon it to trap the air inside). Leave in a warm place until doubled in size. Preheat the oven to 220°C/425°F/Gas 7.

5 Bake the bread for 10 minutes, then lower the oven temperature to 200°C/400°F/Gas 6 and cook for 20 minutes more, or until the loaf sounds hollow when tapped underneath. Allow to cool on a wire rack.

Rye Bread

Rye bread is popular in Northern Europe and makes an excellent base for open sandwiches.

Makes 2 loaves, each serving 10

350g/12oz/3 cups
  wholemeal flour
225g/8oz/2 cups rye flour
115g/4oz/1 cup strong
  white flour
7.5ml/1½ tsp salt
1 sachet easy-blend dried
  yeast

30ml/2 tbsp caraway
  seeds
475ml/16fl oz/2 cups
  hand-hot water
30ml/2 tbsp molasses
30ml/2 tbsp sunflower oil

1 Grease a baking sheet. Put the flours in a bowl with the salt and yeast. Set aside 5ml/1 tsp of the caraway seeds and add the rest to the bowl. Mix well, then make a well in the centre.

2 Add the water to the bowl with the molasses and oil. Gradually incorporate the flour and mix to a soft dough, adding a little extra water if necessary.

3 Turn the dough on to a floured surface and knead for 5 minutes until smooth and elastic. Divide the dough in half and shape into two 23cm/9in long oval loaves.

4 Flatten the loaves slightly and place them on the baking sheet. Brush them with water and sprinkle with the remaining caraway seeds. Cover and leave in a warm place until doubled in size. Preheat the oven to 220°C/425°F/Gas 7.

5 Bake the loaves for 30 minutes until they sound hollow when tapped underneath. Allow to cool on a wire rack.

Soda Bread

Finding the bread bin empty need never be a problem when your repertoire includes a recipe for soda bread. It takes only a few minutes to make and needs no rising or proving. If possible, eat soda bread warm from the oven as it does not keep well.

Serves 8

*450g/1lb/4 cups plain
   flour
5ml/1 tsp salt
5ml/1 tsp bicarbonate
   of soda*

*5ml/1 tsp cream of tartar
350ml/12fl oz/1¹/₂ cups
   buttermilk*

1 Preheat the oven to 220°C/425°F/Gas 7. Flour a baking sheet. Sift the dry ingredients into a mixing bowl and make a well in the centre.

2 Add the buttermilk and mix quickly to a soft dough. Turn onto a floured surface and knead lightly. Shape into a round about 18cm/7in in diameter; place on the baking sheet.

3 Cut a deep cross on top of the loaf and sprinkle with a little flour. Bake for 25–30 minutes, then transfer to a wire rack to cool.

Cook's Tip
Soda bread needs a light hand. The ingredients should be bound together quickly in the bowl and kneaded very briefly. The aim is just to get rid of the largest cracks, as the dough becomes tough if handled for too long.

Malt Loaf

This is a rich and sticky loaf. If it lasts long enough to go stale, try toasting it for a delicious teatime treat.

Serves 8
*350g/12oz/3 cups plain
   flour
1.5ml/¹/₄ tsp salt
5ml/1 tsp easy-blend
   dried yeast
pinch of caster sugar
30ml/2 tbsp soft light
   brown sugar
175g/6oz/generous 1 cup
   sultanas*

*150ml/¹/₄ pint/²/₃ cup
   hand-hot skimmed
   milk
15ml/1 tbsp sunflower oil
45ml/3 tbsp malt extract*

To glaze
*30ml/2 tbsp caster sugar
30ml/2 tbsp water*

1 Sift the flour and salt into a mixing bowl, stir in the yeast, pinch of sugar, brown sugar and sultanas, and make a well in the centre. Add the hot milk with the oil and malt extract. Gradually incorporate the flour and mix to a soft dough, adding a little extra milk if necessary.

2 Turn onto a floured surface and knead for about 5 minutes until smooth and elastic. Lightly oil a 450g/1lb loaf tin.

3 Shape the dough and place it in the prepared tin. Cover with a damp dish cloth and leave in a warm place until doubled in size. Preheat the oven to 190°C/375°F/Gas 5.

4 Bake the loaf for 30–35 minutes or until it sounds hollow when tapped underneath.

5 Meanwhile, make the glaze by dissolving the sugar in the water in a small pan. Bring to the boil, stirring, then lower the heat and simmer for 1 minute. Brush the loaf while hot, then transfer it to a wire rack to cool.

Banana and Cardamom Bread

The combination of banana and cardamom is delicious in this soft-textured moist loaf.

Serves 6

10 cardamom pods
400g/14oz/3½ cups
    strong white flour
5ml/1 tsp salt
5ml/1 tsp easy-blend
    dried yeast

150ml/¼ pint/⅔ cup
    hand-hot water
30ml/2 tbsp malt extract
2 ripe bananas, mashed
5ml/1 tsp sesame seeds

1 Grease a 450g/1lb loaf tin. Split the cardamom pods. Remove the seeds and chop the pods finely.

2 Sift the flour and salt into a mixing bowl, add the yeast and make a well in the centre. Add the water with the malt extract, chopped cardamom pods and bananas. Gradually incorporate the flour and mix to a soft dough, adding a little extra water if necessary.

3 Turn the dough onto a floured surface and knead for 5 minutes until smooth and elastic. Shape into a plait and place in the prepared tin. Cover loosely with a plastic bag (ballooning it to trap the air) and leave in a warm place until well risen. Preheat the oven to 220°C/425°F/Gas 7.

4 Brush the plait lightly with water and sprinkle with the sesame seeds. Bake for 10 minutes, then lower the oven temperature to 200°C/400°F/Gas 6. Cook for 15 minutes more, or until the loaf sounds hollow when tapped underneath. Remove to a wire rack to cool.

Swedish Sultana Bread

A lightly sweetened bread that goes very well with the cheeseboard and is also excellent toasted as a tea bread.

Serves 10

225g/8oz/2 cups
    wholemeal flour
225g/8oz/2 cups strong
    white flour
5ml/1 tsp easy-blend
    dried yeast
5ml/1 tsp salt
115g/4oz/scant 1 cup
    sultanas

50g/2oz/½ cup walnuts,
    chopped
15ml/1 tbsp clear honey
150ml/¼ pint/⅔ cup
    hand-hot water
175ml/6fl oz/¾ cup
    hand-hot skimmed
    milk, plus extra for
    glazing

1 Grease a baking sheet. Put the flours in a bowl with the yeast, salt and sultanas. Set aside 15ml/1 tbsp of the walnuts and add the rest to the bowl. Mix lightly and make a well in the centre.

2 Dissolve the honey in the water and add it to the bowl with the milk. Gradually incorporate the flour, mixing to a soft dough and adding a little extra water if necessary.

3 Turn the dough onto a floured surface and knead for 5 minutes until smooth and elastic. Shape into a 28cm/11in long sausage shape. Place on the prepared baking sheet.

4 Make diagonal cuts down the length of the loaf, brush with milk, sprinkle with the remaining walnuts and leave in a warm place until doubled in size. Preheat the oven to 220°C/425°F/Gas 7.

5 Bake the loaf for 10 minutes, then lower the oven temperature to 200°C/400°F/Gas 6 and bake for 20 minutes more or until the loaf sounds hollow when tapped underneath. Remove to a wire rack to cool.

Poppy Seed Rolls

Pile these soft rolls in a basket and serve them for breakfast
or with dinner.

Makes 12

oil for greasing
450g/1lb/4 cups strong
    white flour
5ml/1 tsp salt
5ml/1 tsp easy-blend
    dried yeast
300ml/½ pint/1¼ cups

hand-hot skimmed
    milk
1 egg, beaten

For the topping
1 egg, beaten
poppy seeds

1 Lightly grease two baking sheets with the oil. Sift the flour
and salt into a mixing bowl. Add the yeast. Make a well in the
centre and pour in the milk and the egg. Gradually
incorporate the flour and mix to a soft dough.

2 Turn the dough on to a floured surface and knead for
5 minutes until smooth and elastic. Cut into 12 pieces and
shape into rolls.

3 Place the rolls on the prepared baking sheets, cover loosely
with a large plastic bag (ballooning it to trap the air inside)
and leave in a warm place until the rolls have doubled in size.
Preheat the oven to 220°C/425°F/Gas 7.

4 Glaze the rolls with beaten egg, sprinkle with poppy seeds
and bake for 12–15 minutes until golden brown.

Variations

Vary the toppings. Linseed, sesame and caraway seeds
all look good; try adding caraway seeds to the dough,
too, for extra flavour.

Granary Baps

These make excellent picnic fare and are also good buns for
hamburgers.

Makes 8

oil for greasing
450g/1lb/4 cups malted
    brown flour
5ml/1 tsp salt
10ml/2 tsp easy-blend
    dried yeast

15ml/1 tbsp malt extract
300ml/½ pint/1¼ cups
    hand-hot water
15ml/1 tbsp rolled oats

1 Lightly oil a large baking sheet. Put the malted flour, salt
and yeast in a mixing bowl and make a well in the centre.
Dissolve the malt extract in the water and add it to the well.
Gradually incorporate the flour and mix to a soft dough.

2 Turn the dough on to a floured surface and knead for 5
minutes until smooth and elastic. Divide it into eight pieces.
Shape into balls and flatten with the palm of your hand to
make 10cm/4in rounds.

3 Place the rounds on the prepared baking sheet, cover
loosely with a large plastic bag (ballooning it to trap the air
inside), and leave in a warm place until the baps have
doubled in size. Preheat the oven to 220°C/425°F/Gas 7.

4 Brush the baps with water, sprinkle with the oats and bake
for 20–25 minutes or until they sound hollow when tapped
underneath. Cool on a wire rack.

Variation

To make a large loaf, shape the dough into a round,
flatten it slightly and bake for 30–40 minutes. Test by
tapping the base of the loaf – if it sounds hollow, it is
cooked.

Wholemeal Herb Triangles

These make a good lunchtime snack when stuffed with ham and salad and also taste good when served with soup.

Makes 8

225g/8oz/2 cups
  wholemeal flour
115g/4oz/1 cup strong
  plain flour
5ml/1 tsp salt
2.5ml/¹/₂ tsp bicarbonate
  of soda
5ml/1 tsp cream of tartar
2.5ml/¹/₂ tsp chilli
  powder

50g/2oz/¹/₄ cup soft
  margarine
250ml/8fl oz/1 cup
  skimmed milk
60ml/4 tbsp chopped
  mixed fresh herbs
15ml/1 tbsp sesame seeds

1 Preheat the oven to 220°C/425°F/Gas 7. Flour a baking sheet. Put the wholemeal flour in a mixing bowl. Sift in the remaining dry ingredients, including the chilli powder, then rub in the margarine.

2 Add the milk and herbs and mix quickly to a soft dough. Turn onto a lightly floured surface. Knead very briefly or the dough will become tough.

3 Roll out to a 23cm/9in circle and place on the prepared baking sheet. Brush lightly with water and sprinkle with the sesame seeds.

4 Cut the dough round into 8 wedges, separate slightly and bake for 15–20 minutes. Transfer the triangles to a wire rack to cool. Serve warm or cold.

Variation
Sun-dried Tomato Triangles: replace the mixed herbs with 30ml/2 tbsp chopped, drained sun-dried tomatoes in oil, and add 15ml/1 tbsp mild paprika, 15ml/1 tbsp chopped fresh parsley and 15ml/1 tbsp chopped fresh marjoram.

Caraway Bread Sticks

Ideal to nibble with drinks, these can be made in a wide variety of flavours, including cumin seed, poppy seed and celery seed, as well as the coriander and sesame variation given below.

Makes about 20

225g/8oz/2 cups plain
  flour
2.5ml/¹/₂ tsp salt
2.5ml/¹/₂ tsp easy-blend
  dried yeast

10ml/2 tsp caraway seeds
150ml/¹/₄ pint/²/₃ cup
  hand-hot water
pinch of sugar

1 Grease two baking sheets. Sift the flour, salt, yeast and sugar into a mixing bowl, stir in the caraway seeds and make a well in the centre. Add the water and gradually mix the flour to make a soft dough, adding a little extra water if necessary.

2 Turn onto a lightly floured surface and knead for 5 minutes until smooth and elastic. Divide the mixture into 20 pieces and roll each one into a 30cm/12in stick.

3 Arrange the bread sticks on the baking sheets, leaving room to allow for rising. Leave for 30 minutes until well risen. Meanwhile, preheat the oven to 220°C/425°F/Gas 7.

4 Bake the bread sticks for 10–12 minutes until golden brown. Cool on the baking sheets.

Variation
Coriander and Sesame Sticks: replace the caraway seeds with 15ml/1 tbsp crushed coriander seeds. Dampen the bread sticks lightly and sprinkle them with sesame seeds before baking.

Curry Crackers

These spicy, crisp little biscuits are ideal for serving with drinks or cheese.

Makes 12

50g/2oz/¹/₂ cup plain
  flour
5ml/1 tsp curry powder
1.5ml/¹/₄ tsp chilli
  powder

1.5ml/¹/₄ tsp salt
15ml/1 tbsp chopped
  fresh coriander
30ml/2 tbsp water

1 Preheat the oven to 180°C/350°F/Gas 4. Sift the flour, curry powder, chilli powder and salt into a mixing bowl and make a well in the centre. Add the chopped coriander and water. Gradually incorporate the flour and mix to a fine dough.

2 Turn onto a lightly floured surface, knead until smooth, then leave to rest for 5 minutes.

3 Cut the dough into 12 pieces and knead into small balls. Roll each ball out very thinly to a 10cm/4in round.

4 Arrange the rounds on two ungreased baking sheets. Bake for 15 minutes, turning over once during cooking.

Variations
These can be flavoured in many different ways. Omit the curry and chilli powders and add 15ml/1 tbsp caraway, fennel or mustard seeds. Any of the stronger spices such as nutmeg, cloves or ginger will give a good flavour but you will only need to add 5ml/1 tsp.

Oatcakes

These are traditionally served with cheese, but are also delicious topped with thick honey for breakfast.

Makes 8

175g/6oz/1 cup medium
  oatmeal, plus extra for
  sprinkling
pinch of bicarbonate of
  soda

2.5ml/¹/₂ tsp salt
15g/¹/₂oz/1 tbsp butter
75ml/5 tbsp water

1 Preheat the oven to 150°C/300°F/Gas 2. Grease a baking sheet. Put the oatmeal, bicarbonate of soda and salt in a mixing bowl.

2 Melt the butter with the water in a small saucepan. Bring to the boil, then add to the oatmeal and mix to a moist dough.

3 Turn on to a surface sprinkled with oatmeal and knead to a smooth ball. Turn a large baking sheet upside down, sprinkle it lightly with oatmeal and place the ball of dough on top. Dust with oatmeal; roll out thinly to a 25cm/10in round.

4 Cut the round into eight sections, ease apart slightly and bake for 50–60 minutes until crisp. Leave to cool on the baking sheet, then remove the oatcakes with a palette knife.

Cook's Tip
To get a neat circle, place a 25cm/10in cake board or plate on top of the oatcake. Cut away any excess dough with a palette knife, then remove the board or plate.

Chive and Potato Scones

These little cakes should be fairly thin, soft and crisp. They are delicious served for breakfast.

Makes 20

450g/1lb potatoes
115g/4oz/1 cup plain flour, sifted
30ml/2 tbsp olive oil
30ml/2 tbsp snipped chives
salt and freshly ground black pepper
low-fat spread, for topping

1 Cook the potatoes in a saucepan of boiling salted water for 20 minutes, then drain thoroughly. Return the potatoes to the clean pan and mash them. Preheat a griddle or heavy-based frying pan over low heat.

2 Tip the hot mashed potatoes into a bowl. Add the flour, olive oil and chives, with a little salt and pepper. Mix to a soft dough.

3 Roll out the dough on a well-floured surface to a thickness of 5 mm/¼ in and stamp out rounds with a 5cm/2in scone cutter, re-rolling and cutting the trimmings.

4 Cook the scones, in batches, on the hot griddle or frying pan for about 10 minutes until they are golden brown. Keep the heat low and turn the scones once. Spread with a little low-fat spread and serve immediately.

Cook's Tip
Use floury potatoes such as King Edwards. The potatoes must be freshly cooked and mashed and should not be allowed to cool before mixing. Cook the scones over low heat so that the outside does not burn before the inside is cooked.

Ham and Tomato Scones

These make an ideal accompaniment for soup. If you have any left over the next day, halve them, sprinkle with cheese, and toast under the grill.

Makes 12

225g/8oz/2 cups self-raising flour
5ml/1 tsp mustard powder
5ml/1 tsp paprika, plus extra for topping
2.5ml/¹⁄₂ tsp salt
25g/1oz/2 tbsp soft margarine
50g/2oz Black Forest ham, chopped
15ml/1 tbsp snipped fresh basil
50g/2oz/¹⁄₃ cup drained sun-dried tomatoes in oil, chopped
90–120ml/3–4fl oz/ ¹⁄₃–¹⁄₂ cup skimmed milk, plus extra for brushing

1 Preheat the oven to 200°C/400°F/Gas 6. Flour a large baking sheet. Sift the flour, mustard, paprika and salt into a bowl. Rub in the margarine until the mixture resembles breadcrumbs.

2 Stir in the ham, basil and sun-dried tomatoes; mix lightly. Pour in enough milk to mix to a soft dough.

3 Turn the dough onto a lightly floured surface, knead lightly and roll out to a 20 x 15cm (8 x 6in) rectangle. Cut into 5cm/2in squares and arrange on the baking sheet.

4 Brush sparingly with milk, sprinkle with paprika and bake for 12–15 minutes. Transfer to a wire rack to cool.

Cook's Tip
Scone dough should be soft and moist and mixed for just long enough to bind the ingredients together. Too much kneading makes the scones tough.

Drop Scones

Children love making – and eating – these little scones.

Makes 18

225g/8oz/2 cups self-raising flour	1 egg, beaten
2.5ml/¹/₂ tsp salt	300ml/¹/₂ pint/1¹/₄ cups skimmed milk
15ml/1 tbsp caster sugar	oil for brushing

1 Preheat a griddle, heavy-based frying pan or an electric frying pan. Sift the flour and salt into a mixing bowl. Stir in the sugar and make a well in the centre.

2 Add the egg and half the milk and gradually incorporate the surrounding flour to make a smooth batter. Beat in the remaining milk.

3 Lightly grease the griddle or pan. Drop tablespoons of the batter onto the surface, leaving them until they bubble and the bubbles begin to burst.

4 Turn the drop scones with a palette knife and cook until the underside is golden brown. Keep the cooked drop scones warm and moist by wrapping them in a clean napkin while cooking successive batches. Serve with jam.

Variation
For a savoury version of these tasty scones, add 2 chopped spring onions and 15ml/1 tbsp freshly grated Parmesan cheese to the batter. Serve with cottage cheese.

Pineapple and Spice Drop Scones

Making the batter with pineapple or orange juice instead of milk cuts down on fat and adds to the taste. Semi-dried pineapple has an intense flavour that makes it ideal to use in baking.

Makes 24

115g/4oz/1 cup self-raising wholemeal flour	1 egg, beaten
115g/4oz/1 cup self-raising white flour	300ml/¹/₂ pint/1¹/₄ cups pineapple juice
5ml/1 tsp ground cinnamon	75g/3oz/¹/₂ cup semi-dried pineapple, chopped
15ml/1 tbsp caster sugar	oil for greasing

1 Preheat a griddle, heavy-based frying pan or an electric frying pan. Put the wholemeal flour in a mixing bowl. Sift in the white flour, ground cinnamon and sugar and make a well in the centre.

2 Add the egg with half the pineapple juice and gradually incorporate the surrounding flour to make a smooth batter. Beat in the remaining juice with the chopped pineapple.

3 Lightly grease the griddle or pan. Drop tablespoons of the batter onto the surface, leaving them until they bubble and the bubbles begin to burst.

4 Turn the drop scones with a palette knife and cook until the underside is golden brown. Keep the cooked scones warm and moist by wrapping them in a clean napkin while cooking successive batches.

Cook's Tip
Drop scones do not keep well and are best eaten freshly cooked. These taste good with cottage cheese.

Peach and Amaretto Cake

Try this delicious cake for dessert, with reduced-fat fromage frais, or serve it solo for afternoon tea.

Serves 8

3 eggs, separated
175g/6oz/¾ cup caster
  sugar
grated rind and juice of
  1 lemon
50g/2oz/⅓ cup semolina
40g/1½oz/scant ½ cup
  ground almonds
25g/1oz/¼ cup plain
  flour

For the syrup

75g/3oz/6 tbsp caster
  sugar
90ml/6 tbsp water
30ml/2 tbsp Amaretto
  liqueur
2 peaches or nectarines,
  halved and stoned
60ml/4 tbsp apricot jam,
  sieved, to glaze

1 Preheat the oven to 180°C/350°F/Gas 4. Grease a 20cm/8in round loose-bottomed cake tin. Whisk the egg yolks, caster sugar, lemon rind and juice in a bowl until thick, pale and creamy, then fold in the semolina, almonds and flour until smooth.

2 Whisk the egg whites in a grease-free bowl until fairly stiff. Using a metal spoon, stir a generous spoonful of the whites into the semolina mixture to lighten it, then fold in the remaining egg whites. Spoon into the prepared cake tin.

3 Bake for 30–35 minutes, then remove the cake from the oven and carefully loosen the edges. Prick the top with a skewer and leave to cool slightly in the tin.

4 Meanwhile, make the syrup. Heat the sugar and water in a small pan, stirring until dissolved, then boil without stirring for 2 minutes. Add the Amaretto liqueur and drizzle slowly over the cake.

5 Remove the cake from the tin and transfer it to a serving plate. Slice the peaches or nectarines, arrange them in concentric circles over the top and brush with the glaze.

Chestnut and Orange Roulade

A very moist roulade – ideal to serve as a dessert.

Serves 8

3 eggs, separated
115g/4oz/½ cup caster
  sugar
½ x 439g/15½oz can
  unsweetened chestnut
  purée
grated rind and juice of
  1 orange
icing sugar, for dusting

For the filling

225g/8oz/1 cup low-fat
  soft cheese
15ml/1 tbsp clear honey
1 orange

1 Preheat the oven to 180°C/350°F/Gas 4. Line and grease a 30 x 20cm/12 x 8in Swiss roll tin. Whisk the egg yolks and sugar in a mixing bowl until thick and creamy. Put the chestnut purée in a separate bowl. Whisk the orange rind and juice into the purée, then whisk into the egg mixture.

2 Whisk the egg whites until fairly stiff. Stir a generous spoonful of the whites into the chestnut mixture to lighten it, then fold in the remaining egg whites. Spoon the mixture into the prepared tin and bake for 30 minutes until firm. Cool for 5 minutes, then cover with a clean damp dish cloth and leave until cold.

3 Meanwhile, make the filling. Put the soft cheese in a bowl with the honey. Finely grate the orange rind and add to the bowl. Peel away all the pith from the orange, cut the fruit into segments, chop roughly and set aside. Add any juice to the bowl, then beat until smooth. Mix in the orange segments.

4 Sprinkle a sheet of greaseproof paper with icing sugar. Turn the roulade out onto the paper; peel off the lining paper. Spread the filling over the roulade and roll up like a Swiss roll. Transfer to a plate and dust with icing sugar.

Cinnamon and Apple Gâteau

Make this lovely gâteau for an autumn teatime treat.

Serves 8

3 eggs
115g/4oz/¹/₂ cup caster
   sugar
75g/3oz/¾ cup plain flour
5ml/1 tsp ground
   cinnamon

For the filling and topping
4 large eating apples

15ml/1 tbsp water
60ml/4 tbsp clear honey
75g/3oz/¹/₂ cup sultanas
2.5ml/¹/₂ tsp ground
   cinnamon
350g/12oz/1¹/₂ cups low-
   fat soft cheese
60ml/4 tbsp reduced-fat
   fromage frais
10ml/2 tsp lemon juice

1 Preheat the oven to 190°C/375°F/Gas 5. Line and grease a 23cm/9in sandwich cake tin. Whisk the eggs and sugar until thick, then sift the flour and cinnamon over the surface and carefully fold in with a large metal spoon.

2 Pour into the prepared tin and bake for 25–30 minutes or until the cake springs back when lightly pressed. Cool on a wire rack.

3 To make the filling, peel, core and slice three of the apples and cook them in a covered pan with the water and half the honey until softened. Add the sultanas and cinnamon, stir well, replace the lid and leave to cool.

4 Put the soft cheese in a bowl with the fromage frais, the remaining honey and half the lemon juice; beat until smooth. Split the sponge cake in half, place the bottom half on a plate and drizzle over any liquid from the apples. Spread with two-thirds of the cheese mixture, then top with the apple filling. Fit the top of the cake in place.

5 Swirl the remaining filling over the top of the sponge. Quarter, core and slice the remaining apple, dip the slices in the remaining lemon juice and use to decorate the edges.

Lemon Chiffon Cake

Lemon mousse makes a tangy and delicious sponge filling

Serves 8

1 lemon sponge cake mix
lemon glacé icing
shreds of blanched
   lemon rind

For the filling
2 eggs, separated
75g/3oz/6 tbsp
   caster sugar

grated rind and juice of
   1 small lemon
20ml/4 tsp water
10ml/2 tsp gelatine
120ml/4fl oz/¹/₂ cup
   reduced-fat fromage
   frais

1 Preheat the oven to 180°C/350°F/Gas 4. Line and grease a 20cm/8in loose-bottomed cake tin, add the sponge mixture and bake for 20–25 minutes until firm and golden. Cool on a wire rack, then split in half. Return the lower half of the cake to the clean cake tin and set aside.

2 Make the filling. Whisk the egg yolks, sugar, lemon rind and juice in a bowl until thick, pale and creamy. In a grease-free bowl, whisk the egg whites to soft peaks.

3 Sprinkle the gelatine over the water in a bowl. When spongy, dissolve over simmering water. Cool slightly, then whisk into the yolk mixture. Fold in the fromage frais. When the mixture begins to set, fold in a generous spoonful of the egg whites to lighten it, then fold in the remaining whites.

4 Spoon the lemon mousse over the sponge in the cake tin. Set the second layer of sponge on top and chill until set.

5 Carefully transfer the cake to a serving plate. Pour the glacé icing over the cake and spread it evenly to the edges. Decorate with the lemon shreds.

Strawberry Gâteau

It is difficult to believe that a cake that tastes so delicious can be low fat.

Serves 6

2 eggs
75g/3oz/6 tbsp caster sugar
grated rind of ¹/₂ orange
50g/2oz/¹/₂ cup plain flour

For the filling
275g/10oz/1¹/₄ cups low-fat soft cheese

grated rind of ¹/₂ orange
30ml/2 tbsp caster sugar
60ml/4 tbsp reduced-fat fromage frais
225g/8oz strawberries, halved and chopped
25g/1oz/¹/₄ cup chopped almonds, toasted

1 Preheat the oven to 190℃/375℉/Gas 5. Line a 30 x 20cm/12 x 8in Swiss roll tin with non-stick baking paper.

2 In a bowl, whisk the eggs, sugar and orange rind until thick and mousse-like, then fold in the flour lightly. Turn the mixture into the prepared tin. Bake for 15–20 minutes or until firm and golden. Cool on a wire rack, removing the lining paper.

3 Meanwhile, make the filling. In a bowl, mix the soft cheese with the orange rind, sugar and fromage frais until smooth. Divide between two bowls. Add half the strawberries to one bowl. Cut the sponge widthways into three equal pieces and sandwich together with the strawberry filling. Place on a serving plate.

4 Spread the plain filling over the top and sides of the cake. Press the toasted almonds over the sides and decorate the top with the remaining strawberry halves.

Tia Maria Gâteau

A feather-light coffee sponge with a creamy liqueur-flavoured filling spiked with stem ginger.

Serves 8

75g/3oz/¾ cup plain flour
30ml/2 tbsp instant coffee powder
3 eggs
115g/4oz/¹/₂ cup caster sugar

For the filling
175g/6oz/¾ cup low-fat soft cheese
15ml/1 tbsp clear honey

15ml/1 tbsp Tia Maria
50g/2oz/¹/₃ cup stem ginger, chopped

For the icing
225g/8oz/2 cups icing sugar, sifted
10ml/2 tsp coffee essence
5ml/1 tsp fat-reduced cocoa
coffee beans (optional)

1 Preheat the oven to 190℃/375℉/Gas 5. Line and grease a 20cm/8in round cake tin. Sift the flour and coffee powder together.

2 Whisk the eggs and sugar in a bowl until thick and mousse-like, then fold in the flour mixture lightly. Turn the mixture into the prepared tin. Bake for 30–35 minutes or until firm and golden. Cool on a wire rack.

3 Make the filling. Mix the soft cheese with the honey in a bowl. Beat until smooth, then stir in the Tia Maria and ginger. Split the cake in half horizontally and sandwich together with the Tia Maria filling.

4 Make the icing. In a bowl, mix the icing sugar and coffee essence with enough water to make an icing which will coat the back of a wooden spoon. Pour three-quarters of the icing over the cake. Stir the cocoa into the remaining icing, spoon it into a piping bag fitted with a writing nozzle and drizzle the mocha icing over the coffee icing. Decorate with coffee beans, if desired.

Quick-mix Sponge Cake

Choose either chocolate or lemon flavouring for this light and versatile sponge cake, or leave it plain.

Makes 1 x 20cm/8in round cake

115g/4oz/1 cup self-
  raising flour
5ml/1 tsp baking powder
115g/4oz/½ cup soft
  margarine
115g/4oz/½ cup
  caster sugar
2 eggs

For the flavourings
Chocolate: 15ml/1 tbsp
  cocoa powder blended
  with 15ml/1 tbsp
  boiling water
Lemon: 10ml/2 tsp
  grated lemon rind

1 Preheat the oven to 160°C/325°F/Gas 3. Grease a 20cm/8in round cake tin, line the base with greaseproof paper and grease the paper.

2 Sift the flour and baking powder into a bowl. Add the margarine, sugar and eggs with the chosen flavourings, if using.

3 Beat with a wooden spoon for 2–3 minutes. The mixture should be pale in colour and slightly glossy.

4 Spoon the mixture into the cake tin and smooth the surface. Bake in the centre of the oven for 30–40 minutes, or until a skewer inserted into the centre of the cake comes out clean. Turn out onto a wire rack, remove the lining paper and leave to cool completely.

Genoese Sponge Cake

This sponge cake has a firm texture due to the addition of butter and is suitable for cutting into layers for gâteaux.

Makes 1 x 20cm/8in round cake

4 eggs
125g/4oz/½ cup caster
  sugar
75g/3oz/6tbsp unsalted
  butter, melted and
  cooled slightly
75g/3oz/¾ cup plain
  flour

For the flavourings
Citrus: 10ml/2 tsp grated
  orange, lemon or
  lime rind
Chocolate: 50g/2oz plain
  chocolate, melted
Coffee: 10ml/2 tsp coffee
  granules, dissolved
  in 5ml/1 tsp
  boiling water

1 Preheat the oven to 180°C/350°F/Gas 4. Base line and grease a 20cm/8in round cake tin.

2 Whisk the eggs and caster sugar together in a heatproof bowl until thoroughly blended. Place the bowl over a saucepan of simmering water and continue to whisk the mixture until thick and pale.

3 Remove the bowl from the saucepan and continue to whisk until the mixture is cool and leaves a thick trail on the surface when beaters are lifted.

4 Pour the butter carefully into the mixture, leaving any sediment behind.

5 Sift the flour over the surface. Using a plastic spatula, carefully fold the flour, butter and any flavourings into the mixture until smooth and evenly blended. Scrape the mixture into the prepared tin, tilt to level and bake for 30–40 minutes, until firm to the touch and golden. Cool on a wire rack.

Madeira Cake

Enjoy this cake in the traditional way with a large glass of Madeira or a schooner of sherry.

Serves 6–8

225g/8oz/2 cups plain
flour
5ml/1 tsp baking powder
225g/8oz/1 cup butter or
margarine, at room
temperature

225g/8oz/1 cup caster
sugar
grated rind of 1 lemon
5ml/1 tsp vanilla essence
4 eggs

1 Preheat the oven to 160°C/325°F/Gas 3. Base line and grease a 20cm/8in cake tin.

2 Sift the flour and baking powder into a bowl. Set the mixture aside.

3 Cream the butter or margarine, adding the caster sugar about 30ml/2 tbsp at a time, until light and fluffy. Stir in the lemon rind and vanilla. Add the eggs one at a time, beating for 1 minute after each addition. Add the flour mixture and stir until just combined.

4 Pour the cake mixture into the prepared tin and tap lightly to level. Bake for about 1¼ hours, or until a metal skewer inserted in the centre comes out clean.

5 Cool in the tin on a wire rack for 10 minutes, then turn the cake out onto a wire rack and leave to cool completely.

Swiss Roll

Vary the flavour of the Swiss roll by adding a little grated orange, lime or lemon rind to the mixture.

Serves 6–8

4 eggs, separated
115g/4oz/½ cup caster
sugar
115g/4oz/1 cup plain
flour
5ml/1 tsp baking powder

**For a chocolate
flavouring**
Replace 25ml/1½ tbsp of
the flour with
25ml/1½ tbsp cocoa
powder

1 Preheat the oven to 180°C/350°F/Gas 4. Base line and grease a 33 x 23cm/13 x 9in Swiss roll tin. Whisk the egg whites until stiff. Beat in 30ml/2 tbsp of the caster sugar.

2 Beat the egg yolks with the remaining caster sugar and 15ml/1 tbsp water for about 2 minutes until the mixture is pale and leaves a thick ribbon trail.

3 Sift together the flour and baking powder. Carefully fold the beaten egg yolks into the egg whites, then fold in the flour mixture.

4 Pour the mixture into the prepared tin and gently smooth the surface. Bake in the centre of the oven for 12–15 minutes, or until the cake starts to come away from the edges of the tin.

5 Turn out onto a piece of greaseproof paper lightly sprinkled with caster sugar. Peel off the lining paper and cut off any crisp edges. Spread with jam, if wished, and roll up, using the greaseproof paper as a guide. Leave to cool completely on a wire rack.

Rich Fruit Cake

Make this cake a few weeks before icing, wrap well and store in an airtight container to mature.

Makes 1 x 20cm/8in round or 18cm/7in square cake

375g/12oz/1¼ cups currants
250g/9oz/scant 2 cups sultanas
150g/5oz/1 cup raisins
90g/3½ oz/scant ½ cup glacé cherries, halved
90g/3½ oz/scant 1 cup almonds, chopped
65g/2½ oz/scant ½ cup mixed peel
grated rind of 1 lemon
40ml/2½ tbsp brandy
250g/9oz/2¼ cups plain flour, sifted
6.5ml/1¼ tsp mixed spice
2.5ml/½ tsp grated nutmeg
65g/2½ oz/generous ½ cup ground almonds
200g/7oz/scant 1 cup soft margarine or butter
225g/8oz/1¼ cups soft brown sugar
15ml/1 tbsp black treacle
5 eggs, beaten

1 Preheat the oven to 140°C/275°F/Gas 1. Grease a deep 20cm/8in round or 18cm/7in square cake tin, line the base and sides with a double thickness of greaseproof paper and grease the paper.

2 Combine the ingredients in a large mixing bowl. Beat with a wooden spoon for 5 minutes until well mixed.

3 Spoon the mixture into the prepared cake tin. Make a slight depression in the centre.

4 Bake in the centre of the oven for 3–3½ hours. Test the cake after 3 hours. If it is ready it will feel firm and a skewer inserted in the centre will come out clean. Cover the top loosely with foil if it starts to brown too quickly.

5 Leave the cake to cool completely in the tin. Then turn out. The lining paper can be left on to help keep the cake moist.

Light Fruit Cake

For those who prefer a slightly less dense fruit cake, here is one that is still ideal for marzipanning and icing.

Makes 1 x 20cm/8in round or 18cm/7in square cake

225g/8oz/1 cup soft margarine or butter
225g/8oz/1 cup caster sugar
grated rind of 1 orange
5 eggs, beaten
300g/11oz/2¼ cups plain flour
2.5ml/½ tsp baking powder
10ml/2 tsp mixed spice
175g/6oz/¾ cup currants
175g/6oz/generous 1 cup raisins
175g/6oz/generous 1 cup sultanas
50g/2oz/⅓ cup dried, ready-to-eat apricots
115g/4oz/⅔ cup mixed peel

1 Preheat the oven to 150°C/300°F/Gas 2. Grease a deep 20cm/8in round or 18cm/7in square cake tin, line the base and sides with a double thickness of greaseproof paper and grease the paper.

2 Combine all the ingredients in a large mixing bowl, snipping in the apricots in strips, using kitchen scissors. Beat thoroughly with a wooden spoon for 3–4 minutes, until thoroughly mixed.

3 Spoon the mixture into the cake tin. Make a slight depression in the centre. Bake in the centre of the oven for 2½–3¼ hours. Test the cake after 2½ hours. If it is ready it will feel firm and a skewer inserted in the centre will come out clean. Test at intervals if necessary. Cover the top loosely with foil if it starts to brown too quickly.

4 Leave the cake to cool completely in the tin. Then turn out. The lining paper can be left on to help keep the cake moist.

Marzipan

Marzipan can be used on its own, under an icing or for modelling.

Makes 450g/1lb/3 cups

225g/8oz/2 cups ground almonds
115g/4oz/½ cup caster sugar
115g/4oz/1 cup icing sugar, sifted

5ml/1 tsp lemon juice
a few drops of almond essence
1 (size 4) egg, or 1 (size 2) egg white

1 Stir the ground almonds and sugars together in a bowl until evenly mixed. Make a well in the centre and add the lemon juice, almond essence and enough egg or egg white to mix to a soft but firm dough, using a wooden spoon.

2 Form the marzipan into a ball. Lightly dust a surface with icing sugar and knead the marzipan until smooth. Wrap in clear film or store in a polythene bag until needed. Tint with food colouring if required.

Sugarpaste Icing

Sugarpaste icing is wonderfully pliable and can be coloured, moulded and shaped in imaginative ways.

Makes 350g/12oz/2¼ cups

1 egg white
15ml/1 tbsp liquid glucose, warmed
350g/12oz/3 cups icing

sugar, sifted

1 Put the egg white and glucose in a mixing bowl. Stir them together to break up the egg white.

2 Add the icing sugar and mix together with a palette knife, using a chopping action, until well blended and the icing begins to bind together. Knead the mixture with your fingers until it forms a ball.

3 Knead the sugarpaste on a work surface lightly dusted with icing sugar for several minutes until smooth, soft and pliable. If the icing is too soft, knead in some more sifted sugar until it reaches the right consistency.

Marzipan Roses

To decorate a cake, shape the roses in a variety of colours and sizes then arrange on top.

Form a small ball of coloured marzipan into a cone shape. This forms the central core which supports the petals. To make the petals, take a piece of marzipan about the size of a large pea, and make a petal shape which is thicker at the base. Wrap the petal around the cone, pressing the petal to the cone to secure. Bend back the ends of the petal to curl. Repeat with more petals, each overlapping. Make some petals bigger until the required size is achieved.

Royal Icing

Royal icing gives a professional finish. This recipe makes enough icing to cover the top and sides of an 18cm/7in cake.

Makes 675g/1½ lb/4½ cups
3 egg whites
about 675g/1½ lb/6 cups
  icing sugar, sifted
7.5ml/1½ tsp glycerine
a few drops of lemon
  juice
food colouring (optional)

1 Put the egg whites in a bowl and stir lightly with a fork to break them up.

2 Add the icing sugar gradually, beating well with a wooden spoon after each addition. Add enough icing sugar to make a smooth, shiny icing that has the consistency of very stiff meringue.

3 Beat in the glycerine, lemon juice and food colouring, if using. Leave for 1 hour before using, covered with damp clear film, then stir to burst any air bubbles.

Storing
The icing will keep for up to three days, stored in a plastic container with a tight-fitting lid in a fridge.

Icing consistencies
This recipe is for an icing consistency suitable for flat icing a marzipanned rich fruit cake. When the spoon is lifted, the icing should form a sharp point, with a slight curve at the end, known as "soft peak". For piping, the icing needs to be slightly stiffer. It should form a fine sharp peak when the spoon is lifted.

Butter Icing

The creamy rich flavour and silky smoothness of butter icing is popular with both children and adults.

Makes 350g/12oz/1½ cups
75g/3oz/6 tbsp soft
  margarine or butter,
  softened
225g/8oz/2 cups icing
  sugar, sifted
5ml/1 tsp vanilla essence
10–15ml/2–3 tsp milk

For the flavourings
Chocolate: Blend 15ml/
  1 tbsp cocoa powder
  with 15ml/1 tbsp hot
  water. Cool before
  beating into the icing.

Coffee: Blend 10ml/2 tsp
  coffee powder with
  15ml/1 tbsp boiling
  water. Omit the milk.
  Cool before beating the
  mixture into the icing.

Lemon, orange or lime:
  Substitute the vanilla
  essence and milk with
  lemon, orange or lime
  juice and 10ml/2 tsp
  of finely grated citrus
  rind. Omit the rind if
  using the icing for
  piping. Lightly tint
  the icing with food
  colouring, if wished.

1 Put the margarine or butter, icing sugar, vanilla essence and 5ml/1 tsp of the milk in a bowl.

2 Beat with a wooden spoon or an electric mixer, adding sufficient extra milk to give a light, smooth and fluffy consistency. For flavoured butter icing, follow the instructions above for the flavour of your choice.

Storing
The icing will keep for up to three days in an airtight container stored in a fridge.

Fudge Frosting

A darkly delicious frosting, this can transform a simple sponge cake into one worthy of a very special occasion. Spread fudge frosting smoothly over the cake or swirl it. Or be even more elaborate with a little piping – it really is very versatile. This recipe makes enough to fill and coat the top and sides of a 20cm/8in or 23cm/9in round sponge cake.

Makes 350g/12oz/1½ cups

50g/2oz squares plain chocolate	*45ml/3 tbsp milk or single cream*
225g/8oz icing sugar, sifted	*5ml/1 tsp vanilla essence*
50g/2oz/4 tbsp butter	

1 Break or chop the chocolate into small pieces. Put the chocolate, icing sugar, butter, milk or cream and vanilla essence in a heavy-based saucepan.

2 Stir over a very low heat until both the chocolate and the butter have melted. Remove the mixture from the heat and stir until evenly blended.

3 Beat the icing frequently as it cools until it thickens sufficiently to use for spreading or piping. Use the icing immediately and work quickly once it has reached the right consistency.

Storing
This icing should be used straightaway.

Crème au Beurre

The rich, smooth, light texture of this icing makes it ideal for spreading, filling or piping onto cakes and gâteaux for all occasions.

Makes 350g/12oz/1½ cups

60ml/4 tbsp water	*with orange, lemon or*
75g/3oz/6 tbsp caster sugar	*lime juice and 10ml/ 2 tsp grated rind*
2 egg yolks	*Chocolate: add 50g/2oz*
150g/5oz/generous ½ cup unsalted butter, softened	*plain chocolate, melted*
	Coffee: add 10ml/2 tsp instant coffee granules, dissolved in
For the flavourings	*5ml/1 tsp boiling*
Citrus: replace water	*water, cooled*

1 Bring the water to the boil, remove from the heat and stir in the sugar. Heat gently, stirring, until the sugar has dissolved. Then boil rapidly until the mixture becomes syrupy, or reaches the "thread" stage. To test, place a little syrup on the back of a dry teaspoon. Press a second teaspoon on to the syrup and gently pull apart. The syrup should form a fine thread. If not, return to the heat, boil rapidly and re-test a minute later.

2 Whisk the egg yolks together in a bowl. Continue to whisk while slowly adding the sugar syrup. Whisk until thick, pale and cool.

3 Beat the butter until light and fluffy. Add the egg mixture gradually, beating well after each addition, until thick and fluffy. For Chocolate or Coffee Crème au Beurre, fold in the flavouring at the end. If you prefer a citrus flavour, follow the instructions above.

American Frosting

A light marshmallow icing which crisps on the outside when left to dry, this versatile frosting may be swirled or peaked into a soft coating.

Makes 350g/12oz/1½ cups

1 egg white
30ml/2 tbsp water
15ml/1 tbsp golden syrup
5ml/1 tsp cream of tartar
175g/6oz/1½ cups icing sugar, sifted

1 Place the egg white with the water, golden syrup and cream of tartar in a heatproof bowl. Whisk together well until thoroughly blended.

2 Stir the icing sugar into the mixture and place the bowl over a saucepan of simmering water. Whisk until the mixture becomes thick and white.

3 Remove the bowl from the saucepan and continue to whisk the frosting until cool and thick, and the mixture stands up in soft peaks. Use immediately to fill or cover cakes.

Glacé Icing

An instant icing for quickly finishing the tops of large or small cakes.

Makes 350g/12oz/1½ cup

225g/8oz/2 cups icing sugar
30 – 45ml/2 – 3 tbsp hot water
food colouring (optional)

For the flavourings
Citrus: replace the water

with orange, lemon or lime juice
Chocolate: sift 10ml/2 tsp cocoa powder with the icing sugar
Coffee: replace the water with strong, liquid coffee

1 Sift the icing sugar into a bowl. Using a wooden spoon, gradually stir in enough water to obtain the consistency of thick cream.

2 Beat until white and smooth, and the icing thickly coats the back of the spoon. Tint with a few drops of food colouring, if desired, or flavour the icing as suggested above. Use immediately to cover the top of the cake.

Simple Piped Flowers

Bouquets of iced blossoms, such as roses, pansies and bright summer flowers make colourful cake decorations.

For a rose, make a fairly firm icing. Colour the icing. Fit a petal nozzle into a paper piping bag, half-fill with icing and fold over top to seal. Hold the piping bag so the wider end is pointing at what will be the base of the rose and hold a cocktail stick in the other hand. Pipe a small cone shape around the tip of the stick, pipe a petal half way around the cone, lifting it so it is at an angle and curling outwards, turning the stick at the same time. Repeat with more petals so they overlap. Remove from stick and leave until dry.

Butterscotch Frosting

Makes 675g/1½ lb/3 cups

75g/3oz/6 tbsp unsalted
butter
45ml/3 tbsp milk
25g/1oz/2 tbsp soft light
brown sugar
15ml/1 tbsp black treacle
350g/12oz/3 cups icing
sugar, sifted

For the flavourings
Citrus: replace the treacle
with golden syrup and
add 10ml/2 tsp finely
grated orange, lemon
or lime rind
Chocolate: sift 15ml/
1 tbsp cocoa powder
with the icing sugar
Coffee: replace the treacle
with 15ml/1 tbsp
coffee granules

1 Place the butter, milk, sugar and treacle in a bowl over a pan of simmering water. Stir until the butter and sugar melt.

2 Remove the bowl and stir in the icing sugar. Beat until smooth and glossy. For flavouring, follow instructions above.

3 Pour over the cake, or cool for a thicker consistency.

Chocolate Fudge Icing

A rich glossy icing which sets like chocolate fudge, this is versatile enough to smoothly coat, swirl or pipe, depending on the temperature of the icing when it is used.

Makes 450g/1lb/2 cups

115g/4oz plain chocolate,
in squares
50g/2oz/¼ cup unsalted
butter

1 egg, beaten
175g/6oz/1½ cups icing
sugar, sifted

1 Place the chocolate and butter in a heatproof bowl over a saucepan of hot water.

2 Stir occasionally with a wooden spoon until both the chocolate and butter are melted. Add the egg and beat well.

3 Remove the bowl from the saucepan and stir in the icing sugar, then beat until smooth and glossy.

4 Pour immediately over the cake for a smooth finish, or leave to cool for a thicker spreading or piping consistency.

Making Caramel

Caramel has endless uses – for dipping fruits and nuts, crushing for cake coating, or drizzling into shapes.

Place 150ml/¼ pint/⅔ cup water in a saucepan. Bring to the boil, remove from the heat and stir in 175g/6oz/¾ cup caster sugar. Heat gently until the sugar has dissolved. Bring the syrup to the boil, boil rapidly until the bubbles begin to subside and the syrup begins to turn a pale golden brown. For praline, add 75g/3oz/¾ cup toasted almonds to the caramel, shake to mix, then pour onto a sheet of oiled foil on a baking sheet. Cool, then crush with a rolling pin, or process in a food processor until finely ground.

Apricot Glaze

It is a good idea to make a large quantity of apricot glaze, especially when making celebration cakes.

Makes 450g/1lb/1½ cups
450g/1lb/1½ cups apricot
jam
45ml/3 tbsp/ water

1 Place the jam and water in a saucepan. Heat gently, stirring occasionally until melted. Boil rapidly for 1 minute, then rub through a sieve, pressing the fruit against the sides of the sieve with the back of a wooden spoon. Discard the skins left in the sieve. Use the warmed glaze to brush cakes before applying marzipan, or use for glazing fruits on gâteaux and cakes.

Glossy Chocolate Icing

A rich smooth glossy icing, this can be made with plain or milk chocolate.

Makes 350g/12oz/1¼ cups
175g/6oz plain chocolate
150ml/¼ pint/⅔ cup
single cream

1 Break up the chocolate into small pieces and place it in a saucepan with the cream.

2 Heat gently, stirring occasionally, until the chocolate has melted and the mixture is smooth.

3 Allow the icing to cool until it is thick enough to coat the back of a wooden spoon. Use it at this stage for a smooth glossy icing, or allow it to thicken to obtain an icing which can be swirled or patterned with a cake decorating scraper.

Sugar-frosting Flowers

Choose edible flowers such as pansies, primroses, violets, roses, freesias, tiny daffodils or nasturtiums.

Lightly beat an egg white in a small bowl and sprinkle some caster sugar on a plate. Wash the flowers then dry on kitchen paper. If possible leave some stem attached. Evenly brush both sides of the petals with the egg white. Hold the flower by its stem over a plate lined with kitchen paper, sprinkle it evenly with the sugar, then shake off any excess. Place on a flat board or wire rack covered with kitchen paper and leave to dry in a warm place. Use to decorate a cake.

Petal Paste

Makes 500g/1¼lb

10ml/2 tsp gelatine
25ml/1½ tsp cold water
10ml/2 tsp liquid glucose
10ml/2 tsp white
    vegetable fat
450g/1lb/4 cups icing

sugar, sifted
5ml/1 tsp gum
    tragacanth
1 egg white

1 Place the gelatine, water, liquid glucose and white fat in a heatproof bowl over a saucepan of hot water until melted, stirring occasionally. Remove the bowl from the heat.

2 Sift the icing sugar and gum tragacanth into a bowl. Make a well in the centre and add the egg white and the gelatine mixture. Mix together to form a soft malleable white paste.

3 Knead on a surface dusted with icing sugar until smooth, white and free from cracks. Place in a plastic bag or wrap in clear film, sealing well to exclude all the air. Leave for about two hours before use, then knead again and use small pieces at a time, leaving the remaining petal paste well sealed.

Meringue Frosting

Makes 450g/1lb/1½ cups

2 egg whites
115g/4oz/1 cup icing
    sugar, sifted
150g/5oz/⅔ cup unsalted
    butter, softened

For the flavourings
Citrus: 10ml/2 tsp finely

grated orange, lemon
    or lime rind.
Chocolate: 50g/2oz plain
    chocolate, melted
Coffee: 10ml/2 tsp coffee
    granules, blended with
    5ml/1 tsp boiling
    water, cooled

1 Whisk the egg whites in a clean, heatproof bowl, add the icing sugar and gently whisk to mix well. Place the bowl over a saucepan of simmering water and whisk until thick and white. Remove the bowl from the saucepan and continue to whisk until cool and the meringue stands up in soft peaks.

2 Beat the butter in a separate bowl until light and fluffy. Add the meringue gradually, beating well after each addition, until thick and fluffy. Fold in the chosen flavouring, using a palette knife, until evenly blended. Use immediately for coating, filling and piping onto cakes.

Marbling

Sugarpaste, or fondant, lends itself to tinting in all shades and marbling is a good way to colour the paste.

Using a cocktail stick, add a few drops of the chosen edible food colour to some sugarpaste icing. Do not knead the food colouring fully into the icing.
When the sugarpaste is rolled out, the colour is dispersed in such a way that it gives a marbled appearance.
Marbled sugarpaste icing can be used to cover novelty cakes. Several colours can be used in the same icing to give an interesting multi-coloured effect.

NOTES

Notes

NOTES

NOTES

N<small>OTES</small>

NOTES

NOTES

NOTES